Evolution and Creation

UNIVERSITY OF NOTRE DAME
STUDIES IN THE
PHILOSOPHY OF RELIGION

Number 4

Evolution and Creation

ERNAN McMULLIN, EDITOR

UNIVERSITY OF NOTRE DAME PRESS
NOTRE DAME, INDIANA 46556

Copyright © 1985 by
University of Notre Dame Press
Notre Dame, Indiana 46556
All Rights Reserved

Manufactured in the United States of America

Library of Congress Cataloging-in-Publication Data

Main entry under title:

Evolution and creation.

   Bibliography: p.
   1. Evolution—Congresses.   2. Creation—Congresses.
3. Evolution—Religious aspects—Christianity—Congresses.
I. McMullin, Ernan, 1924-
QH359.E89   1985   231.7'65   84-40818
ISBN 0-268-00917-1

In memory of
GEORGE N. SHUSTER
(1894–1977)

A man for all occasions

CONTENTS

PREFACE

Modern natural science depends on a few simple organizing ideas, one of these being the idea of evolution, according to which each natural kind has come to be what it is along a path of gradual development that can be traced backward in time. Theology in the Christian tradition likewise can be seen as the working out of a few fundamental ideas, one of which is that of creation, according to which the universe depends on a transcendent God for its being. These two ideas have interacted in complex ways over the ages and continue to do so today.

In recent centuries the tendency has been to see them as opposed to one another. They have been presented as mutually exclusive principles of explanation. In the recent "creationist" debates in the United States the impression has often been given by protagonists on both sides of the issue that one is forced to choose, that one cannot admit both evolution and creation at the same time as complementary approaches to the same natural reality.

The conference from which the core of essays in this book derived was inspired by the conviction that this opposing of evolution to creation betrays a fundamental misunderstanding of one or both concepts. Plans for such a conference go back as far as spring 1972, when George N. Shuster, then assistant to the president of the University of Notre Dame, brought together a group of faculty whose researches bore in one way or another on the interactions of science and religion, to discuss the possibility of a major symposium. The group was enthusiastic, but as often happens, enthusiasm did not translate into immediate action. George Shuster's death in 1977 took away the prime mover, the man who more than any other had labored at Notre Dame to break down the disciplinary barriers that impede the discussion of so many fundamental issues.

The long-planned conference finally took place on March 24-26, 1983, under the joint sponsorship of the Program in History and Philosophy of Science and the Center for Philosophy of Religion at the University of Notre Dame. The Program in History and Philosophy of Science has as one of its special concerns the interactions, both historical and philosophical, between science and religion over the ages. It is one of the few degree programs in history and philosophy of science to have this as a focus of its research and teaching. Hence the topic was seen as a peculiarly appropriate one for the first conference to be sponsored by the program.

The conference was supported by grants from the Lecomte du Nouy Foundation, the Franklin J. Matchette Foundation, and the Center for Philosophy of Religion at the University of Notre Dame. May this volume serve as a tangible expression of gratitude for these generous expressions of support.

The papers delivered at the conference have been revised by their authors in the light of discussions at the conference and afterward. In addition, several papers have been added to supplement the original offerings in areas not covered at the conference. The paper by Phillip Sloan, and the joint paper by Carroll Stuhlmueller, C.P., and Dianne Bergant, C.S.A., were specially written for this volume, and the paper by Christopher Mooney, S.J., which appeared originally in *Chicago Studies*, is reprinted here with permission of the author and editor.

I am grateful to Julie McDonald, who prepared the index, to Ryan Welsh, who can convert the messiest manuscript into neat pages of type, and to John Ehmann and the staff of the University of Notre Dame Press for their patience and their help in bringing this anthology to completion.

ERNAN MCMULLIN

CONTRIBUTORS

William P. Alston is professor of philosophy at Syracuse University. Previously he served on the faculties of the University of Michigan, Rutgers University, and the University of Illinois. He is a past president of the Western Division, American Philosophical Association, of the Society of Philosophy and Psychology, and of the Society of Christian Philosophers. Currently he is the editor of *Faith and Philosophy: Journal of the Society of Christian Philosophers*. His main current interests are philosophical theology, epistemology, and the intersection thereof. Among his recent articles are "Christian Experience and Christian Belief" (1983) and "Concepts of Epistemic Justification"(1985).

William Austin is professor of philosophy at the University of Houston, specializing in the philosophy of science and the philosophy of religion. He has written *Waves, Particles, and Paradoxes* (1967) and *The Relevance of Natural Science to Theology* (1976). Among his recent articles are "Rational Credibility and Causal Explanations of Belief" (1984) and "Theology and Natural Science: Beyond the Truce?" (1984).

Francisco J. Ayala is professor of genetics at the University of California, Davis. Born in Madrid, Spain, he has lived in the United States since 1961 and became a U.S. citizen in 1971. He is author of more than 300 articles and eight books and has edited two other books. The books include *Population and Evolutionary Genetics: A Primer* (1982), *Modern Genetics* (1980), *Evolving: The Theory and Processes of Organic Evolution* (1979), *Evolution* (1977), *Molecular Evolution* (1976), and *Studies in the Philosophy of Biology* (1974). He is a member of the National Academy of Science, the American Philosophical Society, and the American Academy of Arts and Sciences.

Dianne Bergant, CSA, is associate professor of Old Testament studies and director of the Master of Theological Studies Program at the Catholic Theological Union in Chicago. She is the author of *Job and Ecclesiastes* (1982), and *What Are They Saying About Wisdom Literature?* (1982). She is associate editor of *The Bible Today*, general editor of the Collegeville Bible Commentary Series, and a member of the Bishop's Committee on the Liturgy, and the Inclusive Language Lectionary Committee of the National Council of Churches. She is a member of the Congregation of Saint Agnes.

David H. Kelsey is professor of theology at Yale Divinity School, specializing in systematic theology. His books include *The Fabric of Tillich's Theology* (1967) and *The Uses of Scripture in Theology* (1975).

Nicholas Lash is Norris-Hulse Professor of Divinity at Cambridge University. Recent books include *Theology on Dover Beach* (1979) and *A Matter of Hope: A Theologian's Reflections on the Thoughts of Karl Marx* (1981). A director of *Concilium*, he edited (with David Tracy) *Cosmology and Theology* (1983). As a fellow of the Wilson Center, Washington, D.C., in 1986, he will be preparing a study of human experience and the knowledge of God.

John Leslie, professor of philosophy at the University of Guelph, specializes in metaphysics, philosophy of religion, and the philosophy of modern cosmology. His *Value and Existence* (1979) pictures the world as created by the ethical need for it to exist. His articles include "Anthropic Principle, World Ensemble, Design" (1982); "Observership in Cosmology: The Anthropic Principle" (1983); "Cosmology, Probability, and the Need to Explain Life" (1983).

Ernan McMullin is director of the Program in History and Philosophy of Science and occupies the O'Hara Chair of Philosophy at the University of Notre Dame. He is author of *Newton on Matter and Activity* (1978) and editor of several anthologies, including *Galileo: Man of Science* (1967) and *The Concept of Matter in Modern Philosophy* (1978). Some recent articles: "How Should Cosmology Relate to Theology?" (1981), "The Motive for Metaphor" (1982), "Values in Science" (1983), "The Goals of Natural Science" (1984), "Realism in Theology and in Science" (1985).

Christopher F. Mooney, S.J., a member of the Pennsylvania Bar, is academic vice-president of Fairfield University. He has previously served as chair of the Theology Department at Fordham University, president of Woodstock College, and assistant dean at the University of Pennsylvania Law School. He holds doctorates in both theology and law, and in recent years his major interest has become the interface between religious and legal values. He has written five books: *Teilhard de Chardin and the Mystery of Christ* (1966), which won the National Catholic Book Award, *The Making of Man* (1971), *Man Without Tears* (1975), *Religion and the American Dream* (1977), and *Inequality and the American Conscience* (1982).

James Ross is professor of philosophy at the University of Pennsylvania, with interests in medieval philosophy and contemporary metaphysics, philosophy of language, and philosophy of religion. He wrote *Philosophical Theology* (1969, 1980), *Introduction to Philosophy of Religion* (1969), and *Portraying Analogy* (1982) and is currently completing a book on creation of kinds, possibilities, and eternal truths. Two recent articles are "Aquinas on Belief and Knowledge" (1984) and "Believing for Profit" (1984).

Phillip Reid Sloan is an associate professor in the Program of Liberal Studies at the University of Notre Dame, specializing in the history and philosophy of the life sciences, with a particular focus on evolutionary biology. His books include *From Natural History to the History of Nature* (with John Lyon) (1981). Recent articles include "Darwin's Invertebrate Program: Preconditions for Transformism" (1985).

Carroll Stuhlmueller, C.P., is professor of Old Testament studies at the Catholic Theological Union, Chicago. Recently he has published a two-volume commentary on the Psalms, with Donald Senior the book *Biblical Foundations for Mission*, and the three-volume set *Biblical Meditations for Ordinary Time*. He is past president of the Catholic Biblical Association (1978-1979) and of the Chicago Society of Biblical Research (1982-83). In 1973 he was visiting professor at L'École Biblique et Archaeologique, Jerusalem, and has frequently directed graduate study programs in Israel. He is editor of *The Bible Today* and a priest of the Congregation of the Passion.

INTRODUCTION:
EVOLUTION AND CREATION

Ernan McMullin

1. Two Notions

One of the most distinctive features of the new Christian faith that spread through the Mediterranean world nearly two millennia ago was its portrayal of God as "Creator" of the universe, as wholly responsible for the being of all that is. Rejected were the popular dualisms of the day which saw the world as an arena of conflict between evenly balanced forces of good and evil. Matter was to be regarded as God's creature and not as an independent source of suffering and sin. And the universe came to be in stages, under God's hand, instead of being eternal as so many of the Greek philosophers had supposed.

Defenders of the older views were not easily persuaded. The Manicheans of the fourth century, for example, derided the account of creation given in the first chapters of Genesis as childish, not worthy of serious belief. They found various contradictions within it, like the appearance of light before the sources of light (the sun and moon) had begun to be. When the young Augustine decided to reject Manichaeism and return to the Christian faith of his boyhood, these objections to the Christian view of God as Creator, and specifically to the cosmogony of Genesis, were obstacles that he could not ignore. The challenge was not only to develop a theological account of the creation relationship but to provide a set of principles for the reading of texts like Genesis that on the one hand could claim the status of revelation and yet on the other seemed at times to conflict with some well-established beliefs about the world.

Twice Augustine attempted a commentary along allegorical lines on the disputed text of Genesis, but he was unsatisfied with the results. Finally in 415 A.D., after fourteen years of labor, he completed the *De Genesi ad litteram*, a detailed study of all the alleged points of conflict according to the "proper historical meaning", with frequent prescriptions as to how such conflict ought be handled.[1] Among these prescriptions, one was to catch the

1

eye of future generations, most notably that of Galileo when faced with a similar challenge more than a thousand years later. When conflict arises between a literal reading of some Bible text and a truth about the nature of things which has been demonstrated by reliable argument, the Christian must strive to reinterpret the biblical text in a metaphorical way.[2] Since real conflict is impossible between the two sources of truth, revelation and our tested knowledge of the world, the presumption will be that when we are *sure* of our natural knowledge, the apparently conflicting text of the Bible must be read in a way which will eliminate the conflict.

The principle, as it stands, proved a defective one, as Galileo was to discover.[3] But we can reformulate it in such a way as to provide a valuable direction for the contemporary Christian. When an apparent conflict arises between a strongly supported scientific theory and some item of Christian doctrine, the Christian ought to look very carefully to the credentials of the doctrine. It may well be that when he does so, the scientific understanding will enable the doctrine to be reformulated in a more adequate way.

The presumption here of course is that Christian doctrine is to be taken seriously as a cognitive claim about the world. But the further, and equally important, presumption is that it is not a once-for-ever-given; rather, it is capable of indefinite development. And one of the major sources of this development is the impetus given by the sciences of nature and of man. It is in the spirit of this neo-Augustinian principle that the essays comprising this book were put together. The topic is the relation between the theological doctrine of creation and the findings of the evolutionary theories that underlie so much of modern natural science. The topic is one that would delight Augustine, not only because he did more than any other single thinker to elucidate the notion of creation but also because he himself was sympathetic, as we shall see in a moment, to a developmental approach to origins.

By presupposing that the notions of evolution and of creation are at bottom compatible, we are taking for granted from the beginning that the "creation-science" approach which has preempted so much attention in the United States over the past decade is simply misguided. For the so-called "creationists" have assumed that the two doctrines are incompatible, that they present two radically different explanations of how the world and its contents came to be, only one of which can be true. Their hostility to the theory of evolution is predicated on its being incompatible with the words of Scripture and with the entire Christian worldview.

None of the essays in this book will deal with the "creation-science" controversy, not only because it has already been exhaustively discussed in numerous books and articles[4] but even more because the entire effort of the "creationist" movement in the United States presupposes the radical incompatibility of the evolution and creation doctrines. The essays in this book, taken as a single argument, will imply that the two doctrines are not incompatible, that they may indeed be taken to complement one another in important ways. Nevertheless, a further word about the unhappy "creation-science" episode might be worthwhile; I shall return to it later.

My aim in this introductory essay is to look at the concepts of evolution and of creation singly, and then to ask in a very general way how they interrelate, what the points of tension are, and where each may perhaps complement the other. In this way the reader will be prepared for the more detailed analyses to follow.

2. Evolution: Early History

The very first natural philosophers of the Greek world already resorted to types of explanation of a broadly "evolutionary" sort. That is, they tried to explain diversity by postulating an earlier, different stage from which the present diversity developed in an intelligible way. The earlier stage was also seen as *simpler*, so that the explanation worked in two ways: by referring the present to the past and the complex to the simple. This "evolutionary" mode of explanation was a corollary of a more general structural form of explanation, in which the properties of composite bodies were accounted for by postulating a basic "stuff", "seeds", "elements", out of which the bodies are composed. From such an hypothesis it was not a long step to the supposition that coming-to-be-from-the-simpler is true not only of individuals but of the *kinds* of things themselves.

Hippolytus reporting on an early Ionian philosopher of the sixth century B.C. writes:

> Xenophanes thinks that a mixture of the earth with the sea is going on, and that in time the earth is dissolved by the moist. He says that he has demonstrations of the following kind: shells are found inland and in the mountains, and in the quarries in Syracuse he says that an impression of a fish and of seaweed has been found, while an impression of a bay-leaf was found in Paros in the depth of the rock, and in Malta flat shapes of all marine objects. These, he says, were produced when everything was long ago covered with mud, and the impression was dried in the mud. All mankind is destroyed whenever the earth is carried down into the sea and becomes mud; then there is another beginning of coming-to-be, and this foundation happens for all the worlds.[5]

The evidence that the order of things has not always been as it now is supported the inference that since the complex bodies we know are made up of simpler elements, the kinds they represent came to be at some time in the past from these elements. Doubtless, the influence of Eastern religions

might also have been a factor in suggesting views of this sort because of the
cyclical conceptions of history they often embodied. If from the primeval mud
the diversities of the nonliving and the living can come to be and pass away,
there must be some natural processes at work enabling this to happen.

What these might be was not clear. Democritus suggested that atoms could
gradually cluster in more and more complex arrays. But how could a random
process of clustering produce the ordered world, especially the organic realm
where the kinds of living things seem exactly tailored to the tasks facing them?
Empedocles did make an interesting guess that life has gone through an evolutionary sequence beginning from limbs and disjointed organs, which then
came together in random ways and began to reproduce themselves. Only a
few of these combinations were fit to survive. Aristotle summarizes this theory
as follows:

> Wherever, then, everything turned out as it would have if it were happening for
> a purpose, there the creatures survived, being accidentally compounded in a suitable
> way; but where this did not happen, the creatures perished and are perishing still.[6]

Aristotle rejects this view; it runs entirely counter to his own teleological
account of becoming, according to which

> It is both by nature and for an end that the swallow makes its nest and the spider
> its web, and plants grow leaves for the sake of the fruit and send their roots down
> (not up) for the sake of nourishment.[7]

His assumption is that "chance" outcomes are infrequent in their occurrence, whereas "teeth and all other natural things either invariably or normally come about in a given way".[8] Thus natural change cannot be attributed
to chance; since "things are either the result of chance or for an end . . . it
follows that they must be for an end".[9] What he denies, of course, is Empedocles' fundamental point: that random process might in some way give rise
to regularity (when a "suitable" combination is hit upon), a suggestion that
will be amplified triumphantly by Darwin many millennia later.[10]

Aristotle's emphasis on the fundamental place of action-for-an-end, and
thus of teleological explanation, leads him to conclude that the forms which
ground this explanation must be eternal, that there is no process whereby
they could come to be or change. The idea that there might be a more fundamental sort of explanation which could account for the coming-to-be of
the forms themselves escaped him, despite Empedocles' hint. He assumed
that such an explanation could not possibly be teleological. But this is not
so unless we assume that the *only* ends to be served in nature are those of
the forms that *presently* are instantiated in it.

This gives us two basically incompatible alternative accounts of the kinds
of things, organic and inorganic, that constitute the world. One is that they

have come to be as they are now by means of some gradual process, perhaps one still in progress. The other is that they have always been as they now are, and thus that no further account is needed. The evolutionary model implies that the fundamental form of natural explanation is the *genetic* one whereby one accounts for some feature of the world by tracing how that kind of feature originally came to be. The "eternalist" model, on the other hand, *excludes* genetic explanation. When Aristotle lists the four ways in which process is to be explained, he omits the genetic question as to how kinds themselves came to be. This is one of the features that clearly marks off Aristotelian from modern science.

Logically, there was a third alternative besides the evolutionary and the eternalist ones. This was the view that the universe and the kinds of things in it came to be by an act of "making", where the processes of making are extrinsic to the natures made and are proper to the original coming-to-be only. Each different kind of thing makes its first appearance abruptly; from then onward the "natural" sequence of production or reproduction takes over. The analogy would be with the fashioning of products by a craftsman.

The "craft" metaphor was suggested in the myths of origins associated with many early religions, particularly those of the Near East. How was it regarded by philosophers? Was this the metaphor Plato had in mind in the *Timaeus*? He speaks there of a *demiurgos*, or maker, who imposed reason upon an original chaos:

> Desiring, then, that all things should be good, and so far as might be nothing imperfect, the god took over all that is visible — not at rest, but in discordant and unordered motion — and brought it from disorder into order.[11]

The Demiurge recognizes that those visible things with intelligence are better than those without and, further, that intelligence requires soul. Thus:

> When he framed the universe, he fashioned reason within soul, and soul within body, to the end that the work he accomplished might be by nature fairest and best. This, then, is how we must say, according to the likely account, that this world came to be, by the god's providence, in very truth a living creature with soul and reason.[12]

Can the Demiurge be called "creator"? Generations of translators — Jowett among them — have used the Christian term there. But this is misleading, since one of the main themes of the *Timaeus* is that the Demiurge has to contend with a matter not of "his" own making, the realm of necessity which can at best only be "persuaded" by reason. It was crucially important, in Plato's eyes, to postulate such a "matter" in order to explain the evident *failures* of reason, the many ways in which disorder and imperfection appear at all levels of the sensible world. No Greek thinker, least of all Plato, would have allowed the strict notion of creation (i.e., a making "from nothing") into their cosmogony, because it would have laid all the evident imperfection of the sensible realm at the door of reason or the divine.

What Plato was concerned to secure, against the materialist cosmogonies of his Ionian predecessors, was the presence everywhere in the sensible world of the sort of *design* that could only be attributed to reason and to purposive process. Chance and necessity could not produce intelligible order. Organisms could not possibly be the outcome of chance, as Empedocles had supposed.

On the face of it, then, Plato would seem to be embracing the third explanatory model described above, the craft model, as distinct from the evolutionary and the eternalist ones. But the matter is not so simple, as Cornford reminds us.[13] Though Plato makes use of the metaphors of craft and of making throughout the *Timaeus*, he also stresses that what he is giving is a "likely story". He is quite confident of some of its central features, that the world as a whole can be properly regarded as an organism animated by soul and guided by reason, for example. But is he saying that the sensible world had a beginning and that it was fashioned by a maker external to itself, utilizing processes themselves not a proper part of that world?

This "craft" interpretation, not surprisingly, has been favored by Christian commentators early and late. And it is not implausible; it follows after all the letter of the myth.[14] But later in the dialogue time is described as "the moving image of eternity", as the mode in which the eternal presents itself within the order of sense.[15] Perhaps, then, we could take the temporal dimension of the cosmogony of the *Timaeus* (as later Neoplatonism did) to be no more than an image of a relation constitutive of the sensible world: reason and necessity are arrayed over against one another in a ceaseless dialectic. In that case such passages as "the god set water and air between fire and earth, and made them, so far as was possible proportional to one another"[16] would refer not to a past event but to a continuing relationship. Reason would continually act upon disorderly matter to bring about and maintain the "works of intelligence" that Plato is at much pains to discover in the world about us.

The craft metaphor would not in this interpretation imply a separate Craftsman, responsible for the original coming-to-be of a universe of which he is not himself a part. Rather, it would suggest that reason must be supposed to operate continually with the universe, somewhat (but only *somewhat*) as a craftsman might work on recalcitrant materials. But reason is now in some sense *part* of that universe, just as is the matter that is characterized by necessity. And its operation can in some sense be discerned as invariably present in the processes of the sensible world. Is it identical with the reason proper to the world soul? It would seem not, since the world soul is itself said to be a product of this same Demiurge-reason. And yet if it operates as reason within the body of the "animal" that is the world, how do the two agent-reasons differ?[17]

I have labored this issue not in order to rehearse once again a famous point of contention in (Plato) scholarship but in order to bring out some ambiguities that will reappear in modern discussions of evolution. The myth of the _Timaeus_ is not, of course, an evolutionary one. Yet it is not simply a craft metaphor either. If the "works of intelligence" are to be brought about by reason, it may be that the only way in which reason can do so is through a gradual development guided from within, as it were. Plato himself would presumably have opposed any such suggestion because it would attribute too much of a formative role to time and change in the production of intelligibility.

But his critique of the Ionian evolutionary cosmogonies allows us already to recognize two alternative approaches to evolution, one materialist and the other idealist. The former takes the resources of "matter" to be all-sufficient to produce whatever has to be produced to bring about the universe we know. The latter postulates a reason (or mind or soul) working upon matter and somehow transcending it, not a part of it, though in _some_ sense part of the larger cosmic process. Each of these options can be further divided. Within the materialist classification, for example, one might distinguish between a more reductive sort of materialism, of the sort Plato attributed to the Ionians, or a nonreductive type that would allow for the operation of a teleological process within the material order. And the materialist option might also be called "naturalist" if the point of distinction between it and the idealist alternative is to be the extent to which the factor of reason (mind, soul) can be regarded as "natural". Plato does not, of course, have the category of nature available to him, but his linking of reason with the divine, and the sharp contrast he draws between the eternal realm of form (which is prior to reason) and the defective order of the changeable would surely situate him on the nonnaturalist side of the spectrum.

After Plato and Aristotle, the Stoics revived the cyclic notions of earlier thinkers and proposed a universe in which God, reason, soul, and matter are all bound in one. Each cosmic period begins in a fiery state; the _logos spermatikos_ then gradually organizes the four elements from within into the various kinds of things, according to an unchanging set of laws. Then follows decay, dissolution, and a return to the primeval fire. The cyclical cosmogonies presupposed the notion that the universe, of its own natural powers, could generate the diversity of natural kinds, not just once but many times over and always in the same way.

The point of all this is to underline the fact that the _idea_ of evolution was already widely accepted in the ancient world, both in naturalist cosmologies such as those of Ionia and in religious worldviews such as that of the Stoics. By the time Christianity appeared on the scene, the Roman world would have been entirely familiar with the thought that the universe might have gradually come to be as it is. Stoics and Epicureans would have disagreed about the role of reason and soul in this becoming, but they would have been at one in rejecting the other two alternative accounts, the eternalist one and the craft one.

There was no *theory* of evolution, of course, no account of how it might have happened, what laws or regularities would have been required in order that it might come about. Apart from the single imaginative suggestion on the part of Empedocles, a selective survival of the "fit", no other ideas were forthcoming. It was not as though anyone had made a systematic study of the three broad alternatives and had produced evidence favoring one over the other two. There *were*, of course, fragmentary arguments, bearing for instance on the role of reason in the production of order. But religious faith for the most part played a larger part than philosophical argument in inclining people to one or other of the alternatives.

3. Creation

I have already noted that the cosmogonies of most of the peoples of the ancient Near East began from an act of making on the part of a god or gods. The creation narrative of Genesis was distinctive, though it had almost surely been influenced by the cosmogonic myths of the lands in which the Hebrews had sojourned (Egypt, Canaan, Babylon).[18] In these other stories there had been a shaping of a preexistent matter or a generation from the substance of the god. But the Creator in Genesis did not fashion the world out of himself or out of some material. He said: *Let there be* light! Creation was not a shaping; it was a *command*, in response to which the creature sprang into being. Not a *making*, then, in the human sense. No recalcitrant material: the Creator looks at his handiwork and declares it to be good. It is fully what he has commanded it to be, unless, of course, he has given it the power to *resist* his command.

The Genesis narrative was not composed as an answer to a theoretical question as to how the world came to be.[19] Among the people for whom the narrative was intended it would have been assumed that God made the universe. But what needed emphasis was that Jahweh is the Lord of all, the ruler not only of nations but even of the sun and moon, of the seas and mountains. The story of the six days served as introduction to the history of the people of Israel. The gradual progression from the simplest yet mightiest creatures to the most complex and frailest ones led up to the appearance of man and initiated a history in which every stage had a significance for what would come later. The same Creator who brought the universe into being and still maintains it is the one to whom Israel long ago engaged itself by covenant: he is the one on whom Israel may forever unhesitatingly rely.

There was no Jewish *doctrine* of creation, no theoretical development of the hints given in the Genesis story. The Hebrews were not speculatively inclined, and, besides, the story of creation was only background for the more important truths of the Pentateuch. It was only when Christianity began to make its way in the Mediterranean world that the Old Testament it inherited came under serious philosophical scrutiny for the first time. Hans Jonas remarks:

> The doctrine of creation, with all that flows from it concerning the concepts of nature and man, was theoretically close enough to the terms of [Greek] natural theology to fall, as an issue, within the philosophical domain and thus *had* to be taken up by philosophy, whether affirmatively or negatively. On the other hand, the doctrine of the trinity and of incarnation was more alien to the established themes of philosophy; it seemed to defy philosophical assimilation and compel recognition as a supra-rational mystery. In short, the *rational* status of the two components of the Christian complex, and therefore their suitability for philosophical assimilation, were intrinsically unequal. We shall therefore not be surprised by the seemingly paradoxical finding that in a Christian intellectual universe it was the Jewish component which had the major philosophical impact.[20]

Jonas summarizes his point by calling the theme of creation "the cardinal and most obviously Jewish theme thrust on Western philosophy by Christian faith". The *doctrine* of creation that would emerge in those first centuries of Christianity was a Christian one, in the sense that it was elaborated by Christians and soon became a distinguishing mark of the new Christian faith.[21] But Jonas' point is that it took its departure from the Genesis story on which the Jewish religion had been nurtured for centuries. Though Christians might claim credit for the first coherent philosophical doctrine of creation, the doctrine had as its inspiration and partial warrant a specifically Jewish religious belief.

The new metaphysics of creation ran contrary to all of the options inherited from ancient Greece. It took shape only gradually; the theologians of the first four centuries were more concerned with the crucial but (as Jonas notes) conceptually troublesome notions of Incarnation and Trinity. St. Augustine was the first to develop an authentic metaphysics of creation that could hold its own against the Greek challenge. The encounter, in Jonas' words, "elicited from the biblical doctrine its latent implications concerning the whole nature of reality and made these at home in philosophy as an alternative, no less philosophical, view".[22]

There were two main points of disagreement between the creation account and the Greek cosmogonies. First, the Creator (according to Augustine) is responsible not just for the initial coming-to-be but for the entire *being* of all that is. Nothing lies outside his creative power. He does not, like Plato's Demiurge, have to contend with a resistant matter not of his own making. Thus, he is fully responsible for *all* that happens in the world. No Greek thinker had ever postulated a Creator in this strong sense; the Greeks were, as we have already seen, much too conscious of the presence of suffering and defect around them.

The second point of difference between the new doctrine of creation and the classic "eternalist" view of God's relation with the universe (as enunciated especially by Augustine's Neoplatonic contemporaries) was the claim that the world had a beginning. It is not, then, a necessary existent; indeed, it might well never have been. And its history is a single significant story leading up to a unique present moment. Behind this story lies the providence of the creator, constantly made manifest in the details of its daily working out, as in its first remote beginnings.

Augustine thus faced several new and difficult philosophical problems. How could man be truly free if all he does is entirely of God's creating? And how could a good God allow the presence in his world of so much sin and evil? These were to be the legacy of the doctrine of creation to later generations of Christian thinkers. Augustine struggled with these problems throughout his later life: some of his most enduring writings are concerned with the reality of freedom and the nature of evil.

But our concern here is limited to the doctrine of creation itself. The reading of the Bible in the light of the Neoplatonic doctrine that had early captivated him led Augustine to proclaim an omnipotent Creator whose existence is necessary and unchanging: "with Him there is no change nor shadow of alteration".[23] Time is God's creature; it is the condition under which the created world exists, the instrument of his providence.[24] There are two moments, he says, of creation:

> one in the original creation when God made all creatures before resting from all His works on the seventh day, and the other in the administration of creatures by which He works even now. In the first instance, God made everything together without any moments of time intervening, but now He works within the course of time, by which we see the stars move from their rising to their setting.[25]

Calling these "moments" must not lead us to impute time to God. From his point of view there is but a single act of creation in which past, present and future are contained. Yet that act has two "moments" ('aspects' might have been better) which are distinct:

> We should not think of [the first creation of things] as if it were the same as His working now in time. Rather, He made all things together, disposing them in an order based not on intervals of time but on causal connections.[26]

Bringing all things to be initially is not (from *our* point of view) the same as conserving them in being. But Augustine obviously regards both of these as manifestations of the same creative power. Here again the craft metaphor fails:

For the power and might of the Creator . . . makes every creature abide; and if this power ever ceased to govern creatures, their essences would pass away and all nature would perish. When a builder puts up a house and departs, his work remains in spite of the fact that he is no longer there. But the universe will pass away in the twinkling of an eye if God withdraws His ruling hand.[27]

Augustine would be critical of the modern tendency to speak of "the Creation" exclusively as a singular event in the past. There are some who think (he says) that God only made the first things and that everything else since that "is made by the world according to His ordination". Against this he urges the reader in eloquent fashion to:

> believe, and if possible also understand that God is working even now, so that if His action should be withdrawn from His creatures, they would perish. . . . God moves His whole creation by a hidden power and all creatures are subject to this movement: the angels carry out His commands, the stars move in their courses, the winds blow now this way now that, deep pools seethe beneath tumbling waterfalls and mists form above them, meadows come to life as the seeds put forth grasses, animals are born and live their lives according to their proper instincts, the evil are permitted to try the just. It is thus that God unfolds the generations which He laid up in creation when He first founded it; and they would not be sent forth to run their course if He who made creatures ceased to exercise His provident rule over them.[28]

4. Augustine's "Seed-Principles"

And how *were* these "generations laid up in creation"? What did Augustine mean earlier by saying that "God made everything together without any moments of time intervening"? He did not believe that the six "days" of the Genesis account ought to be understood literally: "we should not think of those days as solar days".[29] How could there be solar days before the sun itself came to be? Yet it was created only on the fourth "day". Furthermore, the term 'day' in its ordinary sense is relative to one's position on the earth, since it is night elsewhere when it is day here.[30] Since creation concerns the entire earth at once, the term 'day' must evidently be taken metaphorically. Augustine was relying here on the exegetical principle mentioned at the beginning of our essay: when there is a conflict between the literal reading of a passage in Scripture and a well-established truth about the world, we must take this as a mandate to search for a metaphorical reading of Scripture, on the assumption that this is what the writer must have intended.

Were the "days" indefinitely long periods of time then? Augustine did not think so. In fact, he insisted that the creative action whereby all things came to be was instantaneous; the six "days" refer (he suggests) to stages in the angelic knowledge of creation.[31] In properly temporal terms the "days" reduce to an indivisible instant, so that all the kinds of things mentioned in Genesis were really made simultaneously.[32] The warrant he offers for this is not a philosophical argument but a Scripture text, often repeated: "He created all things together".[33]

Does this mean that all the innumerable kinds of things—stars, earth, seas, plants, animals—came to be, fully formed, in that first moment? Here again Augustine was led by his reading of Scripture to give an unexpected answer. There are two different accounts of creation in the first two chapters of Genesis. Though Augustine considered the possibility that the second simply recapitulated the first, the differences between them were, to his mind, too great to make this a plausible reading.[34] He concluded that the second account must refer to a later stage in God's creative action when the individual kinds of things gradually made their appearance, each at the appropriate time. How, then, could Scripture also say that all things were created together? Here Augustine's reading of the philosophers came to his aid: what were present in the first instant were only the "seed-principles" (*rationes seminales*) of the different kinds.[35] This allowed him to hold both the theses he thought the Genesis text authorized: that the natural kinds were all created in the first instant of time and that they only made their appearance gradually over time.

This reading of Genesis was not an entirely novel one. The Alexandrine Fathers had already defended the view that the universe began from a single divine act and that the six "days" were to be taken allegorically. Gregory of Nyssa went further and argued that what came to be at the beginning were the potencies of all that would come later:

> The sources, causes, and potencies of all things were collectively sent forth in an instant, and in this first impulse of the Divine Will, the essences of all things assembled together: heaven, aether, star, fire, air, sea, earth, animal, plant—all beheld by the eye of God. . . . There followed a certain necessary series according to a certain order . . . as nature the maker (*technike phusis*) required . . . appearing not by chance . . . but because the necessary arrangement of nature required succession in the things coming into being.[36]

What struck Gregory in particular, as it had many of the earlier Fathers, was the way in which the Genesis account spoke of earth and waters "bringing forth" living creatures. It seemed clear that emphasis was being given to the part played by already existing materials in the coming-to-be of living things. God had to act upon these materials in a special way, of course, to bring forth the first instances of each kind. But Gregory took the mention of "earth" and "waters" to imply the prior presence of the requisite potencies only waiting the appropriate moment to be activated. It was not far from this to Augustine's doctrine.

There was one text, in particular, that Augustine liked to recall. The second account of creation begins, in the Old Latin translation he used: "This is the book of the creation of heaven and earth. When day was made, God made heaven and earth and every green thing of the field before it appeared above the earth".[37] Augustine takes this to mean that heaven, earth, plants, and day were made simultaneously at the beginning, but that the plants, at least, could only have been present in potency since they had not yet "appeared above the earth".[38] This supports his hypothesis that all or most things were present only in potency at the beginning.

The "seed-principles" are not, therefore, seeds in the ordinary sense. Augustine admits that his readers will find it difficult to imagine them since they are hidden from view. Yet this is (he says) no different from the principle whereby we grow old, which lies hidden in us when we are young. Though such a principle cannot be seen by the eyes, "by another kind of knowledge we conclude that there is in nature some hidden force by which latent forms are brought into view".[39] The inference to seed-principles is of a similar sort (though motivated differently). And it is aided by analogy: "There is, indeed, in seeds some likeness to what I am describing, because of the future developments stored up in them. Indeed, it is the seed-principle which is the more basic of the two, since it comes before the familiar seeds we know".[40]

He expands on the analogy. Tree comes from seed and seed from tree, and both from earth:

> In the seed, then, there was invisibly present all that would develop in time into a tree. And in this same way we must picture the world, when God made all things together, as having had all things which were made in it and with it when day was made. This includes not only heaven with sun, moon and stars . . . but also the beings which water and earth produced in potency and in their causes before they came forth in the course of time.[41]

Just as seeds may lie dormant until the right conditions are realized, so is it with the seed-principles: "all things were created by God in the beginning in a kind of blending of the elements, but they cannot develop and appear until the circumstances are favorable".[42] It sounds, then, as though the seed-principle is enough of itself, once the environment is right, to produce the new kind in a natural way.

Elsewhere, however, Augustine is not so sure about this. One reason may have been that he takes the Genesis text to imply that the adult forms of each kind came first. And it is obviously harder to imagine how the adult form could come naturally from a seed-principle without going through the normal growth process first. When discussing the origin of the first human body,[43] he asserts that the seed-principles have a *double* potentiality: they may cause slow growth leading in a natural way to maturity (somewhat as ordinary seeds do) or they may do no more than provide for the instantaneous and miraculous production by God of a mature living thing.[44]

But these (we would want to say) are "seed-principles" of two radically different sorts. The first bring about the appearance of new kinds through their own powers, when circumstances of earth and moisture and the like are favorable. The second require a special intervention on God's part to "form" the earth in a miraculous way. Why invoke a seed-principle at all in this latter case? Might not the Creator transform anything into anything, at his will? To say that there was a "seed-principle" present at the beginning for the Creator to form man in a miraculous way at some later time seems too weak to validate the claim that *man* was present in that first instant. Suppose God had simply made the first human body appear, without utilizing the materials of earth? Would there not, even in this case, have been a "seed-principle" for man, in this very weak sense, present beforehand?

Augustine does not think so: "If we should suppose that God now makes a creature without having implanted its kind in His original creation, we should flatly contradict Sacred Scripture which says that on the sixth day God finished all his works".[45] But if God now makes a new kind, was there not a "seed-principle" (or an "obediential potency", as later Scholastic philosophers would call it) for that kind there beforehand, "implanted" in the original creation?

The reason why Augustine excludes this must be because of the role that earth plays in the biblical descriptions of God's making of human and animal bodies. Even if God intervenes in a miraculous way to make man, he does not do it *ex nihilo*, as he did the first creation. He takes earth, which was part of that first creation, and draws on its potencies, even though he goes beyond what earth of its own causal powers could bring about. It was in the first formless matter that the seed-principles resided. Without matter the seed analogy breaks down.

But *was* a special divine intervention needed for the first appearance of the kinds of animals? Granted that there was a seed-principle present beforehand, was it one that led the bodies to form naturally or was it one that required supernatural supplementation? Augustine is not sure:

> In either case, whichever way God made Adam, He did what was in accordance with His almighty power and wisdom. God has established in the temporal order fixed laws governing the production of kinds of beings and qualities of beings and bringing them forth from a hidden state into full view, but His will is supreme over all. By His power, He has given numbers to His creation, but He has not bound His power by these numbers.[46]

The "numbers" here are the laws of nature (by "measure, number and weight") appropriate to each creature.[47] The seed-principles may work according to these "numbers", or they may require the intervention of the Creator to bring about an outcome that would not "naturally" occur. Augustine is at pains to warn us about the ambiguity of the term 'natural' here. When a miracle such as the changing of water into wine described in the Gospels occurs, it does "not happen against nature except for us who have limited knowledge of nature, but not for God, for whom nature is what He has made".[48] Nevertheless, from *our* point of view, there is a very large difference between a doctrine of seed-principles which would hold that all the kinds of things, including the human body,[49] originated through causal powers implanted in matter, and one that would require in addition that the Creator act in a miraculous way in the origination of all (or some) living kinds.

Augustine's theory of seed-principles has obvious affinities with the Stoic *logos spermatikos*, as well as with the equation between *logos* and Platonic ideas in Neoplatonism. But the context is now quite different. The function of the seed-principle is to explain how one can say *both* that God made all things at the beginning *and* that the various kinds of things made their appearance only gradually over the course of historic time. And the warrant for it is almost entirely theological.[50]

Can the theory be described as "evolutionary"? A number of Catholic writers have, over the years, cited Augustine's authority in support of an evolutionary approach to the origin of species.[51] At a time when the attitude of the Church and of Christians generally to the Darwinian theory of evolution was (to say the least) reserved, the support of Augustine was regarded as an important factor. But one has to be careful not to make too strong a claim. Augustine did not hold that one species could arise out of another; his theory of forms as ideas in the mind of God would have rendered such an hypothesis quite implausible[52]. In his view each species arose at the proper time out of its *own* seed-principle. And, as we have seen, he left open the possibility that a divine intervention of a miraculous sort might have been involved in the origination of all, or at least some, animal species. His theory was not proposed as a scientific explanation; though prompted, in part, by seed-analogies, it was not a response to empirical observations suggesting that the kinds of things had only gradually made their appearance.

Nevertheless, there is something to be said for situating Augustine at the head of the lineage not of evolutionary theory but of attempts to show how the notions of evolution and creation may fit together. He clearly saw that a Creator of the sort he envisaged could bring the kinds of things to be in either of two different ways: either by an original miraculous intervention in each case or by the use of the natural order itself to develop the various kinds in a gradual way. He did not try to decide between the two; all he wanted to convey was that Scripture is open to either interpretation. After all, there was virtually no evidence in his day for the gradualist alternative, and it would have seemed almost inconceivable to any who would have reflected upon the issue that there ever could be a way for a man to extend to the distant past the "other kind of knowledge" he refers to in the context of human aging and reveal how the seed-principles could have accomplished their task:

> The principle which makes this development possible is hidden to the eyes but not to the mind; but whether such a development must necessarily come about is completely unknown to us. We know that the principle which makes it possible is in the very nature of body; but there is no clear evidence in that body that there is a principle by which it must necessarily take place.[53]

This was Augustine, the philosopher, speaking!

By interpreting the role of earth in the Genesis account as a causal potency within which the future is at least partially contained, Augustine pointed the way to a new metaphysics which could draw upon protoscientific analogies with seeds and their hidden powers as well as insights into how the Creator might make use of his creature, time, to accomplish his ends. This new metaphysics has elements of both the craft and the evolutionary metaphors; the only model it flatly excludes is the eternalist one of Aristotle. In it the two facets of God's creative action are for the first time clearly outlined. From this beginning all later attempts to show how evolution and creation might complement one another take their origin. It is because of this "seed-principle" lying within Augustine's writings on creation that I have devoted so much attention to them here.

5. Aquinas on Creation

Between the fifth and the thirteenth centuries little attention was paid to the science of nature in its own right. It is in the "hexemeral" literature (commentaries on the work of the six days) that one finds an account of the natural knowledge of the day. The Genesis story of origins provided the occasion for an orderly review of what was known of the heavens, the earth, the plant world, the animal world, and the nature of man.[54] It did not seem important to stress the difference between the two sources of knowledge, the Bible and experience, since both came from God. Encyclopedists like Isidore of Seville moved easily from one source to the other in their chapters on nature. And Augustine's cosmogony continued to find favor. The origin of kinds was thought of not as a discontinuous series of divine interventions over a period of six days but as a gradual unfolding of potencies set within the original matter by God.

The rediscovery of Aristotle's works on nature in the early thirteenth century encouraged a very different perspective. Instead of going to Genesis or to popular encyclopedias the new Aristotelians would have recourse for their knowledge of nature to the works of Aristotle or to scholarly commentaries on those works. They would stress the autonomy of natural science as a distinctive enterprise. Not that they would deny the authority of Scripture, but that the easy blend of considerations drawn from the Bible and from experience might no longer seem unproblematic. The cosmogony of seed-principles, so congenial to a Neoplatonist, would hardly appeal to someone who saw in the eternity of essences the ultimate basis of teleological explanation. In such a perspective the notion of an absolute beginning was hard to accept. But once accepted, an abrupt beginning of each natural kind might well be preferable to a gradual development from seed-principles.

Aquinas tried hard to bridge the gap between Augustine and Aristotle in his account of origins in the *Summa Theologica*. Under each heading he gives the views of Augustine as well as of the earlier Patristic writers who had defended a literal interpretation of the Genesis "days":

> It must, however, be observed that Augustine differs from other writers in his opinion about the production of fishes and birds, just as he does about the production of plants. For while others say that fishes and birds were produced in their mature form on the fifth day, he holds that the nature of the waters produced them on that day in potency only.[55]

So great is his respect for Augustine that he balances the arguments on both sides in order, as he says, to be "impartial".[56] If the notion of seed-principles bothered his Aristotelian sensibilities, he never says so. Perhaps the broadening of the notion of *telos* that he had already undertaken earlier in the *Summa* would have suggested that *telos*-guided development might be extended from the growth of each organic individual to that of each organic species.

Aquinas suggests that the work of the six days can be understood as threefold.[57] First, there is the work of *creation*, when heaven and earth are brought to be but as yet without form. Second, there is the work of *distinction*, occupying the first three days, when the realms of earth and sky and water are separated off from one another. Third, there is the work of *adornment*, occupying the second three days, when the various specific kinds (heavenly bodies, animals, man) are added. He seems prepared to allow that the work of distinction could be regarded as a drawing forth of potencies already implanted in earth and water. The plants, he recalls, are said to be "brought forth" on the third day by the earth under God's command.[58]

But the work of adornment was different. Speaking of the generation of animals, he says that "those things that are naturally generated from seed cannot be generated naturally in any other way".[59] Thus for the first appearance of higher animals[60] a special intervention on the Creator's part would have been needed:

At the first beginning of the world, the active principle was the Word of God
who produced animals from material elements, either in mature form as some holy
writers say, or virtually, as Augustine teaches.[61]

As usual, Aquinas leaves open the choice between Augustine's seed-
principles and the direct fashioning of the mature animal bodies by God on
the fifth day. In the former case an intervention is still required on God's
part since the seed-principles were conceived of as additions to elements of
water and earth that would not possess them on their own account. Aquinas
never does discuss whether the development of the seed-principles from their
virtual beginning could itself be regarded as a *natural* process. This was no
problem for Augustine, but it would have been an awkward topic for an
Aristotelian. Such development is not part of the ordinary round of nature,
and the Aristotelian notion of nature would have had to be stretched considerably to accommodate it. It may have been because of this that Aquinas
never endorsed the Augustinian notion outright.

It is from the Genesis text, rather more than from the biological works
of Aristotle, that Aquinas derives such accounts as this one:

Fish are merely bodies having something in them of soul, while land animals because
of the higher perfection of their life are, as it were, living souls with bodies subject
to them. But the life of man, since it is of the highest kind, is not said to be produced, like the life of other animals from earth or water, but immediately by God.[62]

The elements of earth and water contribute to the coming to be of animals
and even of the human body. But the human soul is "breathed into" the
materials of earth; intellect is of its nature immaterial (Aquinas argues) and
so cannot be constituted from the potencies of matter. There is a notorious
tension here between the Platonic and the Aristotelian notions of soul.[63]
Aquinas appears to draw on both, using the Aristotelian language of matter
and form while attributing, as Plato does, subsistence (independent existence)
to the human soul. What he is concerned with above all, of course, is the
Christian doctrine of immortality. By making the intellect naturally incorruptible he made soul naturally immortal. The Christian promise of resurrection would then bear only on body; even without this promise there would
already have been a form of immortality for individual humans based on their
possession of intellect.[64]

Our immediate concern is not with the credentials of this doctrine but
with its implications for origins and for natural process generally. In his account of the work of the six days Aquinas stresses the role of the potencies
already implanted in the material order in the subsequent bringing to be
of complex forms. He was not, as we have seen, as "developmental" in his
thinking as Augustine had been. Yet the biblical language of "earth bringing forth" influenced him, just as it had done Augustine. Only one thing

could not in any way be brought forth by earth, according to both thinkers, and that was the human soul. Here God had to intervene in a more radical way.

There was, of course, one other doctrine on which an Aristotelian could not readily have compromised. The heavenly bodies according to Aristotle are incorruptible and hence could not have been generated from a prior matter. Origin by "seed-principles" could, therefore, not be allowed.[65] In his discussion of the fourth day Aquinas lists this view of the heavenly bodies, without explicitly making it his own; we know, of course, from his commentaries on Aristotle that it was a crucial part of his own cosmology. But how is this to fit the chronology of the Genesis account?

> The answer must be that the luminaries were substantially created in the beginning, but that their substance, at first formless, is formed on this (fourth) Day by receiving not its substantial form but a determination of power.[66]

It seems a bit strained, but then Aquinas had undertaken a near-impossible task to begin with. Unlike his Augustinian contemporaries, he maintained that without the aid of revelation one could never have known that the universe had had a beginning in time. As far as natural philosophy was concerned, therefore, the eternal universe of Aristotle was still the norm. What he had to do was to show how a universe as like this as possible could more or less abruptly come to be through the action of an omnipotent Creator.

The problem was to know how much relative weight to give the text of Genesis and how much to the works of the philosopher. In the story of the second day the Creator is said to divide the waters beneath from those above by means of a "firmament" or "Heaven". This might (Aquinas remarks) be thought to support the Ionian doctrine that water is the primary element of all things.

> As, however, this view can be shown to be false by solid reasons, it cannot be held to be the sense of Holy Scripture. It should rather be considered that Moses was speaking to ignorant people, and that out of consideration for their weakness he put before them only such things as are apparent to sense. Now even the most uneducated can perceive by their senses that earth and water are corporeal, whereas it is not evident to all that air also is corporeal, for there have been philosophers who said that air is nothing, and called a space filled with air a vacuum. Moses, then, while he expressly mentions water and earth, makes no express mention of air by name, to avoid setting before ignorant persons something beyond their knowledge.[67]

The author of Genesis (whom Aquinas assumed to be Moses) accommodated his manner of writing to the capacities of the uneducated; thus the text is not to be taken literally in all cases. We must search for the true meaning with the help of such other sources of knowledge as natural philosophy. Since

we know from the philosophers that air is an element on a par with earth
and water, and that its natural place is above that of water, we can interpret
the Genesis text as conveying that the "firmament" is the air that lies between the waters below (the seas) and those above (the clouds). And we can
then reinterpret other texts in support of this reading. The passage cited above
continues:

> In order, however, to express the truth to those capable of understanding it, (Moses)
> implies in the words 'Darkness was upon the face of the deep', the existence of
> air as attendant, so to say, upon the water. For it may be understood from these
> words that over the face of the water a transparent body was extended, the subject
> of light and darkness which is, in fact, the air.

Here one can see just how interpretive Aquinas was prepared to be. Taking "Darkness was upon the face of the deep" to convey that air lies above
the waters requires quite a bit of the reader, even of one who is "capable
of understanding the truth". But Aquinas was sufficiently confident in the
best natural science of his day, and in the principle that the truths of science
and of revelation could never contradict, that the imaginative character of
interpretations like this one would not have worried him. Of course, his
assurance that Moses had had revealed to him the sequence of events in those
first days never wavered. How else could the author of Genesis have set down
the story of a time when no human was present to leave a record?
    What gave Aquinas the leeway he needed in reconciling the Genesis text
with the findings of the natural philosophers was his accommodation principle: Moses could not have been expected to make his narrative conform to
the truths of natural philosophy since this would have confused his uneducated
readers. The task of the theologian, therefore, was to reinterpret in the light
of the best natural knowledge of the day the texts thus accommodated. And
the norms governing this reinterpretation were to be quite generous.
    Aquinas' extraordinary effort to bring Aristotle's science of nature and the
truths of the Christian faith together in a single synthesis was challenged even
in his own lifetime. His critics saw in this demonstrative science and in the
notion of nature underlying it a threat to the Christian doctrines of God's
omnipotence and freedom. The rise of "voluntarist" theologies in the fourteenth century saw a more and more energetic assault on the Greek assumption of an invariant natural order. In this climate the Augustinian view that
God had made use of powers originally implanted in nature to bring about
the wondrous diversity of the world lost ground. The new stress on the radical
openness of history to God's free action, untrammeled by considerations of
"essence" or "nature", made it easy to read the Genesis text in a more or
less literal way as a sequence of "miracles", of divine actions lying outside
the bounds set by such human notions as nature or potency or even seed-
principle.

A further impulse to literalism can be discerned two centuries later in the debates surrounding the Protestant Reformation. At the heart of the disagreement between Catholics and Reformers was the question of the interpretation of Scripture: what norms should it follow and under what authority should it be carried on. The "extended" interpretations of earlier generations became suspect, and a "dictation" view of the inspiration of Scripture began to make its way. The topic is an immensely complicated one, and one on which much historical work remains to be done. But it seems safe to say that by the time of Galileo the more relaxed approach of Augustine and of Aquinas to the problem of harmonizing Scripture and natural knowledge had been forgotten in the heat of battle.[68]

6. A New Kind of Scientific Explanation

The first account of cosmic evolution that might perhaps qualify as a scientific theory goes back right to the beginnings of the scientific revolution. It derived from physics, not from biology; it was, after all, far easier to suppose that the main features of the physical world had evolved than that the much more complex structures of the living realm could be accounted for in this way. Descartes was convinced that an adequate physics ought to be able in principle to explain the *origins* of each kind of thing, or to put this in another way, that to explain the *nature* of something is to explain how it might have been brought to be by means of natural processes:

> Just as for an understanding of the nature of plants or men it is better by far to consider how they can gradually grow from seeds than how they were created by God in the very beginning of the world; so, if we can devise some principles which are very simple and easy to know and by which we can demonstrate that the stars and the Earth, and indeed everything which we perceive in this visible world, could have sprung forth, as if from certain seeds (even though we know that things did not happen that way), we shall in that way explain their nature much better than if we were merely to describe them as they are now.[69]

The language of "seeds" is reminiscent of Augustine. But the project Descartes is describing is very different from the Augustinian one. He is confident that the original development of the "seed-principles" can be scientifically explained and that the science required for this is the very same one that governs the everyday action of things. Thus, there are not two different kinds of "natural" process, as Augustine's doctrine had implied, one to bring the natural kinds to be and the other that by which these kinds normally operate. A single account of nature will suffice, Descartes believes, to make the entire story intelligible.

The account is a *mechanical* one, based on the general principles of motion, not (as Augustine might have expected) on concepts drawn specifically from the living world. It is not teleological; like the atomist accounts rejected by Aristotle, it makes no use of such qualifiers as "acting for the good". It might be said to be inspired by the hypothesis of the world as a cosmic machine.[70] Yet this will not quite do since machines do not generate themselves. There is more to it, as we shall see, than a mechanical analogy alone.

But first it should be emphasized that a fifth type of explanation, different in kind from the canonical four "causes" listed by Aristotle in the *Physics*, is taking shape here. It can be called *genetic*, because it explains, not how a nature operates, but how a nature of this sort might have originally come to be through an earlier sequence of traceable stages. Descartes sees genetic explanation as fundamental to our claim to *understand* a nature, and in this he has been followed by later natural science. The break between Descartes and Aristotle is just as decisive on this issue as in regard to the connected notion of teleology.

Aristotle believed that the eternity of natures furnished the only adequate basis for explaining the theological features of natural process. Descartes rejected this starting point. His assurance that the universe began from a moment in the past was what led him to ask how it could have got to be what it now is. The Christian doctrine of creation played a part, therefore, in the shaping of this new kind of question, the genetic question that would find its answer in an evolutionary type of theory.

Descartes realized that two diametrically different accounts of origins were possible. On the one hand, there was the literalist biblical account which had been gaining in favor among theologians over the previous century. An omnipotent God, as Descartes saw, *could* have brought the original diversity of kinds to be in that way. For prudential reasons he was even prepared to allow that this account was the correct one:

> I do not doubt that the world was created in the beginning with all the perfection it now possesses, so that the sun, the earth, the moon and the stars existed in it. . . . The Christian faith teaches us this, and natural reason convinces us that this is true, because taking into account the omnipotence of God, we must believe that everything He created was perfect in every way.[71]

One wonders whether Descartes really *did* believe that "Christian faith" committed him to the literalist account. It seems most unlikely, given the enthusiasm with which he presents the alternative. And the inference from the omnipotence of God is at odds, as the reader would be bound to see, with the entire line of argument elsewhere in the *Principles*. Why could he not have done what Aquinas did and leave the reader free to choose between the literalist account and a gradualist one recalling the precedent of Augustine? Presumably it was his perception of the change of climate in Rome, signified by the trial and condemnation of Galileo, that led him to be so cautious. He *could*, after all, have invoked the authority of Augustine for his gradualist explanation of origins.

He may have been aware that Galileo too had called on Augustine in his own battle to gain discussion space for the Copernican theory.[72] But the theological credentials of the gradualist interpretation of Genesis were far stronger than anything Galileo could have cited in favor of the Copernican doctrine. What Descartes worried about most was the obvious support his cosmogony gave to the notion of a moving earth, explicitly condemned in the 1616 decision of the Congregation of the Index. And so he went to elaborate lengths in the *Principles* to show how the earth might still in a certain (rather strained) sense be taken to be at rest.

Descartes evidently felt that he could not introduce his own evolutionary explanation of origins as an hypothesis on equal footing with the prevailing literalist account. And so he adopted a device: he asked his readers to allow their thought "to wander beyond this world to view another wholly new one", where God is assumed to create an original chaos of particles of all shapes, sizes, and motions.[73] From such a starting point, he asserted, he could show that a world very like our own would necessarily develop, without the need for any further special intervention on God's part. He hoped that this device would enable him to avoid trouble with the theologians of the Sorbonne and at the same time allow readers to make up their own minds about the merits of his proposal.

What he lacked, of course, was a satisfactory method of *comparing* the merits of two conflicting hypothetical claims, where one was based on Scripture and the other on natural science. The principle (partly deriving from Augustine) which had been so often cited in the Galileo debate, that the literal reading of Scripture should prevail except where the conflicting scientific claim could be *demonstrated*, was altogether unsatisfactory.[74] And the Church's reliance on authority to close the gap between hypothesis and the truth made the epistemic situation even more difficult to assess. In the *Discourse* he recalls the program he had set before himself in *Le Monde:*

> I resolved to leave this whole world to their disputes, and to speak only of what would happen in a new world, if God were now to create somewhere in imaginary space enough matter to compose it, and if He agitated the parts of this matter diversely and without order, so that He made of it a chaos as confused as the poets can imagine and if He afterwards did nothing else except lend His ordinary support to nature and leave it to act according to the laws which he established.[75]

He has no doubt at all about what would happen in such a world:

The greatest part of the matter of this chaos must, according to these laws, become disposed and arranged in a certain way which would make it similar to our heavens. . . . Some of its parts must compose an earth, some compose planets and comets, and some others a sun and fixed stars. . . . There is nothing to be seen in the phenomena of this world which would not, or at least which could not, appear in the same way in the phenomena of the world I was describing.[76]

The weakening of "would not" to "could not" suggests that what Descartes was claiming was that *in principle* he could infer from an initially unstructured model to such specifics as "water, air, fire, minerals.[77] Part of his problem here, as elsewhere in his scientific writings, is to know how to deal with hypothesis. According to the notion of demonstration he describes in his early work, the *Regulae*, hypothesis has no proper place in science except perhaps as a temporary stage on the way to demonstration. But how can one demonstrate from effects back to causes? The predicament was a familiar one in the Aristotelian tradition.[78] It was enough for demonstration to show that a postulated cause *could* account for all the observed effects, since another cause might conceivably do so equally well.

Galileo had faced a similar issue just a few years before. Then, too, the notion of hypothesis had proved crucial. Pope Urban encouraged him to proceed with the writing of the *Dialogue* but reminded him that the Copernican system had to be treated as an "hypothesis". Urban was using the term in the sense that had long been customary in mathematical astronomy, namely, a fiction whose sole function is to "save the appearances". But in the *Dialogue* Galileo took the term in the sense familiar to later science: a possibly true account, adequately supported by the evidence given. Descartes, as we have seen, was not going to make the same mistake. And so he advertised himself as following essentially the injunction that Galileo had disregarded.

Even though these things may be thought to be false, I shall consider that I have achieved a great deal if all the things which are deduced from them are entirely in conformity with the phenomena. For if this comes about, my hypothesis will be as useful to life as if it were true [because we will be able to use it in the same way to dispose natural causes to produce the effects which we desire].[79]

The pragmatic tone of these last words are, of course, at odds with the entire tenor of the *Principles*. Only a few lines before he had said:

Certainly, if the principles which I use are very obvious, if I deduce nothing from them except by a mathematical sequence, and if what I thus deduce is in exact agreement with all natural phenomena, it seems that it would be an injustice to God that the causes of the effects which are in nature and which we have thus discovered are false.[80]

It is the *coherence* of the entire argument that he thinks to be an overwhelming indication of the truth of the supposition from which it proceeds.[81]

At the end of the *Principles* he concedes once again that an omnipotent God *could* have brought about things in a different way. But "lest some injury to truth might occur", he feels it necessary to advise the reader that the overall argument of the *Principles* is sufficient to warrant a *moral* certainty.

> Those who notice how many things concerning the magnet, fire, and fabric of the entire world have been deduced here from so few principles (even if they were to suppose that I adopted these principles only by chance and without reason) will perhaps realize that it could scarcely have occurred that so many things should be consistent with one another, if they were false.[82]

What he is underlining here is that he can call not only on the fit between the phenomena and the consequences of his model but also on the *truth* of the principles on which the model is based. We have not discussed these principles here; it would take us too far afield to work through the extraordinarily complex and ingenious details of his cosmogony. But a brief note may help. In *Le Monde* he enunciates three "laws of nature" sufficient of themselves to "untangle the confusion of the chaos".[83] Bodies continue in the same state of rest or motion unless forced to change by collision with other bodies. At collision, motion lost by one body is gained by the other. The tendency of a moving body is to continue its motion in a straight line. These laws derive directly from the immutability of God: "acting always in the same way, He always produces the same effect".[84] Even if all the evidence of our senses concerning the world we know seemed contrary to these laws, we would still be obliged to suppose them to hold in the "new world" whose evolution is to be explored. No other laws are needed for determining all the "effects of nature" except the "eternal truths of mathematics . . . according to which God Himself has taught us He disposed all things in number, weight, and measure". Together, these permit "demonstrations *a priori* of everything that can be produced in that new world".[85]

One additional supposition is needed, and that is that "God will never make any miracle in the new world".[86] What justifies this supposition, once again, is the divine immutability. "It is one of God's perfections to be not only immutable in His nature, but also immutable and completely constant in the way He acts".[87] Once the universe is created, God does nothing but preserve it; thus, the amount of motion given it at the first moment is permanently conserved.

What is implicit in all this, of course, is that God would be unlikely[88] to bring the diversity of kinds to be by a sequence of miraculous intrusions, all the more because such intrusions (Descartes believes he can show) are not required for him to attain his ends. This closes the gap logically. It virtually excludes the literalist reading of the six days, though, of course, Descartes cannot say so. But it was not difficult for the reader to draw such an obvious conclusion.

What follows from all of this is that cosmic evolution is not just possible: it is a conceptual necessity. Even if the details of Descartes' own cosmogony were to prove inadequate, a theory of evolution would still have to be found. This close tie between the doctrines of creation and evolution was new; it was prompted in large part by the mechanical worldview within which the notion of miraculous intrusion was coming to seem an altogether inappropriate way for God to bring about his "natural" ends.

As we read the *Principles* today, the derivations often appear extraordinarily speculative. Take his explanation of terrestrial magnetism, for example:

> There are many pores in the Earth's intermediate region which are parallel to its axis, and through which the grooved particles coming from one pole freely proceed to the other. And these pores have been hollowed out to the measurements of these particles in such a way that those which accept the grooved particles coming from the South pole can in no way admit those coming from the North pole . . . because of course these particles are twisted like the thread of a screw, some in one direction and the others in the opposite one.[89]

This was the kind of invention that Newton had in mind fifty years later when he decried the use of "hypothesis" in science. What gave Descartes confidence in his scheme was his conviction that a *mechanical* explanation had to be possible for all phenomena and for the genesis of all structures. And 'mechanical' was to be construed in the narrowest possible terms; attractions of any sort were to be excluded, and all structures had to be generated by combinations of vortices of particles of the three "elements", called analogously by him fire, air, and earth. Thus, only a narrow range of possibilities was open, and this lent plausibility to those that his limitless ingenuity succeeded in formulating.

Even the living world was to be explained in mechanical terms, and the discovery of the circulation of blood encouraged him to think of animal bodies as complex interacting circulatory systems, analogous with the systems of the heavens.[90] In the *Discourse* he concedes that he does not yet have sufficient knowledge to speak of the formation of animal bodies as he does of the inanimate.[91] He is content for the moment to assume that God formed the human body; he can then show how such a body operates as a purely mechanical system. In the *Principles* he once again sets these topics aside: "I do not know whether I shall ever have sufficient leisure to complete them".[92] Four years later he managed a short tract, *The Description of the Human Body* (1648), which went some way toward showing the approach he intended to adopt. His success in reconstructing the "causes of the formation" of the animal body led him to enthuse: "I have discovered so many new vistas that I have almost no doubt at all that I will achieve all of physics according to my desire".[93]

This first "theory" of biological evolution was thus a part of physics. It could only vaguely suggest how animal bodies might form. But it could not even begin to explain how the diversity of the plant and animal world might have originated. Nor could it explain the adaptations that were so striking a feature of all forms of life. The evolutionary presupposition upon which it depended — that any natural kind can be explained in a developmental (and in this case mechanical) way by tracing lawlike general relations to earlier different stages — seemed to most readers to exclude the operation of providence entirely.

7. The Rise of Physicotheology

The reaction against the Cartesian cosmogony was sharpest among the scientists of the Royal Society, the "virtuosi", as they came to call themselves. Most of these were men of deep religious convictions; many had been influenced by the Calvinist theology of the Puritans. The title of John Ray's immensely popular book *The Wisdom of God Manifested in the Work of Creation* (1691) conveys quite well the spirit with which they approached their investigations of nature. Robert Hooke in his *Micrographia* (1665) echoes their sentiments when he exclaims in wonder at the marvels of design his new microscope reveals in the minute world of the gnat; contemplating these creatures can only lead us to magnify the providence that so clearly works to bring them about.[94]

No wonder, then, that the chief spokesman of the virtuosi, Robert Boyle, would take Descartes to task for his claim that "the ends of God in things corporeal (are) so sublime that it were presumption in man to think his reason can extend to discover them".[95] Effectively this would be to exclude "final causes", explanation in terms of design, from science entirely. In common with most of the virtuosi, Boyle regarded this as a lamentable error, one which "tends much to weaken, if not quite to deprive us of, one of the best and most successful arguments to convince man that there is a God".[96]

And such arguments were coming to be needed. The deep religious dissensions that had been dividing Europe for more than a century had shaken the faith of many. Scripture, it seemed, had served too often to divide. It was attractive, then, for men of faith to seek an uncontroversial basis for belief in God through the commonalities of science.[97] In this way the exasperations of theological disagreement might be avoided, or at least postponed.

At the heart of this new "physicotheology", as its exponents sometimes called it,[98] was the argument from design:

> The excellent contrivance of the great system of the world, and especially the curious fabric of the bodies of animals and the uses of their sensories and other parts, have

been made the great motives that in all ages and nations induced philosophers to acknowledge a Deity as the author of these admirable structures.[99]

Naturalists such as Ray and Nehemiah Grew piled up example after example of adaptation of structure or of behavior in the living world:

> The bee, a creature . . . . (such) that no man can suspect it to have any considerable measure of understanding, or to have any knowledge of, much less to aim at, any end, yet makes her combs and cells with that geometrical accuracy that she must needs be acting by an instinct implanted in her by the wise author of Nature.[100]

Boyle was particularly taken by the differing structures of the eye in insects, frogs, birds, and man. He found great pleasure, he tells us, in the discovery of "hundreds of little round protuberances curiously ranged on the convexity of a single eye" in the common fly, and he had no difficulty in determining what their function might be. It is a tribute to the wisdom of the Creator that he has furnished different species with very different sorts of eyes, suiting them

> both to the rest of their bodies and (which I here mainly consider) to those parts of the great theatre of the world on which He designs that they shall live and act.[101]

The argument was a simple and a persuasive one.[102] Everywhere in living nature we find instances of organic function or species behavior that serve the good of the organism as a whole. Such fitting of means to end can only be explained in terms of an intelligence which *understands* the relationships involved and deliberately designed the organ or the instinct in order to bring the end about. The general laws of mechanics operating upon matter could never suffice to explain how such adaptive structures first came to be, nor how they continue to reappear. The atomists and Descartes, though they begin from very different premises, regard these structures as the outcome of "chance", that is, as needing no special intelligence in their fashioning. The exponents of physicotheology were convinced that this was just bad science. The reductionist principles of Cartesian mechanics (they asserted) had left its author without the resources to explain a good part of the structure of the world.

Boyle was prepared to concede that Descartes might be able to explain the major features of the *inanimate* world. The degree of "contrivance" there is "rarely so exquisite" that "without much improbability", though perhaps only "after many essays", these features might be explained by vortices or the like physical devices:

> I cannot but think that the situations of celestial bodies do not afford by far so clear and cogent arguments of the wisdom and design of the author of the world as do the bodies of animals and plants. And, for my part, I am apt to think there

is more of admirable contrivance in a man's muscles than in (what we yet know of) the celestial orbs; and that the eye of a fly is (at least as far as it appears to us) a more curious piece of workmanship than the body of the sun.[103]

Though most of the virtuosi agreed with Boyle that the argument from design ought to be based on the structures of the living world, there was one distinguished dissenter. In his letters to Bentley (1692-1693) Newton drew upon his newly published *Principia* to show that Descartes was wrong in virtually every single claim he had made for his cosmogony. The formation of a planetary system like ours from an original "chaos":

> I do not think explicable by mere natural causes but am forced to ascribe it to the counsel and contrivance of a voluntary Agent. . . . Why there is one body in our system qualified to give light and heat to all the rest, I know no reason but because the Author of the system thought it convenient. . . . The motions which the planets now have could not spring from any natural cause alone but were impressed by an intelligent Agent. . . . To make this system with all its motions required a cause which understood and compared together the quantities of matter in the several bodies of the sun and planets . . . (a cause) very well skilled in mechanics and geometry.[104]

There is an important difference between Newton's appeal to design and that of Boyle. Boyle had singled out means-end adaptations in the living world that seemed to demand an intelligent agent as their explanation. Newton tries to cast his argument in the same mold, but it does not quite fit. What it really reduces to is the negative claim that the complex and stable structures of the planetary system cannot be explained by the mechanics of the *Principia* alone and thus that some outside agency must be called on. It does not appeal to adaptation, strictly speaking, except in the vague sense that a stable planetary system is desirable as an abode for man. Newton's argument is thus more vulnerable than Boyle's: all that may be needed is a more adequate mechanics. Boyle, on the other hand, could urge that a mechanics could never *in principle* simulate certain sorts of works of intelligence. Only an intelligent agent can build complex means-to-end relationships into its products.

Newton was, of course, right in claiming that the *Principia* could not make room for an evolutionary account of cosmic origins. "The growth of new systems out of old ones, without the mediation of a Divine power, seems to me apparently (evidently) absurd".[105] Later Newtonians like Laplace were able to show that the mechanics of the *Principia* could in fact explain many of the features of the solar system which Newton had held to require a special divine intervention. But Newton was justified in his belief that a cosmogony could never be found for bodies in infinite number spread through infinite

Euclidean space. For that a different sort of space and a quite different sort of mechanics would be required.[106]

Returning to the more persuasive design arguments based on the presence of adaptation in the living world, how did their exponents understand the process by which the Creator brought about such adaptation? Was it an *intervention* in normal natural process? Could it be comprehended in scientific terms? This turns out to be a difficult question to answer, not only because it was not directly addressed in those terms by the virtuosi but also because the notion of "intervention" and its correlative, "invariable nature", would not have been acceptable to them on theological grounds.

In order to explain why, it would be necessary to outline the so-called "voluntarist" tradition in theology which linked Boyle, and many of the other virtuosi, through Calvin to the nominalist thinkers of the fourteenth century. There is space here only for a brief word.[107] The voluntarists saw the work of the Creator in terms of his supreme *will* rather than his intellect. They rejected Aristotelian essentialism as an unacceptable limitation on God's freedom. God is limited only by the principle of noncontradiction. Each occasion is radically different from every other; universals function only as names (nominalism). Where Aquinas saw natural law as an expression of God's intellect and natures themselves as in some sense representative of ideas in the divine mind, the voluntarists saw law in relation to God's command. What makes it "law" for them is not at all its rationality or the regular way in which it manifests itself but the fact that it *obliges*. Aquinas insists that God acts in the world through his creatures, to whom he has delegated real powers. If this were not to be so, "the order of cause and effect would be taken away from created things, and this would imply a lack of power in the Creator".[108] The voluntarists tended to hold that God acts *immediately* in the world, and some of them maintained that no cause-effect relationship could be demonstrated in the sensible world.[109]

On the face of it, it might seem unlikely that anything like this view would be found among the mechanical philosophers. Did not mechanical philosophy itself, and the machine analogies on which Boyle, in particular, liked to dwell, imply a kind of subsistence and stability for the physical order, akin to that of the natures or essences of the Aristotelians? The voluntarism of the virtuosi was, indeed, qualified by their enthusiasm for the machine metaphor, and it becomes very difficult to untangle the threads at times.[110] But they insisted on the *passivity* of matter (against the "naturalists") and emphasized the fact that machines embody design. And above all they saw physical events, even when linked in mechanical sequences, as response to God's commands, as "custom", rather than as manifestations of underlying natures.

Returning, then, to the question from which we began, when the proponents of physicotheology assert that the intelligence of a designer must be discerned in the production of the living, what does this entail? Though they do not stress this point, they are speaking not only of the first appearance but also of the continuing reproduction of each species. The constituents of the living body are governed by mechanical laws, as are those of a clock. It is in the *production* of the living body (as in that of a clock) that the effects of an agent intelligence can be seen. Not that this production runs counter to mechanical law; only that this law *alone* cannot suffice to explain the outcome.

Does God *intervene*, then, in the formation of living bodies? Not really, because every temporal occurrence is equally the creation of his will. There are no "natures" to be overruled or intruded upon by some kind of special action. In this perspective even the term 'miracle' loses its sharp edge. Miraculous events do not, it is true, follow the patterns we are accustomed to. But there is no reason, to begin with, why they should. Pattern is second- ary; what is primary and immediate is God's command which brings each moment into being without constraint from any other moment.

But what does this do to *science*, to our human attempts at understand- ing? Is the inference to a Designer "scientific" in such cases? The inventors of the label 'physicotheology' would have answered that such inference is valid, that it rests on physical evidence and terminates (as did Aristotle's physics) in the assertion of the existence of an original Cause. Was this inference "philosophical" (i.e., scientific)? They would have said Yes. Was it demonstrative, as Aristotelian science had to be? No, because strict demonstra- tion from effect to cause was in any event impossible. Could it be depended on? Boyle gave a sophisticated analysis of the different levels of difficulty in establishing structure-to-function relationships but had no doubt that, in some cases, a convincing case could be made. Of course, the explanation would not be mechanical, but a teleological one could be just as well warranted by the evidence. And in both cases it was in God, whether as Mover or as Designer, that explanation terminated anyway.

Physicotheology did not fit the evolutionary pattern; in fact, it could be said to have been explicitly antievolutionary. It did not explain later stages simply in terms of earlier stages and the lawlike relationship between the two. It invoked an Intelligence that transcended the actual physical process. The problem of bringing the first member of each species to be was treated on a par with that of generating later members: each new conception and growth needed the guidance of the divine Intelligence as much as the first had done. The voluntarists found no difficulty with a literalist reading of Genesis. If the Creator brought forth the first living creatures from earth and water, he has been doing the same ever since. There was no incentive to postulate any sort of gradual development; indeed, given the apologetic aim of physico- theology, there was every reason to oppose any such idea, for it would have imputed exactly the sort of autonomy to the process that had been found so reprehensible in Descartes and the atomists.

Another way to express the difference between the intellectualist and the

voluntarist standpoints would be to note how they regarded *time.* Defenders
of the reality of natures usually agreed with Augustine in regarding the entire created order as issuing from a single act of rational will on God's part.
The rationality of created natures extended to time itself, which is unified
in a hierarchy of patterns. In contrast, voluntarists tended to "atomize" time,
to break it down into moments linked in sequence only through the arbitrary
will of the Creator. Evolution fits readily into the first perspective, much less
easily into the second.

8. The Long Time Scale

   We are now into the eighteenth century. There was as yet no convincing
reason either in physics or biology for postulating a long period of natural
development as the basic explanation of characteristic features of either the
nonliving or the living worlds. A short time scale, consonant with a literal
reading of the Old Testament, was still viable. And the unavailability of a
plausible naturalist explanation could be regarded as powerful evidence for
the necessity of calling on God in some special way and thus of indirectly
affirming his existence. But there *was* one field of scientific inquiry where
the strains would soon begin to show. In fact, they had already begun to
appear in the previous century, although they had not been widely attended
to.
   The signs of a *historical* formation are most clearly to be seen in the structures of the earth's surface. Two evidences of such a formation had long been
noted and were now about to be much more thoroughly investigated. First
were the rock strata which seemed to have been laid down in some sort of
sequence, although the sequences differed from place to place in complicated
ways. Second were the fossils found in these strata which seemed to be the
remains of life-forms quite different from any now known and which
themselves exhibited a sequence.[111] In his *Protogaea*, published posthumously
in 1749, Leibniz drew on predecessors like Steno to argue for a Cartesian type
of cosmogony in which the earth began as an incandescent globe, gradually
cooled, with the deposition of strata under primeval oceans and the recording
in those strata of the life-forms characteristic of the area of deposition. He
did not discuss the time scale necessary for all of this to happen and left open
the possibility of interpreting the deposition processes as being related to the
biblical deluge. In his *Epochs of Nature* (1778) Buffon argued that a
cosmogony of this sort would require a greatly expanded time scale and suggested that human history constituted only the last stage of a much longer
development of life which could be reconciled with Genesis by interpreting
the days of Genesis as "epochs".

In the following decades two separate controversies broke out among the protagonists of the new science of "geology"; in both cases the underlying causes were primarily theological. The "Vulcanist" geology of Hutton and Playfair, which emphasized the role of volcanic processes and presumed the earth's surface to be the end product of a very long sequence of gradual natural changes, was opposed by "Neptunists" such as Kirwan and Jameson who believed that water-related processes were the crucial ones and that these testified to the biblical deluge. The Neptunists attacked the Vulcanists as "atheistical" for two connected reasons. First, Hutton's *Theory of the Earth* (1795) was entirely naturalistic: it attempted to account for all geological features by gradual natural processes, both igneous and depositional, of a kind that can still be discerned and explored. Such an account ran counter to physicotheology since it could not be used to argue for the necessity of a constantly shaping God. Second, it made no attempt to correlate the stages of development with the days of Genesis. The Neptunists were willing to allow that these might not have been literal days, but they were quite sure that the *sequence* of events described in Genesis carried the authority of revealed truth.

In 1796 Cuvier read a paper on fossil elephants which clearly established the fact of extinction of some living forms. Since life is adapted to its environment, these extinctions of the past (and Cuvier went on to document scores of them in later papers in careful terms of comparative anatomy) could only be explained, he argued, in terms of periodic catastrophes. Though his contemporary, Lamarck, had already proposed a sweeping theory of the evolution of species, Cuvier insisted that such an idea was inconsistent with the discontinuities of fossil record.

In England Buckland picked up this idea and developed a "catastrophist" geology to support it. His motives were clear. His inaugural lecture as the first professor of the science of geology at Oxford was entitled *Vindiciae Geologicae or the Connection of Geology with Religion Explained* (1820). His aim was:

> to show that the study of geology has a tendency to confirm the evidences of natural religion; and that the facts developed by it are consistent with the accounts of the creation and deluge recorded in the Mosaic writings.[112]

The catastrophes which had in his view violently shaped the earth, piling animal remains in great profusion in caves and tearing up rock strata, supported a physicotheology, because God must be taken to have operated in special ways in the catastrophic episodes. In addition, the last of these episodes supports the Genesis account and hence the veracity of the Bible as a whole. Other sciences may testify to the intelligence exerted by the Creator at the moment of first creation, and these sciences (Buckland insists) are consistent with the view that no further "interference or continued supervision on the part of a Creator" is needed. However, geology refutes this view because the convulsions required to explain the earth's present surface testify to "final causes":

> When therefore we perceive that the secondary causes producing these convulsions have operated at successive periods, not blindly and at random, but with a direction to beneficial ends, we see at once the proofs of an overruling Intelligence continuing to superintend, direct, modify, and control the operations of the agents which he originally ordained.[113]

The catastrophes witnessed to God's intervention in two rather different ways, as "catastrophic", that is, as violent events outside the normal course of physical causation, and second, as exhibiting an adaptation of means to "beneficial ends", mainly to the appearance of man. Buckland stressed the latter consideration, linking it to more traditional arguments from design, but the former played a larger role in the controversy that followed. So plausible was his blending of evidence from the earlier Neptunists and Vulcanists as well as from the newer researches on fossils that "diluvialism" became the orthodoxy in British geology for a brief period in the 1820s.

Lyell's three-volume *Principles of Geology* (1830-1833) initiated a new stage in the debate. His central theme was that the past could only be understood by postulating agencies of the sort that still operate today. Against the hypothetical method of the catastrophists he urged a sturdy Newtonian inductivism. The "uniformitarianism" he proposed was similar to Hutton's approach earlier but by now had a great deal more evidence in its favor. He allowed that frequent extinction of animal species had occurred and supposed that God had created ancestor pairs for each species in succession at the appropriate times. But he emphatically denied that there had been any progress in animal forms—this would have been too close to the catastrophist thesis—and held, on very weak grounds, that basically the same general sorts of living things have coexisted through the aeons.

One might have expected that someone so developmental in his approach to geology would have embraced an evolutionary approach in biology. But in fact it was the catastrophists who argued for a progressive sequence of species in the strata, though of course excluding a properly evolutionary relationship between them, since each species in the sequence had, in their view, been directly created. Though Lyell rejected physicotheology and effectively undermined the diluvialist geology, he agreed with his opponents that God had to be invoked at the origins of each living species.

It was William Whewell, the most perceptive philosopher of science of his generation and a defender of catastrophism, who most effectively pointed out the inconsistency in a uniformitarian allowing so broad a role to God in the miraculous creation of living species. And if Lyell's inductivism fails here, why not elsewhere? Whewell's challenge is direct. A uniformitarian should explain, by natural causes only, how one could pass from a world filled with one set of animal forms to another in which hardly any of these appear. But such an explanation (Whewell is quite sure) is impossible. He concludes:

> We see in the transition from an earth peopled by one set of animals to the same earth swarming with entirely new forms of organic life, a distinct manifestation of creative power, transcending the known laws of nature: and, it appears to us, that geology has thus lighted a new lamp along the path of natural theology.[114]

A lamp—or a bomb? The exponents of physicotheology had from the beginning been pursuing a dangerous strategy. To make their point they had to show that the coming-to-be of various features of the world we know "transcended the known laws of nature", as Whewell puts it here, but how could they exclude the possibility that laws of nature as yet *unknown* might suffice? A special intervention on God's part would not, then, be needed. Making God a "God of the gaps" is a risky business. Gap-closing is the *business* of science. To rest belief in God on the presence of gaps in the explanatory chain is to pit religion *against* science ultimately, although the physicotheologians would never have seen it in that way.

It is also to make evolution and creation seem like exclusive concepts. Creation is portrayed as a series of interventions in natural process, and evolutionary natural process is held to be in principle insufficient to bring about major features of the world. A theory of evolution thus necessarily appears as a threat to the foundations of religious belief.

It is worth recalling once again that the argument from nature to God's existence took two rather different forms. In one, the adaptation of means to end was taken to show the presence of design and hence the need for an explanation of a different sort to the one normally found in natural science. The emphasis was, thus, on balance a positive one. Whereas in the other, ordinary physical processes were held to be insufficient to account for the origin of some complex feature of the world, such as planetary stability. The laws of nature had to be "transcended". The emphasis in this case is negative; it is on the simple inability of scientific explanation as a matter of *fact* to account for these features. To put the distinction in another way, the design arguments were proposed as a proper part of natural philosophy. Whereas the arguments of Newton and many of the catastrophists seemed to rely upon an *insufficiency* on the part of natural philosophy and the consequent need to postulate a nonnatural intervention.

From the standpoint of voluntarist theology the distinction between the two types of argument is particularly significant. One historian, R. Hooykaas, who draws explicitly on the voluntarist principles of the Calvinist tradition, suggests a fourfold distinction when chronicling the "Genesis and Geology" debate.[115] _Naturalism_ (exemplified by Darwin) holds that "immanent and eternal laws rule over nature . . . no final causes are admitted"; _deism_ (Hutton): "God created matter and endowed it with laws under which the world and all its inhabitants are realized according to the plan originally contrived"; _semideism_ (Lyell, Buckland):

> God created the world and upholds its constant '_natural_ course', but now and again He intervenes in a _supernatural_ way. God's activity is not only evident in the wise design of the fabric of the world, but is also manifested by events which cannot be explained by 'natural' causes and which, in general, are sudden and cataclysmic in character.[116]

What is wrong with all of these views from the voluntarist standpoint is their assumption of an underlying _nature_ and the correlative notion of an "intervention" when the expected order is not followed. Hooykaas' definition of the fourth alternative, what he calls the "biblical position", is worth quoting in some detail:

> God created the world as an expression of His free will, and He sustains it in the minutest detail, so that nothing happens without His 'intervention' in this sense. In His providence, He usually guides the world according to constant rule; but as He is a free agent, He may give deviations from order, as well as order. As God's thoughts transcend human thought, the natural order is not _wholly_ perspicuous to human reason . . . it has to be accepted as given. . . . The Bible does not use the concepts 'natural' and 'supernatural', and it makes much smaller the gap between Law and Miracle. . . . One and the same event may be considered as 'natural' on one level and as wholly miraculous on a different level. Thus in principle there is no predilection either for uniformity of nature nor for sudden catastrophes in nature—both conceptions are recognized to have their place. On one level _all_ are attributed to the Primary Cause; on the other they are explained in terms of the instruments He uses, the secondary 'natural' causes and _by these alone_.[117]

One can see right away why the voluntarist interpreters of the notion of creation would find the language of "laws of nature" being "transcended", and the approach to God through "gaps" in normal scientific argument, theologically suspect. If there is no basic "nature", violations in the expected natural order cannot be used for apologetic purposes. (For many voluntarists, of course, a biblical _faith_ would preclude recourse to a scientific or quasi-scientific approach to God's existence in the first place).

But some puzzles remain. Hooykaas draws a distinction of level (just as the Thomist or the deist would) between the order of secondary "natural" causes and that of the Primary Cause. Furthermore, he maintains that an explanation in terms of secondary causes _alone_ is in principle available. But if this is so, how does this differ from deism, looking at the issue from the *scientist's* standpoint? Exactly the same sorts of explanation will be available under both descriptions. The distinction between the deist and the voluntarist is a *theological* disagreement about the order of intellect and will in God, a disagreement which does not of itself affect the sequence of events on earth. It may, however, affect the choice of *ontology* on the part of the philosopher concerned to understand physical process, since the voluntarist rejects an ontology of natures on theological (and sometimes on empiricist) grounds.[118] Associated with this is the correlative rejection of any claim to a *complete* understanding of any physical phenomenon; there is no nature there to furnish this sort of ultimate intelligibility.

Nevertheless, Hooykaas does allow that God "usually" acts according to a "constant rule" (even though there is *antecedently* no "predilection" for uniformity rather than for catastrophe). This means that departure from this rule might be recognized. Why should such a departure not be used to impress the believer in natures that God's special power is at work? Granted, the argument will not work for the voluntarist, but then he does not need an argument to begin with. As an *ad hominem* argument for the nonvoluntarist, who very likely will accept the existence of something like natures, it would seem to be effective.

The problem with such an argument lies rather in its vulnerability to scientific advance. What made the two-hundred-year history of physicotheology an inevitable prelude to conflict was the way in which religious belief was made to depend on a supposed shortcoming of science or a limitation on "regular" scientific explanation. The age of Boyle and Newton had come to see in natural science the paradigm of rationality generally; it was tempting, then, to cast the reasons for belief in a quasi-scientific mold. But the cost would ultimately come very high.

The collapse of physicotheology in the second half of the nineteenth century has so often been chronicled that it seems unnecessary to run through the story yet again.[119] The adaptations in living nature that had formed the basis of the design argument could now be accounted for, in principle at least, by a naturalist theory relying on processes of selection and differential reproduction. And the "insufficiencies" of physics and geology had fallen, one after another, to the ingenuity of the practitioners of those sciences. Until then most major scientists had been firmly Christian in belief and had been intent on weaving together their two sources of knowledge or on making one the part-warrant of the other. Now, for the first time, there were scientists who saw their science as undermining the grounds for rational belief in God. Many of these, like Darwin, would conclude that evolutionary theory, by displacing physicotheology, had made the Christian hypothesis of a creator unnecessary.

9. Postscript

In this introductory essay I have traced the outlines of the long and complex interaction between ideas, one of them central to Christian theology, the other equally central to modern natural science. The opposition which is so often perceived between them today derives in some part from the persistent attempt over two centuries to build belief in a Creator on the supposed impossibility of an evolutionary account of origins. Augustine knew better!

It seems obvious to those who reflect on the Augustinian heritage today that God can work as easily through evolution as through a sequence of interventions to bring about his ends:[120] as easily and much more appropriately from the perspective of a theology that does take time to be God's creature and "intervention" to be unneeded where an omnipotent and omniscient Creator is concerned. Far more fitting that such a Creator would set the "seed-principles" in the first formless matter for all that would later come and impose no dualities in that later history that would require the powers of the original creation to be somehow supplemented. In that sense evolution *complements* Christian belief. It binds together in cousinship all the created world. The theories of cosmic and biological evolution help us to understand why the scale of the universe has to be what it is in order for human life to come about in a "natural" way.

But this makes it all seem, perhaps, too simple. The theories of evolution *do* pose problems for the Christian. Most of them bear on the nature of the *human* reality. Must we suppose that man has a "spiritual" side and how does this fit in with an evolutionary origin? How is the Christian message of resurrection to be construed in an evolutionary world bound together in a seamless whole? How are the central Christian doctrines of providence, miracle, prayer, grace, to be understood in the new world-picture? How do the themes of original innocence, the fall, redemption, relate to an evolutionary explanation of human origins? If human nature is the result of a long period of evolutionary shaping, could it be that the human practice of religion is itself to be accounted for in evolutionary terms? These are difficult questions, and they will be dealt with systematically by later essays in this book.[121]

But before finishing, there are three topics I would like to mention very briefly because of their special relation to the developments I have chronicled above.

EVOLUTION AND PHILOSOPHY

The success of the evolutionary principle in biology has prompted a variety of evolutionary philosophies.[122] An evolutionary philosophy differs from scientific theory in one or both of two ways. It may be of a high degree of generality; it may extend the limited scientific notion to a wider range of reality. Or it may derive from an insight, a principle, an analogy, whose source is something other than the observed regularities with which science deals. Virtually every philosopher today would allow that species have evolved from a common origin, but not all are "evolutionary philosophers" in the sense of making it their central interpretive principle.

At one end of the spectrum is Spencer's "synthetic" philosophy which generalizes from the evidences of evolution in biology, astronomy, sociology, and other sciences to a "supreme principle" from which all the particular forms of evolution can then be deductively derived. What is taken to warrant this materialistic variety of evolution is the inductive support in the sciences from which Spencer originally takes his start. At the other end of the spectrum is Royce's idealistic version of evolutionary philosophy which is based on his analysis of the self. Like Hegel, he finds his starting point in the structures of mind or spirit, directly known to us and disclosed to us also by history through which the Absolute Spirit manifests itself.

Between these extremes three general types of evolutionary philosophy may perhaps be discerned. Emergent evolutionism (Samuel Alexander and Lloyd Morgan) takes as its central insight the reality of irreducible *levels* in nature and of genuine *novelty* as one passes from one level to the next higher one. Each level prepares for the appearance of the next, but the emergence of the qualitatively distinct new level is in principle unpredictable.[123] "Deity" appears only as the immanent upper level toward which the hierarchy of emergent qualities proceeds as cosmic evolution continues, not as the agent responsible for the occurrence of emergence or of process generally.

The dialectical materialism of Marx and Engels incorporates an emergent evolutionism of this same general sort, though of course without God as its immanent goal. When Dühring pointed out the incoherence of retaining in a materialist system the basically idealist notion of a dialectic in nature, Engels in his *Anti-Dühring* (1878) tried to show how dialectical laws, like the "negation of the negation", can operate at the physical and biological levels. Motion itself (he argues) is contradictory. This ambiguous legacy, balanced uneasily between idealism and materialism, led to deep dissensions in Soviet philosophy in the 1920s, with factions favoring three different emphases, materialist (Bukharin), positivist (Bogdanov), and dialectical (Deborin).[124] The first two (and the associated "mechanism") were outlawed in 1929; the third, after a brief period of triumph, was proscribed by Stalin in 1931, putting an end to serious work in philosophy in the Soviet Union for a considerable time. Our interest here is in the fact that the question of *emergence* became a touchstone of orthodoxy; the mechanist view that scientific theories of evolution were sufficient of themselves to account for the different levels was treated as heretical because it undermined the "dialectical" character of change, so crucial to Marxist political philosophy.

The second cluster of evolutionary philosophies are those that take the metaphor of *organism* as central and rely upon our intuitive grasp of such properties as feeling, apprehension, purposive action. Properties such as these are, in one form or another, attributed to the universe at all levels so that evolution becomes itself a sort of organic growth. The Darwinian account is regarded as at best incomplete because of its mechanistic character. The best-known exponents of this approach are C. S. Peirce and A.N. Whitehead, each of whom built a complex metaphysics around the principle that the universe and its processes are best understood by analogy with the organism. Peirce regarded cosmic evolution as the development of habits; the original chaos of pure feeling and objective chance gradually evolves toward a more ordered state, in which habit replaces feeling and order replaces chance. Whitehead rejected the emergence of irreducible properties and argued instead that the categories of sentience and subjective aim apply at all levels, even that of the molecule. God appears both at the beginning and at the end of process, in two very different ways. The "primordial nature" of God is the order which is immanent in the world itself; actual entities exhibit an urge toward the realization of the forms (or eternal objects), and this is what drives evolution forward. In the process God acquires a "consequent nature" due to the self-realization of actual entities at all levels. God does not create other entities. Rather, God gives the initial impetus toward self-realization to other actual entities and is also (in the consequent nature) an outcome of the creativity of those entities.

The third group of evolutionary philosophies, like the second, attributes the categories of organism to the universe at all levels but also stresses the active role of God who suffuses the entire evolutionary process. The two best-known representatives come from the French vitalist tradition. Henri Bergson criticized Darwin's theory of evolution for its inability to account for coadaptation or for the increase in organic complexity over time. Instead, he proposed a notion of "life-force" (*élan vital*) which our intuition reveals to us within ourselves and which is responsible for our own evolution. The same sort of impetus must have brought about the evolution of complexity both in the nonliving and in the living worlds. Discontinuities of level occur within this development where "leaps" are required, as between animal and man. There was, however, no predetermined plan, though man can in some sense be said to be the "reason" for the entire story. The *élan vital* manifests itself in evolution as a sort of "supraconsciousness" that could even be called "God". In his last writings Bergson moved closer to the orthodox Christian view of God: God is love and exhibits his loving purpose in the evolutionary process.

Pierre Teilhard de Chardin was deeply influenced by Bergson[125] but carried the evolutionary theme much further than his mentor had done.[126] Evolution, he asserted, "has long ago ceased to be an hypothesis, and become a general condition of knowledge, an additional dimension, which henceforth all hypotheses must satisfy".[127] But he found the mechanistic approach to evolution in neo-Darwinian theory unacceptable and postulated a special kind of "radial" or "psychic" energy which is responsible for the progressive and directed character of evolutionary process. This energy cannot be defined in terms of conventional physics and chemistry; it can be recognized only by a "seeing" that grasps purpose and intelligence in a pattern of development of unity in complexity. There are "critical points" along the way when qualitatively new levels appear, notably that of man himself when the power of reflection makes its first appearance. Evolution continues in the convergence of the human group itself toward the "Omega Point", the personal Center to which psychic energy has all along been drawn. God creates by simultaneously complexifying and uniting, through the power of love, at every moment along the way.[128]

The reader has probably noted already some striking analogies between the evolutionary philosophies of the twentieth century and the physicotheology of the seventeenth. Though these philosophies take the label 'evolutionary', they all (with the exception of Spencer's synthetic philosophy) resist the claim of Darwin and his heirs to have an explanation in hand for evolutionary process. Indeed, what might be said to constitute them as "philosophies" is, in part, this insistence that conventional natural science is *in principle* unable to give a complete, or even a halfway adequate, explanation of how evolution occurs. Such an insistence obviously cannot derive from science itself.

Boyle and his colleagues held that living structures exhibiting adaptation cannot be explained in mechanistic terms but require the interposition in some fashion of intelligence. Evolutionary philosophers assert that mechanistic accounts of evolutionary process cannot explain how emergence occurs or how complexity keeps increasing. Some of them would go further and see in evolution over time the marks of an intelligence, ultimately the divine intelligence, at work. The means-end adaptations that Boyle dwelt on would be allowed by most of today's evolutionary philosophers to be explicable in neo-Darwinian terms. But the higher-level transitions from one level to another, the progressive increase in complexity and the overall apparent directedness, would play something of the role for these philosophers that the simpler examples of living adaptations played for Boyle and Ray.

The ambiguities we saw in the descriptions given by physicotheologians of how God operated in the world can be paralleled in evolutionary philosophy also, where notions like *élan vital* and *psychic energy* have been heavily criticized for their vagueness. How do the traditional categories of 'natural' and 'supernatural' fit into the picture? Is psychic energy part of "natural" process? Does emergence imply intervention in philosophies that see God as the "mover" of evolutionary process? One can hear echoes of the older voluntarist debates.

Of course, there are clear disanalogies too. The physicotheologians were themselves scientists and had the support of other scientists. The evolutionary philosophers are, for the most part, not scientists and, even when they are, tend to distance themselves to some extent from "conventional" natural science and insist upon its inadequacy in the face of evolutionary novelty and complexity. They thus quite often evoke hostility from the scientific community. Physicotheology was an *apologetic* enterprise, a marshalling of evidence for God's existence. Evolutionary philosophers are much more varied in their aims. Teilhard de Chardin comes closest perhaps in spirit to physicotheology:

> What Teilhard tried to do was, in principle, praiseworthy and in conformity with a long philosophical tradition: he sought to use science (particularly in its biological branches, essentially linked with history) in order to induce from it, almost experimentally, the existence of God, and from that a religious apologetic.[129]

But something more must be said. In an essay subtitled "The way in which the scientific study of matter can and must help to lead us up to the divine centre", Teilhard notes first that science can never find God by "analytical" procedures that lead down to the atom, outward to the nebula, backward to the past. These procedures of themselves could lead only to reductionist materialism. And matter is nothing more than

> essentially boundless plurality, mere dust. It is therefore impossible to build upon it, and to try to follow it up to its very end would be to move towards nothingness. Matter is not a stable foundation of the world: it is a direction in which things continually disappear a little more as they lose a little more unity. . . . The only consistence beings have comes to them from their *synthetic element*, in other words from what, at a more perfect or less perfect degree, is their soul, their spirit.[130]

The "impotence" of these analytical efforts at explanation on the part of science thus shows us that:

> in the direction in which things became complex in unity, there must lie a supreme centre of convergence and consistence. . . . We should be overcome with joy to note how admirably Jesus Christ . . . fills this empty place which has been distinguished by the expectation of all Nature.[131]

Were we not already Christian, of course, we could not have made this identification. "I would never dream", Teilhard continues:

> of deducing Christian dogmas solely from an examination of the properties our reason attributes to the structure of the world. . . . Although the world can justify our expectation of Christ, he cannot be deduced from it.

This is not, then, an apologetic intended to bring a nonbeliever to belief in God (or in Christ, whom Teilhard often identifies with the Omega Point). Rather, it is intended for the believer in order to show where identifications may be made between elements of Christian belief and certain "holes" in science which may only be *recognized* as holes by the believer (though Teilhard would, I think, insist that *any* scientist ought to see them as holes). What Teilhard offers, therefore, is a *coherence* between science and religious belief, a coherence which may be seen as a reason for belief but which does not, however, function as a full-scale apologetic.

The difficulties that lie in the way of the theological construal of evolutionary philosophy are obvious enough. They are in the first instance theological. The God of evolutionary philosophy is, almost necessarily, an immanent one and thus not at all the transcendent Creator of traditional Christian belief. Creation itself becomes a time-bound affair, in which God is caught up in, indeed may even be constituted by, the successes and failures of his creatures. Process theologians would, of course, see in this an *advantage* of the evolutionary approach.[132] But at the very least it forces a radical reconstitution of long-held views on God's transcendence. Further, the distinction between natural and supernatural gets blurred, though here again perhaps the theological voluntarist may rejoice.

Most worrisome of all, arguments that begin from the inadequacy, in principle, of conventional science have not had a good record. It is by no means clear that such features of the evolutionary process as emergence or progress in complexity are any better indications of the *special* involvement of an intelligence or a cosmic living force than were the animal instincts and adapted organs of earlier physicotheology. Recourse to "special" features of the world and its history that purportedly lie outside naturalist modes of scientific explanation will always continue to spur the scientist to broaden his explanatory schemes to meet the challenge and in that way to extend the notion of the "natural" itself.

EVOLUTION AND PHYSICS

We saw earlier how Descartes tried to formulate an evolutionary cosmogony on the basis of mechanics and how Newton was easily able to show that such a venture could not succeed. In a Cartesian (or, for that matter, a Newtonian) universe it could not, for quite specific reasons. But in the last fifty years the picture has entirely changed.[133] Now one can say that evolution finds almost as secure a home in cosmology as it does in biology, though the principles in the two cases are quite different.

What made the difference were the two major physical theories of the twentieth century, general relativity theory and quantum theory, and one quasi-observational discovery, that of the expansion of the nebulae (Hubble, 1929). Together these have permitted the construction of a plausible account of the early universe when the major structures of the universe we know took shape.

Not only can one show how galaxies, stars, and planets are likely to have come to be, but one can also provide a detailed "evolutionary chemistry" which gives a plausible explanation of how the chemical elements were built up, beginning from the simplest, hydrogen, and how they attained their present abundances in the universe. Admittedly, accounts of the "first three minutes" are speculative; they are essentially thought-experiments against which our latest quantum field theories can be tested for coherence in extreme conditions that can never be realized in the present universe.[134] Nevertheless, they are getting firmer as they are made to yield testable predictions about such (approximately) known data as the cosmic abundance of helium.

One feature of the standard big bang cosmological model is worth noting. Once evolutionary explanation comes to be seen as basic, something like the big bang hypothesis is likely to be reached as the end of a regress that traces later structures back to earlier, simpler, ones. Conceptually there are really only two generic alternatives: a structureless initial "photon" of inconceivably great energy, beyond which no further question about an earlier simpler stage makes sense, or an unchanging "steady-state" universe with no "beginning" (or singularity in past time). It is interesting that these *were* in fact the rival models for a brief time until the big bang model was seen to account much better for the low-temperature microwave radiation pervading the universe (discovered by Penzias and Wilson in 1965).

The point is that these are the alternatives that our mode of explanation forces upon us. A structural cosmic state will always invite the question "But why *that* structure?" and such questioning can cease only when a "simple" first state is reached. But is this possible? And if it is, how could the contingencies of the later universe ever develop from it? Must there not be specifications of that first "photon" that just "are" the way they are? Or ought one assume that explanation must terminate in a a *necessary* state, with boundary conditions that could not have been other than they were?

A great deal of interesting work has been going on in cosmology over the past decade regarding these issues. One outcome was the fascinating debate about the "anthropic principle", initiated by Collins, Hawking, and Carter in 1973-1974. It began to look as though a good deal of "fine-tuning" would have been necessary to obtain the initial conditions from which a life-bearing universe could develop. Until then it had seemed that a long-lived universe with galaxies, stars, planets, water, carbon, and so forth would develop from almost any plausible specification of the initial conditions. But Hawking argued that a universe with the requisites for complex life was almost infinitely improbable, given the immense range of theoretically equally plausible alternatives in which such life could not arise. So why this one? Well, because we are here. If it had *not* been of this sort, we would not have to speculate about it. So in that (admittedly very odd) sense, our presence here "explains" the universe.

I will confine myself here to a brief remark.[135] The anthropic principle has unmistakable overtones, once again, of physicotheology. The initial cosmic features that enabled a universe to develop in which man could one day evolve are so unlikely according to present theory that it is tempting to invoke the plan of a Creator. The presumption is that science will "never be able to explain" how so contingent, yet in a human sense so significant, an initial state could have occurred. Yet in the decade since 1973 at least one theory has been suggested that would greatly reduce the contingency, though this is still a long way from showing that it "had" to be so.[136] This is not to say that this latest meeting-point of the concepts of evolution and creation is without interest to the theologian. But it *is* to say that we have surely learnt by now that in this domain caution is the order of the day!

EVOLUTION AND POLITICS

And now back finally to the United States in the last third of the twentieth century. It is significant that the "creationist" controversy that has been making so many headlines has occurred *only* in the United States. It would be virtually unthinkable in Europe. Two reasons immediately suggest themselves. The first is a biblical fundamentalism with deep roots in many of the immigrant groups that have flowed together to make American society the complicated patchwork it is. The second is a public school system in which advocacy of religious belief in any shape or form is barred on constitutional grounds. The modern extension of the First Amendment (in ways the Founding Fathers could hardly have anticipated) enforces a neutrality on public education that excludes any positive teaching on such matters as the existence of God or the destiny of man. If one is to have a common educational system in a nation as deeply divided along religious lines as is the United States (so it is argued), such an interpretation of the First Amendment is the only alternative.

But the cost is high, and many are not prepared to pay it. Neutrality and indifference are perilously close where the dynamics of belief are concerned. And, of course, in this case the teaching of evolutionary theory does not seem at all neutral to those who see it as inimical to Christian belief. Indeed, as late as 1968 Arkansas still had a (rarely enforced) law on its statute-books barring the teaching of evolution in the public schools. Such laws eventually fell to constitutional challenge.

The recent phase of the controversy began in California as concerned Christian parents, often (though not always) of strongly fundamentalist convictions, argued that the teaching of evolutionary theory in public school as the *only* account of origins, and especially of human origins, excluded the creation account *in principle* and hence could not be neutral from the religious standpoint. To say that evolutionary theory is the best theory is one thing, but to say that it is the only *possible* theory is to exclude God's action in the world as a matter of principle. This (it was argued) is a covert way of teaching atheism.

Efforts were made by various groups to persuade the California Board of Education to allow, or even enforce, the presentation of the creation story in Genesis as an alternative to the evolutionary account.[137] In 1969 the board agreed to recommend this. Years of controversy followed until in 1974 the board reversed itself. The "creationists" (as they had come to be called) were prompted by two different motives: first, the fundamentalist belief that the "true" account of origins was given by a literal reading of Genesis and hence that this text *should* be taught in school, and, second, that an evolutionary account of human origins necessarily conflicted with basic Christian beliefs about the nature of man and thus should *not* be taught.

But it was clear, on constitutional grounds, that the Genesis account could not be taught in public schools because of its religious character. So a different strategy was devised, namely, to construe the Genesis story as *science*, as "creation-science", and to ask for "balanced treatment" of this "scientific alternative". Creation-science was held to explain many features of the geological record that the evolutionary hypothesis could not account for. Two states, Arkansas and Louisiana, enacted "balanced treatment" statutes into law in 1981 under pressure from well-organized creationist lobbies.

But the move to construe the Genesis account as science, understandable enough as a way to get around the legal bar against teaching it as religion, proved disastrous.[138] It enraged theologians, religious leaders, and scientists in about equal measure. A coalition of all three challenged the legality of the Arkansas statute and won their case after a highly publicized trial in December 1981, in which the state was aided by the Institute of Creation Research in San Diego. The argument of Judge William Overton's detailed decision[139] relied on two claims: first, that science can be identified in terms of five "essential characteristics" and that creation-science lacks these characteristics; second, that creation-science is clearly derivative from a literal reading of the Genesis story, and thus teaching it would advance religious belief. Philosophers of science were unhappy about the first of these claims, since it would be fairly generally admitted nowadays that the energetic search for a "principle of demarcation" between science and nonscience, prompted by Popper in the '50s and '60s, failed to establish anything like a set of "essential characteristics" for science and indeed gave good reason to doubt that any such set could exist.[140] The "essential" character of every single one of the characteristics listed by Judge Overton has, in fact, been challenged somewhere or another in the literature of the last twenty years.[141]

It would have been more effective to argue that creation-science is simply *bad* science.[142] Despite its critics' claim that it is untestable and hence not "scientific", it is quite obvious (and indeed this is often mentioned by the same critics) that it *has* been tested, in multiple versions and in multiple ways, and falsified. But the prosecution in Arkansas determined long in advance of the trial to argue that creation-science is simply not science at all and sought expert witnesses who would testify to this. The defense, curiously, did not call philosophers of science on the other side, as they easily might have done, and Judge Overton was persuaded to accept the claim that creation-science is not science.[143] One critic remarks:

> The core issue is not whether Creationism satisfies some undemanding and highly controversial definitions of what is scientific; the real question is whether the existing evidence provides stronger arguments for evolutionary theory than for Creationism.[144]

That is the "real question" for philosophers, of course. But for constitutional lawyers the other component in the judge's argument was the more important one: the act had as a major effect the advancement of religion. This was much easier to show (though it is only sketchily argued in the opinion, far more attention being given to the "nonscience" claim) and could have been helped as much by the conclusion that creation-science is bad science as by the more vulnerable claim that it is nonscience. After the Arkansas act was declared unconstitutional, Louisiana dropped its version of "balanced treatment" with little fuss, and it does not look as though another attempt to mandate the teaching of the Genesis story as science will be made again in the near future.

From the Christian standpoint the whole affair was a tragedy from beginning to end. Creationists acted in defense of their religious beliefs, but they succeeded only in making religion and science seem mutually exclusive. They tried to force a false choice on public school students, an either-or that even the smallest comprehension of the story traced above would have shown to be ill-considered. Here is physicotheology in reverse: the claim that if Genesis is right (in its literal reading), then science must be wrong. Far more likely that students would take the argument in the opposite direction and conclude that since evolutionary theory is "right" (i.e., gives the best available explanation of origins) that the Genesis story (and all that goes with its acceptance) must be wrong.

A particularly unfortunate consequence of this controversy is that the term 'creationist' has been rendered unusable by ordinary Christians, Jews, or Muslims in describing their own beliefs. Yet they believe in God as creator; they profess the faith that the universe is God's handiwork. They are all thus "creationist" in the most basic sense. But they are forced to disavow the extravagant doctrine that its protagonists (and the U.S. media) have agreed to call "creationism". The entire notion of creation has been rendered suspect by an ill-advised literalism that would already have seemed out of place in Augustine's day.

Augustine, indeed, perceived the dangers to the Christian community of precisely the sort of suspicion that the proponents of "creation-science" have fostered. Often, he says, Christians who do not fully understand some point about the earth, or the distances of the stars, or the orbits of planets, or the nature of stones, or the like, will attempt to make their point by arguing as if it were Christian doctrine. The worst, he goes on, is not that such persons will be laughed at but that the Scriptures themselves will be brought into disrepute. If those who are not bound by the authority of the Scriptures

> find a Christian mistaken in a field which they themselves know well and hear him base foolish opinions on the Scriptures, how are they going to believe the Scriptures regarding the resurrection of the dead . . . when they think that the pages of Scripture are full of falsehoods regarding facts which they themselves have learnt from experience and light of reason?[145]

Once again, the man of good sense!

Making sense of creation in the modern evolutionary universe has proved just as great a challenge as making sense of evolution was long ago in Augustine's created universe. Both concepts have shown themselves to be capacious, and each has to some degree shaped the other along the way. We have followed the story of their intricate relationship in detail enough to be sure of one thing at least, and that is that there are surprises still ahead.

NOTES

1. Only recently made available in English translation for the first time: St. Augustine, *The Literal Meaning of Genesis*, 2 vols., translated by J. H. Taylor, S. J., New York: Newman, 1982. (Abbreviated as *LMG* below.)
2. See, for example, ibid., Book I, chapter 21.
3. See McMullin, "How Should Cosmology Relate to Theology?" in A. Peacocke, editor, *The Sciences and Theology in the Twentieth Century*, Notre Dame, IN: University of Notre Dame Press, 1981, pp. 17-57.
4. Two collections of essays are of especial value. In *Is God a Creationist? The Religious Case against Creation-Science* (New York: Scribner, 1983) Roland Frye assembles a set of articles which together make a telling case against the claim of "creation-science" to represent the authentic Christian position. In *Did the Devil Make Darwin Do It? Modern Perspectives on the Creation-Evolution Controversy* (Ames, IA: Iowa State University Press, 1983) David B. Wilson has gathered a variety of essays to help those "who make, who influence, or who are interested in public policy decisions involving the creation-evolution controversy" to understand just what is going on under the surface of that messy debate. A special issue of *Science, Technology and Human Values* (7, Summer 1982) also brought together a useful set of articles illustrating different aspects of the debate, as well as a reading list on "creationism". Two books that argue against creation-science on more specifically philosophic and scientific grounds are Philip Kitcher, *Abusing Science: The Case against Creationism* (Cambridge, MA: M.I.T. Press, 1982), and Michael Ruse, *Darwinism Defended: A*

Guide to the Evolution Controversies (Reading, MA: Addison-Wesley, 1982). A sociological account of the debate is provided by Dorothy Nelkin in *Science Textbook Controversies and the Politics of Equal Time* (Cambridge, MA: M.I.T. Press 1977).

5. *Refutatio* I, 14, 5; G. S. Kirk and J. E. Raven, *The Presocratic Philosophers*, Cambridge: Cambridge University Press, 1957, p. 177.

6. *Physics* II, 8; 198b 29. Oxford translation by R. P. Hardie and R. K. Gaye.

7. *Physics*, 199a 26.

8. *Physics*, 198b 35.

9. *Physics*, 199a 2.

10. Much more would, of course, have to be said about Aristotle's argument here. His choice in this context of frequency of occurrence as a distinguishing characteristic between the two exclusive and exhaustive alternatives, chance and telic (for-an-end) outcomes, was on the face of it an unfortunate one. Much more fundamental was the characteristic which he underlines in earlier chapters of *Physics* II, namely, that action for an end is for the *good* of the nature concerned, whether that nature be capable of conscious deliberation or not. But this more basic distinction would not have served in the argument against Empedocles unless he also assumed that *all* physical change is for an end, i.e., that there are no chance events. But this he explicitly rejects in *Physics* II, 5.

11. *Timaeus*, 30A. Translation in Francis M. Cornford, *Plato's Cosmology*, New York: Library of Liberal Arts, 1957, p. 33.

12. *Timaeus*, 30B. Cornford translation slightly modified.

13. Cornford, *Plato's Cosmology*, pp. 31-41.

14. Cornford is too quick, perhaps, to *exclude* this interpretation (ibid., pp. 37-38). It is important, however, as he himself concedes, not to suppose that we can, if we are clever enough, penetrate the mythic imagery to reveal "a literal meaning which Plato himself would endorse" (p. 38).

15. *Timaeus*, 37D.

16. *Timaeus*, 32B.

17. This question became enormously convoluted in later Neoplatonism, where the Intelligence and Soul are successive emanations from the One, and where the temporal language of emanation and becoming conveys in a metaphorical way the timeless structures of the intelligible world.

18. See the paper by Bergant and Stuhlmueller below.

19. See Claus Westerman, *Creation*, Philadelphia: Fortress, 1974, p. 11.

20. Hans Jonas, "Jewish and Christian Elements in the Western Tradition", in *Creation: The Impact of an Idea*, edited by Daniel O'Connor and Francis Oakley, New York: Scribner, 1969, pp. 241-258; see p. 244.

21. See the essay by David Kelsey below, and Langdon Gilkey, *Maker of Heaven and Earth*, New York: Doubleday, 1965.

22. Jonas, "Jewish and Christian Elements", p. 244.

23. Augustine often quotes this phrase from the Epistle of James I, 17.

24. "With the motion of creatures, time began to run its course" (*LMG*, V, 5; p. 153; see also IV, 20; p. 127). His best-remembered and most detailed treatment of the topic of time is in Book XI of *The City of God*.

25. *LMG*, V, 11; p. 162.

26. *LMG*, V, 5; p. 154.

27. *LMG*, IV, 12; p. 117. Eugene Portalie, S.J., in his useful work *A Guide to the Thought of St. Augustine* (translated by R. Bastian. Chicago: Regnery, 1960) distinguishes strongly between creation and conservation: "Augustine demands the im-

mediate intervention of God for the formation of the universe, something different
from the ordinary divine concurrence. God certainly creates no longer, but His direct
action is sometimes necessary . . . to bring about the full development of such and
such a seed at the desired moment" (p. 141). It must be emphasized, however, that
Augustine also says that "all is simultaneous in the creative act of God"; to speak
of a before and after is to speak from the point of view of the *creature* (*LMG*, IV,
35; p. 145). He does not seem to have fully recognized the tension between his distinction between initial divine creation and subsequent governance and the claim that
God's action brings time itself to be, and thus of itself is not temporally divided.
Scotus Erigena saw this tension very clearly and argued, on clear Augustinian grounds,
that the distinction between creation and governance can be drawn only from the
point of view of the creature.

28. *LMG*, V, 20; pp. 171-172.

29. *LMG*, V, 5; p. 154. It ought be noted that Augustine's usage of the term
'literal' was much broader than ours. The "literal meaning" alluded to in the title
of his book, the meaning he searches for so painstakingly, was the meaning intended
by the original author. 'Literal' for him was opposed to 'allegorical', not to 'metaphorical'. Thus he could claim that 'day' in the Genesis account clearly had to be taken
metaphorically, that this was the author's plain intention. Hence the "literal" meaning here (in his sense) was the metaphorical one. See J. H. Taylor's introduction to
The Literal Meaning of Genesis, p. 9.

30. *De Genesi ad litteram liber imperfectus*, XIII, 43. See also *LMG*, IV, 30; p. 137.

31. He is quite tentative about this interpretation of the "day" metaphor:
"Whoever, then, does not accept the meaning that my limited powers have been able
to discover . . . let him search and find a solution with God's help." *LMG*, IV, 28;
p. 136.

32. *LMG*, IV, 33; see also *The City of God*, XI, 9.

33. Ecclesiasticus, XVII, 1. This was the Old Latin reading. Modern translators
have found the 'simul' here a defective translation and prefer "He created the *entire*
universe".

34. Biblical exegetes today would say that the two accounts derive from different
periods in the composition of the Genesis text. (See the Bergant-Stuhlmueller essay
below.) But Augustine's notion of revelation was of a simpler and more direct sort;
he had to assume that a single author was responsible and that since this author clearly
could not have been present at the events narrated, the story must have come, in
some way, directly from God.

35. He also calls them "causales rationes", "rationes primordiales", "primordia
causarum", "quasi semina futurorum". See *LMG*, footnote 67, p. 253.

36. *Apologetic Treatise on the Hexemeron*, *Patrologia Graeca*, edited by J. P.
Migne, *44*, col. 72; quoted by Messenger, *Evolution and Theology*, p. 24; translation
slightly modified. Messenger provides a useful review of the Greek and Latin Fathers
prior to Augustine, showing how widely shared the assumption was that the "materials"
of earth and water had had a generative role in the original coming-to-be of the different kinds of living things.

37. The 'before it appeared' phrase on which Augustine's argument depends was
rejected by later translators of the Hebrew. There would be general agreement today
on something like: "there was as yet no vegetation upon the earth".

38. Augustine might (it would seem)have taken this phrase to mean that the seeds
of plants (in the ordinary sense of 'seeds') were made in the initial creation, to issue
forth shortly after as plants. But since the first account in Genesis I mentions that

"the earth brought forth the crops, scattering the seeds according to their kinds", he takes mature plants to have *preceded* seeds. The plants themselves must, therefore, have come from the causal potencies implanted from the beginning in the earth.
39. *LMG*, VI, 16; p. 197.
40. *LMG*, VI, 6; p. 185.
41. *LMG*, V, 23; p. 175.
42. *De Trinitate*, III, 9; quoted by Portalie, *A Guide to the Thought of St. Augustine*, p. 138.
43. It is interesting that Augustine disagrees with those who see in the Genesis text a warrant for saying that God formed the human body in a more direct way than he did that of other animals. In both cases, Augustine reminds us, God is said to have formed the body from the earth. The difference between man and animal comes not in the mode of formation of their bodies but in the fact that man is made in God's image (*LMG*, VI, 12; p. 193).
44. *LMG*, VI, 14; p. 195.
45. *LMG*, V, 20; p. 171.
46. *LMG*, VI, 13; p. 194.
47. This was Augustine's influential interpretation of the passage in Wisdom: "Thou hast ordered all things in measure and number and weight" (XI, 21). See *LMG*, IV, 3-5.
48. *LMG*, VI, 13; p. 195.
49. Augustine excluded the human soul from the scope of seed-principles. Being spiritual, the first soul had to have been directly created by God. The Genesis account of Eve's origins invokes God so explicitly that Augustine concluded that God must have intervened directly in the formation of her body as well as the creation of her soul.
50. He says quite explicitly that it was "the words of Scripture" that led him to adopt the distinction between the initial simultaneous creation of all things and the subsequent appearance of the first instances of each kind of natural thing from the seed-principles (*LMG*, VI, 6; p. 184).
51. John Zahm, C.S.C., was one of the earliest of these. His *Evolution and Dogma* (Chicago: McBride, 1896) was well received in the United States but was condemned by the Congregation of the Index in Rome, when an Italian translation appeared. (The book was never officially proscribed.) His biographer, Ralph Weber, remarks that Zahm "defined a liberal interpretation of evolution by emphasizing the possibilities of theistic evolution. . . . More than any other American Catholic, he translated Darwin's theory into terms understandable and at least partially acceptable to his American Catholic audiences" (*Notre Dame's John Zahm,* Notre Dame,IN: University of Notre Dame Press, 1961, p. vii). A later controversial work, which also claimed Augustine for evolution, was Henry de Dorlodot's *Le Darwinisme au point de vue de l'orthodoxie catholique* (Brussels: Lovanium, 1921). This work was translated by E. C. Messenger as *Darwinism and Catholic Thought* (New York: Benziger, 1922). The debate is discussed by Messenger in his *Evolution and Theology: The Problem of Man's Origins* (New York: Macmillan, 1932).
52. *LMG*, IV, 5; pp. 110-111.
53. *LMG*, VI, 16; pp. 197-198.
54. For a fascinating account of one of the last great representatives of this "hexemeral" tradition going back to Augustine, see Nicholas Steneck, *Science and Creation in the Middle Ages: Henry of Langenstein (d. 1397) on Genesis*, Notre Dame, IN: University of Notre Dame Press, 1976. Henry is particularly interesting because

he utilizes the Aristotelian natural philosophy of his own day but in a context of seed-principles which is thoroughly Augustinian.

55. *ST*, I, q. 71, a.1, c. *Basic Writings of St. Thomas Aquinas*, edited by A. C. Pegis, New York: Random House, 1945, vol. 1; translation slightly modified. Aquinas reminds the reader that the order of the "days" for Augustine denoted not a sequence in time but an order of nature.

56. *ST*, I, q. 74, a. 2, c.

57. *ST*, I, q. 70, a. 1, c.

58. The ambiguity, of course, lies in the interpretation of "God's command" here. Did this entail a special intervention on God's part? Or could the first plant seeds form within the earth in a natural way? Aquinas is noncommittal in the *Summa theologica* about this. Messenger notes, however, that elsewhere he appears to imply that a special divine intervention is not needed to bring about the first plants: "The common active principles which belong to the work of distinction suffice for the generation of plants" (*Scriptum in IV Libros Sententiarum*, II, dist. xiv, a. 5, ad 6). For the normal production of plants, "the virtue of the heavenly bodies suffices as father and the virtue of the earth in place of a mother" (*De potentia*, q. 4, a. 2, ad 28). See *Evolution and Theology*, p. 71.

59. *ST*, I, q. 71, a. 1, ad 1.

60. Aquinas followed Albertus Magnus in distinguishing between those animals that are generated by seed and those "lower" animals that are generated by the direct influence of the heavenly bodies, such as maggots in decaying flesh. These latter did not seem to need seeds for their normal propagation, and so would not have needed a special divine intervention for their first appearance. They would not have appeared in the six days, Aquinas suggests, but would have been evoked by the heavenly bodies (the sun's heat, for example) at a later time when putrefaction of an earlier-created living body occurred (q. 72, a. 1, ad 5).

61. *ST*, I, q. 71, a. 1, ad 1.

62. *ST*, I, q. 72, a. 1, ad 1.

63. His argument for the subsistent character of the human soul is neither Platonic nor Aristotelian: "By means of the intellect, man can know all corporeal things. Now whatever knows certain things cannot have any of them in its own nature, because that which is in it naturally would impede the knowledge of anything else" (*ST*, I. q. 75, a. 2, c.). He concludes that the intellect cannot have anything in it of the "material" and hence that soul (whose primary activity is that of intellect) is "immaterial". The argument hinges on an ambiguity in the notion of matter. And the premise that mind must be immaterial or else it could not properly know matter might well seem question-begging. See Wilfrid Sellars, "Being and Being Known", *Proceedings American Catholic Philosophical Association, 34*, 1960, pp. 28-49.

64. See the essay by James Ross below.

65. Aquinas asserts that Augustine is "not at variance" with other writers in regard to the heavenly bodies: "For he says that they were made actually and not merely virtually, since the firmament has not the power of producing luminaries, as the earth has of producing plants" (q. 70, a. 1, c.). But a reference to the text cited from Augustine (*LMG*, V, 5; p. 155) makes this reading seem dubious. Augustine does say there that "on the fourth day, the lights and stars were created", but this is in a paragraph about "those beings which were formed from formlessness (unformed matter) and are clearly said to be created". He appears to be using the term 'created' here in the sense of "drawing forth from a prior matter", the sense that Aquinas wants to exclude.

66. *ST*, I, q. 70, a. 1, ad 1.

67. *ST*, I, q. 68, a. 3, c.

68. See section 1: "Augustine and Galileo" in E. McMullin, "How Should Cosmology Relate to Theology?", pp. 18–25.

69. René Descartes, *Principles of Philosophy*, III, 45; translated by Valentine Miller and Reese Miller, Dordrecht: Reidel, 1983, pp. 105-106. Descartes developed his cosmogony in three texts. He had almost completed *Le Monde* when he learnt of the condemnation in Rome of Galileo's *Dialogue* in 1633. This led him to withdraw his work; *Le Monde* was published posthumously in two parts: *L'homme* (the long final chapter of the original) in 1662 and *Le Monde* in 1664. Meanwhile, Descartes sketched its contents in the fifth part of the *Discourse on Method* of 1637, extending its argument, in principle at least, to the animal world. Then in 1644 he published a much enlarged version of the original *Le Monde* as *Principia philosophiae*, his most ambitious work, and the one on which he hoped his reputation would mainly rest.

70. As Michael Mahoney suggests in the introduction to his useful edition of *Le Monde*, with text and translation on facing pages: *René Descartes: Le Monde ou Traité de la lumière*, New York: Abaris, 1979.

71. *Principles*, III, 45; p. 105.

72. A Latin translation by Elia Diodati of Galileo's *Letter to the Grand Duchess Christina* appeared in Strasbourg in 1636. In the *Letter* Galileo draws heavily on texts from Augustine's *De Genesi ad litteram* to urge that a literal interpretation ought not be given biblical passages referring to the sun in motion or the earth at rest.

73. *Le Monde, Oeuvres de Descartes*, edited by Charles Adam and Paul Tannery, Paris: Vrin, 1967, vol. 11, p. 432; Mahoney, p. 55.

74. See the introduction to *Galileo, Man of Science*, edited by E. McMullin, New York: Basic Books, 1967, pp. 31-35.

75. René Descartes, *Discourse on Method*, Part V, translated by Paul Olscamp, Indianapolis: Bobbs-Merrill, 1965, p. 35.

76. Ibid., p. 36.

77. Ibid, Part VI, p. 52.

78. See section 1: "An Ambiguous Heritage", in E. McMullin, "The Conception of Science in Galileo's Work", in *New Perspectives on Galileo*, edited by R. Butts and J. Pitt, Dordrecht: Reidel, 1978, pp. 211-217.

79. *Principles*, III, 44; p. 105. The material in brackets was added in the first French translation of the *Principles* in 1647, which was carried out by Abbé Claude Picot under Descartes' own supervision.

80. *Principles*, III, 43; p. 104.

81. Ralph Blake, "Experience in Descartes' Theory of Method", in *Theories of Scientific Method*, edited by R. Blake, C. J. Ducasse, and E. H. Madden, Seattle: University of Washington Press, 1960, pp. 75-103; see esp. pp. 89-97.

82. *Principles*, IV, 205; p. 287; translation slightly modified.

83. *Le Monde*, p. 59; *Oeuvres*, 11, 434.

84. *Le Monde*, p. 69; *Oeuvres*, 11, 439.

85. *Le Monde*, p. 75; *Oeuvres*, 11, 442.

86. *Le Monde*, p. 77; *Oeuvres*, 11, 443.

87. *Principles*, II, 36; p. 58.

88. 'Unlikely' or 'impossible'? God's freedom is limited only by the possible. But how exactly in the "possible" to be circumscribed?

89. *Principles* IV, 133; p. 243.

90. This theme is explored in great detail by Richard Carter in *Descartes' Medical*

Philosophy, Baltimore: Johns Hopkins, 1983.

91. *Discourse*, Part V, p. 37.

92. *Principles*, IV, 188; p. 275.

93. Draft of an unaddressed letter from around 1648, *Oeuvres*, V, p. 260; cited in Carter, p. 190.

94. See R. S. Westfall, *Science and Religion in Seventeenth-Century England*, New Haven: Yale University Press, 1958, chapters 2 and 3.

95. Robert Boyle, *A Disquisition about the Final Causes of Natural Things* (1688), *Works*, edited by T. Birch, London, 1744, vol. 4, p. 516.

96. Ibid., p. 521

97. This theme was heavily stressed by Thomas Sprat in his *History of the Royal Society*, London, 1667, when discussing the motives that led to the foundation of the society.

98. The other name for it was the more traditional 'natural theology'. We shall retain the newer term in order to underline the difference between the older natural theology and the newer one. Even though three of the Five Ways of Aquinas (particularly the fifth one, involving the presence of design in nature) are reminiscent of the seventeenth-century arguments, they rested on very different metaphysical premises. And they did not have the fundamental apologetic role they came to take on in Boyle's day. See J. E. McGuire, "Boyle's Conception of Nature", *Journal of the History of Ideas, 33*, 1972, 523-542.

99. Boyle, *Final Causes*, p. 521.

100. John Ray, *The Wisdom of God*, 9th edition, London, 1727, p. 132.

101. Boyle, *Final Causes*, p. 525.

102. James Lennox gives a detailed and helpful analysis of the steps involved in "Robert Boyle's Defense of Teleological Inference in Science", *Isis, 74*, 1983, 38-52.

103. Boyle, *Final Causes*, p. 523.

104. I. Newton, *Four Letters from Sir Isaac Newton to Doctor Bentley*, London, 1756, Letter 1.

105. Newton, *Four Letters*, Letter 3.

106. See E. McMullin, "Is Philosophy Relevant to Cosmology?" *American Philosophical Quarterly, 18*, 1981, 177-189.

107. Eugene Klaaren, *Religious Origins of Modern Science*, Grand Rapids: Eerdmans, 1977, chapter 2: "Voluntarist Theology of Creation".

108. *ST*, I, q. 105, a. 5, c.

109. See Julius Weinberg, *Nicolaus of Autrecourt*, Princeton: Princeton University Press, 1948.

110. Keith Hutchison, "Supernaturalism and the Mechanical Philosophy", *History of Science, 21*, 1983, 298-333.

111. See M. J. S. Rudwick, *The Meaning of Fossils*, New York: Elsevier, 1972, chapter 2.

112. Quoted in Charles C. Gillispie, *Genesis and Geology*, New York: Harper, 1959, p. 103. Mott Greene reminds us how elastic the term 'catastrophist' was in describing a group of positions at bottom very different. See *Geology in the Nineteenth Century*, Ithaca, NY: Cornell University Press, 1982.

113. Buckland, *Vindiciae Geologicae*, Oxford, 1820, p. 19.

114. W. Whewell, "Lyell: *Principles of Geology*", *British Critic, 9*, 1831, 194; quoted by Gillispie, *Genesis and Geology*, p. 146.

115. R. Hooykaas, *New Interactions between Theology and Natural Science*, Unit 11 of the Open University Series on Science and Belief, Milton Keynes: Open University Press, 1974.

116. Ibid., pp. 64-65.

117. Ibid., p. 65. Emphasis his.

118. See R. Hooykaas, *Religion and the Rise of Modern Science*, Grand Rapids: Eerdmans, 1972.

119. See, for example, John Greene, *The Death of Adam*, Ames, IA: Iowa State University Press, 1959; Michael Ruse, *The Darwinian Revolution: Nature Red in Tooth and Claw*, Chicago: University of Chicago Press, 1979; Neal Gillespie, *Charles Darwin and the Problem of Creation*, Chicago: University of Chicago Press, 1979; James Moore, *The Post-Darwinian Controversies*, Cambridge: Cambridge University Press, 1979. This last contains an exhaustive bibliography. For a contemporary critique of physicotheology, see the essay by Nicholas Lash below.

120. Arthur Peacocke gives eloquent expression to this claim in his recent *Creation and the World of Science*, Oxford: Clarendon, 1979. See also Ervin Nemesszeghy, S.J., and John Russell, S.J., *The Theology of Evolution*, Notre Dame, IN: Fides, 1971.

121. See the essays below by Ross, Sloan, Alston, Lash, and Austin, respectively.

122. See James Collins, "Darwin's Impact on Philosophy", in *Darwin's Vision and Christian Perspectives*, edited by Walter Ong, S.J., New York: Macmillan, 1960, pp. 33-103; Eric Rust, *Evolutionary Philosophies and Contemporary Theology*, Philadelphia: Westminster, 1969.

123. See E. McMullin, "The Dialectics of Reduction", *Idealistic Studies*, 2, 1972, 95-115.

124. See David Joravsky, *Soviet Marxism and Natural Science 1917-1932*, London: Routledge, 1961. See also E. McMullin, "Is the Progress of Science Dialectical?" *Hegel and the Sciences*, edited by R. Cohen and M. Wartofsky, Dordrecht: Reidel, 1983, pp. 215-239.

125. Emile Rideau, *Teilhard de Chardin: A Guide to His Thought*, London: Collins, 1967, p. 294.

126. See E. McMullin, "Teilhard as a Philosopher", *Chicago Theological Seminary Register*, 55, 1964, 15-28.

127. Teilhard de Chardin, *The Appearance of Man*, New York: Harper, 1965, p. 211.

128. This conveys very little of the richness of Teilhard's thought in the theological domain. See the essay by Christopher Mooney, S.J., below.

129. Rideau, *Teilhard de Chardin*, p. 247.

130. Teilhard de Chardin, *Science and Christ*, translated by René Hague, New York: Harper, 1968, p. 29.

131. Ibid., p. 34.

132. See Delwin Brown et al., *Process Philosophy and Christian Thought*, Indianapolis: Bobbs-Merrill, 1971. Peacocke gives a sympathetic treatment of Teilhard and the process theologians under the title of "Creation and Hope", *Creation and the World of Science*, chapter 8.

133. See the useful review of this issue by Charles Misner, "Cosmology and Theology", in *Cosmology, History, and Theology*, edited by Wolfgang Yourgrau and Allan Breck, New York: Plenum, 1977, pp. 75-100; see also Edward Harrison, *Cosmology*, Cambridge: Cambridge University Press, 1981.

134. See Steven Weinberg, *The First Three Minutes: A Modern View of the Origin of the Universe*, New York: 1977. See also McMullin, "Is Philosophy Relevant to Cosmology?", section 2.

135. For a full account see the essay by John Leslie below, and Martin Rees, "Our Universe and Others", *Quarterly Journal Royal Astronomical Society*, 22, 1981, 109-124; McMullin, "How Should Cosmology Relate to Theology?", section 4.

136. See Alan Guth, "Inflationary Universe: A Possible Solution to the Horizon and Flatness Problems", *Physical Review D, 23*, 1981, 347-356.

137. See Dorothy Nelkin, *The Creation Controversy*, New York: Norton, 1982, chapter 7.

138. See Langdon Gilkey, "The Creationist Issue: A Theologian's View", *Cosmology and Theology*, edited by D. Tracy and N. Lash, Concilium Series, New York: Seabury, 1983; also *Is God a Creationist*, note 4 above.

139. For the text of the decision see "Opinion in McLean vs Arkansas", *Science, Technology and Human Values*, 7 (40), 1982, 28-42.

140. See Philip Quinn, "The Philosopher of Science as Expert Witness", in *Science and Reality*, edited by James Cushing et al., Notre Dame, IN: University of Notre Dame Press, 1984, pp. 32-53; Larry Laudan, "Science at the Bar: Causes for Concern", *Science, Technology and Human Values*, 7 (41), 1982, 16-19.

141. Larry Laudan, "The Demise of the Demarcation Problem", in *Physics, Philosophy and Psychoanalysis*, edited by R. S. Cohen and L. Laudan, Dordrecht: Reidel, 1983, pp. 111-128.

142. Quinn ("The Philosopher of Science as Expert Witness") argues this in some detail and offers an incisive critique of the argument of the opinion, while not disagreeing with the verdict itself.

143. The testimony he mainly relied on was that of the philosopher and historian of science Michael Ruse, who submitted a number of position papers to the Court. Ruse summarizes his view in "Creation Science Is Not Science", *Science, Technology and Human Values*, 7 (40), 1982, 72-78.

144. Laudan, *op. cit.*, p. 18.

145. *LMG*, I, 19; p. 43.

PART ONE
Evolution

THE THEORY OF EVOLUTION:
RECENT SUCCESSES AND CHALLENGES

Francisco J. Ayala

1. The "Fact" of Evolution

The theory of biological evolution (or, simply, the theory of evolution) encompasses the set of scientific concepts and propositions that apply to the origin of organisms now living on our planet and to the changes that have occurred in the living world since the origin of the first organisms to the present. The statements advanced by the theory can be classified into three subsets, according to the issues they deal with: (1) some general propositions stating that organisms are related by common descent; (2) propositions concerning the degree of relationship and evolutionary history of particular organisms, or groups of organisms, and their parts; (3) propositions concerning the processes, or "mechanisms", by which evolutionary change occurs.

The propositions in the first subset are the most fundamental; they also are the most definitively corroborated by science. These propositions may be summarized as follows.

Nearly two million species of living organisms have been described, and many more remain to be studied. The diversity of organisms encompasses the lowly bacteria, the yeasts and molds, the plants, and the animals. Many other species of organisms lived in the past, some very different from any organism now living. Of the species that lived in the past some became extinct without issue; others have left more or less modified descendants.

Living organisms are related by common descent. The diversity of organisms descended from a single common ancestral species becomes greater as we move further into the past. For example, the last common ancestor of humans and apes lived a few million years ago; earlier there lived a species from which humans, apes, and monkeys have all descended; all vertebrates — mammals, birds, reptiles, amphibians, and fishes — shared common ancestors that lived still earlier; and so on.

The general notion of the evolutionary origin of organisms expressed in the previous statements is supported by many sources of evidence. It is a scientific conclusion established with a certainty similar to that of notions such as the roundness of the earth, the motions of the planets, and the molecular composition of matter. This degree of certainty beyond reasonable doubt is what is implied by scientists when they say that the evolution of organisms is a "fact".

It is unfortunate that the different use of the word 'theory' in science and in ordinary language has misled some people to think that because scientists speak of the "theory of evolution", it must be that the evolution of organisms is not definitely established. In common usage, "theory" is contrasted with "fact". A fact is something considered well-established; a theory is something unlikely to be true or at least something for which evidence is lacking. That the Japanese bombed Pearl Harbor might be considered a "fact"; that the assassination of President Kennedy was planned by a foreign power would be just a "theory". In science a theory is a coherent set of statements that provide explanation for certain phenomena. A theory may be very tentative (in which case it is often called a "hypothesis") or well corroborated. In science a theory is not an imperfect fact, as it is in common language. That all matter consists of molecules is a scientific theory, but it is beyond reasonable doubt. That organic evolution has occurred is also corroborated beyond reasonable doubt (although there are uncertainties in the details of evolutionary history and in the relative importance of various mechanisms of change, as we shall see below).

Seeking evidence for or against the "fact" of evolution actively occupied scientists during the second half of the nineteenth century and the earlier part of the twentieth, up to the 1930s. The cumulative evidence eventually became so strong that this issue stopped being a matter of active concern for a majority of scientists. Additional evidence continues to accumulate as a consequence of scientific discoveries. Indeed, all biological knowledge is consistent with the notion that organisms have evolved, and virtually every biological discipline provides evidence supporting that fact. The only individuals challenging the fact of evolution are some calling themselves "creationists". These promote the teaching in schools, under the name of "creation-science", of a selection of statements from the Book of Genesis.

Creation-science is not science, because it does not have the attributes of science. There are no scientific data that would lead to theories about the origins and diversity of living beings resembling what is said in Genesis. If there had been no Book of Genesis, there would be no creation-science; no one would at present propose that living forms appeared suddenly just a few thousand years ago. The sudden creation of the world and of life are not explanations by natural processes. Neither can one find in creation-science any of the fertility of real science; observations are not used to enhance understanding. Rather, observations and experimental data are ignored or distorted in a futile effort to make them consistent with a point of view that scientific results utterly refute.

Teaching statements taken from religious books as if they were scientific explanations can only hamper education, with great damage to society. In the view of many religious authorities that confusion does great harm to religion as well. Pope John Paul II addressed the Pontifical Academy of Science (October 1981) as follows:

> The Bible itself speaks to us of the origin of the universe and its make-up, not in order to provide us with a scientific treatise but in order to state the correct relationships of man with God and with the universe. Sacred Scripture wishes simply to declare that the world was created by God, and in order to reach this truth it expresses itself in the terms of the cosmology in use at the time of the writer. The Sacred Book likewise wishes to tell men that the world was not created as the seat of the gods, as was taught by other cosmogonies and cosmologies, but was rather created for the service of man and the glory of God. Any other teaching about the origin and make-up of the universe is alien to the intentions of the Bible, which does not wish to teach how the heavens were made but how one goes to heaven.

2. Evolutionary History

The theory of biological evolution goes much beyond the general affirmation that organisms are related by common descent. Scientists try to ascertain the evolutionary relationships between particular organisms and to reconstruct the events of evolutionary history (the second subset of propositions enumerated above) as well as the mechanisms or processes by which evolution takes place (third subset). These are matters of active scientific investigation. Some conclusions are established with considerable certainty; others, less so; still others are conjectural.

The study of fossil remains of organisms living in the past provides definite clues to the evolutionary history (or "phylogeny") of a group of organisms, but the fossil record is always incomplete and often very limited or altogether lacking. Phylogenetic inferences may also be made from the comparative study of living organisms (Simpson, 1953). The logical basis of these inferences is simple. Because evolution is by and large a gradual process, organisms sharing a recent common ancestor are likely to be more similar to each other than organisms with a common ancestor only in a more remote past: relative degrees of similarity are used to infer recency of common descent. Assume, for example, that we compare three species and find that two of them, A and B, are much more similar to each other than they are to C; we would infer that the lineage leading to C separated from a lineage going to both A and B, before this lineage split again into two. Needless to say, the reconstruction of evolutionary history from the study of living organisms is a task far from simple: rates of evolutionary change may be different at different times, or in different groups of organisms, or with respect to different features of the same organisms. Moreover, resemblances due to common descent must be set apart from resemblances due to similar ways of life, to life in the same or similar habitat, or to accidental convergence.

Until about two decades ago the biological discipline that provided most information about evolutionary history was comparative anatomy, but additional knowledge was obtained from embryology, cytology, ethology, and biogeography. These biological disciplines all study the configuration, or "phenotype", of organisms. The advances of molecular biology have made possible, in recent years, the comparative study of proteins and nucleic acids— DNA and RNA (Dobzhansky et al., 1977). The DNA is the repository of hereditary (evolutionary and developmental) information. Proteins are part of the conformation of the organism, but their relationship to the DNA is so immediate that they closely reflect the hereditary information. This reflection is not perfect because the genetic code is redundant, and, hence, some differences in the DNA do not yield differences in the proteins. Moreover, it is not complete because, as we now know, a large fraction (about 90 percent) of the DNA does not code for proteins. Nevertheless, because proteins are so closely related to the information contained in the DNA, they, as well as the nucleic acids, are called "informational macromolecules." Some spectacular advances in the study of evolution have been accomplished in recent years by using the linear sequence of the components of DNA and proteins in reconstructing the phylogeny of organisms. This methodology has also made it possible to time important evolutionary events that occurred in the remote past—what is known as the "molecular clock" of evolution.   ⟵

Informational macromolecules retain, indeed, a considerable amount of evolutionary information. Nucleic acids and proteins are linear molecules made up of units, nucleotides in the case of nucleic acids, amino acids in the case of proteins. The sequence of the units contains information in a similar way as the sequence of letters and punctuation marks in a paragraph contains information. Comparison of two macromolecules establishes the number of units which are different in them. Because evolution usually occurs by changing one unit at a time, the number of differences is an indication of the recency of common ancestry. Changes in evolutionary rates may create difficulties, but macromolecular studies have two notable advantages over comparative anatomy and the other classical disciplines. One is that the information is more readily quantifiable: the number of units that are different is readily established when the sequence of units is known for a given macromolecule in different organisms. The other advantage is that even very different sorts of organisms can be compared. There is very little that comparative anatomy can say when organisms as diverse as yeasts, pine trees, and human beings are compared, but there are homologous macromolecules that can be compared in all three.

Informational macromolecules provide information not only about the topology of evolutionary history—that is, about the splitting of lineages, or *cladogenesis*—but also about the amount of genetic change that has occurred in any given evolution lineage, or *anagenesis*. It might seem at first that quantifying anagenesis for proteins and nucleic acids would be impossible, because it would require the comparison of molecules from organisms that lived in the past with those of living organisms. Organisms of the past are sometimes preserved as fossils, but their DNA and proteins are largely disintegrated. Nevertheless, comparisons between living species provide information about anagenesis. Consider two contemporary species, C and D, evolved from a common ancestral species, B (Figure 1). Assume that we find that C and D differ by x amino acid substitutions in a certain protein, say myoglobin. It is reasonable to assume, as a first approximation, that x/2 substitutions have taken place in each of the two evolutionary lineages, that is, from B to C and from B to D.

The assumption that equal amounts of change have occurred in the two lineages can be removed. Suppose that a third contemporary species, E, is compared with C and D and that the number of amino acid differences between the myoglobin molecules of the three species are as follows:

$$C \text{ and } D = 4$$
$$C \text{ and } E = 11$$
$$D \text{ and } E = 9$$

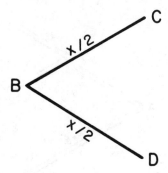

Figure 1. The amount of evolution through time, inferred from comparisons between living species. C and D are two contemporary species having B as a common ancestral species. If the amount of genetic differentiation between C and D is x, we can assume, as a first approximation, that half of the change occurred in each of the two lineages.

If the phylogeny of the three species is as shown in Figure 2, we can estimate the number of substitutions that have occurred in each of its branches. Let us use x and y to denote the number of amino acid differences between B and C and between B and D, respectively, and z to denote the number of differences between A and B *plus* those between A and E. We have, then, the following three equations:

$$x + y = 4$$
$$x + z = 11$$
$$y + z = 9$$

Solving these equations, we obtain x = 3, y = 1, and z = 8.

The procedure becomes more complicated when many more contemporary species are involved, but the conceptual basis for estimating anagenetic change is the same. As a concrete example, consider cytochrome c, a protein involved in cell respiration. The sequence of amino acids is known in many organisms, from bacteria and yeast to insects and humans. In animals cytochrome c consists of 104 amino acids. When the amino acid sequence of humans and rhesus monkeys are compared, they are found to be different at position 66 (isoleucine in humans, threonine in rhesus monkeys) but identical at the other 103 positions. When horses are compared with humans 12 amino acid differences are found, but when horses are compared with rhesus monkeys, there are only 11 amino acid differences (Figure 3).

Even if we did not know anything else about the evolutionary history of mammals, we would conclude that the lineages of humans and rhesus monkeys diverged from each other much more recently than they diverged from the horse lineage (compare Figures 4 and 5). Moreover, it is possible to conclude that the amino acid difference between humans and rhesus monkeys must

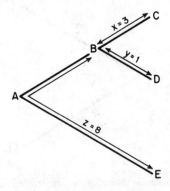

Figure 2. Estimated amounts of change in the evolutionary history of three contemporary species, based on comparisons between the three living species.

```
              1-8   9    10                                              20
Human         ----  Gly-Asp- Val -Glu- Lys -Gly- Lys- Lys- Ile -Phe- Ile -Met-
Rhesus monkey ----  Gly-Asp- Val -Glu- Lys -Gly- Lys- Lys- Ile -Phe- Ile -Met-
Horse         ----  Gly-Asp- Val -Glu- Lys -Gly- Lys- Lys- Ile -Phe- Val -Gln-
```

```
21                              30                            40
Lys -Cys- Ser -Gln- Cys- His - Thr- Val -Glu- Lys -Gly- Gly- Lys- His - Lys - Thr- Gly- Pro -Asn- Leu-
Lys -Cys- Ser -Gln- Cys- His - Thr- Val -Glu- Lys -Gly- Gly- Lys- His - Lys - Thr- Gly- Pro -Asn- Leu-
Lys -Cys- Ala -Gln- Cys- His - Thr- Val -Glu- Lys -Gly- Gly- Lys- His - Lys - Thr- Gly- Pro -Asn- Leu-
```

```
41                              50                            60
His - Gly- Leu- Phe- Gly- Arg- Lys - Thr- Gly- Gln- Ala - Pro - Gly- Tyr- Ser - Tyr- Thr- Ala - Ala -Asn-
His - Gly- Leu- Phe- Gly- Arg- Lys - Thr- Gly- Gln- Ala - Pro - Gly- Tyr- Ser - Tyr- Thr- Ala - Ala -Asn-
His - Gly- Leu- Phe- Gly- Arg- Lys - Thr- Gly- Gln- Ala - Pro - Gly- Phe - Thr- Tyr- Thr- Asp- Ala -Asn-
```

```
61                              70                            80
Lys -Asn- Lys -Gly- Ile - Ile - Trp- Gly- Glu- Asp- Thr- Leu- Met- Glu- Tyr- Leu- Glu- Asn- Pro -Lys-
Lys -Asn- Lys -Gly- Ile - Thr- Trp- Gly- Glu- Asp- Thr- Leu- Met- Glu- Tyr- Leu- Glu- Asn- Pro -Lys-
Lys -Asn- Lys -Gly- Ile - Thr- Trp- Lys- Glu- Glu- Thr- Leu- Met- Glu- Tyr- Leu- Glu- Asn- Pro -Lys-
```

```
81                              90                            100
Lys - Tyr- Ile - Pro -Gly- Thr- Lys -Met- Ile -Phe- Val -Gly- Ile - Lys- Lys- Lys- Glu- Glu- Arg- Ala-
Lys - Tyr- Ile - Pro -Gly- Thr- Lys -Met- Ile -Phe- Val -Gly- Ile - Lys- Lys- Lys- Glu- Glu- Arg- Ala-
Lys - Tyr- Ile - Pro -Gly- Thr- Lys -Met- Ile -Phe- Ala -Gly- Ile - Lys- Lys- Lys- Thr- Glu- Arg- Glu-
```

```
101                             110   112
Asp- Leu- Ile - Ala - Tyr- Leu- Lys - Lys - Ala - Thr- Asn- Glu
Asp- Leu- Ile - Ala - Tyr- Leu- Lys - Lys - Ala - Thr- Asn- Glu
Asp- Leu- Ile - Ala - Tyr- Leu- Lys - Lys - Ala - Thr- Asn- Glu
```

Figure 3. The sequence of amino acids (the structural components of proteins) in the protein cytochrome *c* in humans, rhesus monkeys, and horses. In these organisms cytochrome *c* consists of 104 amino acids (positions 9-112; positions 1-8 are reserved for amino acids that exist in some organisms but not in mammals). The amino acid differences between the sequences (highlighted with shading) are 1 between humans and monkeys, 12 between humans and horses, and 11 between monkeys and horses.

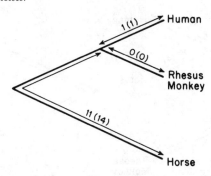

Figure 4. Amino acid (and nucleotide) changes in the evolution of cytochrome *c* from the last common ancestors to humans, rhesus monkeys, and horses. The numbers indicate the amino acid substitutions (and, in parentheses, the minimum number of nucleotide substitutions) that have taken place in each branch of the phylogeny.

have occurred in the human lineage after its separation from the rhesus-monkey lineage (see Figure 4).

The methods developed for estimating genetic change during evolution from the study of informational macromolecules include DNA sequencing, protein sequencing, DNA hybridization, immunology, and electrophoresis (Ayala and Kiger, 1984). Here I will illustrate the power of these methods using a protein, cytochrome c, as an example. The amino acid sequences of the cytochrome c of many organisms are known. Phylogenies can, then, be constructed based on the number of amino acid differences between species. However, the amino acid sequence of a protein contains more information than is reflected in the number of amino acid differences. This is because the replacement of one amino acid by another requires in some cases no more than one nucleotide substitution in the DNA that codes from the protein, but in other cases it requires at least two nucleotide changes.

The minimum numbers of nucleotide differences necessary to account for the amino acid differences in the cytochromes c of twenty organisms are given in Table 1 (Fitch and Margoliash, 1967, 1970). A phylogeny based on that data matrix, as well as the minimum numbers of nucleotide changes required in each branch, are shown in Figure 6. These differences are often fractions. It is obvious that a nucleotide change may or may not have taken place, but fractional nucleotide changes cannot occur. However the values given in Figure 6 are those satisfying best the data in Table 1.

The phylogenetic relationships shown in Figure 6 correspond fairly well, on the whole, with the phylogeny of the organisms as determined from the fossil record and other sources. There are disagreements, however. For example, chickens appear more closely related to penguins than to ducks and pigeons, and men and monkeys diverge from the other mammals before the

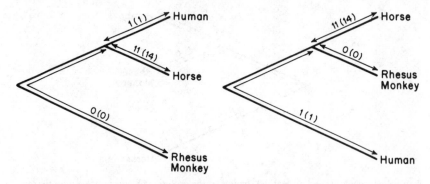

Figure 5. Two theoretically possible phylogenies of humans, rhesus monkeys, and horses. The numbers of amino acid (and nucleotide) substitutions required in each branch to account for the cytochrome c sequences indicate that neither of these two phylogenies is likely to be correct.

marsupial kangaroo separates from the nonprimate placentals. In spite of these erroneous relationships, it is remarkable that the study of a single protein yields a fairly accurate representation of the phylogeny of twenty organisms as diverse as those in the figure. The amino acid sequence of proteins (and the genetic information therein contained) store indeed considerable evolutionary information.

Cytochromes c are slowly evolving proteins. Organisms as different as humans, silkworm moths, and *Neurospora* have in common a large proportion of amino acids in their cytochrome c. The evolutionary conservation of this cytochrome makes possible the study of genetic differences among organisms only remotely related. However, this same conservation makes cytochrome c useless for determining evolutionary change in closely related organisms, since they may have cytochromes c that are completely or nearly identical. The primary structure of cytochrome c is identical in humans and chimpanzees, which diverged about 10 million years ago; it differs by only one amino acid replacement between humans and rhesus monkeys, whose most recent common ancestor lived 40 to 50 million years ago.

TABLE 1

Minimum number of nucleotide differences in the genes coding for cytochromes c *in 20 organisms. (Data from Fitch and Margoliash, 1967).*

Organism	2	3	4	5	6	7	8	9	10	11	12	13	14	15	16	17	18	19	20
1. Human	1	13	17	16	13	12	12	17	16	18	18	19	20	31	33	36	63	56	66
2. Monkey		12	16	15	12	11	13	16	15	17	17	18	21	32	32	35	62	57	65
3. Dog			10	8	4	6	7	12	12	14	14	13	30	29	24	28	64	61	66
4. Horse				1	5	11	11	16	16	16	17	16	32	27	24	33	64	60	68
5. Donkey					4	10	12	15	15	15	16	15	31	26	25	32	64	59	67
6. Pig						6	7	13	13	13	14	13	30	25	26	31	64	59	67
7. Rabbit							7	10	8	11	11	11	25	26	23	29	62	59	67
8. Kangaroo								14	14	15	13	14	30	27	26	31	66	58	68
9. Duck									3	3	3	7	24	26	25	29	61	62	66
10. Pigeon										4	4	8	24	27	26	30	59	62	66
11. Chicken											2	8	28	26	26	31	61	62	66
12. Penguin												8	28	27	28	30	62	61	65
13. Turtle													30	27	30	33	65	64	67
14. Rattlesnake														38	40	41	61	61	69
15. Tuna															34	41	72	66	69
16. Screwworm fly																16	58	63	65
17. Moth																	59	60	61
18. *Neurospora*																		57	61
19. *Saccharomyces*																			41
20. *Candida*																			—

Fortunately, different proteins evolve at different rates. Phylogenetic relationships among closely related organisms may be inferred by studying the primary sequences of rapidly evolving proteins, such as fibrinopeptides in mammals (Figure 7). Genetic changes in the evolution of very closely related species can also be studied by other methods, such as DNA sequencing, DNA hybridization, immunology, and gel electrophoresis.

3. The Molecular Clock of Evolution

It was first observed in the late 1960s that the numbers of amino acid differences between homologous proteins of any two given species was very nearly proportional to the time since their divergence from a common ancestor. If

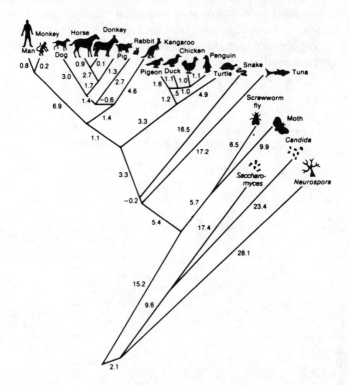

Figure 6. Phylogeny based on differences in the protein sequence of cytochrome *c* in organisms ranging from yeast to man. The numbers are estimates of the nucleotide substitutions in this protein that have occurred during evolution. This pattern agrees well with the pattern of phylogenetic relationships worked out by classical techniques of comparative morphology and from the fossil record. (After Fitch and Margoliash, 1967).

the rate of evolution of a protein or gene would be approximately the same in the evolutionary lineage leading to different species, proteins and DNA sequences would provide a molecular clock of evolution. The sequences could then be used to reconstruct not only the topology of the phylogeny (i.e., the sequence of branching events) but also the time when the various events occurred. Consider, for example, the phylogeny shown in Figure 6. If the rate of evolution of cytochrome c were constant through time, the number of nucleotide changes that have occurred in each branch of the phylogeny would be directly proportional to the elapsed time. If we know from an outside source (such as the fossil record) the actual geological time of any one branching event in the phylogeny, it becomes possible to determine the times of all other events by a simple proportion. That is, once the molecular clock is

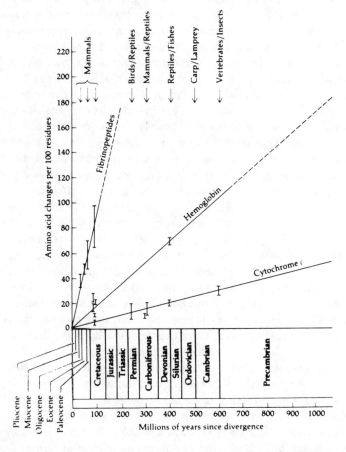

Figure 7. Rates of molecular evolution of different proteins. (After R. E. Dickerson, 1971).

"calibrated" by reference to a single event, it can be used to measure the time of occurrence of all other events in a phylogeny.

The molecular clock would not, of course, be expected to be a "metronomic" clock, like timepieces in ordinary life that measure time exactly, but a "stochastic" clock like radioactive decay. In a stochastic clock the *probability* of a certain amount of change is constant, although some variation occurs in the actual amount of change. Over fairly long periods of time a stochastic clock is, nevertheless, quite accurate. Moreover, each gene or protein would be a separate clock providing an independent estimate of phylogenetic events and their time of occurrence. Each gene or protein would "tick" at a different rate (determined by the slope of lines such as those shown for three proteins in Figure 7), but all genes and proteins would be timing the same evolutionary events. The joint results of several genes or proteins would provide a fairly precise evolutionary clock. The possible existence of a molecular clock of evolution is one more exciting development in modern evolutionary theory.

Whether or not there is a molecular clock and how accurate it is are at present controversial matters. The "neutrality theory" of molecular evolution, which will be discussed below, provides theoretical grounds to expect the existence of a molecular clock of evolution. The neutrality theory predicts that each gene will evolve at a rate that is precisely the rate of mutation to "neutral" alleles of that gene. A number of empirical tests have been performed in order to measure the accuracy of the molecular clock (see, e.g., Ayala and Kiger, 1984). The outcome of these tests may be summarized as follows. The amount of variation observed is greater than is expected from a stochastic clock; that is, the clock is sloppy. But the heterogeneity of evolutionary rates along different lineages is not excessively large. Thus, it is possible in principle to time phylogenetic events with as much accuracy as may be desired, but it is necessary to examine more genes or proteins (about two to four times as many) as would be required if the clock were stochastically constant. The *average* rates obtained for many proteins become a fairly precise clock, particularly when many species are studied and the evolutionary events involve long time periods (of the order of one hundred million years or more). This conclusion is illustrated in Figure 8, which plots the cumulative number of nucleotide changes in 7 proteins versus the paleontological dates of divergence of 17 species of mammals. The overall correlation is fairly good for all phylogenetic events except those involving some primates (at lower left of the figure), which appear to have evolved at a slower rate than the average for the other species. This anomaly is a typical instance of the point made that the more recent the divergence of any two species the more likely it is that the changes observed will depart from the average evolutionary rate. The reason is simply that as time increases, periods of rapid evolution and periods of slow evolution in any lineage are likely to cancel each other out.

4. The Origin of Genes

The origin of "novelty," or the "emergence" of new organs or features, is an old evolutionary question. A new version of these issues arises at the level of genes and DNA. How do new items of evolutionary information come to be? We understand how genes evolve by stepwise replacement of one by another nucleotide in the DNA sequence. Indeed, we can trace, in as much detail as we may want, the evolution of specific genes through time, as they record the evolution of organisms. But where do genes come from in the first place? The amount of genetic information—the number of genes—also evolves. The primordial organisms had only a few genes. Three and a half

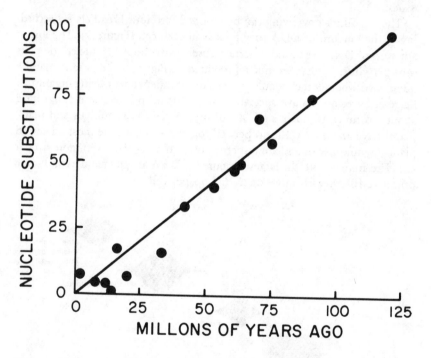

Figure 8. Nucleotide substitutions versus paleontological time. The total nucleotide substitutions for seven proteins (cytochrome *c*, fibrinopeptides A and B, hemoglobins alpha and beta, myoglobin, an insulin c-peptide) have been calculated for comparisons between pairs of species whose ancestors diverged at the time indicated in the abscissa. The solid line has been drawn from the origin to the outermost point and corresponds to a total rate of 0.42 nucleotide substitutions per million years (or 98.2 nucleotide substitutions per 2 × 120 million years of evolution) for the genes coding for all seven proteins. The fit between the observed number of nucleotide substitutions and the expected number (as determined by the solid line) is fairly good in general. However, in the primates (points below the diagonal at lower left) protein evolution seems to have occurred at a slower rate than in most other organisms. (After Fitch, 1976).

billion years later there are organisms with one hundred thousand times more DNA than others, all of which surely have more DNA than their earliest common ancestors. The origin and organization of genes is an onerous, yet exciting, challenge to evolutionary science. Scientists have obtained a few glimpses of the processes involved during the last decade or so, but they are far from a full understanding. The difficulty is, perhaps, that we lack a satisfactory theory to account for the origin of evolutionary novelty. Mendelian genetics coupled with the theories of mutation and natural selection provide an adequate conceptual framework to explain how genes change through time, but they are insufficient for a full understanding of how genes come to be. Be this as it may, I shall now review what we have recently learned about these issues.

The organisms now living can be grouped into four broad classes according to the amount of DNA they possess in each cell (Figure 9). The lowest amounts of DNA are found in some viruses, with about 10^4 nucleotide pairs (np) per virus. Viruses are not represented in Figure 9, because it may be questioned whether they should be considered independent living organisms. Bacteria have, on the average, about 4×10^6 np per cell, and fungi have about ten times as much, or 4×10^7 np per cell. Most animals and many plants have about 2×10^9 np per cell, on the average. The most advanced plants, gymnosperms and angiosperms, often have 10^{10} or even more np per cell. The animals with the largest amounts of DNA are salamanders and some primitive fishes, with more than 10^{10} np per cell.

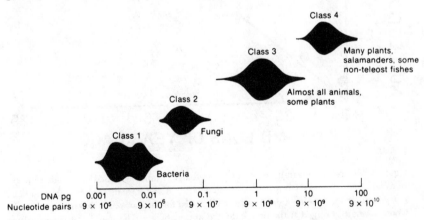

Figure 9. Organisms classified according to their amounts of DNA per cell. The amount of DNA is given by weight (1 pg = 10^{-12}g) and by the number of nucleotide pairs. It ranges within one order of magnitude for most organisms within each group. For all organisms, from bacteria to plants and animals, the amount of DNA varies by more than five orders of magnitude. (After Hinegardner, 1976).

A substantial evolutionary increase in the amount of DNA per cell has occurred from bacteria to fungi, to animals, and to plants. More complex organisms may need more DNA than a bacterium or a mold, but there seems to be no consistent relationship between the amount of DNA in an organism and its complexity of organization. For example, salamanders and flowering plants are not ten times more complex than mammals or birds, although some of the former have ten times more DNA than the latter.

How does the amount of DNA per cell increase during evolution? One process is polyploidy, by which the number of chromosomes of a cell, and hence the amount of DNA, is doubled. Polyploidy is a fairly common phenomenon in plants but rare in animals. In plants as well as in animals increases and decreases of DNA often occur in evolution by duplication or deletion of small DNA segments. Duplications often occur in tandem, that is, with the duplicated segments adjacent to each other in the chromosomes. But there also occur "insertions" of short DNA segments that come from removed regions of the DNA of the organism, or even from foreign DNA elements (viruses or viruslike DNA segments that are now known to exist in all cells, independently of the nuclear DNA of the organism).

A recent exciting discovery is that some genes have arisen by tandem duplications of very small DNA segments. An example is the gene coding for collagen. Collagen is the main structural protein of bone, cartilage, connective tissue, and skin in vertebrates. In the chicken, for example, the collagen gene consists of about 38,000 np, made up of more than 50 small segments ("exons") that code for the protein, separated by larger DNA segments ("introns") that do not code for protein at all. The number of nucleotide pairs in each exon ranges from 45 to 108 but is always a multiple of nine. It seems that this long gene is made up of several hundred duplications of a particular short sequence of 9 np, although nucleotide changes have occurred in this basic sequence in many places during the course of evolution.

A more complex situation exists in some genes coding for antibodies (immunoglobulins). Some of these genes are about 600 nucleotide pairs long that have arisen by 12 tandem repetitions of an ancestral sequence 48 np long. The 48-np building block is itself the result of the association of three segments 14, 21, and 15 np long that are similar in sequence and may have evolved from one another, also after tandem duplication and partial deletion.

Other genes in higher organisms seem to have arisen by the combination of small primordial genes having separate functions; the descendants of the ancestral genes are recognized at times because they constitute different exons (i.e., they remain separated from each other by DNA sequences that do not code for protein) of the modern gene. Each exon codes in these cases for a different protein domain, that is, a part of the protein with a distinctive function homologous to the function of the ancestral simple gene. Some antibody genes, for example, each code for three different protein domains: CH_1, CH_2 and CH_3. Each domain has a distinctive function: CH_3 is involved in cell surface interactions, and CH_2 in complement fixation, whereas CH_1 forms an attachment point. A second example is provided by the hemoglobin genes, which consist of three exons. The middle exon codes for the protein domain containing the contacts that determine the heme binding site (which is involved in association and dissociation with oxygen). This domain may be a remnant of an ancestral miniglobin. The two flanking exons code for elements that wrap the product of the central exon. The gene coding for alcohol dehydrogenase in *Drosophila melanogaster* also consists of three exons, separated by two introns of 65 and 70 np. One exon codes for the 140 residues involved in binding the coenzyme. The longer intron separates this protein domain from the elements involved in the main catalytic activity of the enzyme.

5. The Multiplication of Genes

Complex genes, as they exist in higher organisms, often become multiplied from two to many times in the course of evolution. The fate of the duplicated genes varies from one to another case, but three kinds of outcomes may be identified. (1) Functional conservation: some duplicated genes retain the original function and remain identical in structure to each other. (2) Functional divergence: some duplicated genes gradually diverge and eventually acquire different but related functions. (3) Functional loss: some duplicated genes change in structure in such a way that they can no longer code for functional proteins.

Typical examples of functional conservation are the genes that code for ribosomal RNA or for transfer RNA. The ribosomes are cell organelles that mediate the process by which the information contained in genes of all sorts becomes translated into enzymes and other proteins. Organisms have three kinds of ribosomal RNA encoded by three different kinds of genes. There are many copies of these genes in a given organism. For example, there are 7 copies in the bacterium *Escherichia coli*, about 140 in yeast, 200 in *Drosophila* flies, 500 in the African clawed toad, and 300 in humans. All the copies of a given gene are essentially identical to one another in structure and function. The presence of multiple copies of each gene facilitates the production of the large amounts of ribosomal RNA that are needed by the cells. A similar situation obtains in the case of the transfer RNA genes. There are in each organism at least 20 different kinds of transfer RNA molecules, which like the ribosomes are also involved in the translation of genetic information into proteins. There are about 100 copies of the transfer RNA genes in *Escherichia coli*, 350 in yeast, 750 in *Drosophila*, 7,800 in the African toad, and 1,300 copies in humans.

Functional divergence can be illustrated with the globin genes. Myoglobins and hemoglobins are molecules involved in the storage and transport of oxygen in vertebrates. Myoglobin exists primarily in muscle; the hemoglobins are present in the blood. There are several kinds of hemoglobins. For example, in humans there are three kinds of hemoglobin during embryonic development, a different kind appears later in the fetus, which is eventually replaced by two other kinds shortly after birth. There are at least eight different hemoglobin genes and one myoglobin gene in humans. All or most of these genes are also found in mammals and other vertebrates. The similarity of all the globin genes leaves no doubt that they have arisen by a series of duplications from a common ancestral gene (Figure 10).

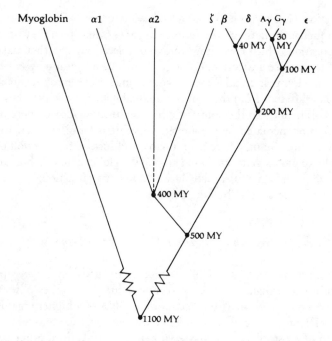

Figure 10. Evolutionary history of the globin genes. The dots indicate where the ancestral genes were duplicated, giving rise to a new gene line. The approximate times when the duplications occurred are indicated in millions of years (MY). In humans the α1 and α2 genes are identical due to "gene conversion", but the presence of the duplicated genes in many, perhaps all, vertebrates suggests that this duplication occurred around the time of the origin of the vertebrates. Similarly, the Aγ and Gγ genes are identical to each other in humans owing to gene conversion. Since they are duplicated in the great apes as well, the duplication must have occurred before the great apes diverged from each other and from the human lineage.

The first duplication made possible the evolution of two kinds of globins: myoglobin specialized in oxygen storage in muscle and hemoglobin for oxygen transport in the blood. The next duplication occurred about 500 million years ago. The presence of two hemoglobin genes made possible the evolution of modern hemoglobin that consists of four protein chains ("polypeptides"), two of each of two kinds, which is considerably more efficient for oxygen transport than is a single-chain molecule. This four-chain structure of hemoglobin is found in all vertebrates except in some primitive fishes. Hence, that duplication must have occurred after the lineage of the primitive fishes split from the lineage leading to all other vertebrates, but before these diverged from each other. Considerations of evolutionary history together with comparisons of the DNA sequences yield the evolutionary history traced in Figure 10. Successive duplications made possible gradual specialization of functions.

Functional loss occurs in the so-called "pseudogenes" — DNA segments with high sequence similarity to the functional genes from which they have arisen by duplication, which have, however, accumulated changes that make them unable to produce a functional protein chain. An intriguing hypothesis, yet unconfirmed, is that pseudogenes may sometimes evolve into functional genes with roles different from those of the original gene from which they are derived. This hypothesis thus proposes that the functional divergence of genes may often be mediated by pseudogenes: before it acquires a new function, the divergent gene may have been unable to function for a period of time. Examples of pseudogenes are found among the globin genes. In humans there is a pseudoalpha gene proximally located to the two functional alpha genes, and a pseudobeta near the beta gene.

6. "Nonsense" DNA and "Horizontal" Transfer of Genes

The kinds of duplicated DNA sequences discussed in the two previous sections do not exhaust all those known to occur, nor do they pose the only unsolved issues. Less than 10 percent of the DNA of a higher organism carries genetic information that becomes eventually translated into proteins. The function of most of the remaining 90 percent is unknown. Some scientists argue that most of this is "nonsense" DNA, which accumulates by duplication but has no functional role whatsoever. It remains in the organism because it replicates along with the other DNA during cell division but fails to be eliminated by natural selection because it imposes only a trivial energy burden on the organism. But it might be that much of this DNA plays some role in maintaining the overall structural organization of the DNA and thus making possible the function of the genes that code for protein. In addition, some

DNA is known to have regulatory functions, that is, it encodes signals that tell when a gene should be activated or deactivated. But it is not known how much DNA is involved in regulatory functions of this sort. In any case a good fraction of the noncoding DNA consists of sequences of variable length that are repeated many times. One example are the "Alu" sequences, each about 300 np long, of which there are about 300,000 copies in each human cell, making up 3 percent of the total DNA. And there is another sequence, 3,400 np long, that occurs in about 3,000 copies spread throughout the human DNA to make up nearly 1 percent of the total; one of the copies is present in the neighborhood of the beta-hemoglobin gene.

One more unsolved puzzle is the recent discovery of genes that exist in evolutionarily distant species but are identical or very similar in DNA sequence. One intriguing possibility is that genes can sometimes be transmitted "horizontally", that is, between species coexisting at a given time, rather than from parents to descendants. Gene duplications increase the DNA of an organism and make possible the evolution of new functions. Duplicated genes follow ancestral relationships coincident with those of the organisms in which they occur: that is, the ancestral and the duplicated genes exist in the same species. It would seem that evolution by the incorporation of a gene evolved in one species into the genome of another is impossible: species are independent evolutionary units because they are reproductively isolated from one another. However, it has been known for several decades that bacteria can incorporate foreign DNA by means of processes known as transformation and transduction. There is recent evidence that genes may transfer from one higher organism to another, although this phenomenon must be very rare even in the evolutionary time scale—if it occurs at all.

Two of the probable instances of horizontal DNA transfer occur between sea urchin species. Certain nucleotides of the highly repeated genes coding for the histones H4 and H3 evolve in several sea urchin species at a rate of 0.5-0.6 nucleotide substitution per million years—similar to the rate observed in single-copy genes coding for proteins. In one species, *Psammechinus miliaris*, the rate of evolution of those nucleotides appears to be 1/100 to 1/200 of the standard rate. One possible explanation is that, for some unknown reason, strong selective constraints in *Psammechinus* reduce the rate of evolution of the nucleotides to less than one-hundredth of their rate in other species. An alternative explanation is that a histone gene cluster has transferred from another species, *Strongylocentrotus drobachiensis*, within the last 1 million years, even though the ancestors of these species diverged some 65 million years ago. Two other sea urchin species, *Strongylocentrotus purpuratus* and *Tripneustes gratilla*, diverged from each other even earlier. The single-copy DNA of these species has diverged at standard rates, but there is a family of repeated sequences that is extremely similar in both species.

One possible explanation is recent horizontal transfer of this family of sequences from one species to the other.

A still more intriguing apparent example of horizontal transfer involves the ponyfish and its bioluminescent bacterial symbiont, *Photobacter leiognathi*. Superoxide dismutase (SOD) is an enzyme engaged in removing harmful oxygen radicals from the cell. An SOD distinctive to higher organisms but present also in bacteria contains manganese. A second SOD exists that in higher organisms contains copper and zinc but in bacteria contains iron. In *P. leiognathi* this SOD resembles the corresponding SOD of its host, the ponyfish, much more clearly than the SOD of any other bacteria. Horizontal transfer from the ponyfish to its symbiont would account for this similarity.

The evidence for horizontal gene transfer is still limited and far from convincing, because other possible explanations have not been fully excluded. If it occurs, the phenomenon of horizontal DNA transfer opens a new avenue for evolution that was thoroughly unsuspected for higher organisms until very recently. In any case, this phenomenon could not be very common even in the evolutionary time scale. Otherwise, organisms would consist of a medley of genes, making it impossible to identify the distinctive degrees of homology and evolutionary relationship found; we would not be able to identify, say, the insects as a clearly separate lineage from the molluscs.

7. *Hereditary Variation*

The scientific study of evolution seeks not only to reconstruct the evolutionary history of organisms but also to discover the processes that account for evolutionary change. The propositions concerned with the mechanisms of evolution constitute the third subset of the evolutionary theory enumerated at the beginning of this paper. Darwin proposed that natural selection — that is, better survival and reproduction — of organisms having favorable traits could explain why evolution occurs, as well as the apparent design of organisms. The science of genetics has provided understanding of the processes of gene mutation and duplication by which new hereditary variations appear. The process of natural selection has been measured in many favorable circumstances, and it can be understood in terms of ensuing genetic changes. But other evolutionary mechanisms have been discovered. The relative importance of natural selection relative to other processes is a matter of active investigation and debate at present. We shall confront some of the issues at stake later. Now, however, I want to review one important recent accomplishment: our ability to measure genetic variation.

The occurrence of hereditary variation in the population of organisms was the starting point of Darwin's argument for evolution by a process of natural selection. Indeed, if there are no hereditary variations, there is no way in which one variant can increase in frequency at the expense of the other and gradually replace it. Evolutionary geneticists have further shown, theoretically as well as experimentally, that the rate of evolution of a population of organisms is proportional to the amount of genetic variation present in the population. Thus, quantifying the amount of variation is the fundamental step in order to evaluate the evolutionary potential of a species and to understand how evolution proceeds.

The evidence for genetic variation can be traced to Mendel's experiments in the 1860s: his discovery of the laws of heredity was made possible by the segregation of genetic variants in the progenies of crosses between plants that differed with respect to certain traits. Since that time the study of genetic variation has been characterized by a gradual discovery of ever-increasing amounts of genetic variation. But the efforts to obtain precise estimates were thwarted for many years because of a methodological handicap imposed by the traditional methods of genetic analysis.

Consider what we need to do in order to find out how many genes are variable in a given population or species. We cannot study every gene of an organism, because we do not even know how many genes there are and because it would be an enormous task. The solution, then, is to look at only a sample of genes. If the sample is random, that is, not biased and thus truly representative of the population, the values observed in the sample can be extrapolated to the whole population. Pollsters do quite well this way: for example, on ⟶ sometimes the basis of a sample of about 2,000 individuals they are able to predict with fair accuracy how millions of Americans will vote in a presidential election.

To ascertain how many genes are variable in a population, we need to study a few genes that are an unbiased sample of all the genes. With the traditional methods of genetics this is impossible, because the existence of a gene is ascertained by examining the progenies of crosses between individuals showing different forms of a given character; from the proportions of individuals in the various classes we infer whether one or more genes are involved. By such methods, therefore, the only genes known to exist are those that are variable. There is no way of obtaining an unbiased sample of the genome, because invariant genes cannot be included in the sample.

A way out of this dilemma became possible with the discoveries in molecular genetics. It is now known that the genetic information encoded in the nucleotide sequences of the DNA of a structural gene is translated into a sequence of amino acids making up a protein. We can select for study a series of proteins without previously knowing whether or not they are variable in a population—a series of proteins that, with respect to variation, represent an unbiased sample of genes of the organism. If a protein is found to be invariant among individuals, it is inferred that the gene coding for that protein is also invariant; if the protein is variable, we know that the gene is variable, and we can measure how variable it is, that is, how many variant forms of the protein exist, and in what frequencies. Direct study of the nucleotide sequence of a sample of genes is also a possible solution to the dilemma: a gene can be sequenced in a number of individuals independently of whether or not the DNA sequence varies among individuals.

In the 1960s a new technique, known as gel electrophoresis, was developed for the rapid survey of different kinds of proteins in many individuals. The results, summarized in Table 2, are astounding. The significant measure is the "heterozygosity," which is the probability that the two genes, inherited one from the father and the other from the mother, for a given trait are different in an individual. The average heterozygosity for the organisms summarized in that table ranges from 6 to 18.5 percent.

One way to appreciate the significance of these figures is the following. Consider our own species in which the heterozygosity estimated by gel electrophoresis is 6.7 percent. If we assume that there are 30,000 different genes in a human being, which may be an underestimate, a person would be heterozygous at $30,000 \times 0.067 = 2,010$ genes. Such an individual can theoretically produce $2^{2010} \doteq 10^{605}$ different kinds of sex cells, or 1 followed by 605 zeros. (An individual heterozygous for one gene can produce two different kinds of sex cells or gametes; an individual heterozygous for n genes has the potential of producing 2^n different sex cells.) This number of sex cells will never be produced by any individual, however, nor by the whole of mankind; the estimated total number of atoms in the universe, 10^{76}, is infinitesimal by comparison.

These calculations, therefore, show that no two human individuals (except those derived from the same egg, such as identical twins) who exist now, have ever existed in the past, or will ever exist in the future are likely to be genetically identical. Herein lies the genetic basis of human individuality. And the same can be said, in general, of organisms that reproduce sexually: no two individuals developed from separate eggs are ever likely to be genetically identical.

The results become more dramatic yet by noticing (1) that gel electrophoresis does not detect all protein differences and (2) that not all genetic differences yield protein differences. The reason for (1) is that gel electrophoresis detects differences by the differential mobility of proteins in an electric field. But some proteins with small differences in composition may have identical electrophoretic mobility. It is not now known how much protein variation goes undetected by electrophoresis. Recent experimental results indicate that the values of heterozygosity at the protein level should be two or three times greater than those given in Table 2.

In addition, some differences in the DNA sequence of genes do not translate into protein differences. This is, first, because of the redundancy of the genetic code. There are from one to six different "words" in the DNA coding for each one of the 20 amino acids that make up proteins. Moreover, not all the DNA of a gene contains information coding for protein. There are, for example, the introns mentioned earlier, which separate the coding segments of a gene. In very recent years it has become possible to isolate individual genes and to clone them in microorganisms so that many identical copies of the gene are produced and the sequence of the DNA can then be obtained. These are the "recombinant DNA'" techniques that adumbrate a new revolution in genetics. The number of genes sequenced in any given species is still limited. But the data already at hand indicate that in terms of the DNA sequence nearly every gene is heterozygous in every sexual organism. The two copies of a gene, inherited one from the father and the other from the mother, differ in about 1 or 2 percent of the nucleotides that make up the DNA. A gene consists of something like 1,500 nucleotides. Hence, the two genes that we have for each trait are likely to differ from each other in about 15 to 30 nucleotides.

The significance of these DNA variations remains to be ascertained. It may be that most DNA differences that do not yield protein heterogeneity are of little significance to the life of the organism, because they do not affect its ability to function, to survive, and to reproduce. But at least some of these differences encode signals that activate or deactivate genes, and these can affect living processes. Only the future will tell the evolutionary importance of this enormous variation in the DNA sequences.

TABLE 2

Genetic variation measured by protein variation.

Organisms	Number of species studied	Average number of genes per species	Average heterozygosity per gene
Animals			
Invertebrates	57	22	0.134
Vertebrates	68	24	0.060
Plants			
Self-pollinating	33	14	0.058
Outcrossing	36	11	0.185

(After Ayala and Kiger, 1984.)

8. Natural Selection and Chance

In *The Origin of Species* Darwin accumulated an impressive number of observations supporting the evolutionary origin of organisms. Moreover, and perhaps most importantly, he provided a causal explanation of evolutionary processes—the theory of natural selection. The principle of natural selection, as Darwin saw it, provides a natural explanation of the adaptation of organisms to their environment. With *The Origin of Species* the study of adaptation—or "the problem of design" as the English natural theologians of the eighteenth and nineteenth centuries would have it—came fully into the domain of science.

The modern understanding of the principle of natural selection derives from Darwin's concept, although it is formulated in a somewhat different way. Natural selection is understood today in genetic and statistical terms as differential reproduction. Differential reproduction is a compound process, the elements of which are differential survival, differential mating success, and differential fecundity. Natural selection implies that some genes and genetic combinations are transmitted to the following generation on the average more frequently than their alternatives. Such genetic units will become more common in every subsequent generation, and their alternatives less common. Natural selection is a statistical bias in the relative rate of reproduction of alternative genetic units.

Natural selection changes organisms in the direction of increased adaptation to the environments where they live. The organisms likely to leave more descendants are those having variations that are more advantageous as adaptations to the environments. Natural selection accounts also for the diversity of life as it promotes the adaptation of organisms to different environments and ways of life. Natural selection is a principle of considerable explanatory power, and its integration with genetics is one spectacular success of the theory of evolution.

The theory of evolution identifies other processes, besides natural selection, that bring about genetic changes. I have already mentioned gene mutation and duplication, the ultimate sources of all genetic variability. The sexual process combines in every individual the hereditary materials that it receives from the previous generation. Then, there is the process known as "genetic drift", by which gene frequencies change due to sampling variation from one generation to the next. The frequency of, say, the gene for the B blood group in a certain generation might be 0.24, but it might increase to 0.25 in the following generation (and the joint frequency of the genes for A and O blood groups decrease from 0.76 to 0.75) because by chance the B gene happens to be present in the sex cells that produce the following generation a little more often than would be expected. Genetic drift occurs simply because populations are finite in numbers, and so sampling errors result in gene frequency changes from one generation to another for reasons analogous as to why one may get more or fewer than 50 heads in 100 throws of a coin.

That the morphological, behavioral, and physiological adaptations of organisms are by and large the result of natural selection is not a question of debate among evolutionists. But what about small differences in DNA sequence or in protein structure, such as those mentioned in the previous section? About a decade and a half ago Motoo Kimura (1968, 1983) and others proposed the hypothesis that most of the protein and DNA variants found in natural populations are functionally equivalent. If so, protein polymorphisms are evolutionary noise; genetic variants encoding protein variation would change in frequency not by the adaptive process of natural selection but rather as a consequence of random sampling through the generations. This hypothesis has come to be known as the neutrality theory of protein evolution.

The neutrality theory recognizes that the morphological, physiological, and behavioral features of organisms evolve by natural selection. Neutralists argue, nevertheless, that evolution at the molecular level (i.e., in DNA and proteins) largely occurs through stochastic events in the form of genetic drift. The neutrality theory acknowledges that a large fraction of all newly arising mutations are unconditionally deleterious. These harmful variants are eliminated or kept at very low frequencies by natural selection. But the neutrality theory proposes that for most genes there are a number of mutants (variants) that are effectively equivalent with respect to adaptation. These are functional variants, any one of which is favorably selected relative to the deleterious ones. However, carriers of alternative genotypes for the adaptively equivalent variants do not differ in their adaptedness to the environment. The frequencies in populations of adaptively equivalent, or "neutral", variants are, therefore, not affected by natural selection. Because natural populations consist of finite numbers of individuals, the frequencies of neutral mutants would change from generation to generation due to the accidents of sampling. Differences between species in proteins and DNA sequences are consequently mostly due to random processes of chance, not to natural selection.

The epistemological characteristics of the neutralist theory are quite interesting. According to the theory, protein variants and the genic variants coding for them evolve for the most part by genetic drift. Since natural selection is not involved, environmental variations as well as other parameters that might affect selective values can be ignored. It is therefore possible to advance evolutionary models that include very few parameters, notably mutation frequencies (which determine the rates at which allelic variants arise in a population), population size (which determines the magnitude of the sampling errors from generation to generation), and time (for situations not in equilibrium). The presence of very few parameters makes it possible to derive precise predictions about evolutionary patterns. The neutrality theory can thus be readily subject to empirical tests by ascertaining whether its empirical predictions agree with the states of affairs observed by experiment. In epistemological terms the neutralist hypothesis is a theory with large empirical (informative) content. This is a most welcome situation in the field of evolution, where theories and models are notoriously difficult to test in their general form. The neutralist hypothesis is a most valuable evolutionary theory precisely because it is readily amenable to empirical testing.

Numerous tests of the neutrality theory have been carried out. Many genetic discoveries have provided additional relevant evidence. But the question is yet far from fully resolved. It now appears that most changes in protein structure, even those not obviously related to function, are adaptively significant and thus largely determined by natural selection. So are, therefore, the changes in DNA sequence that yield protein variations. Many DNA sequence changes that do not translate into protein variations are also known to be subject to the constraints of natural selection. But it remains unresolved whether many other variations within a species and differences between species in the sequence of the DNA have adaptive significance or are the result of random fluctuations. The role of chance in the evolutionary process, particularly at the level of the DNA sequences that encode the hereditary information, remains to be delimited.

9. Gradual and Sudden Evolution

A challenge to evolutionary theory that was flickering for over a decade but has recently flared comes from some paleontologists. The proposition is that morphological evolution as it is recorded in fossils is "punctuated" rather than gradual, this being known as the model of "punctuated equilibrium". This model proposes that morphological evolution happens in bursts, with most phenotypic change occurring during speciation events, so that new species are morphologically quite distant from their ancestors but do not thereafter change substantially in phenotype over a lifetime that may encompass many millions of years. The punctuational model is contrasted with the gradualistic model, according to which morphological change is a more or less gradual process, largely occurs during the lifetime of a species, and is not strongly associated with specification events (Figure 11).

The issues raised deal, in good part, with the history of evolution and might have been discussed earlier when such matters were tackled. But the model of punctual equilibrium, or punctualism for short, includes specific claims about the processes involved: to wit, that morphological change occurs pre-

cisely concomitantly with speciation, the origin of new species, and that it
largely happens by chance as a consequence of the reduction of a population
to very few individuals, which is alleged to be a normal event in the origin
of a new species. In the words of S. M. Stanley (1979, p. 87), "rapidly divergent
speciation interposes discontinuities between rather stable entities (lineages),
and . . . there is a strong random element in the origin of these discontinuities". S. J. Gould, most conspicuous among the punctualists, writes (1982,
p. 85): "Punctuated equilibrium holds that accumulated speciation is the root
of most major evolutionary change, and that what we have called anagenesis
is usually no more than repeated cladogenesis (branching) filtered through
the net of differential success at the species level".

This claimed association of morphological change with speciation I want
to take up first, because it involves, I believe, a blatant fallacy. Species are
groups of interbreeding natural populations that are reproductively isolated

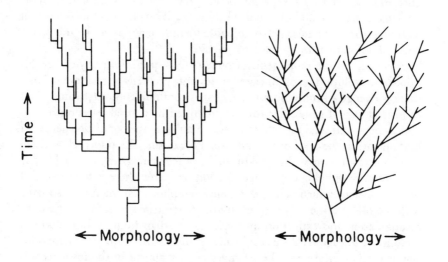

←— Morphology —→   ←— Morphology —→

Figure 11. Simplified representation of two models of phenotypic evolution: punctuated equilibrium (left) and phyletic gradualism (right). According to the punctuated model most morphological evolution in the history of life is associated with speciation events, which are geologically
instantaneous. After their origin, established species generally do not change substantially in
phenotype over a lifetime that may encompass many million years. According to the gradualist
model morphological evolution occurs during the lifetime of a species, with rapidly divergent
speciation playing a lesser role. The figures are extreme versions of the models. Punctualism
does not imply that phenotypic change never occurs between speciation events. Gradualism does
not imply that phenotypic change is occurring continuously at a more or less constant rate
throughout the life of a lineage, or that some acceleration does not take place during speciation,
but rather that phenotypic change may occur at any time throughout the lifetime of a species.

from any other such groups (Dobzhansky et al., 1977). Speciation involves, by definition, the development of reproductive isolation between populations previously able to interbreed. But it is in no way apparent how the fossil record could provide evidence of the development of reproductive isolation. Paleontologists recognize species by their different morphologies as preserved in the fossil record. New species that are morphologically indistinguishable from their ancestors (or from contemporary species) go totally unrecognized. Sibling species (i.e., morphologically indistinguishable from each other) are common in many groups of insects, in rodents, and in other well-studied organisms. Moreover, morphological discontinuities in a time series of fossils are usually interpreted by paleontologists as speciation events, even though they may represent phyletic evolution in an established lineage, without the splitting of lineages.

Thus, when paleontologists use evidence of rapid phenotypic change in favor of the punctuational model, they are guilty of definitional circularity. Speciation as seen by the paleontologist always involves substantial morphological change — and morphological change always happens in association with speciation — because paleontologists identify new species by the occurrence of substantial morphological change.

According to the proponents of punctuated equilibrium phyletic evolution (i.e., evolution along lineages of descent) proceeds at two levels. First, there is change within a population that is continuous through time. This consists largely of gene substitutions prompted by natural selection, mutation, genetic drift, and the other processes familiar to the population geneticist that operate at the level of the individual organism. The punctualists claim that most evolution within established lineages rarely, if ever, yields any substantial morphological change. Second, they say, there is the process of origination and extinction of species. Most morphological change is associated with the origin of new species. Evolutionary trends result from the patterns of origination and extinction of species rather than from evolution within established lineages. Hence, the relevant unit in the study of macroevolution (morphological and other changes as they appear in the fossil record) is the species rather than the individual organism. It follows from this argument that the study of microevolutionary processes provides little, if any, information about macroevolutionary patterns, the tempo and mode of large-scale evolution. Thus, macroevolution is autonomous relative to microevolution, much in the same way as biology is autonomous relative to physics.

Whether phenotypic change in macroevolution occurs in bursts or is more or less gradual is a question to be decided empirically. Examples of rapid phenotypic evolution followed by long periods of morphological stasis are known in the fossil record. But there are instances as well in which phenotypic evolution appears to occur gradually within a lineage. The question is the relative frequency of one or the other mode, and paleontologists disagree in their interpretation of the fossil record.

Be that as it may, punctualists are far from clear or consistent as to what they mean when they allege that the study of macroevolution is autonomous or deny that "the mechanisms underlying microevolution can be extrapolated" to macroevolution. These claims may apply to either one, or both, of the following two issues: (1) whether the microevolutionary processes identified by population geneticists (mutation, random drift, natural selection) are sufficient to *account for* the morphological changes and other macroevolutionary phenomena, or whether additional microevolutionary processes need to be postulated; (2) whether theories concerning evolutionary trends and other macroevolutionary patterns can be *derived* from knowledge of microevolutionary processes. The first is a substantive scientific question; the second is epistemological.

Goldschmidt (1940, p. 183) argued long ago that the incompatibility between micro- and macroevolution is real: "The decisive step in evolution, the first step towards macroevolution, the step from one species to another, requires another evolutionary method than that of sheer accumulation of micromutations." Goldschmidt's solution was to postulate "systemic mutation", yielding "hopeful monsters" that, on occasion, would find a new niche or way of life for which they would be eminently preadapted. The progressive understanding of the nature and organization of the genetic material acquired during the last forty years excludes the "systematic mutations" postulated by Goldschmidt, which would involve transformations of the genome as a whole.

The punctualists' claim that mutations with large phenotypic effects must have been largely responsible for macroevolutionary change is based on the rapidity with which morphological discontinuities appear in the fossil record (Stanley, 1979; Gould, 1980). But the alleged evidence does not necessarily support the claim. Microevolutionists and macroevolutionists use different time scales. Events that appear instantaneous in the geological time scale may involve thousands, even millions, of generations. Gould (1982a, p. 84), for example, has made operational the fuzzy expression "geologically instantaneous" by suggesting that "it be defined as 1 percent or less of later existence in stasis. This permits up to 100,000 years for the origin of a species with a subsequent life span of 10 million years". But 100,000 years encompasses one million generations of an insect such as *Drosophila*, and tens or hundreds of thousands of fish, birds, or mammals. There is little doubt that the gradual accumulation of small mutations may yield sizeable morphological changes during periods of that length.

Anderson's (1973) study of body size in *Drosophila pseudoobscura* provides an estimate of the rates of gradual morphological change produced by natural selection. Large populations, derived from a single set of parents, were set up at different temperatures and allowed to evolve on their own. A gradual, genetically determined, change in body size ensued, with flies kept at lower temperature becoming, as expected, larger than those kept at higher temperatures. After twelve years, the mean size of the flies from the population kept at 16°C had become, when tested under standard conditions, approximately 10 percent greater than the size of the flies kept at 27°C. Assuming ten generations per year, the populations diverged at a rate of 8×10^{-4} of the mean value per generation.

Paleontologists have emphasized the "extraordinarily high *net* rate of evolution that is the hallmark of phylogeny" (Stanley, 1979). Interpreted in terms of the punctualist hypothesis, human phylogeny would have occurred as a succession of jumps, or geologically instantaneous saltations, interspersed by long periods without morphological change. Could these bursts of phenotypic evolution be due to the gradual accumulation of small changes? Consider cranial capacity, the character undergoing the greatest relative amount of change. The fastest rate of net change occurred between 500,000 years ago, when our ancestors were represented by *Homo erectus*, and 75,000 years ago, when Neanderthal man had acquired a cranial capacity similar to that of modern humans. In the intervening 425,000 years cranial capacity evolved from about 900 cc in Peking man to about 1,400 cc in Neanderthal people. Let us assume that the increase in brain size occurred in a single burst at the rate observed in *D. pseudoobscura* of 8×10^{-4} of the mean value per generation. The change from 900 cc to 1,400 cc could have taken place in 540 generations, or, assuming generously 25 years per generation, in 13,500 years. Thirteen thousand years are, of course, a geological instant. Yet, this evolutionary "burst" could have taken place by gradual accumulation of mutations with small effects at rates compatible with those observed in microevolutionary studies.

The known processes of microevolution can, then, account for macroevolutionary change, even when this occurs according to the punctualist model — that is, at fast rates concentrated in geologically brief time intervals. But what about the problem of stasis? The theory of punctuated equilibrium argues that after the initial burst of morphological change associated with their origin, species generally do not change substantially in phenotype over a lifetime that may encompass many million years. Is it necessary to postulate new processes, yet unknown to population genetics, in order to account for the long persistence of lineages without apparent phenotypic change? The answer is No.

The geological persistence of lineages without morphological change was already known to Darwin, who wrote in the last edition of *The Origin of Species* (1872, p. 375), "Many species once formed never undergo any further change . . . ; and the periods, during which species have undergone modification, though long as measured by years, have probably been short in comparison with the periods during which they retain the same form". A successful morphology may remain unchanged for extremely long periods of time, even through successive speciation events—as manifested, for example, by the existence of sibling species, which in many known instances have persisted for millions of years (Stebbins and Ayala, 1981).

Evolutionists have long been aware of the problem of paleontological stasis and have explored a number of alternative hypotheses consistent with microevolutionary principles and sufficient to account for the phenomenon. Although the issue is far from definitely settled, the weight of the evidence favors stabilizing selection as the primary process responsible for morphological stasis of lineages through geological time (Stebbins and Ayala, 1981; Charlesworth et al., 1982).

Now I pose the second question raised earlier: Can macroevolutionary theory be derived from microevolutionary knowledge? The answer can only be No. If macroevolutionary theory were deducible from microevolutionary principles, it would be possible to decide between competing macroevolutionary models simply by examining the logical implications of microevolutionary theory. But the theory of population genetics is compatible with both punctualism and gradualism, and, hence, logically it entails neither. Whether the tempo and mode of evolution occur predominantly according to the model of punctuated equilibria or according to the model of phyletic gradualism is an issue to be decided by studying macroevolutionary patterns, not by inference from microevolutionary processes. In other words, macroevolutionary theories are not reducible (at least at the present state of knowledge) to microevolution. Hence, macroevolution and microevolution are decoupled in the sense (which is epistemologically most important) that macroevolution is an autonomous field of study that must develop and test its own theories. (For further discussion of this matter see Ayala, 1983.)

REFERENCES

Anderson, W. 1973. "Genetic divergence in body size in experimental populations of *Drosophila pseudoobscura* kept at different temperatures." *Evolution*, 27:278–284.
Ayala, F. J. 1983. "Beyond Darwinism? The Challenge of Macroevolution to the Synthetic Theory of Evolution". *PSA 1982* (Philosophy of Science Association) 2: 275-291.
Ayala, F. J., and J. A. Kiger. 1984. *Modern Genetics*. Menlo Park, CA: Benjamin/Cummings.
Charlesworth, B., R. Lande, and M. Slatkin. 1982. "A Neo-Darwinism Commentary on Macroevolution". *Evolution* 36:474-498
Dickerson, R. E. 1971. "The Structure of Cytochrome *c* and the Rates of Molecular Evolution". *J. Molec. Evol.* 1:26-45.

90   Francisco J. Ayala

Dobzhansky, Th. F. J. Ayala, G. L. Stebbins, and J. W. Valentine. 1977. *Evolution*. San Francisco: W. H. Freeman & Co.

Fitch, W. M. 1976. "Molecular Evolutionary Clocks". In *Molecular Evolution*, edited by F. J. Ayala. Sunderland, MA: Sinauer Assoc., pp. 160-178.

Fitch, W. M., and E. Margoliash. 1967. "Construction of Phylogenetic Trees". *Science* 155:279-284.

Fitch, W. M., and E. Margoliash. 1970. "The Usefulness of Amino Acid and Nucleotide Sequence in Evolutionary Studies". *Evol. Biol.* 4:67-109.

Goldschmidt, R. B. 1940. *The Material Basis of Evolution*. New Haven: Yale University Press.

Gould, S. J. 1980. "Is a New and General Theory of Evolution Emerging?" *Paleobiology* 6:119-130.

Gould, S. J. 1982. "The Meaning of Punctuated Equilibrium and Its Role in Validating a Hierarchical Approach to Macroevolution". In *Perspectives in Evolution*, edited by R. Milkman. Sunderland, Mass: Sinauer.

Hinegardner, R. 1976. "Evolution of Genome Size." In *Molecular Evolution*, edited by F. J. Ayala. Sunderland, MA: Sinauer, pp. 179-199.

John Paul II. 1981. "Science and Scripture: The Path of Scientific Discovery." *Origins* 11:277-280.

Kimura, M. 1968. "Evolutionary Rate at the Molecular Level". *Nature* 217:624-626.

Kimura, M. 1983. *The Neutrality Theory of Molecular Evolution*. New York: Oxford University Press.

Simpson, G. G. 1953. *The Major Features of Evolution*. New York: Columbia University Press.

Stanley, S. M. 1979. *Macroevolution: Pattern and Process*. San Francisco: W. H. Freeman.

Stebbins, G. L. and F. J. Ayala. 1981. "Is a New Evolutionary Synthesis Necessary?" *Science* 213:967-971.

MODERN COSMOLOGY AND THE CREATION OF LIFE

John Leslie

1. Some Alleged Weaknesses of Design Arguments

The argument from design tries to prove God's reality by examining the universe. In the form given to it today by those naming themselves "creation scientists" it earns the fury of genuine scientists. I shall show why most reputable thinkers consider it long dead and buried. But afterward I plan to demonstrate that recent developments make it very much alive, though not in any shape which creation science would welcome. (This paper continues a line of reasoning which has led to four others.[1])

Creation scientists try to keep the argument from design alive by giving it a second childhood. The earth, they say, was created only a few millennia ago. God's hand formed all living things, as we can see just by looking at them; we do not need the Bible to tell us of it. The eye, for instance, must be a product of divine workmanship rather than of Darwinian natural selection because the latter, an affair of blind chance, could not possibly create anything intricate and useful. I call all this a second childhood because it reverts to many detailed beliefs about God's activities which every rational, educated adult knows to be wrong. In its first childhood, in contrast, the argument was wondrously vague. Plato thanks Anaxagoras for suggesting that mind directs all things but chides him for not going on to argue that it directs them in good ways—so perhaps even the notion that design *was beneficent* was absent during the argument's early infancy. Later we find Aquinas torn between the view that God directs the world's activities and the Aristotelian picture of things as all directing themselves toward the divine, like bees struggling to reach honey. It is only in the seventeenth and eighteenth centuries that we repeatedly meet with claims that living organisms have a complexity which proves God to have designed each individually. Now such claims were all very well for the rational and educated of those days, but their plausibility has since suffered drastically at the hands of Darwin. Darwin's theory, of course, does not rely on the workings of blind chance because natural selection is conceived as a wind separating the wheat from the vast quantities of chaff to which chance gives birth. Life's evolutionary rise from simple begin-

91

nings is today an established fact, and the ability of natural selection to explain it, even suggesting how the business could have started at a prebiological, chemical level, is almost equally well proven. And though the hypothesis that God occasionally intervenes with a helpful shove would be immensely difficult to disprove, it lacks the charms of simplicity.

The upshot is that many of the ablest modern defenders of design limit themselves to suggesting, first, that it should be understood to mean simply the Creator's choice of a world such that complex life would arise in it naturally, through Darwinian selection, and, second, that *looking on* nature *as* an expression of the divine should come easily to the believer, somewhat as looking on a squiggle as a drawing of a duck rather than of a rabbit comes easily to the duck-loving rabbit-hater. Sometimes, under pressure from a supposed need to "demythologize" religion, they slide toward using such terms as 'God' and 'teleology' to mean nothing more than that nature is indeed able to generate life by its unaided operations. But this amounts to conceding defeat while continuing to make warlike noises.

What reduced them to such a state? A tale now fairly standard among empiricist philosophers runs as follows. With Darwin to open people's eyes it became generally appreciated that the design argument was full of faults, many of them ones which Hume and Kant had noted. Essentially we have here *an argument from analogy*, and all such arguments are insecure. This particular one, though, is far worse than most because its analogy is ludicrously weak. God is conceived on the model of a watch designer. Yet the realm of stars and planets is not much like a watch, neither is the realm of living organisms or the individual organism. Put watches, pumps, and windmills in among earthworms, elephants, and cabbages, and any child can tell the difference. At the opening of the nineteenth century a clever man like William Paley could comment[2] that this only went to show the skill of a designer who could, so to speak, make watches of a sort which moved around, grew larger, and even manufactured more watches like themselves. But the trouble with such a comment is that watchlike things able to manufacture others of their own kind might have started off as comparatively simple affairs, growing to be vastly complex only after billions of years of reproductive trial and error such as Darwin envisaged. (When Paley considers the trial and error theory, it is only in a silly form in which entire plants and animals are imagined as springing into being by chance.) Besides, the rules of analogy tell us *not to jump from the finite to the infinite.* Hence, instead of introducing an omniscient, omnipotent designer, one would better limit oneself to believing in a bungling committee of demigods laboriously developing evermore sophisticated plans.

Faced with such problems (the standard tale continues), defenders of design often retreat to the claim that God designed not the whole organisms but only the natural laws and materials which allow evolution by natural selection to begin and to proceed smoothly. How immense, they exclaim, was the skill that this demanded! Just imagine it, being able to make matter such that life would arise from it automatically! But what facts could there be to support their way of viewing things? Is it not every bit as arbitrary as seeing a duck where others see a rabbit? There is no doubt an excellent fit between *life as we know it* and nature's actual laws and materials, but to praise God for this could be much like praising him for causing large rivers to flow through the world's principal cities. Might it not be that just as more or less any sizable river attracts a largish town, so more or less any world would have given birth to life of some sort or to something else equally interesting? It can often seem that design's supporters are trying to have things both ways. When they see obstacles which life only barely succeeds in overcoming, they applaud the divine intelligence which supplies just the means needed to overcome them; when on the other hand everything runs easily, they again glorify that same intelligence for making easy running possible. Moreover they pick and choose their evidence shamelessly. The frozen desert of the Antarctic is forgotten in favour of a few ponds whose depths are protected by the ice above, ice described as having very providentially expanded as it formed, so as to float. (The marvellous result is that plant and animal cells down below are protected from the damage which results when water expands into ice inside plant and animal cells!) The sun's controlled nuclear fusion is admired; the fact that the principles behind it can lead to fusion of the uncontrolled, hydrogen-bomb kind, is conveniently ignored. The billions of wasted years before complex life evolved are treated as if of no account instead of as aeons of evidence *against* design. The creation of a few men is seized upon, no attention being paid to the Creator's apparent preference for beetles or for life-threatening germs. The huge emptiness of interstellar space, the inferno inside the stars, the uninhabited planets, are dismissed so that our minds may concentrate upon the single tiny habitat that we know — a habitat likely to be the only one in our galaxy if we accept Frank Tipler's recent argument[3] that in a galaxy well supplied with intelligent life earth would long ago have been colonized by aliens or by their self-reproducing von Neumann machines, of which a single one could spread its offspring throughout the galaxy within a mere hundred million years or so.

Underlying all the design argument's idiocies (so the standard story runs) are two horrendous blunders. (1) The first is this. Patterns of evidence collected somewhere in nature are treated as indicating the presence, *not* of other patterns elsewhere in nature, but rather of something supernatural. Yet nature as a whole cannot possibly give evidence of anything beyond it! One reason for this is that the natural world, the universe, is (by definition) a one and only affair; *there cannot be two universes. But a central principle of probability theory is that single cases cannot be made the foundations of probability statements.* To judge that the natural world would be hopelessly "improbable" unless God has chosen it in preference to other, "more probable", worlds is therefore mathematical lunacy. It treats the necessarily unique universe as if it were just one universe among many.[4] (2) Second, the supporter of design overlooks the fact that if the world had been one in which intelligent life could not evolve, then *we should not be here to discuss the matter.* He invites us to feel surprise and awe at how natural laws and materials gave rise to complex organisms over billions of years. But how could we even wonder whether to be surprised if complex organisms such as ourselves had not arisen? This simple logical consideration[5] is decisive. There is no need to probe all the other holes with which his argument is riddled: for instance, his failure to explain anything when he points to God the Reasonlessly Existing Magician.

2. Why Many of the So-Called "Weaknesses" Could Fail to Impress Cosmologists

What I shall now show is that these standard objections against design arguments threaten to delay the development of science. Oddly enough, the threat is greatest if the design hypothesis *is wrong.* For let us take it for granted that reasonable modern defenders of design are not creation scientists and do not even wish to get much mileage out of how ice protects the depths of ponds. What they can instead argue, however, is that there is something crying out for explanation in the sheer fact that our cosmos obeys laws which make Darwinian evolution at all possible. Now, efforts to prove that there could be nothing remarkable in such a fact—that its unremarkableness is guaranteed by probability theory or by the simplest of logic—*would, if successful, do more than just destroy all alleged evidence of design. They would destroy as well the main excuse for developing many-universe cosmologies.* And these cosmologies have very important implications for science and especially for physics.

To illustrate this, let us go back to the earliest instants of the big bang. Everything is unimaginably highly compressed and expanding at tremendous speed. But just what are the properties of this everything? How strong are the forces which govern it? How rapidly does it expand? A possible reply is that the compression is so great that such questions have no definite answers. Quantum theory strikes many physicists as suggesting that at very tiny dimensions space loses its structure: the idea that events have firm positions must be abandoned. Now, the totality undergoing the big bang may have been a totality infinitely large from its earliest instants, but at least everything *in the known universe* — everything inside the horizon which light's speed sets to possible interactions between our bodies and other things—was compressed into a volume so tiny that its spatial structure could well have been blurred, foamy, confused. Hence, to talk of it as expanding at a definite speed is quite possibly nonsense. A definite speed could perhaps be had only later, when individual particles became respectably separated.[6] *It seems plausible that the speed then became decided in the fundamentally probabilistic way which is characteristic of quantum theory. And it is again plausible that the quantity of the material which we now see inside our horizon, and the details of the forces governing it, became decided in similarly probabilistic fashion.* It is thought that the four main physical forces—gravitation, electromagnetism, and the weak and strong nuclear forces—were indistinguishable at early instants, only later taking on the strength differences they have at present. I. L. Rozental has argued in a recent series of papers[7] that the very immensity of these strength differences (they range over forty orders of magnitude) indicates that an intense, exceedingly improbable fluctuation was involved here.

Notice the words "exceedingly improbable fluctuation". (In the simpler case of coin tossing, an exceedingly improbable fluctuation might be that of getting twelve heads in a row. It is of course *probable* that you would get such a fluctuation if the experiment of tossing the coin twelve times *were repeated sufficiently many times.*)

Notice too the implications of *the horizon set by the speed of light.* Philosophers typically define *our universe* as *the sum of everything*, assuming both that there could be no other reasonable definition and that the everything must form a single causal system, its parts all in theory knowable by us and obeying everywhere exactly the same laws. Modern cosmologists often think otherwise. All things visible to us may form only a bubble in a vastly greater whole. The bubble could be isolated from other bubbles by the hugeness of space—isolated maybe only temporarily, with new things constantly appearing on our ever-expanding horizon; but maybe permanently, perhaps because many things were rushing away from us faster than the bubble was expanding. (The general expansion of space would be what carried them away from us, and light's speed cannot limit this according to many theorists.) *The bubble's temporary or permanent isolation, and its tremendous size, would give an excuse for calling it "a separate universe." It might be only one among vastly many universes, extremely varied in their characters, and most of them ones in which life could never evolve.*

Another possibility is that individual universes are born as quantum vacuum fluctuations in a superspace. Heisenberg's uncertainty relation between energy and time allows a thing (e.g., an electron) to pop into existence for a period limited by the amount of energy "borrowed" from the vacuum in order to form it. Now, the total energy of our universe may be zero or very near zero because its gravitational binding energy enters into the total *as a negative quantity*. So the vacuum of a superspace could be peppered with big bangs, each of which "costs nothing in energy or very near to nothing" and gives rise to a universe which may last for billions of years—though it might instead last for only a century, or even only a second, if such characteristics as its speed of expansion were settled probabilistically. A universe which expanded too slowly could well collapse back into self-annihilation far too quickly for life to evolve in it.

Alternatively, systems of events worth calling "separate universes"—systems very largely or entirely isolated from one another and perhaps with very different amounts of matter, very different degrees of cosmic order or disorder, very different ratios between the strengths of their main forces, and so on— could succeed one another in time. In an admittedly highly speculative but still very interesting picture developed by John Wheeler, big bangs give birth to universes whose expansions are slowed by gravity until at last everything collapses together in big squeezes; the collapsing material of a universe escapes self-annihilation, though, by bouncing back in a further big bang, which later gives way to another big squeeze, and so on. At the "knothole" between successive oscillations all structure is lost, and laws and constants and conditions become "reprocessed" so that the next bang is likely to result in a completely new situation, "a new universe". However, the fact that time itself loses its structure at the knothole makes for some difficulty in saying which of two bangs come first, or even whether they are two and not only a single one in which the expanding stuff streams into two separate branches. The resulting picture is thus remarkably similar to another with which Wheeler has also worked, the one presented by many-worlds quantum theory. Here a single bang is visualized as giving birth to a universe that constantly splits into more and more branches. Each branch interacts only slightly with the others, this providing grounds for calling it a separate world or universe. In the case of early splits—those occurring when the structure of space was first becoming firm, or slightly later when perhaps largely indeterministic phase transitions decided the relative strengths of physical forces and the masses of various particles—the universes branching away from one another could differ greatly.

There is a large and ever-growing scientific literature in this area.[8] Its relevance to the argument from design is as follows. Physics as such and cosmology as such may suggest how a large and very varied collection of universes might perhaps have come into being, but they supply us with nothing like strong grounds for a belief in any such collection. And yet we do have our strong grounds. They are these. It is not at all clear that you could alter the details of a universe much and still leave it as a place in which life could evolve. *An impressive sign that ours was only one universe among many could be this: that actual investigations suggested that very tiny altera-*

tions in it would have made it uninhabitable and hence unobservable. For in that case we could reasonably ask how the universe observed by us managed to balance on such a razor edge of observability. A natural answer would be that *if there existed very many universes and if they differed in their details, then it would not be surprising that at least one of them should be observable*, even if observability involved so delicate a balance. And obviously it would be in a universe like that, an inhabitable universe, that people would be asking, "How came we to be so fortunate? Why are our universe's details of the very special sorts which seem required if there is to be anyone to observe it?" Now, many scientists do indeed think that we are observing a universe such that extremely marginal alterations in its details—for instance, a tiny change in its expansion rate at very early times, perhaps by less than one part in a million million—would have made it uninhabitable (in the case of the expansion rate, by making it impossible for the gases of the big bang to form themselves into galaxies of stars and planets). So to these scientists it seems altogether natural to believe in, say, a billion billion universes with different expansion rates. But of course it is natural to believe this only if you are willing to see some sort of problem in the fact that our universe was "just right for life", and *seeing a problem here is something which is central to the argument from design.*

To put this in another way: A cosmologist who says there is "no problem" in how the expansion rate and everything else was "just right", because if there are billions upon billions of universes, "then one or two of them are practically certain to be lucky, life-containing ones, and only those could be observed", is in effect saying that there *is* a problem here, but that it would be very neatly solved by postulating billions upon billions of universes. The neatness of the solution—the way in which it could make it so much to be expected that there should exist somewhere a universe in which living beings could marvel at how the expansion rate and everything else was right—is as fine an indication as you could wish that there really is something here which needs to be explained. For we are not born into the world with very much idea of what needs explanation. Seeing the milk bottles falling off the wall, the philosophical baby might well treat it as an ultimate, inexplicable law that milk bottles do fall at intervals. It is the sight of a stick approaching each bottle in turn, just before it falls, which simultaneously suggests both *an explanation* and *something in need of an explanation.* But recall now that our cosmologist's explanation gets little direct support from physics as such or from cosmology as such. It does not have the backing of any well-established scientific account of how universes come into being. And the man who favors the argument from design has a competing explanation. He too can point to a hypothesis which could make it to be expected that the universe should be right for life. He believes in God.

If the explanation which brings in God is somewhat obscure or for other reasons unsatisfying, then this is not very different from what we find in the case of our cosmologist's explanation. Ockham's razor, for example, could give grounds for not believing in vastly many universes. It might all the same seem plain that one of the two explanations (for it is hard to see how there could be any others) would have to be correct. Saying that no explanation was needed could seem as preposterous as believing that the milk bottles each just happened to fall precisely when the stick approached. It would be saying such things as that a one and only universe had, without any explanation whatever, an expansion rate that was, to within one part in a million million, precisely the rate which allows our two competing explanations to come into play.

Though physics and cosmology may give little direct support to the idea of multiple universes with very varied characteristics, physicists and cosmologists have cause to be interested in this idea. For great variations among universes could occur only if the natures of universes were not settled in any detailed way by some basic set of physical laws, for instance, those of some nonprobabilistic variety of unified field theory. Great variations could occur only if such basic laws either (a) fixed the natures of universes merely in a probabilistic way or (b) specified that there should exist universes having every single one of an entire continuum of possible natures, as is suggested by many-worlds quantum theory. In either of these two cases basic physical theory would be no guide to how large our universe is, how fast its expansion was at very early times, what the strength ratios are of its main forces, what the relative masses are of its elementary particles, and so on. These affairs would have to be discovered by experiments instead of being predictable from basic principles. Conversely, the results of the experiments would shed no light on the basic principles. Obviously all this could be of immense significance to cosmology and to physics. So it is surprising to find so many philosophers so very satisfied with their proofs that the argument from design has no force and that life's existence presents no problem.

Let us see how these proofs of theirs fare against the new background.

(1) Are they right in claiming that any supposed *special need to explain* our universe's life-generating nature *must be derived from a weak argument from analogy*? Agreed, those who argue for such a special need do draw upon scientific findings, and induction, central to science, does depend on viewing various situations as all interestingly analogous; but must it therefore be especially helpful to describe the argument for multiple universes (to take one instance of an argument based on such a supposed special need) as "an argument from analogy"? Surely not. Surely it is better called an argument from probabilities. If there were vastly many universes and if they varied greatly, then it could seem altogether probable that the details of a few of

them should be just right for producing life, and it would be unsurprising that we living beings should find ourselves in a universe from among those few; the fact that very tiny changes in its expansion rate (or in any of a host of other features) would have been disastrous to life's prospects *ought not to startle us; we should have an explanation for it*. But if on the other hand ours is a one and only universe, then such a fact could be very startling indeed: it could seem highly improbable that a one and only universe *should just chance to have features of precisely the kind needed for such an explanation*! Hence it can seem altogether likely that there exist many universes — unless, that is to say, God is a reality, so that it could be expected that even a one and only universe would be exactly right for life. (Probabilistic arguments often do a better job of showing that some explanation is very probably needed than of actually picking out the right explanation. Scientists whose theories make seemingly improbable effects very probable and who then, when these effects are observed, congratulate themselves on being very probably right, are often dismayed to find that other theories predict the same effects equally firmly and have the advantage of actually being right. Nonetheless, arguments of this general type — arguments following the principle that you should favor theories which make seemingly improbable things look more probable — often do manage to add force to hypotheses even when they also add force to competing hypotheses; thus *both* the believer in God *and* the supporter of multiple universes could draw strength from the need to make life's existence look less improbable. Again, such arguments could add force to the God hypothesis even if it somehow managed to be somewhat uncertain that God would prefer a life-containing to a non-life-containing universe, for they require only that a universe should be more likely to be life-containing if God-created than if non-God-created.)

If, however, you do happen to want an argument from analogy here, then one can readily be supplied. Suppose you see light coming through a pinhole in a screen. The rest of the screen is dark. What is it natural to think? Well, either (a) there is just the one pinhole and just one light ray directed at the screen, but (you can see how all this corresponds to the God hypothesis) all is so cleverly designed that the light ray hits that one and only pinhole, or else (b) we have plenty of pinholes but only one light ray (which corresponds to the hypothesis that there are plenty of universes, almost all of them not giving rise to observations), or finally (c) we have just one pinhole but great numbers of light rays striking all around it (which corresponds to the seemingly false hypothesis that observations would be occurring even if our universe were slightly differently placed in the "space" of possible universes with respect to its basic characteristics — its expansion rate at very early instants, its particle masses, the relative strengths of its forces, its degree of turbulence, and so forth). Now, it seems to me that our being able to observe a universe *is* interestingly analogous to the case of seeing the point of light or, again, to the catching of a fish with an apparatus which could not catch fish which were by one million millionth part longer or shorter. We could tidy up the above talk of "correspondences" into a full argument from analogy; the branch of the argument which points toward God would then no doubt have some slight similarity to the argument from analogy which Hume sees when he looks at the argument from design. But little depends on the precise degree of tidiness with which all this could be accomplished, for here is not an area where arguments from analogy *must* be used.

Take an extreme example. Suppose it could be very firmly established that because very small speed differences at early instants produce enormous differences later, our universe's expansion speed at some very early time had to be right to one part in a trillion trillion trillion trillion for life and observership to be possible. It would now seem to me just common sense to suppose that something dramatic such as God or multiple universes would be needed to explain life's existence. "But where is the analogy?" you protest. "How dissimilar it all is from catching a fish with an apparatus which could not catch fish the tiniest bit longer or shorter! *There*, no doubt, we should assume that there were fish of all lengths in the sea or else that divine intervention had created a fish of exactly the right length; but is not the case of finding oneself in an observable universe very different?" I answer that it is indeed very different, but not in any obviously relevant way. For in each case we ought to be guided by the principle that the neatness of an explanation can help show that an explanation is needed. There is no need for us actually to go fishing with an apparatus of the kind described, then learning by experience what ways of reasoning work well in such a situation, so as to be able at last to make a desperate leap to the in many ways *disanalogous* situation of observing a universe!

(2) But now, what about a second standard objection against design arguments? Should not we at least be very bothered by any *leap from a finite world to an infinite God*? My reply is that our explanations should preferably be simple ones, and introducing an infinity often increases simplicity. It is, for instance, very much simpler and more plausible to suppose that there exists a superspace in which infinitely many universes appear as quantum vacuum fluctuations rather than that there exists a superspace in which only 529 universes will ever appear. And whatever the difficulties of the idea that God is an infinite, omnipotent person, it is at least simpler than supposing the universe to have been designed by a committee of five hundred and twenty-nine demigods. (It may well be, though, that great or infinite divine power is best understood if God is not seen as any kind of person. More on this subject later.)

(3) How about another of the standard objections we met with earlier, *that arguments from design wrongly concentrate on life as we know it*? Might

not more or less any universe generate life of some sort or, failing that, then at least something else equally interesting? My first reaction is that I cannot imagine anything which could begin to compete in its intricacy with the products of Darwinian evolution. And an excellent principle, enunciated by Robert Boyle in his *Disquisition about the Final Causes of Natural Things*, 1688, and put to good use by Darwin, is that such intricacy ought to be found specially interesting and in need of explanation. (We ought not to be happy with the idea, say, that the universe has always just happened to contain lions giving birth to other lions, much as it might always just have happened to contain quarks or electrons. Compare how if lacking actual experience of watch factories, we should still be extravagant in thinking that the universe had always just happened to contain watches. Yet living things far excel these in their intricacy.) However, even if something other than life could be in some way equally interesting, it is hard to see how this could harm the design hypothesis. For like its competitor, the many-universes hypothesis, this does not merely offer to explain how there comes to be a world in which very interesting patterns develop; it offers also a reason why there ever exists anyone to observe any patterns. For our purposes the most striking thing about life is that it is a prerequisite of observations. It would be extremely odd if a one and only actual universe simply chanced to have such features as an early expansion rate which was to one part in a million million precisely right for giving birth to observers. This would be equally odd whether or not lifeless universes could be expected to contain other things as fascinating as living beings are.

But might not life and observership of kinds unfamiliar to us be found *in universes very unlike our own*? I answer that advocates of design or of many universes need take up no stance on this issue. They need not estimate the probability that a universe would be life-containing if drawn at random from the field of all logically possible universes; they need consider only universes "in the local area of possibilities", universes all fairly like ours in their laws. If a light ray hits a pinhole in an enormous screen, then there is no need to examine the whole area of the screen before drawing your conclusions. You can say straight away that, almost certainly, *either* there are many other light rays striking the screen *near the pinhole, or else* there are many other pinholes in that particular neighborhood, *or else* the light has been cleverly aimed. (Finding a pin in the center of a painted rosebud on the wallpaper, you have cause to believe that the pin was placed with deliberate care if there are no other nearby pins and if the wallpaper in the vicinity is featureless. Whether or not *distant* parts of the wallpaper are a riot of rosebuds is irrelevant.)

All we need do, then, is to consider the results of fairly minor changes in the actual laws and constants of nature and of various cosmological numbers. Now, the literature already cited[8] presents seemingly very strong evidence that even very minimal changes would have been fatal to life's prospects. Very slight alterations in the expansion rate at the big bang seemingly yield a universe which either recollapses much too fast or flies apart much too quickly. Very slight additions to the initial turbulence make everything millions of times too hot or lead to a universe of black holes. Small revisions in the strength of the strong nuclear force or of the weak force or of electromagnetism or gravitation, or in various particle masses, would have made stars burn too fast or too slowly, prevented the formation of carbon, blocked anything like chemistry, or stopped even protons (without which there could be no atoms) from forming or from resisting decay, and so on. Some of the constraints which have been calculated in this field seem firm to one part in a million or better. Others allow variation over a few percentage points, or sometimes by an order of magnitude, in cases where theory seems unable to explain why the figures should not be a billion times greater or smaller.

Instead of going into the physics and astronomy of all this, let us ask: Does it not perhaps only show that life *of familiar kinds* could not have evolved had our universe been slightly different? Well, that is what G. Feinberg and R. Shapiro suggest in their ingenious *Life Beyond Earth*.[9] Life of kinds entirely unfamiliar to us may well actually exist deep inside the earth, they propose, and in the sun, and in solid hydrogen at temperatures near absolute zero, and in interstellar gas and on neutron stars, and almost everywhere else. If we can swallow this, then it becomes easy to believe that even quite large changes to nature's laws and constants and initial conditions would have been undisastrous. Neutron star life, for instance, would make absolutely no use of carbon or water or even of chemistry; it would have no need, either, for any help from a long-lived, steadily burning star like our sun, because its energy would not come from photosynthesis and its evolution would take only a fraction of a second instead of billions of years. Yet given the choice between, on the one hand, believing in multiple universes or in God and, on the other, accepting life of the exotic types dreamed up by Feinberg and Shapiro, most experts opt for the former. (Still, nobody has much right to be greatly confident in this area, even today. How bizarre it would be for philosophers to teach that Hume and Kant knew all that needed knowing about the argument from design!)

Notice that the scientific debate *is not* exclusively concerned with the prerequisites of *human* life. The big question is instead whether all intelligent life whatsoever must depend on such things as chemistry. Again, the rarity or otherwise of life in our universe is scarcely considered since the issue is instead whether life ever could evolve, anywhere, in a universe slightly differently constituted. It is the razor edge on which life had to balance if our entire universe was not to be permanently lifeless, which provides the main evidence for many universes or for God. How curious to argue that the frozen desert of the Antarctic, the emptiness of interstellar space, the inferno inside the stars, are fairly strong evidence against design![10] As if the only acceptable sign of a universe's being God-created would be that it was crammed with living beings from end to end and from start to finish! As if God would have only one chance to create a universe, so that there would be a need to ensure that it was well packed! As if, moreover, it were obvious that the natural laws of a universe would be compatible with its being well supplied with life from its earliest instants; or as though (despite centuries of being confronted with the problem of evil, especially as presented by natural disasters) theists could only be utterly baffled by how our universe works with natural laws rather than by magic! And as if (despite all that Minkowski and Einstein said) we should have to see it as having once been true *that Reality as a whole was lifeless*, just because some temporal regions shown by a four-dimensional map of the world in space and time would contain no living things![11]

It should be added that the Feinberg-Shapiro speculations would not be fatal to design arguments or to arguments for many universes even if these speculations were attractive so far as concerned their physics—their intriguing accounts of how, for example, neutron star life might be based on the strong nuclear force rather than on the electromagnetism which underlies all chemistry. One reason for saying this is that the way in which life as we actually know it (life based on chemistry and especially on the properties of carbon and water) manages to balance on its razor edge is so tidily explained by the many-universes hypothesis and also (so I shall argue) by its competitor, the God hypothesis. Now, as said earlier, I work on the principle that the tidiness of an explanation can be a reliable sign of something's needing to be explained. And besides, it can look very odd to suppose that in our cosmos *only life as we know it* is very delicately dependent on force strengths, particle masses, and such, whereas other sorts of life could survive quite major changes in these things. It seems not unreasonable to expect (*a priori*) that anything as vastly complex as life would depend on delicate adjustments— whereas it does strike me as unreasonable to suppose that life as we know it (*a posteriori*), life actually dependent on delicate adjustments, is totally unrepresentative of the life in our cosmos. The most plausible story about exotic life forms would thus seem to be that they too would depend on delicate adjustments of some kind. Yet this only succeeds in making it rather odd to believe in a profusion of such life forms.

(4) How strange it can again seem, against the background of the modern debate over multiple universes, when empiricists attack design arguments by saying that our universe *is obviously a one and only universe and therefore not a fit subject for probability talk*! Consistently developed, such reasoning would yield the grotesque conclusion that whereas your average bank-note forger has immense difficulty in hiding his creative acts, a divine

force or person, "transcending" the universe through being its creative ground rather than just a part of it, would find it logically impossible to produce a world which looked as if it were probably God-made. Even *Made by God* written in fiery letters all over it would, we are being told, supply no evidence of its making "because the universe is a one and only universe." But, I ask, is there not some useful sense of "universe" in which there may actually be many and varied universes, ours being a very untypical one? And in any case, can it seriously be thought that we should need to observe other universes, detecting, for example, that almost all of them did not have *Made by God* written all over them, before concluding that our universe, in which (let us for argument's sake suppose) *Made by God* had in fact been written everywhere thanks to the action of nature's forces, was very probably a designed universe in which nature's forces had been selected carefully so as to produce an otherwise highly improbable result? Would it not be enough if we performed thought experiments, examining possible universes in our imagination? Could we not *work it out* that small changes in nature's forces would have yielded a markedly different world?

I am not claiming that life's existence is quite as suggestive as a message in letters of flame. My point is just that it is unacceptably crude to protest, against absolutely any alleged evidence for design (or for many universes), that we *can experience* only one universe, or that there *could be* only one universe, *and that therefore we lack all basis for comparisons, all logical room for talk of probabilities and improbabilities.* (And in fact some who protest in this way declare in their next breaths that a universe with as many evils as ours would be "a highly improbable" product of divine power, even if it might conceivably be such a product.)

(5) Next: How strange it sounds to ears attuned to recent debates among cosmologists when an opponent of design arguments remarks that *if the universe were not life-containing, we should not be here to discuss it,* then suggesting *that no more needs to be said!* For the "anthropic principle"much discussed by today's cosmologists — that intelligent beings would necessarily find themselves in situations in which intelligent life could exist — is not simply left to stand on its own. Instead it has an intimate connection with many-universe ("many-world") cosmologies. It is only when combined with the idea of multiple universes that the principle makes it unsurprising that life is to be found in this universe of ours.

To demonstrate this, let us start with what is known as the *weak* anthropic principle. This opposes the Copernican, or cosmological, principle which suggests that our universe in its entirety is all very much like the scene which meets our eyes. Supporters of the weak anthropic principle object that, on the contrary, we observers could quite expect to be seeing things from a very unusual time and place, specially suited to life. This is because other times and places—such as the first seconds after the big bang started, or the sun's interior, or intergalactic space—would very likely be devoid of observers. Now, the *strong* anthropic principle operates similarly, except that instead of considering *life-containing times and places inside a universe* we are now dealing with *life-containing universes within a set of universes*. If there existed many universes almost all of which were hostile to life, then we should find ourselves observing one of the unusual ones, a universe friendly to it. This could give us our explanation for such initially very startling discoveries as that very tiny changes in the physical constants and initial conditions of our universe would have made it lifeless.[12]

Notice that it may sometimes be hard to say whether an anthropic explanation on these lines is indeed a strong-principle explanation and not a weak-principle one—because it may be hard to decide whether you really are dealing with many separate universes instead of simply with many gigantic, more or less separate parts of a single, supergigantic universe. In effect, this entire distinction will often turn on the rather arbitrary affair of whether we choose to call systems "separate universes" when they interact only slightly. So it would be strange to make use of the weak principle in one's explanations while refusing ever to consider using the strong one. The two kinds of explanation shade into each other! The essence of both kinds is this: they invite us to consider a wider field of realities inside which the situation in which we find ourselves (our time and place inside a universe, or our particular universe inside a set of universes) may be very unusual and yet very much to be expected by us. For in a very large universe, or in a very large set of universes all of them just as real as the universe in which we find ourselves, even the very unusual could be expected to happen somewhere. And if the very unusual is a prerequisite of observations, then we observers must find ourselves in the midst of it.

To say, in contrast, that a situation hostile to life could not be observed and that this *by itself* is enough to show that the friendliness of our surroundings could be no problem is to miss the point entirely. Dismissing the need for all further explanations, whether those of theism or the ones of the many-worlds cosmologist, it invites the following parody. You are machine-gunned from fifty yards away and for fifty minutes. All the bullets miss. Can you conclude that the explanation for this is that the enemy gunner is a pacifist? "Not so," you say, "for if the bullets hadn't all missed, then I shouldn't be alive to observe and discuss the situation, and therefore I need no explanation for it!"

(6) It may be thought, however, that my various counters to the standard objections manage only to do what is, from the viewpoint of a believer in God, quite the wrong job. They may succeed in showing that our universe's suitability for life could indeed be something remarkable, something in special

need of a dramatic explanation, but, it may be protested, their successes should be counted always as successes for many-universe theories; for, with the idea of multiple universes so well able to account for the cosmological evidence in a simple and attractive way, who needs the antiquated and silly notion of design? Clearly I have a duty to say why design strikes me as a nonsilly hypothesis, and even as a simple and attractive one.

For a start, I am not much bothered by two possible objections to it: that it generates no detailed predictions about the world's nature and that it is itself rather vague: for instance, with respect to whether design implies a designer. I am unbothered because very similar things can be said of the competing many-universes hypothesis without damaging it. (a) Thus, the many-universes hypothesis could be scientifically important: for example, by encouraging us to reject nonprobabilistic varieties of unified field theory, even though nobody could have *predicted* that a life-containing universe would have just the mixture of physical laws and constants and initial conditions which we actually discover. All we can say is that the laws and constants and initial conditions actually discovered are such that very minor variations in them would have yielded lifelessness, and the supporter of many universes need not even be claiming that a situation of this delicately balanced kind was predictable. He can instead be offering to explain a situation of that kind now that he has actually come across it. In this he is like the believer in God, who can see force in design arguments while still believing that divine power could easily have created (and maybe did create?) conscious beings (angels?) in a vacuum or in the inferno of the big bang instead of through fine adjustment of such things as the cosmic expansion rate so as to produce stars, planets, carbon, water, and intelligent life evolving in obedience to physical laws. A pin transfixing a painted rosebud can be seen as needing to be explained when the surrounding area of the wallpaper is blank, but the person offering an explanation (that the pin was placed with care, or else that it was just one of many pins placed at random in that neighborhood) cannot automatically be taken as having been willing to predict this state of affairs or as claiming that no pins are placed where the rosebuds are thickly clustered and thus easier to transfix with a clumsy thrust. Similarly when the detective offers to explain the poisoning: you cannot declare that he could in that case have predicted it and therefore has a share in the guilt; neither should he be taken as denying that the murderer had it in his power to use a battle-ax. And praising the skill which threw a dart right into the bull's-eye to win a pint of beer, you need not be disputing that the thrower might alternatively have chosen to steal a pint. (b) Further, the many-universes hypothesis could be defended even if nobody could say quite how the universes were generated. Its being *a vague hypothesis*, an incomplete one, would not ruin it. In this it and the design hypothesis could be alike. (For surely arguments favoring design could be forceful and interesting through tending to establish that a combination of creative power and goodness was behind the universe, even if the arguments themselves went no further. They might, for instance, be one of many elements supporting faith in some particular religion despite their failure to point toward this religion rather than toward another or toward some worldview too abstract to be called religious. Arguments can help support a theory when they make it more likely that some theory *of that general type* is correct.)

On the other hand, the right to be vague does not amount to a right to be precise in absolutely whatever way you please. Not *just any* picture of God and God's creative activity could be acceptable. If forced to choose between *multiple universes* and *God the Reasonlessly Existing, Universe-Designing Person with Ultimately Inexplicable Powers*, I choose the first without hesitation. But I have argued in several places[13] that there is no need to think of God as a person at all, let alone a person who exists reasonlessly. The reason why there exists something rather than nothing could be this: ethical requirements are in some cases creatively effective. Examining from your armchair the quite ordinary idea of an ethical requirement, you get (as J. L. Mackie concedes in a recent chapter discussing my ideas[14]) no guidance on whether ethical requirements, ethical grounds for the existence of this or that, are or are not able to create universes. What you find is only that they might conceivably create them. But examining next the fact that at least one universe exists and the fact that it is life-containing, you may see these two matters as problems. And in that case you may come to believe that an ethical requirement (or, which is another way of saying the same thing, a consistent set of ethical requirements) does have creative power, producing our universe and perhaps also many another life-containing universe. This could be what is best meant by *God* and *design*. It seems to me that we have here an attractively simple and unmysterious picture of creation by God.

However, perhaps God is instead an all-powerful person who owes his existence and his power to his ethical requiredness. Either way the argument from design could ask us to believe in something which was not pure magic.

3. Some Main Lines Which Further Research Could Take

Let us review the situation. The cosmological evidence, I have said, suggests that life's evolution depended on a very dramatic degree of "fine tuning" in physical constants and initial conditions. There are five main ways of reacting to this. (1) Agree with it but deny that life could itself be anything very dramatic. Say that there could not possibly be anything here to justify requests for explanation. (2) Call the evidence inadequate. Argue that more or less any universe would be life-containing, either because calculations indicating a need for fine tuning have gone wrong or else because such calculations are relevant only to life as we know it: life based on chemistry, occurring on planets circling steadily burning stars. (3) Believe in multiple universes, with natural laws and constants and initial conditions varying from universe to universe until life becomes possible somewhere. (4) Believe that a divine person created our universe, giving it characteristics designed to generate life. (5) Say that talk of God or of design, if it is to be retained, should be talk not of a person and his plans but of a creative ethical requirement.

Which among these options is the best?

I have rejected (1). Life certainly could be something to get excited about, because such tidy explanations could be given for it: the God explanation and the many-universes explanation. The availability of an explanation can confirm that an explanation is needed. If the fish's length had to be just right in order for it to be caught, then we ought not to disregard our ability to explain the catching of just such a fish.

This still leaves us with four options. My preference is for the last of them, but my message is that much more research into them is needed.

Consider (2). Here is not the place for long debate on whether life of exotic types could exist in conditions very different from earth's. Instead let us recall what was said earlier. Speculations about *life on neutron stars* and the like *in our universe* can well seem whimsical (though even in this field more research perhaps needs to be done). On the other hand, speculations about *life in universes entirely different from ours*, though fascinating, are irrelevant (since the need to explain why the pin is in the rosebud at the center of an otherwise blank area of wallpaper is a need which is precisely as great whether or not *distant* areas of wallpaper are thick with rosebuds). So our question must be about *life as we know it in our universe*. Does it truly depend very delicately on such things as the cosmic expansion rate at early instants?

The expansion rate is specially worth discussing because here the accuracy required of the fine tuning can seem so extreme if the most generally accepted (but of course still speculative) ideas about our universe's origins are correct. "To within one part in a million million" may well understate the problem. Tiny speed differences early on in the big bang become colossal differences later, so the further we push back the instant at which the tuning is to be carried out, the more dramatic the figures we obtain. In chapter four of *The Accidental Universe*[8] Paul Davies considers the Planck time, 10^{-43} seconds after the bang started, calculating that at this stage a change of one part in 10^{60} would have been disastrous. (That is one part in a million million million million million million million million million million.) Alan Guth,[15] looking at a later stage when particle energies were at 10^{17} GeV, still sees an apparent need for accuracy to one part in 10^{55}. But unlike Davies, Guth considers that this difficulty can be overcome without resort to God or to many universes. His is what he calls "an inflationary universe". In its very early stages it "supercooled to temperatures 28 or more orders of magnitude below the critical temperature for some phase transition"; "a huge expansion factor would then result from a period of exponential growth". The sudden tremendous expansion would explain why the universe is so "flat", so nearly Euclidean in its space; now, its flatness is associated with its being extremely near the border between being "open" (destined to expand forever) and being "closed" (destined to collapse), which in turn means that it expands at just such a speed as allows galaxies to form and life to evolve.

Further, Guth sees his inflationary scenario as solving a very serious "horizon problem". This concerns how the observable universe of today is so free of the effects of early turbulence, and hence of multibillion-degree overheating, when at the 10^{17} GeV stage the standard picture shows it as containing as many as 10^{83} separate regions, regions unable to modify one another's behavior so as to enforce adherence to a pattern of unturbulent development *because they lie over one another's horizons* — causal influences have had insufficient time to move between them. Roger Penrose has estimated[16] that if no physical theory could explain away the seeming threat of cosmic disorder then we should have to take our universe's actual orderliness — its low, life-permitting temperatures and the fact that its matter is not almost all of it accumulated into black holes (whose internal disorder is very high) — as indicating that "the accuracy of the Creator's aim", when he placed his selecting pin inside the space whose points represent the various possible initial configurations of our universe, must have been "at least of the order of one part in $10^{10^{123}}$", which is a figure vastly greater even than the 10^{60} arrived at by Davies. According to Guth's theory, however, calculations supplying such huge figures would be based largely on the false premise that no huge inflation had occurred. Universe parts which people believe to have been causally separated may in reality have been well within one another's horizons prior to the inflation. In short, Guth may indeed be able to explain away the seeming threat of disorder. He may be able to show not only that the cosmic expansion speed had to be just the speed that was needed for producing life but also that the horizon problem is illusory, so that cool, life-encouraging cosmic order was more to be expected than immensely hot, life-excluding turbulence.

How should supporters of design or of many universes react to this challenge to their most beautiful items of evidence? Though Guth claims that his model gets some support from recent grand unified theories, it can be pointed out that these are still very speculative, and even if correct, they would have to be applied extremely speculatively to give such effects as supercooling by a factor of 10^{28}. Furthermore, Guth confesses that the inflationary scenario is plagued by its own tendencies to generate immense turbulence when the inflation ends. This and other problems render his position "at best very unattractive" in its present form, he says. It can seem that his universe would have to be almost as "special", as finely adjusted, as the standardly accepted universe. It would, however, be quite wrong to make beliefs in design or in multiple universes depend on developments in this or in any other single problem area. For, first, the most impressive thing in favor of such beliefs is that there appear to have been *so very many* different features of our universe which needed fine adjustment.[7,8] And second, neither design's supporter nor the supporter of many universes should be dismayed by the suggestion that in our universe some fairly fundamental law has various highly complex repercussions which solve some severe problems which life seemed to face. For there are types of many-universe theory (for instance, John Wheeler's picture of a cosmos undergoing "reprocessing" between its oscillations) in which even quite fundamental laws can vary from universe to universe until there arise laws with complexly providential repercussions. And the believer in design can lay stress on the complexity of the repercussions, their providential character, and the seemingly clear fact that things might well have been different. Suppose, for example, that our universe's expanding at a speed just right for galaxy formation really was a result of its once having inflated tremendously, the inflation being inevitable, for various highly complex reasons, granted that the laws of physics take precisely the form which they do. It would remain sufficiently plain that other possible universes recognizably like ours in their physics would be noninflationary. That is why the correctness of the inflationary scenario is not obvious even to the best physicists!

What really would ruin all the evidence would be that it could somehow be shown that only one system of laws, constants, and initial conditions could be self-consistent, or else that all self-consistent systems would be life-generating ones. In his later writings Wheeler has favored the latter alternative, claiming — with appeals to Bishop Berkeley and to the interaction of observer and observed in quantum physics — that the presence of observers is necessary to a universe's actual existence.[17] But there seems to me little force in his logical, epistemological, and scientific arguments for this startling conclusion. *To exist* simply does not mean *to perceive or to be perceived*, and the interaction of "observer" with "observed" in quantum physics can be illustrated with cameras and other such recording equipment, or even with a photosensitive crystal "observing" a photon, just as well as with conscious beings. Wheeler's lines of thought here look almost as inadequate as his earlier ones[18] in favor of the former alternative, when he suggested that a "calculus of propositions" could by some logical magic lead up to the actual laws of physics via a pregeometry which was totally a priori. Discussions with logicians soon led him to abandon *that!*

My provisional conclusion is that we do have good evidence either of design or else of multiple universes. But, now, which of these two should we prefer? Should it be multiple universes? (1) There is nothing excessively odd in the notion that several universes exist. Why imagine that there should be *only one* gigantic system of causally interacting things? Even Guth's theory has variants in which immensely many permanently isolated universes are a natural result of the inflation. Again, if our cosmos is a huge quantum vacuum fluctuation, then it would be strange to think it the one and only such fluctuation. (2) On the other hand, there would seem to be *no purely philosophical grounds* for believing in universes with widely varying natures. It seems weak to argue, for instance, that in any immense totality of existence we ought positively to expect plenty of them—plenty of regions which were "separate" not only through being huge and more or less isolated but also through obeying very different laws—for this reason: induction, our excuse for thinking that laws do not vary, grows ever weaker as it extends to wider and wider areas. This is too reminiscent of a nineteenth-century calculation by W. S. Jevons, using Laplace's rule of succession, that 5,000 years of sunrise, though making it virtually sure that the sun will rise tomorrow, give only a half chance that it will still be rising 5,000 years hence.[19] Such an approach disastrously omits to attach weight to the *simplicity* of unvarying laws. (3) There is likewise not very much strength in a philosopher's suggestion[20] that absolutely all possibilities *may well* be realized somewhere, or even, I think, in the philosophical doctrine that ontology demands that they *must* all be realized. The first is too mere a suggestion; the second, the ontological doctrine, is fascinating but seems to me mistaken; and both involve seemingly fatal difficulties with induction, difficulties discussed (though not deemed fatal) by David Lewis in some recent essays.[21] For if all possibilities are realized, then there are countless real worlds in which induction fails, and the worlds in which it manages not to fail—worlds like our world as I hope it to be, a world in which I do not disintegrate at the very next logically possible opportunity—form a range considerably more restricted than the range of the points inside a target's bull's-eye. (4) Hence one would much like to see some detailed and well-evidenced physical theories explaining how many and varied universes come into being. But, alas, the various available theories are extremely rough and tentative. And some of them may well offend too drastically against Ockham's razor. Many-worlds quantum theory could be a good example of this fault; its continually branching universe makes the drunkard's lamppost genuinely split into many lampposts (albeit not in any way that conflicts with sober experience, because no two of the lampposts ever inhabit the universe-branch which is *your universe as of now*). (5) But what, then, *is* the excuse for believing in universes in large numbers and with widely varying natures? The answer is that the only thing which speaks at all powerfully in their favor is something which speaks just as powerfully in favor of design. It is that life's evolution appears to have been made possible only by many extraordinarily delicate adjustments of force strengths (e.g., a 1 percent increase or decrease in the power of the strong nuclear force ruins stellar synthesis of carbon), particle masses (e.g., for chemistry to be possible the mass of the neutron must exceed that of the proton, but by no more than approximately a tenth of 1 percent), and so on. Fine tuning of this kind, so I have argued, does need to be accounted for, and one attractive way of accounting for it might be to see it as the eventual outcome when vastly many possibilities are explored in vastly many universes, so that, sooner or later, in some universe or other, conditions would become favorable to life.

Could the fine tuning truly be accounted for like that? Perhaps so—but there are serious horizon problems to be overcome. To as far out as our telescopes can reach, our universe consists of particles with the same masses, obedient to forces with the same relative strengths, and so on. Suppose that these masses and strengths and such were settled probabilistically at some early stage. How came they to be settled identically in maybe 10^{83} regions which had no causal interaction with one another? When affairs *are settled in chance ways* in regions which are fully separate because they lie beyond one another's causal horizons, not even light having had time to pass from one region to another, then the laws of chance suggest strongly that they *will be settled in different ways in different regions*. Could we then expect that regions just now appearing on our ever-expanding horizon would have exactly the same life-encouraging characteristics as the region which we inhabit? Most certainly not; yet this is what we do find. So, while our universe's finely tuned expansion speed and very low degree of turbulence could perhaps be explained in ways *neither* involving any faster-than-light communication betwen regions *nor* resorting to Guth's highly complex and speculative method of ridding us of horizon problems, the plain fact is that our need for explanations extends far beyond the speed and the degree of turbulence. Faced with such difficulties, we could judge it altogether better to reject the many-universes approach, putting our trust instead in the God hypothesis.

What are the latter's strengths and weaknesses?

I cannot agree that it is antiscientific. Scientists are rightly opposed to the notion of divine interference with nature's day-to-day operations, but no such interference is imagined when we say that laws, constants, and initial conditions were selected by God. Most scientists take these laws and constants and conditions as the ultimate basis of all scientific explanations rather than as themselves scientifically explicable. Agreed, some people speculate that such matters may be to a large extent a priori. Penrose, for instance, has developed a theory of twistors, "abstract mathematical entities whose properties are forced by abstract mathematical principles such as holomorphicity" and out of which space and time and particles are built.[22] But it is to be hoped that despite his poetic suggestion that "we are all composed of abstract mathematics", even he would agree that more than one kind of universe obeying principles worth calling natural laws *was mathematically possible*. Introducing God to choose between the possibilities may perhaps be nonscientific, but antiscientific it is not.

What is more, the God hypothesis would not lose all its strength even if a physics of multiple universes came to be well worked out. Although such a physics could destroy one apparently powerful set of reasons for believing in God, we should still face the question of *why there exists something rather than nothing*, and (since "mathematically possible" does not mean *existent*) no mathematical formula of physics could hope to answer *that*. But the God hypothesis might answer it, so long as God is not presented as an inexplicably existing being. Further, there would be the question of *why events conform to anything worth calling laws*. It is fashionable to laugh at Sir James Jeans' picture of God as a divine mathematician; absolutely any universe, his critics point out, would have to obey the rules of mathematics on pain of falling into absurdity; but what they forget is that a universe could easily fail to *illustrate* mathematical themes in the striking way in which ours does. Events fall into elegant sequences which lead us to talk of causation and of physics and to describe the world by differential equations; now, no logic forces them to do so; and to say that they do so "through their own powers" can look like just giving a name to a mystery. It is much as if we had found atoms of the elegant varieties imagined by the ancients—perfect spheres, cubes, and regular polyhedra—and commented that this was because the universe had "intrinsic symmetromorphic proclivities".[23]

Admittedly the most impressive evidence for design is "quantitative", as when we discover that life's evolution depended on the early cosmic expansion rate's being right to one part in 10^{12} or 10^{25} or 10^{60}. We have seen, however, that many-universe theories might explain away such evidence; to counterattack, design's supporters could therefore well point (as I have just done) to arguments from the very general facts that a world exists and that its events conform to laws. Yet intermediate tactics are available also. They involve pointing to how the laws have various providential features which *cannot* very readily be explained as the mere outcome of the kind of long, blind, probabilistic ringing of changes which could eventually have led to a particularly fortunate expansion rate or force strength or particle mass. Thus, (1) we could point to how our universe *is ruled by many competing forces*, forces which could therefore hope to enter into a complex system of checks and balances so that atoms and living things and planetary systems and galaxies neither collapsed inward nor flew to bits with disastrous speed; instead their parts could keep at more or less fixed distances and engage in intricate dances,

giving up their energy of attraction or of repulsion at steady rates which life
could exploit. Look, for example, at the way in which the matter of the stars
transforms itself into light. Thanks to how protons repel one another elec-
tromagnetically until they are forced far enough together to feel a mutual
attraction, this happens only very gradually, over billions of years, so giving
to evolution the kind of time span which Lord Kelvin argued to be an
astronomical impossibility. Look again at how electrons fail to feel the strong
nuclear force so that there can be such a subject as chemistry. Look at how
nuclear forces, first strongly repulsive (so that nuclei do not just collapse) and
then at longer ranges strongly attractive (so that nuclei do not explode either
and the protons of stars can fuse), become at still greater ranges entirely
powerless so that the (very fortunately) much weaker force of gravity alone
has influence here—since the positive and negative charges of electromagnetism (a force roughly 10^{39} times more powerful than gravity) conveniently cancel out in the case of matter en masse![24] (2) The way in which
systems are kept isolated from one another is of course most visible in the
fact that our universe is not all crushed into a single black hole; that, as Bert-
rand Russell noted, causal influences are (for the most part) greater at short
than at long ranges, so that the world can have not just a structure but an
understandable structure; that an object's inertia (which may depend on an
influence exerted by all the other objects in the universe) prevents the slightest
push from accelerating it to tremendous speeds. But it involves also such things
as the cosmic expansion: without this Olbers' paradox would come into play,
and the light of the stars, hitting us from along every line of sight and un-
softened by red-shifting, would fry us. Again, quantum effects (which were
at first considered impossibly counterintuitive) prevent mass-energy from
dissipating itself in an ultraviolet catastrophe in which atoms collapse in a
blaze of high-frequency radiation as their electrons spiral inward. (3) Various
symmetry or gauge-theory principles, very complex in the restrictions they
place on fundamental physics, ensure that *systems need not change radically
whenever they become positioned differently* in space and time. (4) *Particles
come in unvarying types*, so that living machinery can rely on a supply of
standard nuts and bolts. In 1873 Maxwell claimed this as evidence of design;
in 1974 Wheeler wrote that "the miraculous identity of particles of the same
type must be regarded as a central mystery of physics."[25] (5) No matter how
fast the system of a living organism and its environment moves relative to
other systems, its internal operations can proceed on identical lines. Yet the
electromagnetic forces which ultimately govern these operations have to be
transmitted between those parts, and their speed of transmission in no way
depends on the speed at which the parts are moving; in this the forces are
like ripples on a pond, transmitted equally slowly whether they are caused
by a falling leaf or by a high-velocity bullet. *But why, then, can living systems*

all operate efficiently no matter how great the relative velocities at which these systems move? The special theory of relativity answers this, except that why the theory is correct is not explained by the theory itself: relativistic effects are definitely not a priori.[26]

4. One Way of Understanding 'Creation by God'

Finally, how about the competition between God as a person and God as a creative ethical requirement?[27]

First: Remember that the competition might be less radical than it looks, because accepting God-as-a-person does not imply accepting that such a person exists and has benevolence, omnipotence, omniscience, and so forth, *for absolutely no reason.* It strikes me as no compliment to make God into the source of all explanations *in that particular sense.* Presumptuous though it could be to claim that one knew for sure that God existed for such and such a reason, the reverse of the coin is that treating sheer inexplicability as itself a ground for worship could look much like groveling. Perhaps tradition sometimes tends in that direction, but tradition has also tended to find a ground for worship in sheer power and even in power exercised completely arbitrarily, and this, as A. C. Ewing insists, risks being much worse than groveling: "the worship of power as such is evil".[28] Besides, there is a strong tradition that God's reality is necessary; now, to interpret "necessary" as meaning nothing more than "eternal and the source of all explanations" looks wrong because being an eternal source of all explanations is entirely compatible with being mere brute fact. But, then, how is God necessary? Ontological arguments for a logical necessity seem to me not to work for this reason: logic deals only with what properties an existent must have if it is already there and in possession of various other properties. It seems more sensible, and a genuine compliment to God, to adopt Ewing's suggestion that God's existence is "necessary not because there would be any internal contradiction in denying it but because it was supremely good that God should exist". My interpretation of this would be that there was an eternally real ethical requirement for the existence of a divine person, the truth of the matter being that such an ethical requirement *was creatively sufficient,* that is, was by itself adequate to account for the existence of such a person. Though such a truth of the matter could not be proved, there could still be a sense in which it *could not be otherwise.* It might be *synthetically necessary* (necessary absolutely, but in a way not provable by conceptual analysis), rather as is I think the case with various truths of intrinsic goodness: for example, that agonizing pain does not have intrinsic goodness, whereas the pleasures of music do.

But second: Must God in fact be a person (or else some hard to understand combination of two or more persons)? A further strong tradition, influential not only among the religious but among surprisingly many of those who call themselves nonreligious, holds that although there exists no omnipotent, omniscient person, there is a creative ground of all being, a power combining goodness with responsibility for the world's existence. Though I may not belong to any religious movement, my talk of *creative ethical requirement* places me firmly in this tradition, and I sometimes mark this fact by using the word 'God'. Using 'God' like that has the approval of a long line of Platonic theologians. It is compatible with calling God *personal*, on the grounds that the unity of power and goodness, the ethical requirement which creatively requires our universe, is imagined as acting much as a benevolent person would, as expressing itself most fully in its creation of persons (and, for Christians, in its creation of one person in particular), and so on. (Notice that if the life of an omniscient person were the ethically ideal kind of life and if supremely important ethical requirements are creatively effective, then there is a problem as to why reality does not consist solely of omniscient persons.)

Third: Is not an ethical requirement too abstract to act creatively?

Well, if by *being abstract* one just intends *having no practical power* (perhaps on the rather dubious excuse that *to be* equals *to be powerful*), then it is thoroughly question-begging to classify all ethical requirements as abstract. For have we discovered that no world exists, or that our world is obviously not of a sort which creatively powerful ethical requirements would produce? Or is it that *requirements for the existence of things* are clearly the wrong sorts of reality for actually bringing them into existence?

If the complaint is instead that a requirement which did not issue from some already-existing object, such as an inexplicably existing person, "wouldn't be real enough to act creatively", then the natural reply is that *only* a requirement which did not issue from some already-existing object could possibly bear ultimate responsibility for the fact of there existing at least one object and, further, that it can look monstrous to imagine that an ethical requirement for the existence of a good world could ever be *unreal*. As if the sudden annihilation of all existing things would lead to a situation in which it *could not really matter* that they had been annihilated! And anyway, just how should we conceive the creative activity of an already-existing, inexplicable person? Would he just *will* the existence of a world, his act of volition setting up a requirement much more ontologically respectable, much more likely to be powerful, than any mere ethical requirement?

What is really giving the trouble here is that there clearly is *some sense* in which an ethical requirement *as such* could not possibly be creatively active. For by "the reality of an ethical requirement as such" we could well mean simply that it really would be an excellent affair, a fulfillment of a need, if such and such were to exist. Now, this really could be so regardless of whether there were any realities of creative activity. It could therefore seem certain that no ethical requirements as such could act creatively. But the reply to this is that it is equally clearly the case that, *in some sense* of the words, *a cow as such* is female but not brown. Just as a complex reality can be divided into an abstraction, brownness, and another abstraction, cowness, so a complex reality having ethical and creative aspects could be divided into an ethical and a creative requirement. But the division would be in thought only.

One stumbling block is that though *cows as such* might sometimes be treated as colorless abstractions, *cows* are reassuringly concrete, and their concreteness has given rise to an utterly uncontroversial sense in which even a cow as such could actually be brown (meaning that it did not just look brown to the victim of jaundice, was not an invisible cow under a coating of brown paint, and so forth). But ethical requirements are not concrete. Moreover, talk of God and of creation is rather a poorly regulated area, and the issue of whether a requirement *would be acting as an ethical requirement* when creating a universe is not ordinarily talked about by the ordinary men who create ordinary language. Therefore, setting up your own linguistic laws, you could very firmly limit yourself to saying "that a complex reality of requirement, real eternally and unconditionally, has ethical and creative aspects". Talk of "an ethical requirement which was itself creative" would then never be permitted to pass your lips. There would be nothing wrong in such fastidiousness. But where people stumble is in not seeing that there would also be nothing especially right in it. It would instead be nothing more than quite all right. It would be merely permissible, rather than especially desirable, to set up your linguistic laws like that.

Fourth: We do not in any straightforward way experience the universe-creating activity of ethical requirements. Even the ethical requirements met with in everyday morality (things like needs for acts of kindness which, according to standard attempts to counter the problem of evil, can be *overruled* by such other needs as the need for the world to be one in which people make decisions freely) are not "experienced" in any ordinary sense. Instead they are realities *in which we believe*, thereby coming to see some of our actions as having behind them an authority beyond that of mere desires — even consistent and natural and socially approved desires. Mackie misrepresents positions like mine when he suggests that they must involve accepting an ethical requiredness which is "objective" in the sense that "we are in some unexplained way able to detect it and respond to it."[29] What I have in fact always said is that ethical requiredness, as well as not being "invented", is not "discovered" either. My ground for believing in it is not that I "detect" it, but it is just that I sincerely hope that some of my actions do have behind them an authority beyond that of mere desires. And what could be the ground for the further belief that such requiredness can be creatively active in the case of an entire universe where hugely many ethical requirements come together compatibly (and hugely many others are unfortunately overruled)? It is that this offers either the only way or else far the simplest way of explaining affairs which I think of as needing explanation. For here is a possible solution to *why there are any existents at all, and why events conform to any laws, and why nature's actual laws, physical constants, and initial conditions are ones complexly conspiring to produce life's evolution*. And in order to accept the solution we need only accept that ethical requirements, when not overruled by other, stronger ethical requirements, are successful rather than unsuccessful in what they require: namely, the existence of such and such. Now, success and lack of success *are equally simple alternatives* here.

This is because there would be no *mechanism whereby* any supremely important set of ethical requirements came to take on creative effectiveness rather than creative ineffectiveness.

Correspondingly, there would be no a priori probability of any such mechanism's failing or succeeding in its work. From our armchairs, without opening our eyes on this strange world of ours, we could say nothing about the likelihood or unlikelihood of an ethical need's creating a universe or universes.

NOTES

1. "God and Scientific Verifiability", *Philosophy*, 53, 1978, 71-79, later worked up into chapter 7 of *Value and Existence*, Oxford: Blackwell, 1979; "Anthropic Principle, World Ensemble, Design", *American Philosophical Quarterly*, 19 (2), 1982, 144-151, and with some misprints corrected in 19 (4); "Cosmology, Probability and the Need to Explain Life", in N. Rescher, editor, *Scientific Explanation and Understanding*, Lanham and London: copublishers the Center for Philosophy of Science, University of Pittsburgh, and University Press of America, 1983, 53-82; "Observership in Cosmology: The Anthropic Principle", *Mind*, 92 (368), 1983, 573-579.

2. *Natural Theology*, chapter 2, first published 1802: see vol. 3 of *The Works of William Paley*, edited by R. Lynam, London: Baynes, 1925, 7-12.

3. "Extraterrestrial Intelligent Beings Do Not Exist", *Quarterly Journal of the Royal Astronomical Society*, 21, 1980, 267-281.

4. This is argued by, for example, D. H. Mellor's "God and Probability", in K. Yandell, editor, *God, Man and Religion*, New York: McGraw-Hill, 1973, 472-481. Also by J. Hick in *Philosophy of Religion*, 2nd edition, Englewood Cliffs, NJ: Prentice-Hall, 1973, 27-28.

5. The consideration is urged by M. Scriven, for instance, in *Primary Philosophy*, New York: McGraw-Hill, 1966, 129: the absence of sensate beings would have meant that "there would be no one to discuss the teleological argument", alias the argument from design.

6. Many regard the Planck length of 10^{-33} cm. as the fundamental length char-

acterizing quantized space. See, e.g., the preface to C. J. Isham, R. Penrose, D. W. Sciama, editors, *Quantum Gravity 2*, Oxford: Oxford University Press, 1981.

7. For instance, in "Seven Numbers That Determine the Structure of the Universe", a 1982 preprint of the Space Research Institute, USSR Academy of Science, Moscow. See also his more readily available "Physical Laws and the Numerical Values of Fundamental Constants", *Soviet Physics: Uspekhi*, 23 (6), 1980, 296-305.

8. Key readings include: B. Carter, "Large Number Coincidences and the Anthropic Principle in Cosmology", in M.S. Longair, editor, *Confrontation of Cosmological Theories with Observational Data*, Dordrecht: Reidel, 1974, 291-298; S. W. Hawking, "The Anisotropy of the Universe at Large Times", ibid., 283-286; B. J. Carr and M. J. Rees, "The Anthropic Principle and the Structure of the Physical World", *Nature*, 278, 1979, 605-612; P. C. W. Davies, *Other Worlds*, London: Dent, 1980, especially chapters 8 and 9, and *The Accidental Universe*, Cambridge: Cambridge University Press, 1982, and *God and the New Physics*, London: Dent, 1983, especially chapter 12; F. Tipler and J. Barrow, *The Anthropic Cosmological Principle*, expected from Oxford: Clarendon Press; J. Barrow, "Anthropic Definitions", *Quarterly Journal of the Royal Astronomical Society*, 24, 1983, 146-153; J. Wheeler, "From Relativity to Mutability", in J. Mehra, editor, *The Physicist's Conception of Nature*, Dordrecht: Reidel, 1973, 204-207; B. S. DeWitt and R. N. Graham, editors, *The Many Worlds Interpretation of Quantum Mechanics*, Princeton: Princeton University Press, 1973; the very exciting papers of I. L. Rozental, most of them not readily available (see footnote 7); J. Demaret and C. Barbier, "Le principe anthropique en cosmologie", *Revue des Questions Scientifiques*, 152 (2), 1981, 181-222, and 152 (4), 1981, 461-509. On the perhaps largely random allocation of force strengths and particle masses in phase transitions see S. Weinberg, "Beyond the First Three Minutes", *Physica Scripta*, 21, 1980, 773-781.

9. New York: Morrow, 1980.

10. For argument on these lines see K. V. Nelson, "Evolution and the Argument from Design", *Religious Studies*, 14, 1978, 423-444. Even Richard Swinburne shows, on page 136 of *The Existence of God*, Oxford: Oxford University Press, 1979, that he is impressed by "the evident paucity of organisms throughout the universe".

11. See John Leslie, "The Value of Time", *American Philosophical Quarterly*, 13, 1976, 109-121; and on the problem of evil see chapter 5 of *Value and Existence* (see note 1).

12. The anthropic principle is defined, and its "weak" and "strong" versions distinguished, in B. Carter's seminal paper (see note 8).

13. Apart from *Value and Existence*, see "The World's Necessary Existence", *International Journal for Philosophy of Religion*, 11, (4), 1980, 207-224; "Efforts to Explain All Existence", *Mind*, 87, (346), 1978, 181-194; "The Theory That the World Exists Because It Should", *American Philosophical Quarterly*, 7, (4), 1970, 286-298.

14. Chapter 13 of *The Miracle of Theism*, Oxford: Clarendon Press, 1982.

15. "Inflationary Universe: A Possible Solution to the Horizon and Flatness Problems", *Physical Review D*, 23, (2), 1981, 347-356.

16. "Time Asymmetry and Quantum Gravity", in *Quantum Gravity 2* (see note 6), 244-251.

17. See, e.g., C. M. Patton and J. A. Wheeler, "Is Physics Legislated by Cosmogony?" in C. J. Isham, R. Penrose, D. W. Sciama, editors, *Quantum Gravity*, Oxford: Oxford University Press, 1975, pp. 538-605.

18. In C. W. Misner, K. S. Thorne, J. A. Wheeler, *Gravitation*, San Francisco: Freeman, 1974, pp. 1208-1212.

19. *The Principles of Science*, 2nd edition, London: Macmillan, 1877, pp. 257-261.
20. See chapter 2 of Robert Nozick, *Philosophical Explanations*, Cambridge, MA: Harvard University Press, 1981.
21. David Lewis, *Philosophical Papers*, Oxford: Oxford University Press, 1983; see especially "Postscripts to 'Anselm and Actuality' ", pp. 21-25.
22. "Twisting Round Space-Time", *New Scientist*, 82 (1157), 1979, 734-737.
23. See chapter 6 of *Value and Existence* and "Does Causal Regularity Defy Chance?" *Idealistic Studies*, 3 1973, 277-284.
24. For some details see F. J. Dyson, "Energy in the Universe", *Scientific American*, 225 (3), 1971, 51-59; E. J. Squires, "Do We Live in the Simplest Possible Interesting World?" *European Journal of Physics*, 2, 1981, 55-57; V. F. Weisskopf, *Knowledge and Wonder*, New York: Doubleday, 1962; S. Weinberg, *The First Three Minutes*, New York: Bantam, 1977, especially pp. 126-127; G. Wald, "Fitness in the Universe", in J. Oro et al., *Cosmochemical Evolution and the Origins of Life*, Dordrecht: Reidel, 1974, pp. 7-27.
25. *Gravitation* (see note 18), p. 1215.
26. Chapter 7 of *Value and Existence* discusses this in more detail, pp. 123-127.
27. This section will bring together some main themes from the writings listed in note 13.
28. In chapter 7 of his *Value and Reality*, London: Allen and Unwin, 1973, especially pp. 156-157 and 161.
29. *The Miracle of Theism*, p. 239.

THE QUESTION OF NATURAL PURPOSE

Phillip R. Sloan

> It is an astounding fact that no canonical writer has
> ever made use of nature to prove God. They all strive
> to make us believe in Him. David, Solomon, etc.,
> have never said, "there is no void, therefore there is
> a God." They must have had more knowledge than
> the most learned people who came after them, and
> who have all made use of this argument. This is
> worthy of attention.
>
> Pascal, *Pensées* 243[1]

Sustained discussions of the question of evolution and creation, once
the issues have moved beyond the issues of biblical inerrancy and "creation-
science" controversies, at some point come up against the fundamental question of natural purpose or natural teleology. As it bears directly on the question of evolution and creation, the issue concerns the difficulty that even if
it is granted that God could create the world through a gradual, transformative historical process rather than by a creation of the existing order in
a given moment of time, there are inherent objections, arising from evolutionary theory itself, that imply lack of direction and eventual purpose in
the process. Readers of the popular scientific literature are undoubtedly aware
of these problems as raised in such works as Jacques Monod's *Chance and
Necessity.*[2] That Monod is giving expression to views encountered in less obvious ways in the scientific, historical, and textbook literature of evolutionary
biology is perhaps less appreciated.

This essay will seek, through a combined historical and critical analysis,
to examine the roots of this question and the degree to which these claims
can be seen to be warranted by empirical and theoretical aspects of evolutionary biology. I will first survey briefly the prehistory of the problem as
it developed in the seventeenth and eighteenth centuries. Darwin's own views
will then be examined in detail on the question of natural purpose. A concluding section will survey briefly the changes in evolutionary theory since
Darwin, with comments on the degree to which these support a fundamental
challenge to the deeper understanding of the doctrine of creation.

121

This essay presumes at the outset that in spite of specific points of empirical and conceptual difficulty, neoselectionist evolutionary theory remains the best scientific explanation of the range of natural phenomena that it seeks to deal with.[3] The argument will proceed by granting the assumptions of that theoretical position.

1. Historical Review

In his recent comprehensive synthesis of biological thought the leading theorist of evolutionary biology in the English-speaking world, Ernst Mayr, summarized his conclusions on the bearing of evolutionary biology on the issue of natural purpose:

> The acceptance of evolution made the problems of a well-ordered world particularly acute. . . . Yet, to convince someone who is not familiar with the evolutionary mechanisms that the world is not predetermined and—so to speak—programmed seems hopelessly difficult. 'How can man, the porpoise, birds of paradise, or the honey bee have evolved through chance?' is the standard question one receives surprisingly often even today. . . . Natural selection not only eliminated the need for a designer but it also spelled the end of cosmic teleology (finalism). Eventually it became clear that the term 'teleological' had been applied to a very heterogeneous medley of phenomena, some of which, but not cosmic teleology, are valid scientific processes. . . . [4]

Several claims are made in this statement that I will address in this paper. First, it is assumed that a purposive understanding of the origin of organisms implies some kind of preprogramming. Second, our naive intuitions of order and design in nature are considered to be ultimately deceptive, and chance events, rather than intelligent plan, underlie this order. Finally, it is claimed that any purpose attributed to organisms is not to be understood in the framework of classic teleological purposiveness of either an internal or external variety. To deal with the apparent orderliness and goal-directedness of organisms, Mayr, in keeping with many other theoreticians of biology, goes on to deal with this by appeal to the nonteleological concept of *teleonomy*, meaning by this a causally determinate account that is able to explain the phenomena without use of classic finalism.[5]

1.1. FINAL CAUSATION AND SEVENTEENTH-CENTURY SCIENCE

To develop the necessary tools for analyzing these arguments, a brief review of the issue of final causation and natural purpose as these concepts were formulated at the beginning of the modern scientific period is in order. Although it is common knowledge that Galileo, Bacon, Harvey, and Hobbes had questioned the value of received versions of final and formal causation in scientific explanation, the Cartesian critique is more directly relevant to the precise formulations I wish to explore. Unlike Bacon and the other critics of these concepts, who challenged them for their practical fruitlessness, Descartes had raised a challenge at a deeper foundational level, closely tying his rejection of final causes to a quest for certitude in natural philosophy.[6]

In his attempt to defeat epistemological skepticism and probabilism, and to establish unshakable metaphysical foundations for natural philosophy, Descartes had rejected an appeal to natural design and teleological purposes as part of his effort to demonstrate the existence of God independent of any appeal to an empirical and material order. In relying on the ontological proofs set out in the *Meditations*, Descartes made the existence of a nondeceiving God, and the dependency of the world on his creative and sustaining act, the necessary precondition for a natural philosophy. Only this theological foundation gave him the basis for the concept of natural law, the principle of inertia, the existence of matter, and the possibility of epistemological certitude. At the same time it implied that natural knowledge was possible only under sharply limited conditions, restricted to the "clear and distinct" dimensions of nature accessible to analytic reason.[7]

This epistemological requirement, implying the elimination from natural philosophy of all inherent teleological principles, self-creative activity, and vital forces, undermined the internal finality of Aristotelian biology by eliminating the connection of teleological purposiveness and substantial form. Descartes' matter is inert, deprived of principles of inherent activity. By rejecting the hylomorphic conception of matter even organic beings were only inert, material entities, lacking any inherent entelechy or *anima* in the Aristotelian sense that could serve as a principle of internal finality. In putting forth his mechanistic model of the organism Descartes was quite explicit on this point. Writing in his posthumously published *Traité de l'homme:*

> I desire you to consider, further, that all the functions that I have attributed to this machine . . . follow naturally in this machine entirely from the disposition of the organs—no more nor less than do the movements of a clock or other automaton, from the arrangement of its counterweights and wheels. Wherefore it is not necessary, on their account, to conceive of any vegetative or sensitive soul or any other principle of movement and life than its blood and its spirits, agitated by the heat of the fire which burns continually in its heart and which is of no other nature than all those fires that occur in inanimate bodies.[8]

With this extirpation of internal principles of natural purposiveness only the external teleology of God who designed this organic machine was at issue in Descartes' philosophy, and even if this divine origin was granted, Descartes raised the point that such an appeal was neither necessary, given the a priori proofs of the existence of God as a precondition of natural philosophy, nor even epistemologically warranted in the light of his restrictions on natural knowledge.

A rich tradition of appeals to such external finalism, it should be noted, was readily available in the medical writings of the sixteenth and seventeenth centuries, deriving particularly from the writings of Galen and the Renaissance medical writers.[9] Representing a different tradition than the Aristotelian-Scholastic writings, which had emphasized internal finality, the medical writings drew heavily on the external teleology of the Neoplatonic and Stoic traditions, which frequently explained biological form and function by appeals to the wise designing power of an intelligent "nature".[10]

In his express attacks on the use of natural phenomena to determine some kind of larger purpose in nature, Descartes seems to have had this use by the medical writers clearly in mind. In the work of William Harvey he had a paradigmatic case of the fertility of an approach to biological questions that at least bracketed, if it did not exclude, questions of final causation in favor of exploration at the level of material and efficient causation.[11] Replying to Pierre Gassendi's appeal to the design of the heart as an argument for "excellent contrivance and marvellous providence", Descartes commented:

> The arguments you adduce on behalf of final causality are to be referred to the efficient cause; thus it is open to us, from beholding the uses of the various parts in plants and animals to regard with admiration the God who brings these into existence . . . but that does not imply that we can divine the purpose for which He made each thing. . . . Certainly in Physics, where everything should rest upon the securest arguments, it is futile to do so. We cannot pretend that certain of God's purposes rather than others are openly displayed; all seems to be equally hidden in the abyss of His inscrutable wisdom.[12]

The practical difficulties in following Descartes in this astringent approach to natural philosophy were to reverberate through seventeenth-century science and philosophy. In the eyes of pious scientist-theologians, such as the English naturalist John Ray, Descartes had eviscerated the grand argument from design and substituted for it arguments too abstract for the ordinary reader. The threat in this, Ray argued, was that the result would be a fully dysteleological natural philosophy. As he comments in his enormously influential *The Wisdom of God Manifested in the Works of the Creation*:

> [Descartes eliminates] the best *Medium* we have to demonstrate the Being of a Deity, leaving us no other demonstrative Proof but that taken from the innate *Idea*; which, if it be a Demonstration, is but an obscure one, not satisfying many of the Learned themselves, and being too subtle and metaphysical to be apprehended by vulgar Capacities, and consequently of no force to persuade and convince them.[13]

Reading the arguments of Ray against Descartes quickly leads one to conclude that he had not sufficiently considered the possible justifications for

Descartes' cautions, nor had he foreseen potential pitfalls that his own reliance on a strong form of the design argument might hold. Furthermore, in rejecting Descartes' approach it was also easy for authors like Ray to defend an opposing view with arguments that subtly altered the Christian doctrine of creation.

This leads us to an interesting and important issue in the natural theology of the seventeenth century. Examining the writings of the classic British physicotheological tradition reveals that on one hand they were inclined to follow Descartes in his exclusion of internal, Aristotelian finality in nature. In their own eclectic versions of the "mechanical philosophy" matter was inert, typically atomic, and acted upon by contact forces, and organisms were only complex arrangements of such matter. The issue that then separated them from Descartes was the role of external teleology, and the ability of man to determine empirically God's purposes from a natural order composed of inert material objects.

Once the issues were conceived in this way, it was very easy for the British physicotheologians to formulate a set of arguments that I would characterize as generically "Stoic" rather than Christian, and the issues posed become those that generally had in antiquity served to separate the natural theologies of ancient Stoicism from the nonteleological philosophy of Epicureanism. In the classic debate both Stoic and Epicureans accepted the fundamentally material nature of reality. The argument between them then became a debate over the source of its empirical order, with Epicureans relying on the spontaneous *clinamen* of the atoms and Stoics seeing this order as the product of a wise, providential, and designing *phusis*, or "Nature".

Consequently, although many important differences can be cited between the natural philosophy of ancient Stoicism and that of the British scientist-theologians of the seventeenth century, the acceptance by this latter group of several key assumptions about matter, mechanical action, and the nature of organisms made the Stoic arguments easily assimilable. Simply by substitution of 'God' for 'Nature' the arguments of Ray, Boyle, William Derham, and Samuel Clark could be almost interchanged with those found in the treatises of Cicero, Seneca, Varro, and Galen.[14]

This has profound implications for the understanding of the doctrine of creation in the writings of these seventeenth-century scientist-divines. While typically affirming at some point that God is the Creator of the universe of matter, the emphasis of these writers, like that of their Stoic predecessors, was not on the notion of a creation of a material universe *ex nihilo*, but on the *organization* at some historical moment of a preexisting atomic chaos. Newton's statement in the *Opticks* that "God in the Beginning form'd Matter in solid, massy, hard, impenetrable, moveable Particles"[15] is classic in its ambiguity over the degree to which God's action is conceived as an existence-giving act at all. Order, not being, is the focus of these natural theologies.

This shift of emphasis from concern with ontological existence to a primary concern with teleological ordering takes on a convincing rationale in the context of a natural philosophy in which matter is accepted as inert and without self-ordering principles. Faced with the alternatives that the empirical order of the world has come about either by intelligent planning or else by classic Epicurean chance, there would seem to be little reason to favor the latter thesis. Robert Boyle argues this pointedly in attacking Epicureanism:

> I think that the wise Author of nature did not only *put matter into motion*, but, when he resolved to make the world, did so regulate and *guide the motions* of the small parts of the universal matter as to reduce the greater systems of them into the order they were to continue in. . . . So that, according to my apprehension, it was *at the beginning* necessary that an intelligent and wise Agent should contrive the universal matter into the world . . . and settle the laws according to which the motions and actions of its parts upon one another should be regulated.[16]

No other explanation of this empirical order is considered. The only options are design and chance, and chance seems clearly absurd. As John Ray argues in utilizing an argument from Cicero's *De natura deorum* that still appears in modern dress in popular antievolutionary literature:

> A wonder then it must needs be, that there should be any man found so stupid and forsaken of reason, as to persuade himself, that this most beautiful and adorned world was or could be produced by the fortuitous concourse of Atoms. He that can prevail with himself to believe this, I do not see why he may not as well admit, that if there were made innumerable figures of the one and twenty letters, in gold, suppose, or any other metal, and these well shaken and mixed together, and thrown down from some high place to the ground, they when they lighted upon the earth would be so disposed and ranked that a man might see and read in them *Ennius's Annals.*[17]

Within the framework of this kind of thinking, the structures and functions of organisms, even more than the ordered motions of the heavenly bodies seemed a decisive proof of purposeful design and ordering. Like Galen before him, Ray could see in the world of living things endless examples of design and function pointing to the superintendence of a God functioning almost identically with Galen's "Nature".

However, by this interpretation of the issues the real force of the argument rested upon the difficulty of imagining alternative accounts within the assumptions of the mechanical philosophy of the seventeenth century. As that century closed, the adequacy of this framework was increasingly brought under severe challenge. The critical issues raised by the rise of Newtonian mechanics for the mechanical conception of nature are well known. Less well known are the independent challenges to the assumptions of mechanistic science presented by its inability to deal adequately with the main biological phenomena—growth, generation, regeneration of lost parts, animal heat pro-duction, and embryological formation—which suggested that perhaps the teleological vitalistic biology of Aristotle, and even the hylozoic biology of the pre-Socratics, were not as bankrupt as had been claimed by the mechanists.[18] From these difficulties of dealing with organic beings in mechanical terms clear alternatives to mechanism emerged with powerful influence in biomedical circles of the early eighteenth century.

1.2. NATURE AND NATURAL PURPOSE IN EIGHTEENTH-CENTURY BIOLOGY

The theoretical critiques of mechanistic assumptions and the reemergence of dynamic and teleological conceptions of the organism in the writings of Ralph Cudworth, Nehemiah Grew, Francis Glisson, Leibniz, Georg Ernst Stahl, and the lesser French medical vitalists at the University of Montpellier form a complex series of events in the history of the life sciences and involved a deep reorientation of metaphysical, theological, and empirical inquiries in these sciences.[19] Definable by specific doctrines, such as the belief in the latent "sensibility" and "irritability" of the elementary constituents of organisms, these new biological traditions were also closely tied to the reemergence of the concept of *nature* as an active, explanatory cause of organic process, an intermediate causal order that relieved God of direct creative action in bringing about the phenomena of growth, formation, and development. In the place of the Cartesian-mechanist concept of nature as "the order and disposition of created things", Greek and Renaissance conceptions of an active *natura naturans* became an important feature of eighteenth-century scientific and philosophical thought.[20] Furthermore, with this third alternative there was available an account of natural order that at the same time allowed for the emergence of attacks on the concept of natural design and purpose. Through the close connection of these issues with biological problems these attacks also had specifically biological reference that will be important for our theme.

Following on the design-mechanism of the seventeenth century, the revival of dynamic conceptions of nature in the eighteenth century raised two possibilities that can be followed out in the writings of Enlightenment authors. In one respect this revival reestablished the concept of *nature* as an inter-mediate causal order, possessed of autonomous powers and able to act as an intermediate creative agency that eliminated the need for God's direct ac-tion, while remaining subordinate to divine natural laws. To this extent it did not involve greatly different assumptions than those found in the writings of the Scholastics, such as Aquinas. However, it also opened for some the possibility of a fully autonomous, self-creative order with sufficient inherent power to abolish the need for the traditonal God. Rather than reinforcing the acceptance of teleological causation as operative in the world on an immanent level, as the first option would suggest, it raised for some the possibility that nature may have no larger purpose, while still possessing causal efficacy to create order. Within these latter assumptions we encounter the emergence of pointed attacks on the concept of natural purpose in a form that will illuminate Darwin's later arguments for us. Two authors, both writing after the 1750s, can be singled out for discussion, and both of them were read by Darwin in his most creative period.

1.3. BUFFON: NATURE AS SUBSERVIENT TO DIVINE LAW

A conservative use of this concept of natural activity can be seen in the writings of Buffon (1707-1788). Widely read by his contemporaries to an extent unsurpassed by perhaps any other natural philosopher in the 1750s and 60s, Buffon's reflections on cosmology, geology, and natural history in his *Histoire naturelle* (1749-1765 with supplements) set in motion a train of naturalistic speculation that was pursued subsequently by Diderot, Kant, La Place, Blumenbach, and Lamarck.[21] In Buffon's work we can also see an interesting interplay between the conception of nature as an intermediate agency with limited self-creating powers and the emergence of attacks on or at least fundamental difficulties with, the evidence for purposive intention in the construction of organisms.

Buffon made his conception of nature the subject of extended discussion in two essays included in the later volumes of the *Histoire naturelle* in 1764 and 1765. He there expounds a concept of a creative but still dependent and law-governed, order standing in subordination to divine agency:

> Nature is that system of laws established by the Creator for regulating the existence of bodies, and the succession of beings. Nature is not a body; for this body would comprehend every thing. Neither is it a being; for this being would necessarily be God. But Nature may be considered as an immense living power, which animates the universe, and which, in subordination to the first and supreme Being, began to act by his command, and its action is still continued by his concurrence or consent. This power is that portion of the divine power which manifests itself to men. It is at once the cause and the effect, the mode and the substance, the design and the execution. Very different from human art, whose productions are only dead works, Nature is herself a work perpetually alive, an active and never ceasing operator who knows how to employ every material, and, though always labouring on the same invariable plan, her power, instead of being lessened, is perfectly inexhaustible. Time, space, and matter, are her means; the universe her object; motion and life her end.
>
> The phaenomena of the universe are the effects of this power. The spring she employs are active forces, which time and space can only measure and limit, but never destroy . . . . With such instruments, what can limit the operations of Nature? To render her omnipotent, she wants only the power of creating and annihilating. But these two extremes of power the almighty has reserved to himself alone.[22]

In this extraordinary set of passages, blending an appeal to Newtonian concepts with an almost intentional directedness of an intermediate agent standing between God and matter, Buffon has given autonomy to the action of nature. God's action is largely confined to the establishment of laws. Even the origin of the cosmos, as he argues in other essays, is by means of natural causes which God only initiates.[23] At the same time Buffon argues that not only God's purposes but also those of "Nature" remain hidden. Against the rational purposiveness presumed evident in the organized structure of animals by the British physicotheologians, Buffon raised these doubts most forcefully in discussing the unusual anatomy of the pig in an article of 1755:

> To circumscribe the sphere of Nature is not the proper method of acquiring the knowledge of her. We cannot judge of her by making her act agreeably to our particular and limited views. We can never enter deeply into the designs of the Author of Nature, by ascribing to him our own ideas. . . .
>
> Why should we imagine, that, in each individual, every part is useful to its neighbour, and necessary to the whole? Is it not enough that they exist together, that they never injure each other, that they can grow and expand without mutual destruction? . . . It is the intentions of true philosophy to instruct us *how* objects exist, and the manner in which Nature acts: but we pervert this intention, by attempting to investigate *why* objects are produced, and the ends proposed by Nature in producing them.[24]

Like many features in Buffon's natural philosophy this shows a strong Cartesian influence. The difference is that there are now two sets of purposes that are unknown and presumably unknowable, those of God and those of "Nature," which stand as separable causal orders. "Nature" can now bring being into existence, but it does so in ways that reveal no larger intentionality discernible by reason. At the same time God has been located simply as a first cause and establisher of this nature, which then works in history by its own powers. The importance of this appeal in the late eighteenth century to a nature with creative powers, but hidden ends, once it is freed from the restraints of the divine limitation still operative in the Newtonian natural philosophy of Buffon, can be seen in the arguments of David Hume.

1.4. HUME: NATURE AS PROFLIGATE MOTHER

Hume's philosophically potent and important critique of natural theology is important for several reasons in this disussion. His posthumous *Dialogues Concerning Natural Religion* was read by Darwin at the time when his evolution theory was taking its mature shape, and I will argue later that some of Darwin's reflections on the question of creation and natural purpose show a possible debt to Hume's argument. Furthermore, Darwin had at least one encounter with these arguments through the summary of them in his grandfather Erasmus Darwin's *Zoonomia*. It is of interest to see how Erasmus Darwin had summarized Hume's basic argument in 1794:

> The late Mr. David Hume, in his posthumous works, places the powers of generation much above those of our boasted reason; and adds, that reason can only make a machine, as a clock or a ship, but the power of generation makes the maker of the machine; and probably from having observed that the greatest part of the earth has been formed out of organic recrements [*sic*] . . . , he concludes that the world itself might have been generated, rather than created; that is, it might have been gradually produced from very small beginnings, increasing by the activity of its inherent principles, rather than by a sudden evolution of the whole by Almighty fiat.[25]

This interpretation by a contemporary of David Hume brings out a point that is seldom noticed in discussions of Hume's attack on the design argument. The possibilities being raised by Erasmus Darwin depend on the assertion he sees in Hume that "nature" is not a passive mechanical system, but a dynamic, self-actuating system with inherent powers of activity.[26] In other words, Hume's arguments would seem to draw their force and plausibility from the possibility of an *activity* of nature quite different from that presumed by the seventeenth-century natural theologians.

We can see the justification for Erasmus Darwin's reading of Hume as we pursue closely the arguments of the *Dialogues Concerning Natural Religion*. I would suggest that we can see in some of these arguments an extension of one line of argument found in Buffon's position. In these arguments nature is not simply an intermediate causal order for Hume. It has the potential to act as a replacement for God's creative power. At the same time the intentions of this dynamic, creative power remain generally inscrutable, and there can be no inference from any empirical order sufficient to decide if it is God or creative nature that is behind the world.[27]

The effectiveness of Hume's arguments against the "Stoical" arguments of the British physicotheologians is dependent on this potential for an ordering principle other than intelligent creative design by a benevolent God or by a clearly rational and benevolent "Nature". His own alternatives depend on his positing as a possibility a vital dynamism of "nature", which does not disclose larger rational ends. In Section VIII of the *Dialogues* Philo, generally considered to represent Hume's own position, poses the possibility that the universe may simply be a system supplied with inherent active powers, with the adjustment of means to ends in organisms a product of the working out in accidental circumstances of this inherent dynamism:

> It is vain, therefore, to insist upon the uses of the parts in animals or vegetables, and their curious adjustment to each other. I would fain know how an animal could subsist, unless its parts were so adjusted? Do we not find, that it immediately perishes whenever this adjustment ceases, and that its matter corrupting tries some

new form . . . till in a great, but finite succession, it fall[s] at last into the present or some such order?[28]

As evidence of this lack of evident intentionality in the organic world, Philo, with help from Demea, develops the argument that nature presents to the careful observer not evidence of harmony and purpose, but rather that of perpetual warfare, strife, and disorder:

> The whole earth, believe me, Philo, is cursed and polluted. A perpetual war is kindled amongst all living creatures. Necessity, hunger, want, stimulate the strong and courageous: Fear, anxiety, terror, agitate the weak and infirm. The first entrance into life gives anguish to the new-born infant and to its wretched parent: Weakness, impotence, distress, attend each stage of that life: And it is at last finished in agony and horror.[29]

Philo then replies with an example that will figure prominently in Darwin's own discussions. Parasitism, particularly as one finds it manifested among the parasitic wasps, gives a striking example of the underlying cruelty of nature:

> Observe too . . . the curious artifices of nature, in order to embitter the life of every living being. The stronger prey upon the weaker, and keep them in perpetual terror and anxiety. The weaker too, in their turn, often prey upon the stronger, and vex and molest them without relaxation. Consider that innumerable race of insects, which either are bred on the body of each animal, or flying about infix their stings in him. These insects have others still less than themselves, which torment them. And thus on each hand, before and behind, above and below, every animal is surrounded with enemies, which incessantly seek his misery and destruction.[30]

To Cleanthes' claim, representing the response of the physicotheological argument, that at least some kind of intentional purpose can be seen in nature, Philo replies by an appeal to the ambiguity of the adaptations of organisms, which seem to have no higher purpose than mere adaptation to circumstance and reproductive survival:

> You ascribe, Cleanthes (and I believe justly) a purpose and intention to nature. But what, I beseech you, is the object of that curious artifice and machinery, which she has displayed in all animals? The preservation of individuals and the propagation of the species. It seems enough for her purpose, if such a rank be barely upheld in the universe, without any care or concern for the happiness of the members that compose it.[31]

Rather than the dynamism of biological phenomena working to reinforce a belief in teleological purpose, Hume draws exactly the opposite conclusion. The combination of the inherent fecundity of nature, the empirical evidence for purely utilitarian fitting of form and function, and the evidence of a general warfare of nature, suggest a potentially purposeless process:

Look round this universe. What an immense profusion of beings, animated
and organized, sensible and active! You admire this prodigious variety and fecundity. But inspect a little more narrowly these living existences, the only beings worth
regarding. How hostile and destructive to each other! How insufficient all of them
for their own happiness! How contemptible or odious to the spectator! The whole
presents nothing but the idea of a blind nature, impregnated by a great vivifying
principle, and pouring forth from the lap, without discernment or parental care,
her maimed and abortive children.[32]

In this preliminary historical discussion my intent has been to emphasize
three points. First, I have suggested that there is a shift in the seventeenth
century away from an understanding of creation as fundamentally an existence-
giving act of God to a primary focus on creation as teleological ordering of
matter. This shifted issues away from the traditional Christian and biblical
understanding to what I would term generically the "Stoic" understanding
of the issue. Second, while this was not necessarily a naive or untenable position for seventeenth-century mechanists to adopt in terms of a universe based
on mechanical action, it is one that was greatly weakened once the "inert-
ness" of matter and of "nature" were rejected after the 1750s for empirical
as well as philosophical reasons. Third, the introduction of the activity of
nature as an intermediate category of explanation did not necessarily imply
a return to the teleological conceptions of classical biological thought, even
though it restored a limited purposiveness to organisms. At the hands of
philosophical critics the activity of nature provided a means by which
arguments against natural design, purpose, and teleology could be raised.
With this as a background we are now in position to examine the views of
Darwin on these issues.

2. Natural Purpose in Darwin's Biology

The complexity of Darwin's biological thought, extending over the period
from 1826-1883, requires careful and delimited discussion, and many uncertainties still remain about the background of his biological thinking in spite
of the voluminous scholarship that has surrounded his work.[33] I have argued
elsewhere that his thought is best approached as a set of interacting layers
rather than simple historical stages,[34] and I feel a similar analysis is useful
in examining his views on natural purpose in relation to his theory of evolution. Critics of Darwin have often pointed out that his language and concepts are often heavily intention-laden.[35] While acknowledging this, I would
suggest that this can be highly misleading if the different historical layers
in his arguments are not carefully separated. I will therefore separate out the
"intentional" dimension of his discussions and then indicate the relation of

this aspect to a more complex nonintentional discussion of the question. I would also acknowledge that for a proper understanding of the critique made by modern evolutionists of the concept of natural purpose, it is the second, rather than the first, set of Darwin's arguments that need to be considered.

2.1. NATURE AS SELECTING DEMIURGE

In a line of argument that can be followed from Darwin's earliest notebooks on transformism, dating form the 1837-1839 period, into the published *Origin of Species* and even to his later works, Darwin seems to place heavy reliance on the concept of *nature* as a selective and teleological agency endowed with wisdom and foresight. Furthermore, these reflections represent more than simply loosely metaphorical appeals.[36] We have seen in the previous section that the revival of active conceptions of nature represented one of the profound breaks with the assumptions of seventeenth-century mechanism in the Enlightenment, and Darwin's use of these concepts represents his acceptance of a common framework of biological theory in the early decades of the nineteenth century. This framework is evident in the context in which Darwin was educated, and it is implied in many of the scientific works he actually read in his formative years.[37]

We can illustrate this context by comments appearing in a review of contemporary physiology prepared for the 1834 meeting of the *British Association for the Advancement of Science* by the Cambridge professor of physiology, William Clark. Reviewing the history of physiological science since antiquity, Clark saw his contemporary scientific community as having emerged from the fruitless dominance of mechanistic concepts, and he affirmed the need for biological science to explain phenomena by a "vital power imparted to organic matter . . . and exemplifying its faculties by means of the organs which it has developed through the force of nutrition."[38] Furthermore, this generally pervasive natural agency is seen by Clark as operative not simply at the level of specific organic function, but also as a more pervasive, creative agent which brings forms in existence:

> Thus does the vital power, manifesting itself in the assimilative process, occasion all the forms of life upon the earth. Each living thing, according to the nature of that original power (of which we can know nothing but by its effects), requires its own modifications of the common conditions of life, and presents an organization (upon which classification is based) adapted to the region and element in which it is destined to exist.[39]

With these ambitious claims offered routinely as majority scientific opinion only a few years previously, there is nothing particularly surprising or even unusually speculative in Darwin's statement in an early transmutation notebook in 1838:

There is one living spirit prevalent over this world (subject to certain contingencies of organic matter[,] chiefly heat), which assumes a multitude of forms each
having [an] acting principle according to subordinate laws. — There is one thinking sensible principle intimately allied to one kind of organic matter . . . which
is modified into endless forms of the living beings.[40]

More theoretically significant in such early notebook reflections is the role
Darwin was then willing to give a dynamic, superintending "nature" in his
original conception of natural selection. The intentionality and *telos*-laden
character commentators and critics were to see in the presentation of this concept in the published *Origin* is transparently present as this is followed in
the early draftings of the transformist theory between 1842 and 1859.

As is well known, the original argument of the *Origin of Species* was
developed around a direct analogy between man's intentional selection of
domestic plants and animals to produce the existing breeds and varieties, and
the selection exercised by "nature" over a longer range of time and space.
Following the emergence of this analogy from 1842 to 1859 reveals that it
is not simply poetic metaphor, for this analogy is clearly linked with Darwin's reliance on the activity of nature as an inherently creative, and even
intentional, power. In the early 39-page draft of the transformist theory in
1842, the analogy between man's intentional acts and those of a selecting
nature is direct and unproblematic. Nature indeed selects, but at a deeper
and more fundamental level:

> Nature's variation far less, but such selection far more rigid and scrutinising.
> Man's races not [even so well] only better adapted to conditions than other races,
> but often not [?] one race adapted to its conditions, as man keeps and propagates
> some alpine plants in garden. Nature lets [an] animal live, till on actual proof
> it is found less able to do the required work to serve the desired end, man judges
> solely by his eye, and knows not whether nerves, muscles, arteries, are developed
> in proportion to the change of external form.[41]

In the 200-page 1844 draft this passage is amplified and presented by means
of the hypothesis of a wisely selecting, superintending Being:

> Let us now suppose a Being with penetration sufficient to perceive differences
> in the outer and innermost organization quite imperceptible to man, and with
> forethought extending over future centuries to watch with unerring care and select
> for any object the offspring of an organism produced under the foregoing cir-
> cumstances; I can see no conceivable reason why he could not form a new race . . .
> adapted to new ends. As we assume his discrimination, and his forethought, and
> his steadiness of object, to be incomparably greater that [*sic*] those qualities in
> man, so we may suppose the beauty and complications of the adaptations of the
> new races and their differences from the original stock to be greater than in the
> domestic races produced by man's agency . . . With time enough, such a Being
> might rationally (without some unknown law opposed him) aim at almost any
> result.[42]

As we follow these reflections directly into the long "Natural Selection" manuscript begun in 1854, from which the published *Origin* was largely an abstracted version, Darwin makes explicit his concept of *nature* as a secondary causal order, similar to Buffon's "Nature" in being subordinate to divinely established laws but possessing formative and selective powers of its own sufficient to bring about development and transformation of species:

> See how differently Nature acts [compared to man]: By nature, I mean the laws ordained by God to govern the Universe. She cares not for mere external appearance; she may be said to scrutinise with a severe eye, every nerve vessel & muscle; every habit, instinct, shade of constitution, — the whole machinery of the organization. There will be here no caprice, no favouring: The good will be preserved and the bad rigidly destroyed, for good & bad are all exposed during some period of growth or during some generation, to a severe struggle for life. Each being will live its full term and procreate its kind, according to its capacity to obtain food and escape danger. . . .
>
> Can we wonder then, that nature's production bear the stamp of a far higher perfection than man's product by artificial selection. With nature the most gradual, steady, unerring, deep-sighted selection, — perfect adaptation to the conditions of existence. . . . If we admit, as we must admit, that some few organic beings were originally created, which were endowed with a high power of generation, and with the capacity for some slight inheritable variability, then I can see no limit to the wondrous and harmonious results which in the course of time can be perfected through natural selection.[43]

The extraordinarily teleological language manifest in this passage, and the clear impression it gives of a teleologically ordered system bringing organisms into "perfect" adaptations with their conditions of existence, directing them to ends more wisely chosen than the limited ends man could foresee, is not simply the survival of metaphor from an earlier period in his thought. Repeatedly in the argument of the *Origin of Species* Darwin appeals to man's artificial selection as a microcosmic case by which to understand natural selection,[44] and the force of this analogy would often seem to rest on the kind of intentionality manifest in this passage.[45]

However, I have developed this dimension of Darwin's thought with a clear recognition of a distinct tension between this intention-laden language and a second level of argument that involves Darwin in an open critique of teleological directedness. Darwin will develop this second line of reasoning to arrive at many of the positions we earlier saw stated by David Hume.

2.2. POST-MALTHUSIAN DARWIN: NATURE AS INERTIAL SYSTEM

This second dimension of Darwin's thought on natural teleology is to be understood in terms of the ramifications of the "Malthus discovery" resulting from his reading of the *Essay on the Principle of Population* in September

1838. Postdating, but only slightly, Darwin's early reflections on the concept of a dynamic, purposive "nature" impelling and guiding transformative change, the Malthus reading introduced new features into Darwin's reflections on several levels, sufficiently distinct to form a second current in his argument. As they bear on this discussion, I would focus on the novelty of Malthus' claim that organic beings have an inherent and incessant tendency to increase geometrically to a maximum. Furthermore, it is the function of this principle as an axiomatic premise in Malthus', and subsequently Darwin's, arguments that requires close attention.

The seemingly self-evident character of the Malthusian principle in modern thought has, unfortunately, tended to obscure this point. Nevertheless, prior to the late eighteenth century a long tradition of reflection on the principles governing the "economy of nature" had assumed a very different point — namely, that animal and plant numbers were controlled by an inherent self-limiting or conserving principle that prevented them from exerting anything like the Malthusian pressures on their environment.[46]

Malthus' claims were made possible by the revival in the eighteenth century of the dynamic and self-actuating conceptions of nature we have previously spoken of. By granting an inherent, nonconserving fecundity to nature Malthus could shift the focus from inherent self-limitations of animal numbers to external control exerted on populations under a continuous internal pressure to expand.

We see this reliance on the inherent, creative power of "nature" in the opening discussion of Malthus' *Essay* of 1798:

> Through the animal and vegetable kingdoms, nature has scattered the seeds of life abroad with the most profuse and liberal hand. She has been comparatively sparing in the room and the nourishment necessary to rear them. The germs of existence contained in this spot of earth, with ample food and ample room to expand in, would fill millions of worlds in the course of a few thousand years. Necessity, that imperious all pervading law of nature, restrains them within the prescribed bounds.[47]

Concerning his reliance on an intrinsic fecundating power of nature the point I wish to emphasize is the role it then gives the principle of population as a quasi-inertial principle in a form that could be utilized subsequently by Darwin. My meaning is explained by drawing an analogy with Newton's system of dynamics. Newton's use in the *Principia* of the principle of inertia, the opening axiomatic law of his physical system, sidestepped a complex set of metaphysical and even theological questions concerning the foundations of this physical principle in seventeenth-century mechanics. Once it is granted the status of a foundational axiom, the focus of Newtonian dynamics could then be on the explanation of all the empirically observable *noninertial* behavior of bodies, such as circular motions. The controls exerted on this initial inertial state of bodies provided the framework for introducing the concepts of centripetal forces, gravitational attraction, distinctions between mass and weight, and the other specific ingredients of Newton's natural philosophy.

In a similar way the Malthusian principle functions as a kind of inertial motion of natural populations, with all tending to increase to some world-encompassing maximum. Once granted, what then needs explanation is the empirical evidence that natural populations *do* in fact seem to exist in reasonably well-balanced and harmonious numbers. Control of this inherent tendency, rather than the explanation of the tendency itself, becomes the central issue.

Once Darwin had seen this principle clearly in 1838, we find in his writings an increasingly common imagery that would almost suggest a conception of a system of organisms, moving "inertially" in time by their great powers of natural increase, and almost colliding with great force against the limited external conditions of life. By this forcible collision they either "wedge" tightly into the conditions of life or else fail to fit and perish. Given this conception of the natural world, the "purpose" evident in the relation of organisms to these conditions would seem to be simply survival and continued reproduction. A passage in the fourth, or "D," transmutation notebook, inserted in September 1838 on the occasion of the Malthus reading, expresses this in metaphors that will later appear in the published text of the *Origin of Species:*

> Population is increase[d] at geometrical ratio in FAR SHORTER time than 25 years — yet until the one sentence of Malthus no one clearly perceived the great check amongst men. . . . One may say there is a force like a hundred thousand wedges trying [to] force every kind of adapted structure into the gaps in the oeconomy of nature, or rather forming gaps by thrusting out weaker ones. — [48]

Even though we can still see in this passage some notion of a larger purposive telos in the "final cause" of this system, the structure of the argument makes this functionally unnecessary. Assuming, as Darwin does, that the "gaps" in the natural order are simply the complexes of external conditions forming available niches, with these undergoing slow, Lyellian changes, directional change is then primarily a case of organisms tracking the lines of least resistance to the degree made possible by their available variation. The analogy with man's selective actions on the domestic animals is, in the case, fundamentally misleading, since in the one case intentional action is clearly involved, whereas in the other it is more a case of a dynamic population of organisms being molded under great pressure onto a natural "template" given by the complex of external environmental and ecological factors. Consequently, Darwin's frequent appeal to the nonteleological example of astronomical motions is neither purely rhetorical nor without good warrant. [49]

The changed meaning this insight gave to Darwin's concept of natural selection can be seen by attending to a crucial example given in chapter four of the *Origin of Species* in all editions. Following an opening discussion in the chapter that would lead the reader to think that Darwin was simply relying on a personified "nature" to ground his concept of natural selection, we see that he has in mind by the use of this example something quite different. Darwin poses as a "thought experiment" the example of an insect-plant relationship. Assuming as a hypothetical initial state a nectar-feeding insect and a nectar-producing flower which is dependent on insects for fertilization, their initial association might be simply fortuitous, possibly the product of the introduction of one form or another into a new area. Furthermore, Darwin assumes that neither form changes to benefit the other. All changes must, in this case, be initially due to benefits accruing independently to each organism, never because it is beneficial to the other form.

In the long-term interaction of these two forms, with the flower being fertilized as the insect seeks to reach the nectar, and the insect surviving through its nourishment by this nectar, each form undergoes a change of structure as slight variations arise that are favorable to both goals. The "pressure" for this change is the incessant populational pressure. In time, Darwin hypothesizes, there results a group of insects which are seemingly remarkably adapted to feed on these specific plant forms with elaborate feeding mechanisms, and conversely one finds a group of plants with potent nectar-secreting structures at the base of long and complicated entry ways.

The truth content, or even the testability, of this kind of evolutionary story is not my concern at this point. More important is its function as an idealizing example of Darwin's concept of natural selection. In it we surely see acknowledgment of some kind of purposive character of organisms. At the same time one is hard-pressed to argue that it suggests any larger purpose in the sense assumed in the Stoic design argument. The fitting of form to function, rather than necessary evidence of intelligent planning, is more a case of the parallel tracking of one form by the other to an end that seems no higher than survival. Consequently, although it was ultimately to be an unfortunate borrowing, Darwin's insertion in the fifth and sixth editions of the *Origin of Species* of Herbert Spencer's term 'survival of the fittest' as a direct synonym of his term 'natural selection' is not as confused or as tautological as has sometimes been claimed.[50] It does indeed make functionally unintelligible the reliance on the artificial-natural selection analogy as anything more than a loose metaphor. But it also indicates the growing awareness on Darwin's part that a nonteleological account of this principle could be given.

2.3. DARWIN'S CRITIQUE OF NATURAL PURPOSE

Suggesting that Darwin's concept of natural selection can be understood in nonteleological terms cannot itself be said to imply a nonteleological universe any more than these implications could be said to emerge from the nonteleological physics of post-Galilean mechanics. Nevertheless, there was available to Darwin after Malthus a framework of arguments that could easily be assimilated to some of Hume's skeptical arguments against the foresight and benevolence of the natural order and the support this order could give to natural theology. Malthus' "inertial" concept of population pressure can be seen to give greater theoretical warrant to Hume's speculations about the purposeless fecundity of nature. Darwin's gradual abandonment of the concept of "perfect" adaptation of organisms by a wise, selecting "nature", and the substitution of the post-Malthusian view of organic beings as forced into situations of purely relative adaptation by the struggle for existence, also makes Hume's skeptical comments on the overall purposive character of this order easily assimilated. That Darwin very early saw the possibility of connecting the Malthusian principle with Hume's arguments is seen from his marginal comment on the passage from Erasmus Darwin summarizing Hume's arguments quoted previously.[51]

Other than by indirect inference, it is difficult to assess the full impact the reading of Hume may have had on Darwin's arguments. I would suggest it is not inconsequential. The result of the reading would not seem to have been a clear decision on Darwin's part for or against some kind of natural purposiveness, but only a tension in his thought between a Humean skepticism and the insights of his originally deistic, if not theistic, views on natural design. This tension manifests itself in the distinct ambiguity in Darwin's public statements on the question. Writing in 1860 to Asa Gray in response to Gray's argument that Darwinian theory was fully compatible with a sophisticated understanding of a guided creation, Darwin responded with even the same example used by Hume in the *Dialogues*, the parasitic wasps:

> With respect to the theological view of the question. This is always painful to me. I am bewildered. I had no intention to write atheistically. But I own that I cannot see as plainly as others do, and as I should wish to do, evidence of design and beneficence on all sides of us. There seems to me too much misery in the world. I cannot persuade myself that a beneficent and omnipotent God would have designedly created the Ichneumonidae with the express intention of their feeding within the living bodies of Caterpillars, or that a cat should play with mice. Not believing this, I see no necessity in the belief that the eye was expressly designed. On the other hand, I cannot anyhow be contented to view this wonderful universe, and especially the nature of man, and to conclude that everything is the result of brute force. I am inclined to look at everything as resulting from designed laws, with the details whether good or bad, left to the working out of what we may call chance. Not that this notion *at all* satisfies me. I feel most deeply that the whole subject is too profound for the human intellect.[52]

While not abandoning the concept of some larger purpose behind the establishment of natural laws, Darwin increasingly saw himself in possession of an account which seemed able to explain empirical order in organisms purely through immanent causes. In his final response to Asa Gray in 1868 Darwin made this argument in public print. Gray had attempted to argue in a series of essays that evolution did not exclude some kind of purposive guidance, either in terms of selective agency or in the guidance of the causes of variation. Darwin replied at length:

> An omniscient Creator must have foreseen every consequence which results from the laws imposed by Him. But can it be reasonably maintained that the Creator intentionally ordered, if we use the words in any ordinary sense, that certain fragments of rock should assume certain shapes so that the builder might erect his edifice? If the various laws which have determined the shape of each fragment were not predetermined for the builder's sake, can it be maintained with any greater probability that He specially ordained for the sake of the breeder each of the innumerable variations in our domestic animals and plants; many of these variations being of no service to man, and not beneficial, far more often injurious, to the creatures themselves? . . . But if we give up the principle in the one case, — if we do not admit that the variations of the primeval dog were intentionally guided in order that the greyhound, for instance, that perfect image of symmetry and vigour, might be formed — no shadow of reason can be assigned for the belief that variations, alike in nature and the result of the same general laws, which have been the groundwork through natural selection of the formation of the most perfectly adapted animals in the world, man included, were intentionally and specially guided. However, much as we may wish it, we can hardly follow Professor Asa Gray in his belief "that variation has been led along certain beneficial lines," like a stream "along definite and useful lines of irrigation." If we assume that each particular variation was from the beginning of all time preordained, then that plasticity of organisation, which leads to many injurious deviations of structure, as well as the redundant power of reproduction which inevitably leads to a struggle for existence, and, as a consequence, to the natural selection or survival of the fittest, must appear to us superfluous laws of nature. On the other hand, an omnipotent and omniscient Creator ordains everything and foresees everything. Thus we are brought face to face with a difficulty as insoluble as is that of free will and predestination.[53]

From this extended comment we see that Darwin has interpreted the concept of purposeful evolution to be inextricably linked with an interventionist guidance of concrete natural processes in historical time, an intervention he sees as unwarranted. Instead, he can appeal to a nonteleological order of natural laws, while still grounding these in some kind of divine causation. Within the framework defined by these laws, however, there is no evident teleological design. This view is expressed forcefully in a comment made late in life to a critic who had argued that natural laws imply purpose:

> The chief [defect in your argument] is that the existence of so-called natural laws implies purpose. I cannot see this. Not to mention that many expect that the several great laws will some day be found to follow inevitably from some one single law, yet taking the laws as we now know them. . . , I cannot see that there

is then necessarily any purpose. Would there be purpose if the lowest organisms alone, destitute of consciousness, existed in the moon?[54]

But does this imply that the natural system as a whole lacks some larger purpose? Here Darwin was much less certain. The question remained in his mind as a great antinomy, which permitted plausible arguments on both sides. Writing in the same year to another correspondent:

> On the other hand, if we consider the whole universe, the mind refuses to look at it as the outcome of chance — that is, without design or purpose. The whole question seems to me insoluble. . . . [55]

Beginning with remarks on the seventeenth-century context, we have followed out a line of argument that presumes that the fundamental issue in the acceptability of concepts of creation and purposiveness has to do with issues of order. The classic physicotheological position assumed that only one explanation of this, intelligent divine action, was possible. This relied, however, on the assumption of a monocausal order. Once another source was posited, the action of nature, or the selection by conditions of life based on a natural overproduction of offspring, this argument lacked convincing force. Before turning to some concluding remarks on the framework in which these issues have been interpreted, comments on new features added by contemporary biology to this discussion are necessary.

3. Purpose and Evolution: Necessary Clarifications

I have commented at length on the historical views of Darwin both with the aim of bringing into sharp focus the basis for the Darwinian arguments against a common interpretation of natural purposiveness, and also to give a background against which we can see what new features may have been added to Darwin's own conclusions by the more developed theoretical structure of modern biology.

Recent discussions of evolutionary theory with reference to its bearing on teleology and teleological explanation would seem to have settled on a majority view that classic teleology can be eliminated from evolutionary theory.[56] Under the influence of cybernetic and information-theory approaches to biology, it is now common to encounter the substitution of the concept of *teleonomy* to designate the goal-seeking and apparently purposeful behavior of organisms, while still denying that this involves endorsement of either internal (Aristotelian) or external (Platonic-Stoic) finality.[57] In any case, the issue here concerns generally the more limited issue of the explanation of purposive behavior rather than a larger finalism, and even biologists who might embrace an Aristotelian concept of teleology to deal with the more limited case often make disclaimers regarding any larger purpose.[58]

Along with the nonteleological analysis of natural selection which I have argued is warranted by Darwin's mature understanding of his principle, other theoretical developments have certainly tended to remove many of the residual conceptual difficulties to be found in Darwin's account. Rather than the vague reliance on the dynamic vitality of "nature" to provide the "push" behind the Malthusian tendency of populations, the deeper understanding of energetic relationships holding between chemical and solar energy input and the biosynthetic activities of organisms has provided a quantifiable physical account of this underlying dynamism.[59]

Darwin's need to rely on "unknown" causes of variation and laws of inheritance has also been substantially reduced as an issue by the development of classical and molecular genetics, with variations interpreted as grounded in genetic mutation dependent largely, if not entirely, on high-energy input into specifiable genetic materials, with this input based on such stochastic processes as random cosmic radiation. The stability and self-reproducibility of highly complex organic energy configurations involved in genetic replication and protein synthesis has been explained by means of order-maintaining microforces, such as hydrogen bonds, which presumably give the key to the "order from order" laws of biology.[60]

Specific points of debate that are still occurring in this reductive program in biology are not of direct interest here since these are generally taking place among biologists still accepting the underlying programmatic assumptions of these theoretical trends.[61] More directly at issue is the extent to which even the possible *completion* of this theoretical program in biology would warrant claims that would seem to bear on the issues of theological creation and the possibility of a larger purpose in the creation of the world.

To deal with this issue requires that a careful distinction be made between the Judeo-Christian understanding of creation and its Stoic look-alike. I have emphasized that in the latter argument the primacy placed upon the issues of material order, rationally evident anatomical purpose, and demiurgic "guidance" renders this argument directly susceptible to the criticisms of Hume, Darwin, and more contemporary evolutionists. Sufficient theoretical apparatus would now seem available to warrant the claim that the known phenomena can be accounted for by nonteleological principles that are consistent with the general framework of explanation used in the physical sciences.

But even granting this point, does it bear in the way that is commonly affirmed in the literature on the theological understanding of creation? It is easy to find in the essays of biologists claims such as the following:

> It is upon the notion of *randomness* that geneticists have based their case against a benevolent or malevolent deity and against their being any overall purpose or design in nature.[62]

This kind of argument, popularized in *Chance and Necessity* by the Nobel Prize-winning geneticist Jacques Monod, obtains its force by a concentration on order once again. But is *order* the real issue?

I would suggest that within the Christian understanding of creation, whose radical character derived precisely from the differences between it and the accounts of cosmology and cosmogony that were found in the Greek philosophers, these popular interpretations of the issues are quite beside the point. As has been repeatedly emphasized by Christian theologians and philosophers of both Catholic and Protestant persuasion, the central issue in the doctrine of creation is not the historicity of the creation event at some datable moment in time, nor is it the establishment of intelligible order in a preexistent chaos.[63] Creation is fundamentally an *existence-giving* act, an act establishing an ontological dependency of the world on a free act of the Jahweh of Exodus 3:14. This Christian, rather than Stoic, understanding is well summarized in St. Augustine's query from the *Confessions*: "What exists, for any reason except that you exist?"[64]

Consequently, it cannot be considered a decisive argument against this understanding of creation to point out that the empirical processes taking place within an existent material order in time occur by means that have no directly evident purpose. It is the *existence* of these events in *any* order whatever that is at issue, and a decisive critique of the possibility of a larger purpose in creation would need to deal directly with this issue. Interpreted in this way, evolutionary biology has very little real relevance to the central problem, since it seeks to describe the material processes by which the existing order of life may have come about but says nothing about the *ontological existence* of that order itself.

A second set of issues on which I feel greater clarification is needed concerns the questions of theodicy that are commonly raised as presumed consequences of the opportunism and apparently nondirectional character of evolution by natural selection.[65] If creation is understood solely as the ordering of a material chaos by a deity, acting in time as an intervening demiurge, the workman of Plato's *Timaeus*, these kinds of questions carry some force. They do indeed strike at the design arguments utilized by figures like John Ray, William Derham, and of course William Paley.

However, this is again to substitute Stoic understandings for those of the Judeo-Christian tradition. As the quotation from John Henry Newman cited by Nicholas Lash in this volume should indicate with some clarity, the Christian tradition has been quite aware of a "fallenness" of nature within a created order that is attributed to a benevolent God. The interpretation of the consequences of this deficiency in its bearing on questions of epistemology, the possibility of natural theology, and the reason-faith and the grace-nature relationships have, of course, been issues of great controversy within the Christian tradition, not only between Catholics and Protestants but also between Augustinians and Scholastics within the Catholic tradition. However, even within the epistemologically optimistic tradition of neo-Scholasticism that has played an important role in Catholic circles for the past century, it could still be argued that the Galen-Paley-Ray version of the design argument has little real significance for the possibility of natural theology. For those in a more Augustinian tradition, which might include Pascal and Newman in the Catholic tradition, or Calvin and Barth in the Protestant tradition, there would certainly be little warrant for assuming that the kinds of issues raised by Darwin present some kind of decisive critique, or even that the arguments raised by the existence of maladaptation, extinction, parasitism, or evolutionary "dead-ending" add something new to the awareness of a world in which death, evil, pain, suffering, and imperfection have deep theological significance. These arguments succeed as critiques only if it is assumed that Christian theology implies a natural order without evident defect or deficiency, able to reveal God's purposes and benevolence in some direct way without need at some point of a faith-response. Seen in this light, the warnings of Descartes against the easy reading off of God's purposes from natural objects are as much the cautions of an orthodox believer as they are a warrant for a non-teleological natural philosophy.

NOTES

1. Pascal, *Pensées* (Brunschvicg numbering), translated by W. F. Trotter, New York: Modern Library, 1941, p. 87.

2. Jacques Monod, *Chance and Necessity*, translated by A. Wainhouse, New York: Knopf, 1971.

3. This is stated in full light of the recent challenges to orthodox neoselectionist evolution theory by such authors as Stephen Jay Gould ("Is a New and General Theory of Evolution Emerging?" *Paleobiology*, 6, 1980, 119-130; also S. J. Gould and Richard Lewontin, "The Spandrels of San Marco and the Panglossian Paradigm: A Critique of the Adaptationist Program", *Proceedings of the Royal Society of London* (B), 205, 1979, 581-598.) These arguments, while of interest, do not yet have sufficient foundations in a cohesive biological theory.

4. Ernst Mayr, *The Growth of Biological Thought*, Cambridge, MA: Belknap Press, 1982, pp. 516-517.

5. See below, p. 29.

6. On Descartes' confrontation with seventeenth-century skepticism see Richard H. Popkin, *The History of Scepticism from Erasmus to Descartes*, revised edition, New York: Harper, 1964, chapter 9. I have discussed some of the implications of this for scientific issues in Phillip R. Sloan, "Descartes, the Sceptics and the Rejection of Vitalism in Seventeenth-Century Physiology", *Studies in History and Philosophy of Science*, 8, 1977, 1-28.

7. Descartes, *Meditations on First Philosophy*, in Elizabeth Haldane and G. R. T. Ross, editors, *The Philosophical Works of Descartes*, New York: Dover, 1955, I, 185, hereafter cited as *Works*. In practice this meant explanations in terms of micro- and macromechanisms.

8. Descartes, *Treatise of Man*, translated by Thomas S. Hall, Cambridge: MA: Harvard University Press, 1972, p. 113. See also comments in Sloan, "Descartes, the Sceptics and the Rejection of Vitalism".

9. The importance of this tradition for the natural theology of the seventeenth century needs exploration. Particularly in Galen's anatomical writings, such as his *Usefulness of the Parts*, strong emphasis is placed on the use of anatomy to provide a compelling argument for external intelligent design, and this line of argument can be readily followed into the writings of sixteenth- and seventeenth-century medical writers like Vesalius and Fabricius of Aquapendente. The deep importance of Galen for medical education into the seventeenth century gave his arguments a social structure through which this external teleology, rather than the immanent teleology of the Aristotelian-Scholastic writers, could be transmitted to students in a dogmatic way.

10. See, for example, Fabricius of Aquapendente's *De venarum ostiolis*, (1603), translated by K. J. Franklin, in Mark Graubard, *Circulation and Respiration*, New York: Harcourt, Brace and World, 1964, pp. 119-125. "Nature" in this treatise functions as an external craftsman, designing the valves of the veins to fulfill intelligent purposes.

11. Harvey's attitude to final causation is particularly relevant since he dealt with biological phenomena in a treatise clearly important for Descartes' own approach to biology. Although Harvey does not exclude formal and final causation, in his *De motu cordis* of 1628 we see Harvey place these at the level of *speculative* explanations that may be considered after an analysis of the phenomena on the level of material and efficient causes. Furthermore, the discussions of formal and final causes are put off to such an extent in Harvey's treatise that one never gets to them in any satisfactory way.

12. Descartes, "Replies to Objection V", in *Works*, II, 223.

13. John Ray, *The Wisdom of God Manifested in the Works of the Creation*, 5th edition, London: Walford, 1709 (1st edition 1671), p. 44. Ray's work went through thirteen editions, reaching into the nineteenth century.

14. This general use of Stoic arguments and sources by seventeenth-century authors has also been noted by R. N. Hurlbutt in his *Hume, Newton, and the Design Argument*, Lincoln: University of Nebraska Press, 1965, esp. pp. 107-112.

15. Newton, *Optics*, Query 31, New York: Dover, 1952, p. 400.

16. Robert Boyle, *The Origin of Forms and Qualities According to the Corpuscular Philosophy*, in M. A. Stewart, editor, *Selected Philosophical Papers of Robert Boyle*, New York: Barnes and Noble, 1979, p. 70.

17. Ray, *The Wisdom of God*, pp. 39-40.

18. For the fundamental discussion of this issue see Jacques Roger, *Les sciences de la vie dans la pensée française du xviiie siècle*, Paris: Colin, 1971, pp. 418-439, and in more extended detail see François Duchesneau, *La physiologie des lumières: empirisme, modèles et théories*, The Hague: Martinus Nijhoff, 1982.

19. Duchesneau, *La physiologie des lumières*, chapter 1.

20. James E. McGuire has discussed the voluntarist and even nominalistic conception of nature of seventeenth-century mechanism and pointed out some of the contrasts with the medical tradition in his "Boyle's Conception of Nature", *Journal of the History of Ideas*, 33, 1972, 523-542. He has made the very important point that the seventeenth-century mechanical philosophers did not envision an autonomous

"nature" of matter in motion. This was an eighteenth-century development. I have
not attempted to deal with the complex contributions of both Leibniz and Spinoza
to this issue.

21. I have discussed these issues in the introduction to John Lyon and Phillip Sloan,
editors, *From Natural History to the History of Nature: Readings from Buffon and
His Critics*, Notre Dame, IN: University of Notre Dame Press, 1981.

22. Buffon, "Of Nature: First View," in William Wood, editor, *Natural History,
General and Particular*, translated by William Smellie, London: Cadell, 1812, vol.
3, pp. 447-448, hereafter cited as *Natural History*.

23. Buffon's account of the formation of the solar system in the first volume of
the *Histoire naturelle* in 1749 had posited the formation of the system from a collision of a comet with a sun, which broke off portions of the sun's material, moving
it in a similar trajectory by inertia. The gradual cooling of these masses and the attractive action of the sun then established the various planets moving in orbits in the
same approximate plane of rotation. By the *Époques de la nature* of his supplemen-
tary volumes of 1778 Buffon had integrated naturalistic cosmology with accounts of
organic origins, the formation of the earth, and other important cosmogonic speculations. For a summary of Buffon's planetary theory see Stanley Jaki, *Planet and Planetari-
ans*, Edinburgh: Scottish Academic Press, 1978, pp. 96-106. Even though through
the 1760s Buffon separates God and Nature as two orders, the testimony of Hérault
de Seychelles, following his interview with Buffon in 1788, indicates that Buffon was
willing late in life to substitute completely the action of "Nature" and natural forces
for God's creative action. See *Journey to Montbard*, translated in Lyon and Sloan,
From Natural History to the History of Nature, p. 367.

24. Buffon, "The Hog," in *Natural History*, vol. 4, pp. 312-314.

25. Erasmus Darwin, *Zoonomia, or the Laws of Organic Life*, 2 vols., London:
J. Johnson, 1794-1796; I, 509. Darwin reports having greatly admired this work as
a student in Edinburgh (1825-1827), and he reread the first volume of the *Zoonomia*,
annotating it, in late March 1839. Dating for these readings can be found in the partial publication of Darwin's reading notebooks in Peter J. Vorzimmer, "The Darwin
Reading Noebooks (1838-1860)", *Journal of the History of Biology*, 10, 1977, p. 121.
Retrospective comments on his early admiration for Erasmus' work are found in Darwin's *Autobiography* in Francis Darwin, editor, *The Autobiography of Charles Darwin and Selected Letters*, New York: Dover, 1958 (first published 1892), p. 13. On
the subsequent Hume readings and the annotations on this passage see below, p. 139
and note 51.

26. Full exploration of the sources of these biological metaphors in Hume's work
goes beyond this essay. Suffice it to note that Edinburgh was the primary English-
speaking center of medical vitalism in the late eighteenth century, particularly through
the writings of Hume's contemporary William Cullen. The strong similarity of some
of Hume's comments to the philosophical uses of these vitalistic concepts found in
the writings of Diderot, especially in his *Rêve D'Alembert*, would suggest Hume's
awareness of attempts to utilize French versions of vitalistic medical theory for
philosophical ends. Hume was in Paris in contact with both Diderot and Buffon from
1760-1762. Although the main body of the *Dialogues concerning Natural Religion*
dates from the 1750s, revisions were made until 1776, and the particularly interesting
passage on the fecundity of nature has been dated to one of his last insertions. See
the critical edition, edited by John Valdimir Price, Oxford: Clarendon, 1976. Hume's
interesting interplay between God and nature in the *Dialogues* has been in part analyzed in George J. Nathan, "Hume's Immanent God", reprinted in V. C. Chappell,

editor, *Hume: A Collection of Critical Essays*, Notre Dame, IN: Universtiy of Notre Dame Press, 1968, esp. pp. 421-423.

27. This is a theme repeatedly developed in Philo's discussions. The best that he feels can be concluded is that there is some remote analogy between human intention and the ordering principle of the world. But as he suggests in chapter 12, this need have no other basis than a common principle which might underlie "the rotting of a turnip, the generation of an animal, and the structure of human thought", and the analogy is closer to the structuring processes involved in works of man's art and contrivance than to works of moral benevolence. (*Dialogues Concerning Natural Religion*, edited by Norman Kemp Smith, Indianapolis: Bobbs Merrill, 1947, pp. 218-219.) See Nathan, "Hume's Immanent God".

28. Hume, *Dialogues Concerning Natural Religion*, p. 185.

29. Ibid., p. 194.

30. Ibid., p. 195.

31. Ibid., p. 198. See also ibid., pp. 207-208, where Hume describes nature as a rigorous taskmaster adapting organisms purely to the immediate needs of life without sufficient provision for new contingencies. The "Stoic" character of the British physico-theological argument, as found in an author like Samuel Clark, makes Hume's argument particularly effective. Norman Kemp Smith has pointed out the clear parallelisms in the structure of Hume's dialogue and the Stoic-Epicurean-Skeptic format of Cicero's *De natura deorum*.

32. Ibid., p. 211. See above, note 26.

33. Some of these deficiencies will be removed with the forthcoming publication of the critical edition of Darwin's correspondence, including many unpublished letters from his early years bearing on religious issues.

34. See my forthcoming "Darwin's Invertebrate Program, 1826-36: Preconditions for Transformism", in David Kohn, editor, *The Darwinian Heritage: A Centennial Retrospect*, Princeton: Princeton University Press; and Wellington, New Zealand: Nova Pacifica, 1985 (in press).

35. See the critical attack on evolutionary biology by the Thomistic philosopher Etienne Gilson, *From Aristotle to Darwin and Back Again: A Journey in Final Causality, Species, and Evolution*, translated by John Lyon, Notre Dame, IN: University of Notre Dame Press, 1984, chapter 3. Unfortunately Gilson has not taken adequate care to delimit the complex layerings in Darwin's thought, nor has he considered to a sufficient degree biological developments since Darwin.

36. This is not to disagree with the important role of Darwin's metaphorical imagery in his anthropomorphic descriptions of nature, as brought out by Edward Manier, *The Young Darwin and His Cultural Circle*, Dordrecht and Boston: D. Reidel, 1978, chapter 10. I would only add that the appeal to intentional and creative natural powers, and even to a creative "nature," were acceptable explanations of a variety of biological, physiological, and chemical phenomena in the early nineteenth century and do not represent an unusual feature of Darwin's thought. Manier has brought out the linkage of this with the Romantic movement. I am currently exploring the tie of this with the more specific incursion of post-Kantian German *Naturphilosophie* into England through the medical circles.

37. I am developing these points in detail in my "Darwin, Vital Matter, and the Transformism of Species"(*Journal of the History of Biology*, in press).

38. William Clark, "Report on Animal Physiology", *Report of the British Association for the Advancement of Science*, 4, 1834, 108.

39. Ibid., p. 110.

40. Gavin R. De Beer, M. J. Rowlands, and B. M. Skramovsky, editors, "Darwin's Notebooks on Transmutation of Species, Pages Excised by Darwin", *Bulletin of the British Museum (Natural History) Historical Series, 3*, 1967, 151. I have continued this quote from the excised pages of the "C" notebook with the following passage from the intact notebook as given in Gavin R. De Beer, editor, "Darwin's Notebooks on Transmutation of Species", *Bulletin of the British Museum (Natural History) Historical Series, 2*, 1960, 108. A new edition of this and the other transmutation notebooks, edited by David Kohn, Frederick Burckhardt, Sandra Herbert, and Sydney Smith, is forthcoming. Darwin's comments here follow the reading between February and July 1838 of Carl Gustav Carus' speculative views on the vital unity of nature as summarized in his "On the Kingdoms of Nature", translated in Richard Taylor, editor, *Scientific Memoirs*, London: Taylor, 1837, I, 223-254. See comments in "C" Notebook, edited by De Beer, p. 93.

41. Francis Darwin, editor, *Foundations of the Origin of Species*, Cambridge: Cambridge University Press, 1909, pp. 9-10. Brackets and parentheses as printed. See further discussion of this intentionality in Manier, *The Young Darwin*, and less adequately in Robert M. Young, "Darwin's Metaphor: Does Nature Select?" *Monist, 55*, 1971, 442-503.

42. Francis Darwin, *Foundations of the Origin of Species*, pp. 85-86.

43. Robert C. Stauffer, editor, *Charles Darwin's Natural Selection, Being the Second Part of His Big Species Book Written from 1856 to 1858*, Cambridge: Cambridge University Press, 1975, pp. 224-225. This work should necessarily be consulted for critical analyses of the often brief and weakly documented arguments of the published *Origin*. The similarity of this definition of "Nature" to that of Buffon's quoted previously should be noted. Darwin had read Buffon's *Natural History* in June 1840, although it is not indicated which essays he read at that time. (Vorzimmer, "The Darwin Reading Notebooks", p. 124.)

44. Darwin's use of this analogy is often present at critical points in his argument, and it functions as an accessible empirical case for reasoning to his larger argument. For example, in arguing that characteristics of species can revert to those of an ancient progenitor, he notes that this "will be most readily understood by looking to our domestic races". Similarly, in arguing that instincts can also be selected and developed, this "possibility, or even probability. . . will be strengthened by briefly considering a few cases under domestication". *The Origin of Species by Means of Natural Selection*, 1st edition, edited by J. W. Burrow, Baltimore: Penguin, 1968, pp. 195, 238. Several examples can be cited. On the importance of this intentionality for Darwin's conception of "perfect" adaptations see Dov Ospovat, "God and Natural Selection: The Darwinian Idea of Design", *Journal of the History of Biology, 13*, 1980, 169-194. While I generally agree with Ospovat, I feel that he fails to take sufficiently into account the possibility of a more naturalistic intention in these early reflections through utilization of the conception of a teleologically acting "nature" that takes over much of the role of divine action.

45. That is, by assuming that this analogy is only a weak one, intended simply to make the reader generally familiar with a fundamentally different process taking place in the natural situation, the appeal to domestic examples at critical junctures as if they were similar in kind and generalizable *ceteribus paribus* to the natural state, loses real force. Modern evolutionary theory, which has dropped all appeal to this analogy in favor of appeal to micro test cases in natural populations, is on firmer ground.

46. This formed part of a providentialist conception of the "economy of nature" with roots in the Stoic tradition that was developed in detail by figures like William

Derham and especially Linnaeus in the eighteenth century. Against this framework Malthus' novel claims would appear untenable without the reemergence of nonmechanical views of nature after 1750. Only by granting an inherent power or force to living nature could the principle be maintained prior to the deeper understanding of energetics which was possible only after the 1840s. For summary remarks on this tradition see Frank N. Egerton, "Changing Concepts of the Balance of Nature", *Quarterly Review of Biology, 48*, 1973, 323-350.

47. Thomas Malthus, *An Essay on the Principle of Population*, edited by Philip Appleman, New York: Norton, 1976, p. 20. Malthus clearly reveals in this passage that he had accepted one feature of preformationist biological theory, associated with the mechanical philosophy, namely, the concept of created "seeds" or "germs" formed primordially by God at creation. He has then, unlike the traditional mechanists, attributed to these a dynamic, nonconserving and creative force.

48. Darwin, "D" Notebook, excised pages, edited by De Beer et al., "Darwin's Notebooks", pp. 162-163.

49. For example, the final paragraph of the *Origin of Species*. Darwin's argument would seem to be that just as the planets do not move in their structured orbits for immediate teleological purposes, but do so only as a consequence of the combined effect of their inertial motions, masses, and the action of the centripetal force exerted by the sun and other planets in the system, similarly organisms are forced into given complex conditions of life and are shaped and adapted to these to the degree permitted by their available variability. The close fitting of structure to function would be no more intentional than the tracking of a precise curvilinear orbit by a given planetary body.

50. Darwin utilized this concept precisely to help clarify the point that he did not intend to personify nature, and he inserts this phrase in the context of the insertion of clarifying remarks on his meaning of "nature". These changes can easily be followed by comparing parallel passages from the first and sixth editions of the *Origin*. Unfortunately, the term 'fittest', as has been frequently pointed out, is thoroughly intention-laden, and more recent biology would have used the term 'relatively fit' in its place. This has given rise to a frequent, but generally unfounded, charge that Darwin is guilty of circular and tautological reasoning. Important clarification on this is to be found in Michael Ruse, "Natural Selection in *The Origin of Species*", *Studies in History and Philosophy of Science, 1*, 1971, 311-351. Ruse in my view fails to take seriously the persistence of the intentional language and arguments in Darwin's discussion which continue through his mature period. I do not feel that Darwin had fully clarified in his own thinking the relationship of the intentional language and nonintentional understandings of natural selection, particularly as this related to a larger teleology of nature. See quotes below, pp. 139-141.

51. Darwin had reread Erasmus Darwin's treatise in March 1839, and it was apparently at this reading that he annotated the family copy, now located in the Cambridge University Library. Alongside the passage quoted (note 25), Darwin marks this passage and writes: "Aided by endless attempts which only few are preserved. Vide Hume's Works". (Quoted by permission of the Syndics of Cambridge University.) The *Reading Notebooks* show that Darwin read both the *Natural History of Religion* and the *Dialogues on Natural Religion* in late September 1839 (see Vorzimmer, "The Darwin Reading Notebooks", p. 122).

52. Letter of Charles Darwin to Asa Gray, May 22, 1860, in Francis Darwin, editor, *The Life and Letters of Charles Darwin*, New York: Appleton, 1888, II, 105. Gray had written three reviews of the *Origin*, and Darwin was instrumental in having these

published in England under the title *Natural Selection Not Inconsistent with Natural Theology* in 1861. On the Gray-Darwin relationship see especially James R. Moore, *Post-Darwinian Controversies*, Cambridge: Cambridge University Press, 1979, pp. 269-284. I owe a deep debt to these excellent discussions for this section of the paper.

53. C. Darwin, *Variation of Plants and Animals Under Domestication*, New York: Appleton, 1897 (first published 1868), II, 427-428.

54. Letter of Darwin to W. Graham, 3 July, 1881, in *Life and Letters*, edited by F. Darwin, I, 285.

55. Letter of Charles Darwin to Thomas Henry Farrer, 28 August, 1881, in Francis Darwin, editor, *More Letters of Charles Darwin*, London: Murray, 1903, I, 394.

56. See Mayr, *The Growth of Biological Thought*, pp. 47-51; Michael Ruse, *The Philosophy of Biology*, London: Hutchinson University Library, 1973, esp. p. 196n. This argument is made polemically throughout Monod's *Chance and Necessity*.

57. This concept was introduced into the literature in Colin Pittendrigh's paper "Adaptation, Natural Selection, and Behavior," in Anne Roe and George G. Simpson, editors, *Behavior and Evolution*, New Haven: Yale University Press, 1958, pp. 391-394, as a substitute for what he considered the discredited notion of teleological purpose. This is embraced by Mayr, *The Growth of Biological Thought*, p. 48.

58. The majority of literature on the question of teleology has concerned itself with such issues as the logical status of functional explanations and intentional language, following upon the attempts of analytic philosophers to translate or reformulate these in terms of nonteleological language. Francisco Ayala has dealt more directly with the question at issue in this paper in his "Teleological Explanation in Evolutionary Biology", *Philosophy of Science*, 37, 1970, 1-15. Ayala defends a critical Aristotelian finalism, while at the same time arguing that this has little bearing on the issue of a more general purposiveness.

59. As a classic statement see Harold F. Blum, *Time's Arrow and Evolution*, Princeton: Princeton University Press, 1951, especially chapter 7. Consequently, few biologists see violations of conservation or thermodynamic principles in evolutionary biology.

60. I am adopting this phrase from Erwin Schrödinger's 1943 lectures published as *What is Life?* Cambridge: Cambridge University Press, 1967 (first published 1944). In a limited respect Schrödinger's program for a physicalistic explanation of these laws was to terminate in the DNA work of Watson and Crick.

61. For example, the debate over selectionist and "punctuated equilibrium" evolutionary mechanisms which has received attention in the popular press is not an argument over the validity of evolutionary theory, the need for a genetic basis of inheritance, or the general framework of modern post-Darwinian biology, all of which is being accepted by both parties.

62. Peter B. and J. S. Medawar, *The Life Science: Current Ideas of Biology*. New York: Harper and Row, 1977, p. 167.

63. Useful, if brief, remarks on this important issue were made in the paper delivered at the Darwin centennial in 1959 by the Protestant theologian Jaroslav Pelikan, "Creation and Causality in the History of Christian Thought", in Sol Tax, editor, *Evolution After Darwin*, Chicago: University of Chicago Press, 1960, III, 29-40. See also the paper by Nicholas Lash in the present volume.

64. *The Confessions of St. Augustine*, translated by John K. Ryan, New York: Doubleday, 1960, Bk. XI, chapter 5, p. 281.

65. See George Gaylord Simpson, *The Meaning of Evolution*, revised edition, New Haven: Yale University Press, 1967, esp. chapters 12-13, for an influential presentation of these issues by a leading evolutionary biologist.

PART TWO

Creation

CREATION ACCORDING TO THE OLD TESTAMENT

Dianne Bergant, C.S.A.,
and Carroll Stuhlmueller, C.P.

Introduction

Creation in biblical thought cannot be separated from Israel's unique appreciation of God and particularly of God's action as savior in their midst. Therefore, as we will conclude in this study, it is more appropriate to focus upon "Creator" than on "creation", upon the person and motivation of the Creator than upon the origin and form of the created world.[1] This emphasis upon Creator brings up another important distinction. The word 'Creator' in the Hebrew language is a participle, literally "the one [who is] creating", and qualifies whatever else is being discussed.[2] God the Creator is *present with* the other action. The Hebrew word 'Creator', therefore, deals primarily with the present moment and its promise for the future, and only secondarily with the past. Because the Creator is acting *now* within the contemporary world, the Bible will not normally attend to *creatio ex nihilo* as a single, unique event of the past. The closest that the Bible comes to the idea of "nothing" is the "chaos" out of which the Creator brings life, good order, balance, and security.[3] This sequence of order out of chaos is how the *New American Bible* reads the opening verses of the Bible:

> In the beginning, when God created the heavens and the earth, the earth was a formless wasteland, and darkness covered the abyss, while a mighty wind swept over the waters. (Gen. 1:1-2)[4]

Another aspect of the Bible, perhaps still more evident than the preceding and certainly pertinent to the question of Yahweh-Creator, is its general *historical* orientation. Religious truths are usually not presented in our Western, more theoretical or logical form of treatises on worship, humanity, morality, and such. The Bible orients its doctrine and explanations in a setting of biographies, epics, and stories.[5] The Torah, or first five books of Moses, are contextualized within a narrative about the patriarchs (Gen. 12-50) and the achievements of Moses (Exodus through Deuteronomy). Other books from Joshua through Second Kings center their message and ideas around great heroes: Joshua, the Judges, Samuel, David, and others. "Salvation history" provides the setting for Israelite thinking on almost every subject except wisdom, found in the sapiential books. In the extensive series of prophetical books (according to the rabbis, Joshua, Judges, 1-2 Samuel, and 1-2 Kings are included in this category) all of post-Mosaic time is evaluated by Israel's obedience and disobedience to the covenant at Sinai and to the covenant with David at Jerusalem. Concern about Yahweh-Creator was always secondary to Israel's preoccupation with Yahweh-Savior. Salvation, moreover, was generally restricted to Israel, "my special possession, dearer to me than all other people" (Exod. 19:5).

Creation, consequently, was subordinate to Yahweh-Creator; Yahweh's role as Creator, moreover, complemented his work as Savior. Yahweh appeared as Savior almost exclusively in the context of saving Israel. We note, therefore, a healthy tension between the primary and the secondary, or according to the rubric in this chapter, between the centripetal or "inside" concern for harmony, identity, and continuity within Israel and this people's history, and the centrifugal or "outside" concern for enrichment, expansion, and growth due to the impact of God's creative power and his redemptive designs for the universe.[6]

Yahweh's covenant with Israel, therefore, was primary and central; this covenant gradually included Yahweh's and Israel's interaction with other nations, their salvation and their doctrine about creation. This latter, secondary, or "outside" momentum toward universal salvation and cosmic creation remained peripheral to major Old Testament books and theologies. It entered only to enrich and expand the covenants with Israel and with David. Eventually, in the New Testament, an area outside the scope of this chapter, the Mosaic covenant was transformed into a "new covenant" with all peoples. Creation then came to be seen as "new", achieved by Jesus' resurrection.

This tension between the centripetal concentration upon Israel's salvation and the centrifugal interaction with other nations and cosmic creation shows up in the two segments of our study of Yahweh-Creator in the Old Testament. Professor Dianne Bergant, C.S.A., investigates the mainline, orthodox theology of the Pentateuch (what we call "centripetal" or "inside"). The more diffuse, more universal, less historically rooted theology of the sapiential literature (what we call the "centrifugal" or "outside" group) is not treated here because of limitations of space. Professor Carroll Stuhlmueller, C.P., attends first to the classical prophets who vigorously challenged Israel's "inside" religious institutions, priesthood and royalty. He then studies the psalms with their wider outreach. While many psalms were composed for the "inside" ceremonial at temple or sanctuary, honoring Yahweh, Savior of Israel, still this rich body of song and poetry flashes signals of a more sweeping concern for Yahweh's creative presence across the cosmos.

To summarize our findings, the belief in Yahweh-Creator in the Bible developed from a tension between a striving for identity as God's chosen people and an outreach toward the foreign nations and even toward the cosmos for enrichment. The Pentateuch and the prophets represent the major internal movements, the psalms move back and forth between internal and external interests, and the sapiential books of Proverbs, Job, and Ecclesiastes are generally outside the main development of Old Testament salvation history and sought their own unity or interrelation of main ideas. For the most part the Old Testament theology of Yahweh-Creator is expressed (1) in the early chapters of Genesis, (2) in occasional passages from the prophets, (3) in those psalms in praise of Yahweh, King and Creator, and (4) in several places within the sapiential literature. While all four are located more on the periphery or outreach of Israelite thinking, the first three kept closer contact with the more internal or central interest in Yahweh as covenant God and Savior of Israel. In this study we concentrate upon the first three areas.

1. Creation in Genesis

Over the centuries the traditions about creation in the Book of Genesis have been understood and explained in many different ways. For instance, medieval exegesis spoke of four senses of Scripture: the historical or literal, where the text means exactly what it says; the allegorical or Christological, where both Hebrew and Christian Scriptures are understood in terms of Christ or the Church; the anthropological or moral, where everything is applied to the individual soul; and the anagogical or eschatological, where the primary focus is fulfillment and the endtime. On the other hand, reckoning that the biblical traditions developed as a people's testimony to belief in their encounter in God, contemporary scholarship has employed the historical-critical method in an attempt to discover the original theology articulated in the traditions about creation. Because most of the writing is narrative in form and the arrangement of these stories suggests a kind of historical sequence, some have erroneously concluded that the bulk of the material is factual. One can presume that Ancient Israel shared many of the cosmological perceptions of neighboring peoples. However, while the framework and content of the accounts about creation may reflect these perceptions, the primary theological focus is not cosmological.

The creation narratives found within Genesis 1 and 2 are examples of Priestly and Yahwistic theology respectively. Each is a product of a different period of Israelite history, a period with its own specific concerns and needs. Although they may both borrow from a common literary storehouse and a common theological tradition, the issues that they are addressing are peculiar to their own situations. While it is true that close attention must be paid to literary expression, it is the theology that is our main concern. As we shall see, the traditions about creation are subordinated to the principal or "inside" theology of covenant, God's covenant with Moses and especially with David.

1.1. GENESIS 2

The account of creation that is found in Genesis 2 is the literary and theological product of a much earlier generation. It reflects the concerns of the united kingdom of David and his successor Solomon. Unlike the Priestly teaching which grew out of the exilic experience of dissolution, this tradition reveals biblical Israel's appropriation of royal ideology and its development as a national entity.

The traditions of the founding of the people Israel describe the gradual integration of a federation of loosely knit tribes. The threats from a common enemy convinced them that centralization was their only hope for survival. Such a position was judged by some as apostasy. Had not their God protected them in the past? Had they lost all hope for continued protection in the future? Besides, royal ideology itself was sacrilegious. In it the sovereign was presumed divine, with power over both heaven and earth. No loyal worshipper of the God of the tribes of Israel could entertain such a view.

The theology that emerged from tenth-century Israel contains a refashioning of royal ideology that both legitimized the monarchy and at the same time held it accountable to the Mosaic law. The creation narrative found within this tradition, like its companion in Genesis 1, is an anthropological and theological rather than a cosmological statement.

The narrative in Genesis 2 consists of various distinct yet related primordial themes. Apparent inconsistencies and the presence of doubts is evidence of this. There are two descriptions of the earth. In the first (2:5-6) it is arid, with only a mist or subterranean spring coming up from the ground, while in the second (2:8-10) it contains a garden with trees and a river that branches out in four directions. Twice the Lord God places the human creature[7] in the garden (2:8, 15); twice the man names the woman (2:23, 3:29); twice he is driven from the garden (3:23, 3:24). Surely this was not meant to provide an explanation of the origin of the world.

The actual account of human creation is told in a manner quite different from that found in Genesis 1. Here the order of the cosmos is not described, the luminaries have not been set in the heavens, and the human creature is brought into a world depicted as a wilderness. Without rain and human toil the earth cannot bring forth vegetation (2:5). This theologian, known as the Yahwist, proposes a terrestrial, not a celestial, focus. "In the day that the Lord God made the earth and the heavens" (2:4b) is followed by an explanation for the barrenness of that earth. The desolation of the land is due to the lack of rain and the absence of a human being to till (serve) the ground. Rain, so necessary for life, is supplied by God alone. It seems, however, that the earth is incomplete without someone to work the land and thereby enable the herb of the field to sprout forth. The verb that expresses this working is ῾ābad, which also means "to serve", and which implies a certain kind of relationship. The one who works the land is working for another. This tiller of the ground is not its servant but is serving it for another. The selection of this word highlights the Yahwist's anthropological understanding. The human serves God by serving the ground.

V. 7 is often called the *locus classicus* of ancient Israelite anthropology. After God caused the mist or spring to come up from the earth and give drink to the ground, God took some of the dust from the ground and formed a human creature as a potter would form an object. In the Yahwist tradition the word used to describe this creation is yāṣar, a verb which denotes the activity of a potter.[8] The human creature is formed or fashioned as a piece of pottery is fashioned. Likewise, as pottery is molded from clay material, so this creature is molded from clay of the ground. ῾āpār (dust) denotes the dry surface of the ground. It also refers to the ground of the grave and thus has the added nuance of commonness or worthlessness.

The relationship between this creature of the ground and the ground itself can be seen from the account of the creative act (being formed), from the material employed therein (dust from the ground), and from the play on words between 'ādām (man or humankind) and adāmâ (ground). The human creature who has been taken from the ground will in turn work the ground that has now been watered by God. Thus the herbs of the field will be able to sprout forth.

This human creature is not yet a nepeš ḥayyâ (a living being). Only by means of a second creative act is this accomplished. It is when God breathes the breath of life into the nostrils that the creature comes alive. This does not imply that the other creatures lack the breath of life. One must remember that these accounts are narrative symbols for anthropological realities and are not to be understood literally. The author has set out to show both the affinity between human beings and other earth-creatures and the special character of the former in respect to the latter. The author chose this way of accomplishing that twofold goal.

In the present narrative no life existed before the human creature, and this creature did not live before receiving the breath of life from God. God is the source of life, but life comes to the earth through human agency. Such a theology has profound implications for the people Israel struggling to incorporate elements of royal ideology into their theological view. It can be seen as a polemic against those who would cast the human ruler in the role of divine benefactor. At the same time it leaves no doubt about the indispensability of human instrumentality.

The reason given for the creation of the animals is that the human creation is not to be alone (2:18). However, these animals are unfit to serve as ʿēzer (helper) for this unique being. The word ʿēzer appears in other biblical passages where the context is usually one of blessing after deliverance, and where the ʿēzer, or mediator of blessing, is God.[9] In this creation account, since no animal was found fit to serve as a source of blessing, God made the woman. The word 'alone' comes from the verb bādad and means "to separate" or "to divide" and, therefore, carries the meaning "incomplete" rather than "by oneself". It is not good that the man remain incomplete, and so God will make someone like this man who will act as a mediator of blessing for him.

It is in the woman that the man finds a helper. She is like the man because since taken from him, she is made of the same substance. Her origin is from him as his origin is from the ground. The play on words ʾîš (man)/ʾiššâ (woman) and ʾadāmâ (ground)/ʾādām (man) illustrates this. Another play on words, found in the Sumerian account of the creation of Ninti "the woman of the rib" and "the woman of life", fails in this Hebrew version. The linguistic similarity that was obvious in the Sumerian, where the roots for 'rib' and 'life' are the same, is absent in the Hebrew where the connection is missing. The Yahwist has retained the link between the woman and the rib, even though the linguistic reason for this link is no longer present.

V.23a is an obvious poetic construction. The word pair 'bone and flesh' is of the type that is characteristically coupled.[10] While this expression probably originated in the ancient idea of the family or kinship, its use in the Hebrew tradition is not limited to this context.[11] The bond is deeper than a merely physical tie. There is a conventional implication.[12] This nuance carries the added connotation of loyalty and responsibility stemming from choice. The very words 'bone' and 'flesh' have psychological as well as physiological meanings. The first has the root meaning of "power", while the second refers to "weakness". When coupled, they embrace the two extremes and everything between. This antithetical construction is a comprehensive expression and is used to speak of a person's total range of interaction with another. The man recognizes that the woman is one with whom he can interact in his totality: he is no longer incomplete.

V. 23b is also poetic but is independent of v. 23a. A careful analysis will show that it too suggests a relationship broader than a purely physiological one. If the tradition intended to describe the actual origin of the woman, then the word for man should be the same as the one used throughout the narrative up to this point. Such is not the case. Instead, the word here is

'îš, a term that is not generic, as is 'ādām, but relational. It has the connotation of male vis-à-vis female, or husband vis-à-vis wife. It did not appear earlier in the account because the man was not yet in an interpersonal
relationship. Only by entering into a relationship of loyalty and responsibility
did he become 'îš to 'iššâ, male to female, husband to wife.

1.2 GENESIS 1

The exile was a devastating experience for Israel both politically and
theologically. Those who survived the trauma faced a period of reconstruction and reinterpretation of covenant and ancient promise. They had to reassert
their belief in their God's power over chaos. One way that this could be
achieved was in their rendition of creation. The tradition that originated in
the Priestly schools of the time was a version of earlier Ancient Near Eastern
myths reshaped in such a way as to portray the God of Israel establishing
the cosmos in an orderly fashion for the elect people Israel. The rekindling
of confidence in this God rather than the reporting of the history of primordial times was the intent of the narrative. Theology and anthropology, not
cosmology, underlie the account.

From a careful look at the tradition we conclude that this is not an account of *creatio ex nihilo* nor is it a summary of some evolutionary process.
The text itself illustrates this. Light appears on the first day (1:3-5). From
whence does it emanate? There are no luminaries until the fourth day
(1:14-19). On the second day God made the firmament to separate the waters
(1:6-8). There has been no mention of the creation of these waters. Instead,
they seem to have been present before the creative activity began (1:2). On
the third day God gathered the waters, and thus the dry land appeared
(1:9-10). This cannot mean that the earth was created then, for the earth had
already been in existence, but void and without form before the light appeared
(1:2). These few examples show that the intent of the account was not cosmological. Its purpose was, rather, to remind the people of God's ability to
bring order out of disorder and to establish the regularity and harmony of the
universe. It also served as a statement of their anthropological understanding.

The structure of the document has carefully been arranged in order to set
forth the Priestly teaching about the restoration of Israel. The sequence of
the acts of creation seems to proceed from what is farthest from God to what
is closest, beginning with chaos and continuing to the appearance of
humankind.[13] The anthropological passage is Genesis 1:26-27. A simple
analysis of the structure of vv. 20-28 enables one to see the place of humanity within the entire plan of creation.

narrative description	v. 20	"and Elohim said . . ."
of creation of water	v. 21	"and Elohim created . . ."
animals	v. 22	"and Elohim blessed . . ."
narrative description	v. 24	"and Elohim said . ."
of creation of land	v. 25	"and Elohim made . . ."
animals		
narrative description	v. 26	"and Elohim said . . ."
of creation of humans	v. 27	"and Elohim created . . ."
	v. 28	"and Elohim blessed . . ."

Vv. 20-28 described three different acts of God:"and God said . . . and blessed." All of these actions are directed toward the *nepeš ḥayyâ* (living beings) of the waters and the birds of the air. Vv. 24-25 pertain in the same way to the *nepeš ḥayyâ* of the earth. One would expect v. 26 to relate the blessing of the land animals, but it does not. The pattern is resumed in vv. 26-28. Whether this pattern was original with the writer or was a reworking of an older creation account, the fact remains that the final form contains the pattern, and it is this form that has been handed down as Priestly teaching.

A significant point to note is the expression used to refer to the entire group of animals. That designation (*nepeš ḥayyâ*) is not applied directly to humans (v. 26). Since the blessing which completes the pattern (vv. 22, 28) is missing after v. 25, the account of the creation of the land animals either has been cut short by the account of human creation or has been extended to include it. Our conclusion is that the pattern has been adjusted in order that humankind be included with the *nepeš ḥayyâ* of the land, thereby indicating the existence of a bond between them. Humans are a kind of beings of the earth.

Further, the *nepeš ḥayyâ* of the waters and the birds are created "according to their kind" (v. 21). The *nepeš ḥayyâ* of the earth, further classified as cattle, creeping things, and living things of the earth, are also made "according to their kind" (v. 25).[14] This phrase is absent in the account of human creation. In its place we read that humankind is created in God's image and according to God's likeness. In keeping with the rest of the interpretation of Genesis 1, this point should also be understood as an anthropological rather than a biological statement. While acknowledging human affinity with the creatures of the earth, the early Israelites recognized that there was a dimension to this earth creature that transcended the purely material.

The blessing of the *nepeš ḥayyâ* of the waters and the birds is "increase and multiply and fill the waters . . . and the earth" (v. 22). The blessing that one might associate with the *nepeš ḥayyâ* of the earth is found in the blessing of the humans along with the commission to "subdue it (the earth) and dominate the fish of the sea and the birds of the heavens and all the

living, the creeping things of the earth" (v. 28). By incorporating the blessing of the land animals with that of the humans the author has linked the
two species. At the same time and in the same verse the commission to subdue and to dominate has bestowed upon the humans the distinction of rulers
over the land and the animals, thereby indicating human superiority.[15]

The use of the technical creation verb *bārā'* is another indication of the
uniqueness of the human creature. The verb denotes extraordinary divine
activity and contains the notion of newness and of awesome or epochal production.[16] The term *'ādām* as used in vv. 26-27 is singular with the collective
meaning of humankind. Since both sexes are required in order to "increase
and multiply and fill the earth", one can conclude that the remainder of the
commission ("subdue it and dominate") was intended for the whole of
humankind, male and female.[17]

Vv. 26-27 also speak of creation in God's image and according to God's
likeness. Immediately after the mention of this image and likeness the commission is stated. It would seem that there is a relationship between the image and likeness and the ability to bring the earth into submission and to
rule over the animals. *ṣelem* is the word used to refer to molten images,
painted pictures, or some kind of physical representation cut out of material.[18]
demût is less concrete in meaning and denotes a likeness or similarity in ex-
terior appearance.[19] It would seem that the Priestly writers found the connotations of *ṣelem* too physical in meaning to express their anthropology,
and so they coupled it with a word having a less concrete nuance. This does
not mean that the image/likeness of God is restricted to a spiritual entity.
Rather, it transcends the physical/spiritual alternative without denying
either.[20] Hebrew thought seldom separated the physical and spiritual but considered the human in its entirety. It is this whole human being that was created
in the image and according to the likeness of God, and both male and female
were so created.

Very little is said about the nature of the image/likeness. More attention
is given to its purpose. Even this is not clearly stated, and there are different
scholarly and doctrinal opinions on the point.[21] Contemporary scholars hold
that the special functions of conquest and domination which are stated in
the text attest to the presence of, but are not to be identified with, the im-
age/likeness of God in humankind.

It appears that Israel, like its neighbors, understood image/likeness in relational terms. The primary significance of this notion was divine relationship,
not the possession of a divine element. The ancient ruler was often spoken
of as the image of the god[22] and was thought to be the direct descendant
of the god. This sovereign functioned in the place of the god as ruler in the
land and over the land. It is in this capacity, as a result of such a relationship, that humankind is understood in royal terms in Genesis 1. Women

and men are not the menial slaves found in the creation myths of other Ancient Near Eastern civilizations. Instead, they are the representatives of God in the realm of creation. They exercise dominion in God's place for they are in the image and according to the likeness of God.

This image/likeness explains not only the human relationship with God but also their relationship with the animals and the land. Though closely associated with the land animals at creation, humans are commissioned to dominate them along with all the other living creatures and to subdue the earth (vv. 26, 28). Though this relationship is one of superiority, there is still limitation or restriction. This is implicit in the idea of image/likeness. They are representatives of, but not identical with, the true sovereign. Women and men must act as regents of the true ruler, not as absolute rulers in their own right. They are responsible for the earth and for the things of the earth.

If the people in exile understood their national humiliation and spiritual desolation as due punishment for their infidelity to the solemn covenant with God and for their prostitution of the land that had been given to them as a gift, then this anthropological interpretation might serve several purposes. It could reinforce Israel's faith in God's ability to bring order and life out of chaos, even a chaos such as they were then experiencing; it could remind them of their fundamental but violated relationships and forgotten responsibilities; and it could instill in them a hope that the creative power of God would once again form them into a faithful people, assuming responsibility for the rest of the created world. These ideas converged in forming the theology of the Priestly account of creation. Creation has been interpreted in the light of God's covenant with Israel and the promise of land; thus creation theology is found close to the heart of Israel's religion.

It is clear from this brief look at the creation traditions of biblical Israel that the sacred authors were well acquainted with the myths of the Ancient Near Eastern world. Imbued with faith in their own God and occupied with national as well as theological matters, they refashioned these myths so as to address their own particular concerns. Political, sociological, and cosmological references are discernible, but they serve the theological interests of the covenant between God and Israel and should be appreciated as such.

2. Creation in Prophecy and Psalms

2.1 PROPHECY AND CREATION

We limit our discussion to the classical prophets with books to their name. This extraordinary series of individuals can be defined not only by their books (generally edited by disciples; cf. Jer. 36:32) but also by shared personal characteristics. We offer this descriptive definition:

individuals thoroughly members of their Israelite community and institutions, closely in touch with its earliest and most basic intuitions, personally and even mystically united with Yahweh, the God who chose Israel as "my special possession dearer to me than all other people" (Exod. 19:5), eloquent in expressing the divine ideals for the people, so that as a result they challenged Israel from its earliest ideals, purified the institutions, and eventually, expanded the mission of Israel to heroic dimensions.[23]

Prophecy enlarged Israel's mission to include Yahweh's creating for Israel "new heavens and a new earth" (Isa. 65:17).

Even within classical prophecy we must restrict ourselves further by investigating only one of Israel's two major prophetic traditions, that of the north; the southern tradition of Jerusalem will enter our discussion later, but only minimally, with the psalms. The north was the site of Israel's principal settlement in the land under Moses' aide and successor, Joshua ben Nun (Josh. 1:1; 3:7; 4:14).[24]

Amos, first in the long series of classical prophets and first in our study, remains a typical classical prophet and at the same time an ambiguous individual. Amos was *typical* in that he loyally challenged Israel's institutions, and in doing so he offered some appreciation of Yahweh as Creator and universal Savior. Ambiguity shows up in the text and personality of this prophet. Although from the village of Tekoa, southeast of Jerusalem (Amos 1:1), he actively prophesized in northern cities and sanctuaries. He accepted Israel's institutions of prophet and nazirite (2:11), but he also counteracted by his denial: "I myself am *no prophet* nor a member of any prophetic band", and then he quickly reverses himself, "The Lord said to me, 'Go, *prophesy* to my people Israel' " (7:14-15).[25] Amos refused to be categorized within an institution, legitimate but corrupt; he would develop his own, new form of prophesying.

Amos, moreover, interacted with the major internal tradition of the exodus (2:10; 3:1; 9:7), while arriving at conclusions befitting an "outsider". After quoting the stereotyped liturgical phrase "I brought [you] up from the land of Egypt", he drew unexpected conclusions. While the people presumed that the exodus always led to new blessings, Amos reasoned from exodus to being "crushed into the ground and fleeing naked" (2:13, 16) and to being "punished for all your crimes" (3:2). In the third occurrence he neutralized the traditional exodus motif as a special grace, unique to Israel:

> Are you not like the Ethiopians to me,
>   children of Israel, says the Lord?
> Did I not bring the Israelites from the land of Egypt
>   as I brought the Philistines from Caphtor
>   and the Arameans from Kir? (9:7)

Amos is reducing Israel's exodus to a common experience shared with other nations: all peoples have had their migrations! Sarcastically, Amos is asking the people Israel, "Why do you preem yourself as superior to other peoples because of your exodus?" In extending Israel's theology of redemption to the world, Amos was paving the way for the entire world being understood as Yahweh's creation.

This question of Amos in 9:7 – "Are you not like the Ethiopians, Philistines and Arameans to me, children of Israel?" – was so radical that it was originally expunged from the collection of the prophet's sermons and then was reinstated in an appendix of "one-liners" (9:7, 8, 9, 10) before the epilog or proverbial happy conclusion was added still later (9:11-15). Within the peripheral section, the appendix, never integrated with Amos' longer, more developed sermons, the prophet announced this universal outreach for biblical religion.[26]

Another example of outreach beyond Israel, this time related still more closely to the topic of creation, is once again located within an editorial addition. Amos has just enunciated a series of indictments or disciplinary punishments from God, each with the refrain "Yet you returned not to me". He then reached the verdict of "Guilty!"

> So now I will deal with you in my own way, O Israel!
> . . . Prepare to meet your God! (4:12)

The editor then added a refrain from an ancient hymn.[27] The style is typically hymnlike with the use of participles (always a continuous action, irrespective of time) to draw attention to God's creative action:

> [Yahweh!] The one forming the mountains and
>   creating [bōrē'] the wind,
>   declaring to each one their thoughts,
> Turning darkness into dawn,
>   striding upon the heights of the earth;
> The Lord, the God of hosts, by name. (4:13)

This hymnlike fragment even includes the word bara' – to create,[28] perhaps for the first time in recorded biblical tradition. The poetry not only evokes the haunting memories of mountains and morning horizons, but it interweaves Canaanite idioms of the gods "striding upon the heights".[29] The God who chose Israel and "favored [them] more than all the families of the earth" (2:1-2) is summoning Israel to think about all these other lands of the earth. Creation, like a flash of lightning, momentarily illumines the universe. The clouds close in at once. Amos' sermons return to a "lament [over] the house of Israel", "the remnant of Joseph" (5:1, 15). Creation remains on the "outside". Creation is introduced to expand the scope of Yahweh's redemptive action and to praise Yahweh in domesticated forms of Canaanite hymnology.

As we turn to a more indigenous northern tradition in the prophecies of Hosea and Jeremiah, creation and its opposite, chaos, are still more closely tied to Israel's religion, particularly to the people's fidelity or infidelity to the Mosaic covenant. Israel's obedience renews the universe; Israel's disobedience destroys it. We quote two texts from each prophet, to see the positive and negative side of covenant/creation. The first is from Hosea:

I will make a covenant for them [i.e., Israel] on that day,
  with the beasts of the field,
With the birds of the air. (Hos. 2:20)

Because "the Lord has a grievance against" Israel for violating the decalogue[30] by "false swearing, lying, murder, stealing and adultery" (4:1-2), creation is undone:

Therefore, the land mourns,
  and everything that dwells in it languishes:
The beasts of the field,
  the birds of the air,
  and even the fish of the sea perish. (4:3)

This same extension of the covenant, positively and negatively, to the earth shows up still more persistently a century later in the longer prophecy of Jeremiah. The "new convenant" (Jer. 31:31-34) reaches outward:

sun to light the day,
moon and stars to light the night,
the sea till its waves roar,

with the refrain similar to lines already quoted from Amos: "whose name is Lord of hosts" (Jer. 31:35). Jeremiah, moreover, is to be credited with the earliest recorded direct statement of Yahweh's creation of the universe:[31]

Thus says the Lord of hosts, the God of Israel. It was I who made the earth, and man, woman and beast on the face of the earth, with my outstretched arm. (27: 5a)

We note how Jeremiah associates creation with the Lord's "outstretched arm", normally extended to redeem Israel, especially in the context of the exodus (cf. Deut. 4:34). The "outside" notion of creation (more precisely, of creation's undoing) is being drawn into the "inside" covenant theology and linked with the historical moment of Israel's sin and exile. Jeremiah concludes the passage:

I can give them to whomever I think fit. Now I have given all these lands into the hand of Nebuchadnezzar, king of Babylon. (27:5b-6)

Jeremiah is inferring, What God created and then reduced to chaos can be re-created again. He announces the time of the new creation when Nebuchadnezzar's kingdom will collapse (27:7) after Israel's "seventy years" in exile (25:11-12; 29:10; 28:1).

When the exile was nearing its end, another prophet appeared in the tradition of Deuteronomy, Hosea, and Jeremiah. The prophet's name is unknown. The poetry was added to the scroll of Isaiah and so is called Second or Deutero-Isaiah (chapters. 40-55). Advised by God to "speak tenderly to Jerusalem [because] her service [as an exile] is at an end", Second Isaiah hears heavenly voices crying out for the creation of "the way of the Lord" in the wasteland, with valleys filled in and mountains leveled so that "the glory of the Lord" in Israel's return to the re-created promised land "be revealed [to] all humankind" (Isa. 40:1-5).

Second Isaiah's reference to Yahweh's re-creating the earth (cf. 40:25-26) are explicitly linked with Israel's redemption. The classic vocabulary for creation (i.e., *bārā', yāṣar, nāṭāh, rāqa', 'āśah*)[32] occurs repeatedly, generally to embellish a poem on Israel's redemption, usually within the introduction or conclusion:

> But now, thus says the Lord,
>   creating you, O Jacob, and forming you, O Israel;
> Fear not, for I redeem you;
>   I call you by name; you are mine. (43:1)

> Everyone who is called by my name,
>   whom I create for my glory,
>   I form and I make. (43:7)

Second Isaiah draws upon the Canaanite creation-myth of Baal's struggling against the chaotic gods of the sea and ocean currents to announce Yahweh's drying up the Red Sea so that the redeemed people Israel may pass over to freedom (51:9-10).[33] The "Red Sea" in this case is the barrier of the Arabian desert, separating Israel from its promised land; the military forces barring the way are those of Babylon instead of Egypt.

Finally, within the Songs of the Suffering Servant (43:1-7; 49:10-7; 50:4-9a; 52:13-53:12) when all seemed lost:

> I thought I had toiled in vain and for nothing, uselessly spent my strength (49:4),

Second Isaiah draws upon two extraordinary insights, up till now "outside" or peripheral to Israel, the creation of the universe and the salvation of the nations:[34]

> Thus says God, the Lord,
>   creating the heavens and stretching them out,
>   spreading out the earth with its crops, . . .

I, the Lord, call you [Israel] for the victory of
   my justice. . . .
I form you, . . .
   a covenant of the people,
   a light for the nations. (42:5-6)

Universal salvation is still more explicit in the second Servant Song (49:6).[35]

In the golden poetry of Second Isaiah the "outside" theologies of cosmic creation and world redemption blend with the "inside" theology of the covenant and the exodus, to transform the latter, not to destroy or submerge it. For this prophet covenant theology provided the line of continuity; creation theology enriched this line and so made it ever more worthy of survival.

Prophecy continued its evolution during the postexilic period. Under God's inspiration the "inside", or institutional, theology of covenant and temple occasionally reached outward, to the peripheral idea of Yahweh-Creator, usually in times of persecution and chaos. At such moments survival was possible only by Yahweh's creating "new heavens and a new earth" (Isa. 65:17) and inviting all "the families of the earth" "to worship the King [and Creator], the Lord of hosts, and to celebrate the feast of Booths [amidst creative abundance]" (Zech. 4:16-17; cf. vv. 6-9). In the most dreadful moment of all, the persecution by Antiochus IV Epiphanes of 167-164 B.C., the "inside" theology survived only by God's most extraordinary creative intervention, raising the persecuted saints back to life (Dan. 7:13-18, 23-27; 12:1-3). Thus the pharisaic author of *Second Maccabees* pictures the mother of seven sons as she encouraged each of them to martyrdom:

> I beg you, child, to look at the heavens and the earth and see all that is in them; then you will know that God did not make them out of existing things; and in the same way the human race came into existence. Do not be afraid of this executioner, but be worthy of your brothers and accept death, so that in the time of mercy I may receive you again with them. (2 Macc. 7:28-29)

The mother is not necessarily relying on a common doctrine of *creatio ex nihilo* (up till now unheard of in the Bible), but rather her words ought to be interpreted of creation out of chaos.[36] She is insisting that the child's bones and ashes can be revived on the day of resurrection.

2.2. THE PSALMS AND CREATION

As we turn from prophecy to the psalms, the interaction of Israel's "inside" theology of Yahweh-Savior with the peripheral theology of Yahweh-Creator continues its classic tension, but in different ways. It is helpful to compare the psalms with Israel's earliest poetry and creeds as found in Gen.

49: 2-27; Exod. 15: 1-18; Deut. 26: 1-11; 32:1-43; Judg. 5:2-31.[37] In these latter we find very little, if any, explicit attention given to Yahweh as King and Creator. The lists of major feastdays, moreover, in Exod. 23:14-17; 34:18-24; Lev. 23; and Deut. 16:1-17, center upon Yahweh's intervention as redeemer in Israel's early existence.[38] Although these redemptive events are associated with Canaanite harvest festivals, little or no trace is found of Canaanite emphasis upon creation and fertility in these biblical accounts.

Turning to some of the earliest poetry in the psalter—like Pss. 8; 19:2-7; 29; 89:6-19; 104—we find the emphasis decidedly shifting from "Yahweh-Savior" to "Yahweh-Creator". While the Pentateuch focuses upon "Savior", these early psalms put more stress upon "Creator".[39] We are not following the position of Sigmund Mowinckel,[40] John Eaton,[41] and others who posit a preexilic feast honoring Yahweh, King and Creator, identifiable with the feasts of New Years or Tabernacles. Israel's earliest psalms, like the architecture for her temple (1 Kgs. 5:15-32), and in fact almost all her cultural achievements, were absorbed and adapted from the native, highly civilized Canaanite. Even though the "inside" theology highlighted Yahweh as Israel's savior and even supported a crusade against Canaanite city-states and their petty kings as well as against Canaanite creation and fertility rites, nonetheless, creation theology degenerated when Canaanite fertility rites spread rapidly and popularly among the people at large. It even found its way into the official worship which we have been calling the "inside", orthodox form of Mosaic covenant religion (cf. Ezek. 8). Popular religiosity gravitated toward creation rather than toward the more ancient, austere desert spirituality of Moses and Joshua (Exod. 32; Num. 25; Jer. 3:2). Its extremes were combatted by prophets like Elijah (1 Kgs. 18) and Hosea (chaps. 1-3).

The early creation psalms, along with myths and folklore in the Yahwist or "J" traditions of the Pentateuch (Gen. 2-3; 6:1-4; 11:1-9), contain the most visible expressions of polytheism of any section of the Bible. This fact corroborates its normally peripheral, "outside" status. Such polytheistic expressions are not to be found in Israel's early creeds (Gen. 49: 2-27; Deut. 26:1-11). Invocation of or allusion to lesser, tutelary gods/goddesses is found in psalm passages dealing with creation:

> You have made humankind little less than the gods,
>   and crowned this one with glory and honor. (Ps. 8:6)
> The sun comes forth like the groom from the bridal chamber
>   and like a giant joyfully runs his course.
> From one end of the heavens he comes forth,
>   and his course is to their other end;
>   nothing escapes his heat. (Ps. 19:5b-7)
> Give to the Lord, you children of the gods,
>   Give to the Lord glory and praise. (Ps. 29:1)

The heavens proclaim your wonders, O Lord,
   and your faithfulness, in the assembly of the holy ones.
For who in the skies can rank with the Lord?
   Who is like the Lord among the children of gods? (Ps. 89: 6-7)

The phrases 'children of gods' and 'holy ones' evoke the religious language and theology of the Canaanites and refer to an assembly of lesser gods and goddesses around the main deity (cf. Ps. 2:4; 8:5; 11:4; 82; 104:1-4; Exod. 19:11; 1 Kgs. 2:10-23).[42] Such biblical polytheism, of course, never degenerated into the complex and (to us) weird system of Canaanite gods and goddesses. The Bible subjects all other gods to Yahweh, or else it allocates them to foreign nations as in Deuteronomy:

When you look up to the heavens and behold the sun or the moon or any other star among the heavenly hosts, do not be led astray into adoring them and serving them. These the Lord, your God, has let fall to the lot of all other nations under the heavens, but you he has taken and led out of that iron foundry, Egypt, that you might be his very own people. (Deut. 4:19-20; cf. 29:25; 32:8-9)[43]

This is a surprising statement from Deuteronomy, a book which gave to Israel its clarion call of monotheism:

Hear, O Israel! The Lord is our God, the Lord alone. (Deut. 6:4)

In Deuteronomy the references to polytheism are incidental, those to monotheism, certainly more central. Together these citations from Deuteronomy and the psalms represent the two sides of biblical religion, the mainline theology of salvation and its strong monotheism as well as the popular religiosity of the masses who favored creation and who enhanced the mysterious forces of fertility with deification.

Writers representing the orthodox, or "inside", theology found it necessary to correct the moderately polytheistic language of the early psalms. When Ps. 96 was composed in the postexilic age, as an anthology of bits and pieces from other sources,[44] it quoted the opening verses of Ps. 29 but with a discreet change:

Give to the Lord, *you families of nations*, give to the Lord glory and praise. (Ps. 96:7)

"Children of gods" in Ps. 29 has become "families of nations"! The Greek Septuagint went a step further in its attempt to cleanse and strengthen the wording of the Bible. In Ps. 8:6 the verse "little less than the gods" is translated into the Greek equivalent of "for a little while less than the angels". The Greek, therefore, reduces "gods" to the status of "angels", who were being accepted within Israel's postexilic theology. It also introduces a note of messianic expectation. In just "a little while" the world and particularly Israel's segment of it will be re-created.

While the northern area of Israel stressed the more ancient forms of biblical religion, with the Mosaic or desert traditions as "inside", and with Canaanite agricultural fertility rites as "outside", the southern area at Jerusalem had its own brand of "polytheism" and creation theology. Creation, as pointed out already, generally involved a battle with sea monsters, considered to be gods and goddesses (Ps. 89:10-13; Isa. 51:9-10). Jerusalem attached Canaanite religious and cultural ideas to its temple. The temple was considered the center of the universe (Ps. 48; Ezek. 38:12), the bulwark of support, security, and good order against the sea monsters (Ps. 46: 2-4, 9-11; Ps 93), the source of all life, symbolized by a sacred river or spring (Ps. 46:5-7; Ezek. 47).[45] An extraordinary example occurs in Ps. 66, adroitly combining exodus and settlement, Canaanite battles against sea monsters, national and personal trials, restoration of new life, holocausts of total adoration, belief in Yahweh's bonded love or *ḥesed*, which is the very last word in the psalm. Such richness of insight, combining creation theology with salvation theology, was integrated within this single, complex, yet well-structured psalm.[46]

Another similar example occurs in Ps. 68 which I think migrated from the northern shrine at Mount Tabor to the central Jerusalem temple.[47] This early psalm does not explicitly acclaim Yahweh as King, Creator, and Ruler of the universe, but these titles are implied by use of Canaanite words and images:

the earth quaked; it rained from heaven at the presence of God.
You have ascended on high, taken captives
    [combining Yahweh's heavenly sanctuary
    with the earthly one at Jerusalem]
I will fetch them [the defeated Israelites] from the
    depths of the sea.
Rebuke the wild beasts of the reeds.

Creation, we notice, is not seen as the initial act of forming the universe but as continuous, sustaining power, struggling against sea monsters. From reading the entire Ps. 68 we are impressed by its "inside" theology which remains staunchly loyal to the Mosaic covenant (vv. 2-11) and to the Davidic dynasty (vv. 16-19).

We turn to a series of late, postexilic psalms, namely, Pss. 96-98 and possibly Ps. 99. In these passages Yahweh is acclaimed explicitly and persistently as Cosmic King and Creator. These psalms tend to be anthological in style, quoting phrases or even full lines from other, earlier sources or incorporating ideas more at home elsewhere or from a common reservoir of liturgical phrases, as in the case of Ps. 96.[48] We also note that the key acclamation "The Lord is King" reads in the Hebrew *Yahweh mālak* (Pss. 93:1; 96:10; 97:1; 99:1). The shout of enthronement, *Yahweh mālak*, moreover, reverses the normal word order of Hebrew grammar, which generally places the verb first, then the subject (cf. 2 Sam. 15:10; 1 Kgs. 1:11). The emphasis is decidedly upon the person of Yahweh and only secondarily upon the enthronement of Yahweh as King and Creator. The phrase, therefore, should read "It is Yahweh [and no other] who rules as King".[49] Once more, the more ancient, "inside" theology of the Mosaic covenant is the line of continuity, absorbing and controlling the "outside", more Canaanite, forms of popular religiosity.

These psalms also emphasize the Lord's justice, as in Pss. 96: 13 and 99:9, where "he comes to judge the earth", with the Hebrew word *shāphaṭ*, meaning to fulfill "justly" the redemptive promises for Israel, with repercussions across the earth. Such is the way that Yahweh acts as King and Creator. The Mosaic covenant held to Yahweh as a personal deity, always alive. Yahweh did not die and rise each year with the agricultural seasons and so did not stand in need of a dramatic return to life and a new enthronement as King.

In the same postexilic period, which saw a marked evolution in understanding Yahweh as King and Creator, two other closely related developments show up at the end of the prophetic movement. One of these we call eschatology, Israel's expectation of a final, definitive victory on a cosmic scale; the other we recognize as a clear belief in bodily resurrection. The first proclaims the re-creation of the universe; the second, the resuscitation of each individual just person. We already noted this development in Daniel and Second Maccabees.

Conclusion

At this point we refer back to Dianne Bergant's investigation into the theology of creation in Genesis 1 and 2. The first account of creation in Genesis 1 was attributed to the Priestly tradition; the second account in Genesis 2, to the Yahwist tradition. Each drew upon ancient myths, not to repeat the myth or to copy the mythological religion but rather to offer insights into the central, "inside" theological synthesis that Yahweh chose Israel and remained faithful to the divine covenant with Israel. The Priestly account in Genesis 1 reached its final form during the exile, or immediately afterward, and served to strengthen the faith of Israel in the re-creation of their land, thoroughly destroyed and reduced to chaos by the Babylonian conquerors in 587 B.C. The Yahwist account of creation in Genesis 2 reached its final form much earlier and was intended to support and direct the concept of royalty within Israel. Israel's king was never to be considered divinely equal to Yahweh, but the king was God's instrument for securing unity, stability, and fertility in the Land and among its people. The king symbolized God's continuous presence as Creator and preserver of life.

Turning to prophecy and the psalms, we arrive at these conclusions about Yahweh as Creator. The person of Yahweh as *Creator*, rather than the material object of creation, is central. Yahweh's personal concern is focused upon the chosen people Israel who were saved from slavery and extinction. These special, redemptive moments, liturgically commemorated, produced Israel's salvation history. As this history involved foreign nations, Yahweh is also appreciated as re-creator of Israel's everexpanding world. This development to re-creator of the cosmos is clearly visible in Isa. 40-55. In its final development Yahweh-Creator is acclaimed eschatologically, that is, as transforming the cosmos in the final age and as bringing the just person back to life in the resurrection.

From the beginning Israel's liturgy centered upon salvation history. Yet, faced with advanced Canaanite culture, Israel adopted Canaanite religious architecture and also absorbed aspects of creation-theology from the Canaanites, particularly in popular religiosity but also within sanctuary worship.

Another type of conclusion from this study of prophecy and psalms is that creation is *not* presented as a cosmological account of the origins of the universe, nor is creation treated for its own sake, independent of faith or religious confession. Prophecy and psalms speak of Creator rather than creation and, therefore, refer to the created world, like the land of Israel, only as a means to fulfill Yahweh's revealed promises of redemption to a personally chosen people. Only when this fulfillment was seen to evolve across a cosmic panorama, when a wholly new world had to be created out of total chaos, did Israel's official "inside" theology of redemption absorb what had long existed on the "outside" especially in popular religiosity, in the fascination with fertility, healing, and afterlife. At this final moment the line of continuity was not simply enriched, but the "outside" influence of Yahweh-Creator enabled the people Israel to persevere through the crisis of severe persecution, as we see in Daniel and Second Maccabees.

Throughout its history, then, creation theology focused first of all upon Yahweh, the God of Israel, not upon the material universe. It enhanced and helped to sustain the basic theology of Israel as God's chosen people. Creation-theology, which developed more on the "outside", enabled the "inside" theology of the covenant to survive severe testing and to reach outward to include the salvation of all the world.

NOTES

1. Cl. Westermann, "Die Reden von Schöpfer und Schöpfung im Alten Testament", *Das Ferne und Nahe Wort*, BZAW, 105; Festschrift L. Rost; Berlin, 1967, pp. 238-244. Zachary Hayes, O.F.M., *What Are They Saying about Creation?* New York: Paulist, 1980.

2. C. Stuhlmueller, "The Participle and Dt-Is' Theology of Creative Redemption", in *Creative Redemption in Deutero-Isaiah*, Rome: Biblical Institute Press, 1970, pp. 48-56.

3. B. W. Anderson, *Creation Versus Chaos. The Reinterpretation of Mythical Symbolism in the Bible*, New York: Association Press, 1967.

4. The translation of *The Torah. A New Translation of the Holy Scriptures according to the Masoretic Text*, Philadelphia: Jewish Publication Society, 1962, reads similarly: "When God began to create the heaven and the earth—the earth being unformed and void, with darkness over the surface of the deep and a wind from God sweeping over the water—God said, 'Let there be light' "

5. Gene M. Tucker, *Form Criticism of the Old Testament*, Philadelphia: Fortress Press, 1971. See chapter two and the explanation of Myths and Folktales, Saga, History, Legend and Novelette.

6. For the interaction of the "inside", or central theology of covenant within Israel, and the "outside", or peripheral theology of universal salvation, see Donald Senior and Carroll Stuhlmueller, *Biblical Foundations for Mission*, Maryknoll, NY: Orbis Books, 1983, pp. 15-32; David L. Petersen, *The Roles of Israel's Prophets*, Sheffield: Journal for the Study of the Old Testament, Supplement Series, 17, 1981, pp. 111-112, fn. 23.

7. Phyllis Trible, *God and the Rhetoric of Sexuality*, Philadelphia: Fortress Press, 1978, p. 80, contends that sexual differentiation did not appear until the creation of the woman.

8. Cf. Is. 29:16; 41:25; 43:1; 43:7; 45:9; 45:18; Jer. 18:4; 18:6.

9. Cf. Ex. 18:4; Dt. 33:7; 33:26; 33:29; Is. 30:5; Ezek. 12:14; Pss. 20:3; 33:20; 70:6; 115:9; 115:11; 121:1; 121:2; 124:8; 146:5.

10. Stanley Gevirtz, *Patterns in Early Poetry of Israel*, Chicago: University of Chicago Press, 1963, pp. 140-161.

11. *Cf.* Gen. 29:14; Jg. 9:2; 2 Sam. 5:1; 19:13.

12. The following ideas are found in Walter Brueggemann, "Of the Same Flesh and Bone (Gn 2, 23a)," *Catholic Biblical Quarterly*, *32*, 1970, 532-542.

13. Werner Schmidt, *Die Schöpfungsgeschichte der Priesterschrift*, Neukirchener-Vlyun: Neukirchener Verlag, 1964, p. 188.

14. The exact meaning of this phrase is not clear from the text. Perhaps it has to do with creation of a species rather than an individual member of the species.

15. Schmidt, *Die Schöpfungsgeschichte*, p. 187.

16. Ludwig Köhler, *Old Testament Theology*, 3rd revised edition, London: Lutterworth Press, 1953, pp. 136, 144.

17. Two excellent studies on this point are Phyllis Trible, *God and the Rhetoric of Sexuality*, and Phyllis A. Bird, " 'Man and Female He Created Them': Gen 1: 27b in the Context of the Priestly Account of Creation", *Harvard Theological Review*, 74, 1981, 129-159.

18. Francis Brown, Samuel R. Driver, and Charles A. Briggs, editors, *A Hebrew and English Lexicon of the Old Testament*, Oxford: Clarendon Press, 1907, pp. 853f.

19. Ibid., p. 198.

20. G. von Rad, "*eikōn*, D. The Divine Likeness in the OT", *Theological Dictionary of the New Testament*, edited by Gerhard Kittel, translated by Jeffrey Bromiley, Grand Rapids, MI: Eerdmans, 1967, vol. 2, p, 391.

21. They include the appearance of both sexes, the human's ability to stand upright, to think and will and love, to create, etc.

22. Aage Bentzen, *King and Messiah*, London: Lutterworth Press, 1955, p. 43.

23. For a more extensive discussion see C. Stuhlmueller, *Thirsting for the Lord*, New York: Image Doubleday, 1979, chapters 2-7, especially p. 36.

24. For the background of these types of prophetic movement see Robert R. Wilson, *Prophecy and Society in Ancient Israel*, Philadelphia: Fortress, 1980, pp. 135-295; Alan W. Jenks, *The Eloist and North Israelite Traditions*, SBL Monograph Series, Chico, CA: Scholars Press, 1977.

25. The *New American Bible* translates in the past tense: "I was no prophet, nor have I belonged to a company of prophets"; yet in Zech. 13:5 it uses the present tense in an almost identical phrase: "I am no prophet, I am a tiller of the soil." The new translation of the Jewish Publication Society uses the present tense.

26. H. W. Wolff, *Joel and Amos*, Hermeneia Series, Philadelphia: Fortress, 1977, pp. 347-349. The book of Amos is divided stylistically into these major sections: oracles, 1:3–2:16; speeches, chaps. 3–5; woe discourses, 5:7–6:14; visions, 7:1–8.3; three longer additions of different stylistic pattern, 7:10-17; 8:4-14; 9:1-6; the "one-liners", 9:7-10; and the "happy conclusion" of a much later date, 9:11-15.

27. Cf. James L. Crenshaw, *Hymnic Affirmation of Divine Justice*, SBL Dissertation Series, 24, Chico, CA: Scholars Press, 1975.

28. Cf. Bergman, Ringgren, Bernhardt, Botterweck, "bara'", *Theological Dictionary of the Old Testament*, edited by G.J. Botterweck and H. Ringgren, revised edition, Grand Rapids, MI: Eerdmans, 1975, vol. 2, pp. 242-249.

29. Cf. Wolff, *Joel and Amos*, 224.

30. Cf. R. V. Bergren, *The Prophets and the Laws*, Cincinnati: Hebrew Union College, 1974.

31. According to W. Foerster, "ktizo", *Theologisches Wörterbuch zum Neuen Testament*, vol 2, p. 1005, Jer. 27:5-6: "ist zum ersten Mal die absolute Geschichtsmächtigkeit auf sein Schöpfersein zurückgeführt". Although Gen. 1:1–2:4a introduces the Torah and the "Priestly Tradition" within it and is influenced by early traditions, nonetheless its present form is recognized as late, as is the case generally with the "Priestly Tradition". Its position in the Bible is due to late editing.

32. Cf. C. Stuhlmueller, *Creative Redemption in Deutero-Isaiah*, chapter 9, "Creation Vocabulary in the Book of Consolation".

33. Ibid., pp. 82-94.

34. It is the position of this study that the references to creation in Genesis are clear only at the beginning of the book (chapter 1-2), elsewhere incidental, like Melchizedek's blessing upon Abram (Gen. 14:19-20). The explicit statement in chapter 1 reached its final, edited form only in the postexilic period, ca. 450-400 B.C.

35. For the development of Second Isaiah's thought and particularly for the emergence of the new creation within the theology of Israel's redemption, I refer to other works of mine, particularly, "Deutero-Isaiah: Major Transitions in the Prophet's Theology and in Contemporary Scholarship", *Catholic Biblical Quarterly 42*, January 1980, 1-29; again, "The Painful Costs of Great Hopes: The Witness of Isaiah 40-55", in *Sin, Salvation and the Spirit*, edited by Daniel J. Durken, Collegeville, MN: Liturgical Press, pp. 146-162.

36. See footnote 4 and the accompanying text.

37. Cf. Frank Moore Cross, Jr., and David Noel Freedman, *Studies in Ancient Yahwistic Poetry*, SBL Dissertation Series, 21, Chico, CA: Scholars Press, 1975.

38. J. Van Goudoever, *Biblical Calendars*, 2nd edition, Leiden: Brill, 1961; E. Otto and T. Schramm, *Festival and Joy*, Biblical Encounters Series, Nashville: Abingdon, 1980.

39. For a longer explanation see the commentaries on Pss. 93, 96-99, along with

commentaries on Pss. 8, 19, 29, in C. Stuhlmueller, *Psalms I-II*, Wilmington, DE: Michael Glazier, 1983.

40. S. Mowinckel, *The Psalms in Israel's Worship*, Nashville: Abingdon, 1967, esp. chapter 5.

41. John Eaton, *Vision in Worship: The Relation of Prophecy and Liturgy in the Old Testament*, London: SPCK, 1981; "The Psalms and Israelite Worship", *Tradition and Interpretation*, edited by G. W. Anderson, Oxford: 1979, pp. 238-273.

42. Cf. H. W. Robinson, "The Council of Yahweh", *Journal of Theological Studies*, 45, 1944, 151-157; F.M.Cross, "The Council of Yahweh in Second Isaiah", *Journal of Near Eastern Studies*, 12, 1953, 274-278.

43. Cf. P. Buis et J. Leclercq, *Le Deutéronome*, Sources Bibliques, Paris: Gabalda, 1963, pp. 57-61.

44. Cf. C. Stuhlmueller, *Psalms II*, p. 87.

45. Cf. *The Bible Today*, n. 97, October 1978, for five articles on Jerusalem; F. S. Frick, *The City in Ancient Israel*, Chico, CA: Scholars Press, 1977; R. A. F. MacKenzie, "The City and Israelite Religion", *Catholic Biblical Quarterly*, 25, January 1963, 60-70; J. J. M. Roberts, "The Davidic Origin of the Zion Tradition", *Journal of Biblical Literature*, 92, September 1973, 329-344; R. deVaux, "Jerusalem and the Prophets", *Interpreting the Prophetic Tradition*, edited by H. M. Orlinsky, New York: Ktav, 1969, pp. 275-300; R. J. Sklba, *The Faithful City*, Chicago: Franciscan Herald Press, 1976.

46. Cf. L. Jacquet, *Les psaumes et le coeur de l'homme*, Bruxelles: Duculot, 1977, 2nd ed., pp. 319-329.

47. J. Gray, "A Cantata of the Autumn Festival", *Journal of Semitic Studies*, 22, Spring 1977, 2-26.

48. In Ps. 96, v. 1 is taken from Isa. 42:10; v. 2 is found also in Isa. 40:9; 52:7; v. 4, from Pss. 48:2; 95:3; vv. 7-9, from Ps. 29:2-3; v. 10a, from Ps. 93:1; v. 10b, from Ps. 9:9b; v. 11a, from Ps. 97:1; v. 11b, from Ps. 98:7a; and v. 13, from Pss. 9:9a and 98:9.

49. Cf. E. Lipiński, *La royauté de Yahwé dans la poésie et le culte de l'ancien Israël*, Brussel: Paleis der Academiën, 1965, chapter 5.

THE DOCTRINE OF CREATION FROM NOTHING

David Kelsey

Most Christian communities affirm the creation of the world by God from nothing (see appendix). As we shall see, while Christians have always affirmed that the world was created, they have not always affirmed that it is God's creation *ex nihilo*. What is being said when the doctrine of *creatio ex nihilo* is affirmed? In particular, what is the force of the phrase *ex nihilo*? In order to get at this topic, it will be useful to ask two questions of the doctrine. (1) What is its scope? That is, in affirming the doctrine what sorts of things does one express or claim? (2) What warrants the doctrine theologically? That is, what considerations lead Christian communities to affirm the doctrine? And under what conditions would these affirmations fail as Christian doctrine?

1. Scope

In affirming the doctrine of creation what sorts of things is one saying? One is doing at least the following: claiming that a peculiar relationship obtains between God and all that is not God; making certain performative utterances; and perhaps making the claim that a singular event occurred.

GOD'S WORLD-RELATEDNESS

The most obvious thing done in affirming the doctrine of creation is to claim that God is related to the world in a peculiar way. Its peculiarity consists in its being unique and free. To affirm this is to make three interrelated claims.

(1) To affirm that God "creates" the world "from nothing" is to claim that God is related to all that is not God in a continuously active "productive" way. Anselm brings this out in his *Monologium* when he gives a classic analysis of the phrase 'from nothing' (chap. 8). It could, he says, be understood in any of three ways. (a) It might mean "nothing was created at all." But that is unintelligible as a formulation of a claim about, precisely, the creation of the actual world. (b) "Created from nothing" might mean that the world

176

was created from nothing itself (*de nihilo ipso*), as though "nothing" were somehow an existent substance from which something could be created. But this is self-contradictory. (c) "Created from nothing" means instead: "Created, but not *from* anything". This is, admittedly, a peculiar way to describe a relationship. It says two things at once. It claims that the world ("all that is not God") is passively related to God in a relationship of absolute dependence for its existence. And it claims that God actively relates to the world in a way that actualizes it. This relationship of active productivity in which God stands to the world is one that obtains continuously as long as there is a world. God's creativity is continuous, coterminal with the world. God's world-relatedness is more properly a continuing relating.

(2) Anselm's analysis brings out a second claim. God's relation to the world is strictly unique. Anselm points out (chap. 11) that to say that God creates the world but "not from anything" is to say that divine creating is not like any productive, generative, shaping, or making relationship we know of between an agent and a patient. All such analogies presuppose something that, as patient, undergoes the production, generation, shaping, or making. But that is precisely what the phrase *ex nihilo* excludes in regard to the Creator-creation relationship. Thus in claiming that God stands in a peculiar relationship with the world, the doctrine of creation from nothing employs an analogy for that relationship and then qualifies the applicability of the analogy very severely. It suggests that the relation is more like one broad class of relationships than it is like others. It is not like a logical relation (as though the world were deduced from God), or like a spatiotemporal relation (as though God were X billion light years away from the world). It is more like the relation one has to an object by virtue of one's intentional acts of shaping and making it. Nonetheless, this likeness is very limited. In particular, God's "productive" and "causal" relation with the world is strictly unique, and so we are bereft of analogies by which to suggest *how* God is "creative".

(3) Anselm's discussion illustrates a third claim about God's world-relatedness made in affirmations of the traditional doctrine of creation from nothing. To say that God creates the world, but not from anything, is to insist that God's world-relating is not necessitated by any reality other than God. God's world-relating is not restricted or required by the nature of anything that is real apart from creation and out of which God creates. In that sense God's world-relating is free.

To affirm the doctrine of creation from nothing is to do two broad kinds of things in regard to the world (i.e., "all that is not God"). As Donald Evans showed in exhaustive detail in *The Logic of Self-Involvement*,[1] it is at once to commit oneself to a number of attitudes and interests in regard to the world and to make certain truth claims about the world. Evans brings this out by adapting J. L. Austin's analysis of the performative force of our utterances, that is, what we *do* in what we say. To affirm the doctrine of creation is undoubtedly to use language to make claims (in this case about the world) that invite assessment of their truth and falsity. But it is also and at the same time to use language to imply that one has certain attitudes and that one holds certain intentions or commitments to behave in certain ways (again, in this case in regard to the world). The relation between these two sides of affirmation of the doctrine of creation (between truth-claiming and existential self-involvingness) is probably the root of most of the difficulties besetting efforts to give a perspicuous account of the meaning of the doctrine. If the existentially self-involving force of affirming the doctrine is stressed exclusively and the fact-claiming ignored or "translated" wholly into the former, then the doctrine ceases entirely to make any serious claim on anyone's credence and is reduced to being an expression of feelings that could equally well be expressed in many other ways. It is trivialized. If the existentially self-involving force of affirming the doctrine is ignored and the truth-claiming alone expressed, the claims by themselves seem so vast and, perhaps, vague that it is difficult to see what of importance is at stake in making them. No consequences for anything else one believes to be true or for the shape of one's life would flow from them. That would be particularly troubling at the point of apparent incongruence between the theological truth-claim about the "goodness" of creation and the manifest fact of evil in the world. We cannot hope to explore thoroughly these two aspects of the doctrine. The most we can do is outline major features of each and explore the main ways in which they are interrelated.

(1) To affirm the doctrine of creation is to make at least two major kinds of *claims* about all that is not God. First, it is to claim that the world is intelligible, and that in two distinguishable senses. It is intelligible in the sense that for all its variegation and changeability it exhibits regularities that can be discovered to an end. The world can be understood in terms of God's purposes for it in creating it. This is tied up with the claim that the freedom of God's active relating to the world finds better analogues in the relationships between persons and artifacts constituted by purposeful human productive actions than in those provided by logical, spatial, or nonpersonal causal relationships.

Second, to affirm the doctrine of creation is to claim that the world is genuinely other than God. Given major themes in the Christian understanding of God which are logically independent of the doctrine of creation, that has several implications. It means that our experience of the world as a plurality

of variously powerful particulars, complexly interrelated and often conflicting, is no illusion. Such experience is not a misapprehension of a deeper
underlying divine unity. The world's diversity is irreducibly real in its own
way. Furthermore, given that the creator is good, these concrete particulars
are good precisely in their particularity and in the conditions that in fact
characterize particularity in this world. To be material, temporal, and genuinely separate from one another is good. Furthermore, such a world cannot
be described as a kind of reality somehow antithetical to God. All that is
other than God is genuinely other than God, but not antithetical to God;
it is simply different from God.

Can the nature of the difference be conceptualized? Trying to do so has
led to a third implication. Given that the hallmark of divine reality is
"necessary existence", the most general characteristic of all that is not God
has been said to be "contingent existence".[2] The claim here is that all that
is not God stands constantly in a relation to God of dependence on God's
continuing productive activity for its very existence. It is precisely that God-
relatedness that constitutes it as creature.

What sorts of claims are these? As we shall see, these doctrinal claims seem
logically tied to a large range of attitudes, intentions, and dispositions that
shape the personal identities and the behavior of those who affirm the doctrine. But it seems clear that these claims cannot be reduced to or translated
without remainder into expressions of those practical commitments. In some
way these are truth claims. Moreover, they are important truth claims because
they are presuppositions of the Christian enterprise in its practical aspects.
It is very difficult to make the case that they are in any direct way grounded
in or inferred from experience. Perhaps it would be possible, though difficult, to specify conditions under which experience would tend to disconfirm the claim that the world is teleologically intelligible. It is notoriously
difficult to say how we would experience the world differently were it not
"contingent" on God for its existence. These claims seem rather to be claims
about absolutely general features of the world, so general that they are the
conditions of any experience of any part of it rather than claims somehow
"based" on experience. They are metaphysical claims. To believe them is to
hold metaphysical beliefs.

(2) To affirm the doctrine of creation from nothing is to take on oneself
a range of attitudes toward, and intentions to behave in certain ways in, the
world. To affirm it is a self-involving utterance. Thus, in affirming the doctrine of creation one not only claims that the world is intelligible but also
implies that one has and cultivates the disposition actively not only to pay
attention to it in delight but also to understand it. More particularly, it implies that one is disposed to think about it and to act in it in ways that are
appropriate to the ends to which it is ordered. In traditional Christian language

it would have been said that the ultimate end to which creation is ordered is the glorification of God. Hence one implies intentions to construe the world and act in the world in ways that express God's glory. In traditional language it would have been said that the proximate end to which the creation is ordered is the realization of the well-being of the several kinds of creatures in their particularity, since it is precisely their well-being that most fully expresses in a creaturely mode the glory of God. Hence, in affirming the doctrine of creation one implies that one has taken on oneself intentions to act in creation in ways that nurture and preserve the well-being of the several kinds of creatures. Of course, it has also been the case that having intentions to act in the world in generally the same kinds of way has not kept Christians from disagreeing strongly about just what specific actions are in fact the appropriate enactments of intentions to nurture and preserve the well-being of the several kinds of creatures.

In affirming the doctrine of creation one not only claims that the world genuinely is other than God but also implies one has the attitude of respect rather than reverence toward all that is not God. Reverence is an attitude appropriate to what is divine. Creation is other than God. There is no aspect or component of creatures that is unqualifiedly "divine". They are utterly secular, deserving respect as God's creatures but not reverence. This has important negative implications regarding all claims, religious or other, that the way by which human beings may find release from suffering and realize happiness is to recognize and seek union with the divine dimension ingredient in themselves and in all nature.

In affirming the doctrine of creation one not only claims that the physical particularity, variety, and variability that characterize all that is not God is not evil, but one also implies that one has the attitude of gratitude for it. One has toward it the attitude that is appropriate to have toward a gift. The combination of reverence and gratitude is a specific kind of wonder or awe that is appropriate to something that is in some deep way mysterious. Not that the world is claimed to be mysterious in the sense of being unintelligible. On the contrary, to affirm the doctrine of creation is to claim that the world is intelligible. Rather, it is an awe that is appropriate to grace, to that which is given for the well-being of the recipient and is neither earned by the recipient nor compelled by the circumstances of the giver.

CREATION AS AN EVENT

For the overwhelming majority of Christians until at least the eighteenth century, and for very many even up to the present, to affirm the doctrine of creation from nothing has been to make a claim about the occurrence of a singular event in the more or less distant past in which the world originated.

It is a claim about cosmogony and not only about cosmology, about the historical genesis of the universe and not merely about the universe's intelligible unity in its continuing relation of dependence on God. The history of Christian theological reflection on the topic of creation is a story of shifting relations between cosmogonic and cosmological claims. In the very earliest period affirmation of the doctrine involved claiming both that the world stood in continuing dependency relation to God and that the world originated in a singular event. And the two claims were not clearly differentiated.[3] As we shall see in the next section, polemical considerations led to an emphasis on the interpretation of creation as an event.

It has been a matter of controversy just how this interpretation should be expressed. Until the early twentieth century it would have been common to say that what was being asserted was that the world had a "beginning in time". But that phrase is open to misunderstanding. Augustine, the most influential writer on this topic from the fourth to at least the sixteenth centuries, argued that time itself must be said to come into existence through this singular event. There would thus have been a first moment of time, the moment of the singular event of creation. However, under the impact of Newton's mechanics theological formulations began to change in the seventeenth century. In the new framework space and time are absolute and without beginning, though of themselves without content. God's creative act could thus be thought of as the introjecting (as it were) of matter into the previously empty framework of space and time. A "beginning in time" would then be a first moment for the material world *in* time but not a first moment *of* time.

A second ambiguity came to light more recently. To say that the world had a beginning in time was traditionally thought to be equivalent to saying that the world's temporal duration had been finite. Discussions of this topic before the present century shared the assumption that time is a single well-defined framework and that it is indifferent which sort of motion be chosen as the basis for its measurement. One of the implications of Einstein's theory of relativity, one that was not immediately noted, is that time is not a single unique framework and that it does make a difference what type of motion is chosen for its measurement. There is thus an ineliminable element of conventionality about assertions regarding the passage of time. It may after all not then be a matter of fact as to whether the lapse of time since the creation-event comes out as finite or as infinite. It depends on whether the basis of the measure is a cyclical (countable) process, such as atomic vibrations, or a continuous one, such as the expansion of the universe itself. The former could give a finite measure, whereas the latter could come out as infinite.[4] This unexpected conventionality makes it even more difficult to formulate clearly what the implications of the doctrine of creation are for the notion of a "beginning in time."

INTERRELATIONS

We have seen that the scope of the Christian doctrine of creation includes three kinds of truth claims (about God's continuing relatedness to the world, about the world's continuing relatedness to God, and about the occurrence of a singular event) and several kinds of performative, self-involving force (implying attitudes, intentions, and dispositions at the very least). Are there logical relationships among any or all of these?

Given the central task of Christian theology, what is centrally important in the affirmation of the doctrine of creation is expressed in the various types of self-involving force. It is the attitudes, intentions, dispositions, and the like that are expressed in that fashion that shape the specific forms of human identity, personal and communal, which Christian doctrine seeks critically to describe. Clearly, the beliefs stated in the truth-claims that are made in affirming the creed are also essential to that which doctrine critically describes. But how are they related to affirmations of doctrine as self-involving performative utterances?

How are such attitudes as respect and gratitude for the world and intentions such as the intention to care for the well-being of fellow creatures related to the claim that the world stands in a relation of dependency on God? They are not implied by the claim. There would be no inconsistency in making the claim and holding contrary attitudes and dispositions. Nor would there be any inconsistency if one added the claim that the God on whom the world depends loves the world. One might still quite consistently believe the loving God is nonetheless unlovable and hold contrary attitudes to the world, disrespect, say, or disinterest. Nor does personal avowal of the attitudes and intentions necessarily imply a claim about the world's God-relatedness. One could consistently avow the attitudes and claims, affirm the world lovable, and yet deny that the world is God-related. Nonetheless, it is clear that Christian doctrines of creation from nothing insist that the truth-claiming and the performative force of what is done in affirming the doctrine are not accidentally and arbitrarily held together. How is their inseparability to be understood?

Donald Evans has made the suggestion that the doctrine of creation, taken as a complex whole, may be understood as an elaborated "parabolic onlook".[5] It is an "onlook" in that it has the same logical form as such familiar expressions as: 'I look on Harry as my brother' and 'I look on the State as my father'. Such expressions have the form 'I look on x as y.' In each case there is implied both a *similarity of attitude* and a *similarity of fact* that makes the similar attitudes appropriate. What is said is, "X is *such that* (implied truth-claim) the *attitude* appropriate to y is similar to the attitude appropriate to x." The onlook expressed by the doctrine of creation is "parabolic" in the sense that the attitude known to be appropriate to y is a parable or analogue for the attitude to x.

Not all expressions of the form 'I look on *x* as *y*' are parabolic. But the ones involved in affirming the doctrine of creation seem to be. Thus, as we have seen, the doctrine framed in the form 'I look on the world as something made freely and in love as a gift' implies that I have toward the world attitudes and intentions appropriate to a gift made for us. But the addition "but not made from anything" reminds one that one has no adequate analogue for the "making" or the "giving". The relation between the attitude one has toward an ordinary gift and that about the gift in virtue of which the attitude is appropriate is only a parable for the relation between the attitude the believer has toward the world and that about the world (i.e., its God-relatedness) that makes the attitude appropriate. In affirming the doctrine of creation one is not *justifying* certain implied attitudes, intentions, dispositions, and the like by inferring them from claimed truths. Nor is one *founding* the truth-claims by showing them to be the necessary formal conditions for the attitudes and such. One is simply expressing the interconnected beliefs, on the one side, and attitudes, intentions, and dispositions, on the other, which together are constituent of Christian forms of life.

The same analysis can be made of the relation between the attitudes and intentions implied in affirming the doctrine of creation from nothing and the truth-claim (made in the same affirmation) that the world originated in a singular event in the past. In general, whereas the claim about the world's dependency relation on God is a metaphysical claim, the claim about the world's absolute origination is a historical claim. Two points need to be made about the role of this historical claim within the inner logic of the doctrine of creation. The first is that making the claim does not involve the introduction of any new parables into expression of the onlook. Both the claim that the world stands constantly and universally in a dependency relation on God and the claim that the world as it is is the end result of a long history originating in a singular event "caused" by God are formulations of the "such that" about the world that makes certain attitudes and intentions toward it appropriate. The second point is that the historical claim implies no additional attitudes or intentions not also implied by the metaphysical claim. Nor does it rule out any attitudes or intentions that might be made along with making the metaphysical claim were the latter made alone.

Finally, in affirming the doctrine of creation from nothing how are the metaphysical and the historical truth-claims related to each other? Let us give the question an edge: Could one retain the claim about the dependency relation (metaphysical) and abandon the claim about an originating event (historical), without either internal inconsistency in one's theology or an unwarranted revision of the meaning of the metaphysical claim itself? The answer seems to be Yes.

The claim that the world has its absolute origination in a singular event in the past might imply that the world ever since stands constantly in a dependency relationship on God. That this is so in the Christian framework is reflected in the history of Christian doctrine. When the claim about "creation" has been identified with a claim about an originating event, it is always insisted that its necessary corollary is a doctrine of preservation (the metaphysical claim).[6]

But the claim that the world stands in a dependency relation on God does not necessarily imply the claim that there was an originating event. The lapse of time during which the world has stood in this relation might be infinite. The added qualification *ex nihilo* does not contradict this. As we have seen, its force is to qualify the adequacy of every analogy for divine creativity. It does not bear on the question whether duration of the world's God-relatedness is finite or infinite.

Hence, the historical claim is logically detachable from the metaphysical claim and could be dropped without introducing incoherence into the doctrine or tacitly altering the meaning of the metaphysical claim. This point is implicit in the history of the doctrine in debates about whether the "eternity" of the world could be proved. Medieval debates were sparked by recovery in the thirteenth century of Aristotle's texts in which the "eternity" of the world was taught. Christian theologians would all have agreed that biblical revelation veridically teaches the cosmological claim that the world had a "beginning in time". Some theologians, like Bonaventure, thought that Scripture's claim could be demonstrated philosophically and Aristotle's claim disproven. Others were in the awkward position of holding that Aristotle's demonstration was valid but has to be superseded by revelation's claim. Others, like Thomas Aquinas, thought that it could be shown philosophically that neither position could be demonstrated. What is noteworthy here is that the claim about an absolute origination of the world was included in the doctrine of creation by all these theologians solely on the grounds that, in their view, it is taught by Scripture. Debates about the validity of the contrary view, that the world is eternal, were conducted entirely as philosophical arguments. Nobody argued that any other part of the doctrine, or any other Christian doctrine, would be undercut were Aristotle's view to be validated. The only theological issue at stake, and it is not unimportant, was faithfulness to biblical revelation.

2. Theological Warrants

There are at least two kinds of assessment that must be made of every Christian doctrinal proposal: Is it properly "Christian", that is, is it the sort of proposal that a Christian community ought in all self-consistency to adopt to guide its life and thought? And, in any case, is it true? Obviously, one may not simply assume that in every case an affirmative answer to one of these questions implies an affirmative answer to the other. The matter would have to be examined case by case, however much one might trust that in fact what is properly "Christian" will turn out to be true as well and vice versa. In this section we will continue to confine ourselves to the inner logic of Christian doctrine and ask only: By what sorts of appeals have Christians warranted the doctrine of creation from nothing as the doctrine Christians ought to affirm? So far as Christian theology is concerned, what are its warrants?

As the doctrine was slowly being worked out into its classical formulations during the first five centuries of Christian thought, it would have been said that the decisive appeal was to the biblical writings which teach divinely revealed truth. Two comments need to be made about this. Their joint consequence, I hope to show, is that what have warranted the doctrine's Christian appropriateness are considerations that go well beyond anything a simple appeal to Scripture alone could provide and that leave the doctrine open to several kinds of possible failures.

First, appeal was made to Scripture interpreted according to credal formulae. It is commonly accepted that credal formulae are very ancient in the life of the Christian movement. There probably were credal formulae that antedated the writing of the New Testament texts and are quoted in them. They were used in the context of acts of worship performed to glorify God. They functioned, among other things, to describe who God is. They did not characteristically make claims *that* God does various things. Rather, they expressed trust in God ("We believe in one God") *who* does thus and so ("maker of heaven and earth"). It is as though the mention of things God does came in answer to the unstated question Who is the One you worship? They served to sum up the Christian understanding of God. When interpretation of Scripture is guided by such credal formulae, the description of God given by the formulae serves as something like a rule by which to unify the otherwise very diverse materials in the Bible: construe it all as in one way or another contributing to a description of the self-same God. Accordingly, some of the earliest formulations of Christian claims about creation (e.g., in sermons in Acts 14:15 and 17:24-28 and, arguably at least from its structure, Justin Martyr's mixture of Scripture and Platonic doctrine very early in the second century) are more about God and God's world-relatedness than about the world and its God-relatedness. It is not accidental that they are claims about creation but *not* claims of *creatio ex nihilo*.

Moreover, when interpretation of the Bible is governed by credal formulae, Scripture tends to be construed as a call to a distinctive way of being human and of living a human life. Credal formulae not only describe who God is, but they also describe who we are: we are the people whose lives are given distinctive shape by our response to this God's presence. Interpreted in the light of such formulae, Scripture's description of God's world-relatedness is seen not so much as the basis for a cosmology as the basis for an account of the forms of life that are appropriate responses to God. Accordingly, the Christian doctrine of creation, insofar as it is addressed to Christian communities themselves, is ordered to the practical matter of helping the community to be true to its own identity. Undoubtedly, then, the "Christianness" of the doctrine of creation was warranted by appeal to Scripture. But the interpretation of Scripture was itself "ruled" by credal expressions. Insofar as that was the case, the doctrine had as its audience the Christian communities themselves, and its aim was to guide reflection on the nature of Christian identity by elaborating some claims about the One to whom Christian life is a response.

In fact, the doctrine of creation from nothing was never merely a restatement of cosmologies found in the Bible. Nor, I think, can it be otherwise today. Theologians appeal to biblical texts interpreted in the light of modern critical scholarship. This reveals a diversity among the canonical texts but provides no basis for deciding which to make normative. While there are one, perhaps two, New Testament texts that imply creation from nothing (Rom. 4:17; perhaps Heb. 11:3), the text traditionally made central because of its place in the most extensive creation narratives, namely Gen. 1:1-2, does not clearly imply creation from nothing. Genesis 1:1 may equally well be translated in either of two ways: (a) "In the beginning God created the heaven and the earth". When translated that way, verse 2 reports the immediate effect of God's creativity: "And the earth was without form and void and darkness was upon the face of the deep". Or (b), "When God set about to create heaven". When translated this way, verse 2 comes in as a parenthesis — describing what the conditions were when God began to create, namely, "the world being then a formless waste, with darkness over the seas and only an awesome wind sweeping over the water" (Speiser). The first translation arguably at least implies creation from nothing. The second — and now very widely adopted — translation clearly contradicts it: God begins, not with nothing, but with formless waste. The exegetical controversy about this text is unresolved and perhaps unresolvable.[7] This would frustrate any effort to warrant the Christian appropriateness of the doctrine of creation from nothing by direct appeal only to biblical texts interpreted in the light of critical scholarship. The doctrine can no more be treated today as an elaboration of biblical cosmology than it ever was. If Christian communities are going to continue to affirm it, it must be on other and more complex grounds having to do with its ties to the description of the One the communities worship and to the corporate identity shaped in them by worshipping that One.

The second point that needs to be made is that the doctrine of creation from nothing was formulated in polemical contexts. Its purpose was not only to guide faithful Christian communities. It was also designed to refute non-Christian religious and philosophical movements and to correct Christian communities who were deemed to have become confused by those non-Christian movements. The *ex nihilo* clause was a defense against teaching that was attractive to some Christians but was also—as the polemic was designed to show—implicitly contrary to the communities' understanding of God and of themselves as expressed in their credal formulae.

Some pagan thinkers, for example, held that matter is coeternal with the world. The eternity of matter appeared to be compatible with credal formulae and with the teaching of some Christian thinkers like Justin Martyr, for whom the doctrine of creation says only that God made the world. That is compatible with the view that God made it "out of" matter coeternal with God. However, to other early Christian thinkers like Theophilus of Antioch (c. 175 A.D.), who seems to have been the first of the Fathers to insist on the *ex nihilo* clause,[8] the eternity of matter implicitly contradicts the description of God given in credal formulae. To affirm the coeternity of God and matter seems to posit two ultimate principles of reality in contradiction to the credal ascription of absoluteness to One alone. In order to make it clear that Christians' description of God excludes the eternity of matter and hence a second ultimate principle, the *ex nihilo* clause began to be added to the claim about God's world-relatedness: God is actively related to the world, producing it, but not *from* anything.

A second example: by the early third century some Christian spokespersons[9] developed theologies that assumed a sharp antithesis between spirit and matter. What is spiritual was assumed to be akin to God, and what is material was assumed to be antithetical to God. This dualism was reflected in their contrast between the Savior God and the Creator. The high God who alone deserves our worship is pure spirit and can have no positive relation to matter. The world of material things cannot be coeternal with the high God. Nor can it have been created by the high God. Its creator must therefore be a being lesser both in power and goodness. We are spiritual beings, akin to the high God, exiled in this material world but saved from it by the high God. Against this the doctrine that the material world was created by God *ex nihilo* was formulated to insist that materiality is itself God's good gift and that material things are good precisely in their materiality and not somehow in spite of it. The *ex nihilo* clause was designed in part to point out that the Savior/Creator dualism implicitly contradicts the description given by credal formulae of the God Christians worship.

Thus in different polemical contexts the *ex nihilo* clause had the force of rejecting different teachings taken to be contradictory of Christian understanding of who God is and who Christian communities are. When efforts were made to warrant the clause's Christian appropriateness, it became necessary to move beyond appeal to Scripture in at least three ways. Each of these ways brings with it a way in which the doctrine of creation from nothing might fail.

For one thing, some proponents of the views being rebutted themselves appealed to Christian Scripture to warrant their views. For example, those who contrasted the Savior to the Creator accepted only the "apostolic witness" of the New Testament as authentic Christian Scripture and contrasted the God it described as Savior with the God described in Hebrew Scripture as the Creator. Clearly this controversy could not be adjudicated by simple appeal to Scripture. Now the issue is: What counts as authentic Christian Scripture and how is its interpretation certified? One way to answer this question was to appeal to institutional teaching authority in the Christian communities. Irenaeus provides a classic example of this. Writing in the early third century against a variety of thinkers whom he calls "Gnostics" and who reflect the dualistic views we have noted, Irenaeus claims that the Christian appropriateness of his formulations is warranted by the universal teaching of bishops in the churches.[10] Christ had entrusted right teaching to the apostles. They established bishops in each church to whom this teaching was entrusted, and they handed it down from generation to generation. Unbroken succession of the office of bishop in the church constitutes an institutional teaching authority by which to settle such questions as what counts as Christian Scripture and how it is properly to be interpreted.

In general this kind of appeal is vulnerable to historical disconfirmation. It rests on a picture of Christian beginnings as characterized by a high degree of uniformity in faith and practice among widely scattered communities. Modern historical research tends to invalidate that picture.[11] If the "Christianness" of the doctrine of *creatio ex nihilo* were largely established by an appeal specifically to the Christian canon of Scripture, and if the decision about which texts belong in the canon and the determination of how the canon is to be interpreted as a whole were warranted by appeal to belief and practice allegedly universal in the earliest period of the Church, then historical research could deprive the doctrine of this warrant.

The "Christianness" of the *ex nihilo* clause has also been at least partly warranted by a quite different kind of extrabiblical appeal. When Theophilus of Antioch stressed '*ex nihilo*' in the second century to reject the doctrine of the eternity of matter, he urged its Christian appropriateness by claiming that the prophets had taught it "with one consent".[12] This involved a subtle but very important shift in the way Scripture was construed. He takes Scripture to speak, not so much of God and God's world-relatedness (as credal formulae tend to do), but of the world and its God-relatedness. More exactly, focus is shifted from Scripture's witness to God to Scripture's cosmogony. As Jaroslav Pelikan has shown, throughout the development of the doctrine of creation it has been acknowledged that in the biblical stories "creation" may refer either to a relation between God and the world, or to an event of absolute world-origination, or to both. But during much of that history the stress has fallen so strongly on the originating event that the *ex nihilo* clause often came to be identified with that claim. That tendency seems to have begun with Theophilus. Its Christian appropriateness was partly warranted by appeal to biblical creation stories construed mainly as revealed information about the absolutely originating event.

That put the doctrine of creation from nothing on a logical par with nontheological cosmological and, especially, cosmogonic doctrines. That, in turn, suggested another strategy for warranting the doctrine's Christianness. If God created the world, then whatever truth we can discover about the world by whatever means is true because God created the world that way. Accordingly, one way to show the Christian appropriateness of a doctrine is to show that it comports well with the best understanding we have of the world. By the late fourth century Augustine had followed this strategy in the doctrine of creation in a way that was enormously influential on the subsequent development of the doctrine. For him the polemical target of the doctrine was the Manichean dualist cosmogony. According to it our world is marked by discord because it originated in cosmic strife between the Father of Light and the Archons of Darkness. Central to the Manicheans' cosmology was a commitment to rationality. They ridiculed Genesis' creation stories as irrational. Augustine's formulation of the doctrine of creation has as part of its background his earlier attraction to the Manichean's cosmology and his own commitment to "rationality". Accordingly, in his commentary on Genesis, *De Genesi ad litteram*, he attempted to show the consistency of the biblical cosmology with the best "scientific knowledge" of his time. His own theory of knowledge led him to stress the literal meaning of the biblical text.

A major problem arose, however, whenever the literal meaning of the text conflicted with claims about the physical universe that were widely accepted as "demonstrated". Augustine concluded that formulation of claims about creation must be answerable to those "scientific" claims. Where there is such a conflict, it is a sign that the text should be interpreted allegorically rather than literally.[13] Thus there is a criterion other than the biblical texts by which a doctrine is to be warranted. On this strategy any warranting of the Christian appropriateness of the doctrine of creation from nothing must include reference to demonstrated truth, at least by exhibiting the consonance of the doctrine and that truth.

This way of warranting the doctrine of creation opens it to a corresponding way in which it might fail. It might be shown not to be cogent as a cosmogony. This could happen in a couple of ways. Analysis might show that its key concepts are too vague or confused to be useful. And it might show that inferences from one proposition within the doctrine to the next are il-legitimate. Although one could not specify in advance when this would hap-pen, persumably there would come a point when conceptual confusion and incoherence would lead to abandonment of this way of talking. The doctrine would then have failed.

Even if the doctrine survived such analysis, it might fail by being shown to be in severe tension with our best scientific understanding of the origins of the universe. If the Christianness of the doctrine is partly warranted by extrabiblical truth, then scientific enquiry into the origins of the physical universe might disconfirm rather than confirm the doctrine. A case in point: it seems to be held in some quarters that the big bang model of the origin of the physical universe tends to confirm the theological doctrine.[14] That is highly problematic, both theologically and scientifically.[15] Whatever else the model claims, it does not claim that the universe was brought into being in a single event *by God*, which is what the doctrine claims. It cannot be claimed that the big bang model *supports* the doctrine of creation. Nonetheless, as Ernan McMullin puts it, *"if* the universe began in time through the act of the creator, from our vantage point it would look something *like* the big bang cosmologists are now talking about".[16] But now suppose that new discoveries lead to the abandonment of the big bang model and the adoption in its place of a very different model according to which the notion of a singular originating event is unintelligible. If the big bang model could not confirm the theological doctrine of creation, the new model could not disconfirm it. However, would not the apparent dissonance between the two tend to be abandonment of the theological claims about an absolute originating event? Probably it would.

It would probably result in abandonment of the theological claim about creation as a singular *event*, but it would probably not lead to an abandon-ment of the *doctrine* of creation from nothing. As we have taken pains to show, the doctrine as a complex whole is not simply a reformulation of biblical cosmology. The claim about an originating event is, in the light of critical scholarship, only tenuously rooted in Scripture. Furthermore, as we argued in part 1, although making truth-claims about the world is an irreducible and essential part of what is done in affirming the doctrine, the particular claim about an originating *event* is not logically indispensable. It could be dropped without introducing incoherence into the doctrine and without alter-ing what is done by and to Christian communities in their affirming the doctrine.

In addition to appeals to institutional teaching authority in the Church and to our best scientific knowledge about the world, efforts to warrant the Christian appropriateness of the doctrine of creation from nothing have in-volved a third kind of extrabiblical appeal. It has been very powerful in the history of Christian theology, I believe, but this is admittedly very difficult to document. It is in a way an appeal to Christians' experience of the world. More particularly, it is an appeal to the wonder, gratitude, and sense of radical contingency with which Christians experience the world. It is an appeal to their experience of the world as grace. This is, not a substitute for appeal to Scripture, but rather an indirect appeal to Scripture. Experience is always conceptually shaped. When biblical writings are genuinely appropriated personally, their concepts, images, and narratives can shape the attitudes, dispositions, beliefs, etc. that comprise the personal identities of the persons who appropriate them. A community whose identity is decisively shaped by biblical narratives and the images and concepts they employ is a community of persons who experience the material context of life in a distinctive way, namely, as gift at once mysterious and loving. Put abstractly, refutation of what are deemed profoundly misleading doctrinal formulations then goes like this: Are not these formulations incoherent with our credal expressions' description of our own corporate identity? These misguided formulations would imply fear and loathing of material things, but our actual experience of material things is one of wonder and gratitude. Thus, for example, the Christian appropriateness of laying stress on the goodness of matter is directly warranted by appeal to its coherence with that experience of wonder and gratitude and indirectly warranted by appeal to biblical writings that, when personally appropriated, shape that experience.[17]

This brings with it another and perhaps decisive way in which the doctrine might fail. I have adopted the suggestion that the doctrine of creation from nothing is, as a complex whole, the expression of an onlook, at once an *avowal* of attitudes and intentions to God and world and *claims* that God and world are *such that* these attitudes and intentions are appropriate. The theological doctrine is ordered to practical matters: elucidation of the attitudes, intentions, and the like that comprise Christian personal identity, communal and individual. The doctrine's logic reflects this. The truth-claiming done in affirming the doctrine is not reducible to the self-involving performative force of affirming the doctrine. It is nonetheless limited to the claims that elucidate certain attitudes and intentions by clarifying what it is in the nature of things that makes them appropriate. It is the self-involving and performative force of affirmation of the doctrine that is theologically central.

Now a self-involving performative utterance may fail, not by being falsified by evidence, but—to use the quasi-technical term J. L. Austin employed when he drew attention to these matters—by being *infelicitous*. It may suffer "infelicity" if I am insincere, lacking the attitude or intention I express. Or it may suffer "infelicity" if what I involve myself in is a promise and, however sincere I may be, I am unable to carry it out. Clearly, then, if the community that uses the doctrine to help elucidate its credal expression of its own self-identity lacks deep dispositions toward the relevant attitudes and intentions (say, gratitude or a commitment to care for the well-being of creatures), then its doctrine of creation fails by "infelicity". Affirming the doctrine would no longer be an authentic expression of the truth of the community.

This might come about as a result of a deep revulsion at moral horrors like the Holocaust or revulsion at physical suffering caused by persistent starvation and disease. Such revulsion might make it impossible to have or to enact the dispositions that are central to the way Christian communities are "set" in the world and are elucidated in the doctrine of creation. They might lead people to adopt a quite different personal "set" than the Christian ones. And that, of course, would be a matter of conversion to another way of being set into the world, perhaps a conversion to another religion. That surely is one decisive and fatal way in which the doctrine of creation from nothing could fail: that it should simply cease in fact to express the most basic way a community of persons is set into the world. Then its affirmation could not be anyone's self-involving utterance by which the deepest of dispositions are taken on and personal identity is shaped. Then the affirmation of the doctrine would indeed be null and void, and our lives a kind of personal chaos over which it would only be right that there should brood a deep silence.

Appendix

Christian communities vary, of course, in the degree to which they are prepared to hold themselves accountable to earlier doctrinal formulation, whether by Church councils or by institutional teaching authorities. Nonetheless, it may be useful to note here classic formulations regarding creation to which reference is frequently made in various communities when this topic is under discussion.

The following are customarily given considerable weight in Roman Catholic discussions. The translations, from the thirteenth edition of Henry Denzinger's *Enchiridion Symbolorum*, are by Roy J. Deferrari, in *The Sources of Catholic Dogma*, St. Louis: B. Herder, 1957.

The Lateran Council IV, 1215 (Denzinger, 428): "Firmly we . . . confess . . . the true God . . . who by His own omnipotent power at once from the beginning of time created each creature from nothing, spiritual and corporal, namely, angelic and mundane, and finally the human, constituted as it were, alike of the spirit and the body".

The Council of Florence, 1441, in the Bull "Cantata Domino" (Denzinger, 706): "Most strongly it believes, professes, and declares that the one true God, Father, Son and Holy Spirit, is the creator of all things visible and invisible, who, when He wished, out of His goodness created all creatures, spiritual as well as corporal; good, indeed, since they were made by the highest good, but changeable, since they were from nothing, and it asserts that nature is not evil, since all nature, in so far as it is nature, is good".

The Vatican Council, 1870, in the "Dogmatic Constitution concerning the Catholic Faith" (Denzinger, 1782-1783): "there is one, true, living God, Creator and Lord of heaven and earth, . . . who, although He is one, singular, altogether simple and unchangeable spiritual substance, must be proclaimed distinct in reality and essence from the world". "This sole true God by His goodness and 'omnipotent power', not to increase His own beatitude, and not to add to, but to manifest His perfection by the blessings which He bestows on creatures, with most free volition 'immediately from the beginning of time fashioned each creature out of nothing, spiritual and corporal, namely angelic and mundane' ".

Pius X, in a response of the Biblical Commission, on "The Historical Character of the Earlier Chapters of Genesis", 1909 (Denzinger, 2123): *"Question III:* Whether in particular the literal and historical sense can be called into question, where it is a matter of facts related in the same chapters, which pertain to the foundations of the Christian religion; for example, among others, the creation of all things wrought by God in the beginning of time; . . . *Reply:* In the negative".

These were all formulated in particular polemical contexts and need to be interpreted in the context of their respective controversies.

Lutheran formulae were also produced in polemical contexts. Controversies at the time of the Reformation centered on Christological, soteriological, and ecclesiastical issues. Accordingly, while the doctrine of creation from nothing is by no means denied, it is not prominent in the confessions and catechisms most frequently cited in Lutheran discussions. The following examples come from John H. Leith, editor, *Creeds of the Churches*, Atlanta: John Knox Press, 1982.

Martin Luther's "Small Catechism", 1529, on the First Article of the Creed (Leith, p. 115): "What does this mean? Answer: I believe that God created me and all that exists; that he has given me and still sustains my body and soul, and limbs and senses, my reason and all the faculties of my mind, together with food and clothing, house and home, family and property; . . . All this he does out of his pure, fatherly, and divine goodness and mercy, without any merit or worthiness on my part. For all of this I am bound to thank, praise, and obey him". Clearly the stress here is on the self-involving force of affirming the doctrine.

The Augsburg Confession, 1530, from Article I (Leith, pp. 67-68): "We unanimously hold and teach, in accordance with the decree of the Council of Nicea, that there is one divine essence . . . and that there are three persons in this one divine essence . . . : God the Father, God the Son, God the

Holy Spirit. All three are one divine essence, eternal, without division, without end, of infinite power, wisdom, and goodness, one creator and preserver of all things visible and invisible". It is worth noting that in neither of these Lutheran formulations is there any sign of an interest to distinguish between creation as an ongoing relationship between God and the world (creating and preserving are treated as two aspects of the same thing) and creation as an event of absolute origination of the world.

The controversies in which many Calvinist formulations of the doctrine arose often centered on questions about God's providence and predestination and human freedom, as part of debates about the nature of God's grace. These topics were characteristically treated in the context of the larger canvas of God's governance of nature and history generally. Accordingly, they offer somewhat more emphatic statements of the doctrine of creation. The following are frequently cited in discussions of this topic by theologians in the Reformed tradition. They come from Philip Schaff, editor, *The Creeds of Christendom*, vol. 3, New York: Harper, 1919.

The Heidelberg Catechism, 1563 (Schaff, p. 315): "That the eternal Father of our Lord Jesus Christ, who of nothing made heaven and earth, with all that in them is, who likewise upholds and governs the same by his eternal counsel and providence, is for the sake of Christ his Son my God and my Father, in whom I so trust as to have no doubt that he will provide me with all things necessary for body and soul". Here too no distinction is drawn between creation as a relation and creation as an event, and the stress falls on the self-involving force of affirming the doctrine, not on cosmological truth-claiming. Among Calvinist formulations of the doctrine the latter characteristic of the Heidelberg Catechism stands in sharp contrast to the formulations that came out of Westminster, which follow.

The Westminster Confession of Faith, chapter 4, "Of Creation", 1647, (Schaff, p. 611): "It pleased God the Father, Son, and Holy Ghost, for the manifestation of the glory of his eternal power, wisdom, and goodness, in the beginning, to create or make of nothing the world, and all things therein, whether visible, in the space of six days, and all very good.

The Westminster Shorter Catechism, question 9, "What is the work of creation?" 1647 (Schaff, p. 677): "The work of creation is God's making all things of nothing, by the word of his power, in the space of six days, and all very good".

"Anabaptist" communities generally do not recognize the authority of any creed or confession. Nonetheless it is worth noting that at the time of the Reformation certain such groups found it necessary to formulate confessions in which a doctrine of creation is affirmed. The following is from the Mennonite *Dordrecht Confession*, 1632 (Leith, p. 293): "Him we confess as the Creator of all things, visible and invisible; who in six days created and prepared 'heaven and earth, and the sea, and all things that are therein'. And we further believe, that this God still governs and preserves the same, together with all His works, through His wisdom, His might, and the 'word of His power' ".

NOTES

1. Donald Evans, *The Logic of Self-Involvement*, London: SCM Press, 1963.
2. The notion of "necessary existence" is undoubtedly problematic and so is the contrast "necessary existence/contingent existence". In certain kinds of neo-Thomism a great deal of effort was made to giving precise ontological content to both of them. But the notions are not the invention of that intellectual tradition, and that particular kind of ontology is not identical with the Christian doctrinal point being made. The latter, it may be suspected, profits from a certain creative ambiguity. Cf. Etienne Gilson, *The Spirit of Medieval Philosophy*, New York: Charles Scribner's Sons, 1940, chapters 3-5 for a good example of the neo-Thomism referred to.
3. Cf. Jaroslav Pelikan, "Creation and Causality in the History of Christian Thought", in Sol Tax and Charles Callender, editors, *Evolution after Darwin*, vol. 3, *Issues in Evolution*, Chicago: University of Chicago Press, 1960, pp. 29-41.
4. Ernan McMullin, "How Should Cosmology Relate to Theology?" in A. R. Peacocke, editor, *The Sciences and Theology in the Twentieth Century*, Notre Dame, IN: University of Notre Dame Press, 1981, p. 35.
5. Evans, *The Logic of Self-Involvement*, pp. 124-235; 220-228.
6. Cf. Pelikan, "Creation and Causality", p. 36.
7. E. A. Speiser, *Genesis*, Garden City, L. I., NY: Doubleday, 1964,, p. 3. Speiser discusses the problems confronting translator and interpreter on pp. 8-13. That Genesis 1 must be translated in a way that expresses precisely the *ex nihilo* clause is argued, *contra* Speiser, on form-critical and internal theological consistency grounds by Brevard Childs, *Myth and Reality in the Old Testament*, London: SCM Press, 1960, pp. 30-42, and by Gerhard von Rad, *The Problem of the Hexateuch and Other Essays*, Edinburgh: Oliver & Boyd, 1966, pp. 131-144.
8. Cf. Pelikan, "Creation and Causality", p. 34.
9. The usual generic name for these movements has been "Gnostic". However, there are so many differences among these movements that it is far from clear that any such common term is useful. It seems, for example, to have been quite possible for some "Gnostics" to hold a doctrine of *creatio ex nihilo*. Clearly, rejection of the doctrine of creation is not itself a characteristic helping to define a "Gnostic". See Gerhard May, *Schöpfung aus Dem Nichts*, Berlin: Walter de Gruyter, 1978. I am indebted to Professor Robert Wilken for this reference.
10. Irenaeus, *Adversus Haereses*, 3,2,2; 3,3,3; 3,4,1.
11. See Robert Wilken, *The Myth of Christian Beginnings*, Notre Dame, IN; University of Notre Dame Press, 1980, for an excellent discussion of this point.
12. See Pelikan, "Creation and Causality", p. 34ff., for the following discussion.
13. Augustine, *De Genesi ad litteram*, II, 9.
14. See an allocution by Pope Pius XII, *Bulletin of the Atomic Scientists, 8*, 1952, 143-146, and, perhaps, Robert Jastrow in his popular book *Until the Sun Dies*, New York: Norton, 1977. Jastrow is not terribly precise in his expression of his views, but it seems a possible and not unfair reading of him.
15. Central among the scientific problems with this influence is that there seems

to be nothing in the Big Bang model that could rule out the possiblity that the Big Bang itself was preceded by a "different" universe, all traces of which might have been obliterated by the Big Bang, but which nonetheless would have been the "material" for the next stage. Which is to say that it is far from clear that one can fairly infer from the Big Bang an *absolute* beginning in time.

16. McMullin, "How Should Cosmology Relate to Theology", p. 39; emphasis added.

17. The philosophical theologian Austin Farrer explicitly set out to evoke just this way of "experiencing" the world as the precondition for being able to make his speculative theology credible. See *Finite and Infinite*, London: Dacre Press, 1943.

GOD'S ACTION IN THE WORLD

William P. Alston

1. The Problem

In this essay I seek an understanding of the notion of God's acting in the world, where this is to be understood as going beyond God's creation and preservation of the world, and as involving God's doing things with respect to his creatures, intentionally producing various particular effects in the world. The general notion covers a wide variety of putative cases. On the one hand, there is a variety of ways in which God is thought to deal "directly" with human beings: communicating messages to them, judging them, forgiving them, sustaining them, enlightening or guiding them, and so on. Then there are more public displays, the Cecil B. De Mille spectaculars, such as parting the waters of the Sea of Reeds, sending the plagues on Egypt, and raising the dead to life. In my discussion I will be taking this whole spectrum into account, though at times I will narrow the focus.

It goes without saying that this problem will assume different forms, depending on how we view God and how we view the world. Let me explain the setting within which I am raising the question. God is the ultimate source of being for everything other than himself: everything other than God exists only because of the divine creative activity. And it is not simply that God initially brings each creature into existence; God's creative or sustaining activity is continually required to keep the creature in being. God's existence, on the other hand, depends on nothing outside himself. God exists necessarily; he exists in every possible world. God is unlimited in every perfection: knowledge, power, goodness, and so on. As such he is immaterial, not limited by the conditions of corporeality. I also think of God as not himself being in, or moving through, time, but the details of my discussion will not reflect that conviction. I shall take it that talk of God as a temporal agent, at least my talk of God as a temporal agent, can always be translated into talk of God as a timeless agent that produces temporal effects. In most of these respects I am siding with classical theism against the "process theology" of Whitehead, Hartshorne, and their followers.

Moreover, I think of God as literally a "personal agent". By a "personal agent" I mean a being that acts in the light of knowledge to achieve pur-

197

poses, a being whose actions express attitudes and are guided by standards and principles, a being that enters into communication and other forms of personal relations with other personal agents. In saying that God *literally* acts in the light of knowledge and purposes, I do not mean to imply that knowledge, intention, and other psychological states and processes are realized in God in the same way they are realized in human beings. What it is for God to intend something may be, and undoubtedly is, radically different from what it is for a human being to intend something. But this is quite compatible with the basic sense of terms like 'know' and 'intend' holding constant across the divine-human gap. For example, despite the radical differences in divine and human nature, the existence of an intention (together with the power to carry it out) can have the same sort of implications in both cases. Thus, from "God intends to establish his kingdom on earth", together with "God is omnipotent", we can infer that God's kingdom will be established on earth. In taking God to be literally a personal agent my view is distinguished from pansymbolists like Paul Tillich and John Macquarrie. If I were to agree with Tillich that divine will and intellect are "symbols for dynamics in all its ramifications and form as the meaningful structure of being-itself",[1] and that providence is the "divine condition which is present in every group of finite conditions and in the totality of finite conditions, . . . the quality of inner directedness in every situation",[2] I would not draw such implications from attributions of intentions to God.

I will not say much about the world. I use the term to designate the whole of creation, the totality of everything that exists other than God. In this essay I will be focusing on the physical universe, including human beings, leaving to one side whatever else there may be to creation. No doubt, the details of an account of God's action in the world will differ somewhat from one cosmology to another, but I doubt that any of the issues I will be discussing are affected by detailed differences between cosmologies. In the course of the discussion I will consider both sides of one issue about the creation, whether everything that happens is determined to happen in just that way by natural causes.

2. Determinism and Divine Agency

The most basic issue that arises when, against this background, we try to understand the action of God in the world is this. Must we think of *everything* that happens in the world, including those happenings that are due to natural causes, as actions of God, as something that God does? Or is it only some, perhaps very small, subclass of happenings that deserves that appellation? We are pulled both ways here. On the one hand, as we shall see in a moment, there is a considerable case to be made for the thesis that everything that happens in the world (with the possible exception of free voluntary acts of created agents) is God's doing. But, on the other hand, it seems that when we take some particular occurrence to be an action of God, we mean to be contrasting it with more humdrum happenings that are purely the work of created agents. When the waters of the Sea of Reeds part to let the Israelites through, but close when the Egyptians seek to follow, that is seen as an act of God. But the normal rippling of the water before and after this event is not thought of as God's doing, at least not in the same way. We single out an act of God against a massive background of the purely worldly. In the remainder of this section I will look at the case for holding that everything, or almost everything, is done by God. The rest of the paper will be devoted to exploring the idea that happenings of some relatively small subset are actions of God in some special sense.

There is a widespread view in Christian theology that I will call "omnidetermination". This is the thesis that God wills, intentionally brings about, every detail of creation. It can boast such distinguished adherents as Augustine, Aquinas, Calvin, and Luther. For example, Aquinas argues that all things are subject to the divine government, including contingent events and things that happen by chance.[3] To say that something happens by chance is simply to say that it is not determined by some particular kind of natural causes; to say that something happens contingently is to say that its proximate causes are not sufficient to determine it uniquely.[4] But nothing falls outside the order instituted by the divine will. God, as first cause and first mover, is responsible for all existence and all activity. And since God's causation is by his will, guided by his intellect, every activity in the world was willed by God and so carries out a divine intention. This even includes human volition, which, Aquinas insists, is free, but free in the sense that no created being outside the agent causes the agent to will one alternative rather than another, and contingent in that its proximate causes, the created will in question, is not determined by its nature to will in just one way.[5] Since God wills every created happening, God is the agent of every happening. "God works in every agent".[6]

Thus Aquinas seeks to establish omnidetermination, and hence universal divine agency, from very general considerations concerning the nature of God and the relations he must have to *any* created world. I do not find the arguments convincing, but to explain why I would have to go deeply into Thomistic theology and philosophy, something I have no time for in this essay. I shall simply assume that the fundamental nature of God, as briefly adumbrated at the beginning of this section, leaves open the extent to which God determines every detail of his creation. God could determine everything; he has the power to do so. But he also has a choice as to whether to be omni-determining. His nature does not constrain him either way. It is quite conceivable that he proceeds as Augustine, Aquinas, and others suppose. but it is also quite conceivable that God has deliberately refrained from deciding certain details, for example, the free voluntary choices of human beings.

Proceeding in that spirit, I shall explore the prospects for universal divine agency on one or another assumption about the universe. And first I shall indicate how universal divine agency follows from a certain possible feature of the universe, namely, *causal determinism*. Determinism is the thesis that everything that happens in the universe is uniquely determined to happen in just that way by natural causes. Thinking of the universe in this way, let us consider a particular naturally determined event. A cow eats some grass and is thereby sustained. We would say, of course, that the cow is nourished by the grass and that the grass does the nourishing. Does that rule out God's doing the nourishing? By no means. After all, God instituted and maintains the natural order by which this nourishing takes place. God created the entities involved and established the laws by which their behavior is governed. Since he did this knowingly and since he acts purposefully, we must suppose that he set all this up in order, *inter alia*, that this cow should be nourished by this grass at this time.[7] Thus we must hold that God used the grass to nourish the cow and hence that God is the ultimate doer of the deed, just as when I use a hammer to drive in a nail, it is I who drove in the nail, even though I used a hammer to do so. In the latter case I intentionally bring about certain dispositions of the hammer vis-à-vis the nail in order to get the nail imbedded in the wood. In the former case God, via creating and sustaining the natural order, intentionally brings about a certain disposition of the grass vis-à-vis the cow in order to get the cow nourished. Thus in both cases the agent who intentionally brings about the immediate cause of E in order to produce E is rightly said to have produced E. Indeed, God has, if anything, a better right to be regarded as the nourisher of the cow than I have to be regarded as the driver of the nail, for he is more fully responsible than I for the intended effect. I merely make use of an instrument I find ready to hand, whereas God is responsible for the existence of his instrument. Even if I forged the hammer, I merely transformed preexisting materials. I did not bring them into existence out of nothing, nor am I responsible for their continuation in existence.

Indeed, we do not even need the doctrine of continuous divine presentation to arrive at the conclusion that God brings about every effect. Suppose that God simply brings created substances into existence, ordains deterministic laws that govern their behavior, and then leaves them alone. It is still the case that God intentionally set up the natural order as he did, knowing how it would work out at every time and place. We can hardly deny that he did this in order to accomplish his purpose, and hence that in exercising his creative activity, he was intentionally bringing about what ensues in the world. We have as much reason, on this hypothesis, to say that God nourished the cow as we have for saying that the person who booby trapped a car killed the driver. In both cases some arrangements were made in order to lead to a result, and after a passage of time they did lead to that result, even though the agent did not actively intervene after the initial arrangements were made. If God continuously sustains everything in being, this gives his agency, so to say, more immediacy, but it is not required for the pervasive reality of divine agency.

Note that the doctrine of divine agency in the world, as I have been presenting it, is not simply the doctrine of creation and preservation expressed differently. The thesis that God is the intentional agent of all worldly happenings follows from the doctrine of divine creation (and preservation) *provided* that it is conjoined with (a) the thesis of determinism and (b) the assumption that it is God's purpose to bring about all that he does bring about.

To be sure, since God's claim to have nourished the cow rests on the fact that God intentionally and knowingly brought about a state of affairs that led to that nourishment, we cannot limit the instrument God used for this action to the grass ingested. For God no more directly brought about the ingestion than he did the resultant bovine metabolism. That herbaceous ingestion was itself brought about by the use of a previous state of affairs, and that, in turn, all the way back to the Big Bang, or back indefinitely if the universe is temporally infinite. But it is hardly a matter for surprise that God should use instruments on a cosmic scale.

It is sometimes thought that universal divine agency is incompatible with the reality of created agency, so that if we hold that God nourished the cow, we must deny that the grass did. To dispel this impression we only need note that the action involves different roles for different agents and that the filling of one role by no means implies that the others are empty. Whenever an agent uses an instrument to do something, both the (ultimate) agent and the instrument are doing something, and if they were not both doing their job, the effect would not be forthcoming, at least not in that way. The hammer will not pick itself up and drive in the nail, but neither can I drive the nail by my bare hands. Just so, the grass will not nourish the cow unless God endows it with its properties and sustains it in being. To be sure, God could perfectly well bring it about that the cow is sustained without using grass or any other created agency. However, if God chooses to nourish the cow by the ingestion of grass, the grass must do its thing metabolically if God is to do it that way. Similarly, suppose that I could drive the nail with my bare hands if I so choose. Even so, when I choose to use the hammer, the hammer has an essential role to play; if the hammer did not knock the nail in (propelled and guided by me), then I would not drive the nail in that way, by using a hammer. Thus we must reject the theological version of the National Rifle Association principle: "Diseases don't kill people; God kills people". We can recognize that both God and the disease kills, both God and the grass nourishes, each in its distinctive way.[8]

Thus far I have been proceeding on the assumption of determinism. Here the case for divine agency, on the assumptions of classical theism, is quite straightforward. But many thinkers today hold that the results of quantum mechanics show that no physical events are strictly causally determined, though for macroscopic events the chances of things having come out differently are negligible. It would be interesting to explore the bearing of a quantum mechanical point of view on the case for universal divine agency. Could we think of God as having nourished the cow if he used means that are only very, very, very likely to bring it about? I would think so. But here I want to concentrate on another kind of possible exception to causal determinism, human voluntary actions. If they are causally determined, the above account of bovine nourishment applies equally to them. We would all be divine instruments in the same straightforward sense as the grass. But what if, as libertarians think, human voluntary actions are not causally determined? On that assumption can God be said to perform those actions? Aquinas, as we have seen, insists that God intentionally brings about every event, whether uniquely determined by natural causes or not. But having set aside that position, we want to know what follows concerning divine agency of human voluntary actions, from the tenets of classical theism as set out in section 1, plus a libertarian account of human voluntary action.

There is no doubt but that the situation is significantly different from what it is on the thesis of complete determinism. Here we cannot say that God instituted the natural order knowing that it would lead to my freely choosing to become a professional philosopher. Hence we lack that reason for holding that God is the agent of that choice. Even if God foreknows all free human actions, it does not follow that he intentionally brought them about in order to achieve his purpose. It is true that God cannot escape all responsibility for a given naturally undetermined event, for example, that choice of mine. For, being omnipotent, he could have made it impossible, either by creating a wholly deterministic universe that excluded it, by refraining from allowing some of the conditions of its possibility (for example, not endowing me with the capacity to make such a choice), or by interfering before I could bring it off. Thus God bears the kind of responsibility for naturally undetermined events that I bear for something I could have prevented but did not, for example, my small child's beating his fists on the wall in rage. But the fact that I could have prevented that action does not imply that I did it, that *I* beat my son's fists against the wall; the same point holds for God and human free action.

This last result underlines the point that the doctrines of divine omnipotence and continuous divine conservation do not by themselves imply that everything that happens in the world is done by God. For free autonomous created agents, as much as other creatures, exist and exercise their powers only because God continuously sustains them in existence. And the divine omnipotence extends to them as much as to other creatures; God could have refrained from creating them as autonomous agents, and he can interfere with their activities at any time. But despite all that, the above considerations show that God is not properly regarded as the agent of their actions.

I cannot discuss the status of human voluntary actions in this essay, but I want to consider the bearing of the libertarian position on the extent of divine agency. I have already noted that causally undetermined human actions or volitions cannot be regarded as divine actions in a full sense. But, in addition, the libertarian position greatly complicates the case for divine agency of causally determined happenings. Recall that the case for universal divine agency, given universal determinism, rested on the thesis that every worldly happening issued from the order God instituted in order to produce those happenings. But in allowing some created agents a say in what they do, God is also giving them a share in causally determining other sorts of events. Human voluntary actions themselves have effects as much as any other worldly happenings. At least on or near the surface of the earth very little happens that is totally causally independent of past human activity. That leaves the rest of the universe; yet apart from the prospects for human exploration outside our solar system, if there are free created agents elsewhere in the universe, a like situation obtains there. To be sure, there are gross features of the environment that are, thus far, independent of human manipulation. We have not yet altered the cycle of the seasons or the location of the seas. But even here the precise details of the weather or of the sea level are affected by our doings. So there are a vast number of causally determined happenings whose causal determinants did not stem solely from God's choice. In fact, the above-mentioned bovine nourishment is undoubtedly one of them. Assuming that this is a domesticated cow, she would not have been in just that place, in a position to eat just the grass, apart from the voluntary activity of husbandmen. So what is the case for divine agency of those causally determined happenings that are influenced by free human choices?

Let us remind ourselves that we have a problem here because the earlier case for universal divine agency depended on the assumption that God *chose* *all* worldly happenings by creating the constituents of the world and ordaining laws governing their interaction. But since that cow would not be eating that grass if some human had not made certain choices that God did not determine, even indirectly, the previous argument does not apply. So what is God's role in a happening that partly depends on free human choices? It is still true that God partly determines the event; human choices make a partial contribution at most. If God had not endowed cows and grass and numerous other things with the powers they have no cow would be eating any grass anywhere. But the crucial difficulty here comes not from the extent of divine causal involvement in the outcome, but rather from divine intentions. Can we think of God's having intended just this outcome, considering the role of human free choice in producing it? We cannot, as before, hold that God knew that this result would be forthcoming just by instituting the natural order. Of course, it is conceivable that God acts directly to shape the situations that are influenced by human voluntary activity. But at this point we are confining ourselves to happenings that are determined by natural causes.

Let us make a fresh start. It seems clear that God can intentionally produce an effect that is completely determined by created causes only by way of his institution of the causal order. Is there any way in which God could do that if other, independent sources of determination are involved? (Even if those sources owe their independent voice to God's permission, they still make their contribution in ways not specifically chosen by God.) This could happen if God could foresee those independent contributions *and on the basis of that* adjust the details of the natural order so that the outcomes of those creaturely choices would always be in line with his intentions: not necessarily in line with what he would have chosen had he been calling all the shots (his antecedent will), but at least in accordance with his intentions, given that free created agents will act as they will (his consequent will). But if God is to adjust the natural order in light of this knowledge, it cannot be direct intuitive knowledge of the actual occurrence of the free actions, whether this is a contemporaneous awareness of them in the divine eternal now (on the assumption that God is timeless) or a special cognitive power of directly intuiting what will happen in the future (if God is temporal). For the direct intuition of the actual occurrence of the free choice is logically posterior to that choice; it presupposes the constitution of that choice. But that means that it also presupposes the constitution of the causal order that produced the situation in which the choice was made. Human free choices, even if not uniquely determined by their natural environment, are surely heavily influenced by that environment. If my natural environment were different from what it is in certain respects, I would not even have the same alternatives from which to choose. In an appropriately different environment I would not have the opportunity to choose whether to be a professional philosopher. Moreover, given those alternatives, various features of my situation determine what influences me one way or the other. Hence if God's only "foreknowledge" of human free choices is an intuitive awareness of the actual choices, this "comes too late" to permit him to adjust the natural order so as to carry out his intentions in the light of those choices. He would already be stuck with one natural order rather than another.

Thus it seems that if God is to produce intentionally the sustenance of the cow, via the institution of the natural order, he will have to know how free created agents *would* act in various possible situations, as well as knowing how they will act in actual situations. That is, he will have to have "middle knowledge".[9] (God's "middle knowledge" is his conditional knowledge of future contingent events. The controversial doctrine of *scientia media* was devised originally by Molina in an attempt to secure both God's foreknowledge and the reality of human freedom, the latter of which he thought to be undermined by the standard Thomistic accounts.) I myself am dubious about the possibility of such knowledge, not because I think God might be limited in his cognitive powers, but because I doubt that there are any true-or-false propositions, any facts of the matter to be known, about how free agents would act in this or that situation. There may well be truths to the effect that the probability of a given free agent doing A in situation S is so-and-so. But I doubt that there are any truths as to precisely what a free agent would do in a given situation. How could there be such truths if the agent does indeed have a free choice in such a situation? How could there be such a truth if the agent were not somehow determined to do A in that kind of situation? But be that as it may, it would seem that only if God has middle knowledge, could he adjust the laws of nature in the light of human free choices. God needs that knowledge of how the agent would act in various situations if he is to have a realm of possibilities within which the free choice and the laws of nature can be mutually adjusted so as to produce consequences in line with his intentions.

But even in the absence of middle knowledge, and given libertarian assumptions about human voluntary action, it can still be true that God intentionally brings about various not completely specific features of causally determined states of affairs influenced by human voluntary action. God can limit the scope of human free choice, so as to prevent it from threatening various features of his world he wishes to preserve. And he can see to it that his world contains enough counterinfluences to prevent the most disastrous possible consequences of human sin. But on those assumptions God would not unqualifiedly be the agent of all naturally determined happenings.

Let me summarize the results of this section. Given an unrestricted thesis of determinism, there is a straightforward derivation of universal divine agency of worldly happenings from the classical theism we are presupposing. If there are naturally undetermined happenings, whether human voluntary actions or otherwise, this line of argument does not apply to them, and God is not their agent unless he directly produces them. Furthermore, it is only on the assumption that God has "middle knowledge" that he could be the agent of naturally determined happenings that are causally influenced by naturally undetermined happenings. Finally, even where God is not, in the full sense, the agent of certain happenings, he could still see to it that they do not deviate too widely from his intentions.

3. Is Direct Divine Intervention Possible?

Now for the opposite pull, the conviction that some happenings are acts of God in a way in which most happenings are not. Believers sometimes single out particularly noteworthy happenings as acts of God in a special sense. For example, when a boy is the only survivor of a highway collision and then in later life discovers a cure for some dread disease, one may be inclined to regard his survival of the wreck as an act of God in a way in which the collision itself and the dispersion of the wreckage are not. But if all naturally determined happenings are acts of God in a quite straightforward and full-blooded sense, what is this special sense in which only a small subclass deserves that appellation?

To be sure, in the previous section I expressed doubt about the doctrine of middle knowledge that is required if God is to be the agent of all naturally determined happenings, assuming human free will in the libertarian sense. Of course, even if we reject middle knowledge, God will be the agent of many naturally determined happenings that we do not pick out as "acts of God" in a special way, and we will still be faced with the question of the basis on which those special items are picked out. But to simplify the discussion I shall henceforward stifle my doubts about middle knowledge and take God to be the agent of all naturally determined events, even those influenced by free human acts.

There is a well-known traditional answer to the question of what makes special divine acts special, and I am sure you have been impatiently wondering why I had not mentioned it earlier. Only some events are acts of God in the strongest sense, because only in these cases is God *directly* bringing about some effect in the world rather than using natural causes to do so. God normally works through the natural order he has created, but from time to time he bypasses this and brings about some state of affairs just by willing it. These cases are marked out by the fact that things happen otherwise than they would if produced in the usual way by natural causes: a man walks on water, water suddenly becomes wine, the sun remains fixed in the heavens, a blind man regains his sight at the touch of a hand, and so on. It is because we realize that something is happening contrary to the usual course of nature that we are impelled to credit the effect to the direct action of the Creator.

This, in brief, is the traditional view of "miracles". And there is no doubt that this view embodies a sense of "(direct) act of God" different from that in which section 2 shows all naturally determined events to be "acts of God". This traditional view has encountered some stormy seas in the last 200 years or so. First there was the Humean argument that we can never have sufficient reason for supposing that an act of God in this sense (indeed, anything outside the usual course of nature) has occurred. Naturalists have condemned the belief in miracles as contrary to determinism. And underneath these theoretical arguments is the fact that belief in special divine interventions runs counter to the deeply rooted modern faith that for any occurrence, no matter how bizarre, it is in principle possible to find a scientific explanation. In these latter days many theologians have gone over to the opposition and decried the belief in miracles as "unacceptable to the contemporary mind".

> The traditional conception of miracle is irreconcilable with our modern understanding of both science and history. Science proceeds on the assumption that whatever events occur in the world can be accounted for in terms of other events that also belong within the world; and if on some occasions we are unable to give a complete account of some happening — and presumably all our accounts fall short of completeness — the scientific conviction is that further research will bring to light further factors in the situation, but factors that will turn out to be just as immanent and this-worldly as those already known.[10]

Indeed, some of their statements branding the belief as "unintelligible" or "meaningless" go beyond anything to be found in the pages of atheists, who typically are willing to concede that the belief in miracles gets so far as to be false.

> I want to emphasize that the problem we are considering does not arise in the first instance out of difficulties connected with conceiving a transcendent agent; it is rather the difficulty — even impossibility — of conceiving the finite event *itself* which is here supposed to be God's act. . . . An "event" without finite antecedents is no event at all and cannot be clearly conceived; "experience" with tears and breaks destroying its continuity and unity could not even be experienced . . . it is impossible to conceive such an act either as a natural event or as a historical event, as occurring either within nature or history; in short it is impossible to conceive it as any kind of event (in the finite order) at all. Our experience is of a unified and orderly world; in such a world acts of God (in the traditional sense) are not merely improbable or difficult to believe: they are literally inconceivable. It is not a question of whether talk about such acts is true or false; it is, in the literal sense, meaningless; one cannot make the concept hang together consistently.[11]

> Miracles cannot be interpreted in terms of supranatural interference in natural processes. If such an interpretation were true, the manifestation of the ground of being would destroy the structure of being; God would be split within himself.[12]

I am afraid I do not find any of this very impressive as an argument for denying that divine interventions do, or can, occur. Let it be granted that the belief in such interventions runs counter to various features of the contemporary mind-set. But unless we have reason to think that our age is distinguished from all others in being free of intellectual fads and fancies, of attachments to assumptions, paradigms, and models that far outstrip the available evidence, of believing things because one finds one's associates believing it, and so on, this is hardly of any probative value. I fear that theologians who appeal in this way to the contemporary climate of thought are doing nothing more intellectually respectable than considering what it takes to sell the product, or rather, what would inhibit the sale of the product.

> It is this traditional account of the distinctiveness of miracle that makes the concept very difficult for modern minds, and might even suggest to the theologian that "miracle" is a discredited and outmoded word that ought to be banished from his vocabulary. The way of understanding miracle that appeals to breaks in the natural order and to supernatural interventions belongs to the mythological outlook and cannot commend itself in a post-mythological climate of thought.[13]

And even in this they are misguided. A little market research would surely reveal that the most flourishing business is done by fundamentalist sects for whom direct divine interventions are a matter of course and who have scant respect for "the modern understanding of science and history" and the "post-mythological climate of thought".[14]

The more respectable arguments for the impossibility of miracles invoke the doctrine of determinism, directed not against causally undetermined happenings, but against happenings that are determined by supernatural rather than natural causes. But I think it is fair to say that this doctrine is accepted on faith by its devotees. It is true that with the progress of science we have greatly advanced in our knowledge of the natural conditions on which one or another outcome depends, but we are almost as far as we were 1,000 years ago from being able to show in a particular instance that the outcome was causally determined in the last detail. For example, by now we fairly much know the conditions of the putrefaction of meats. But that by no means implies that we have established such laws of putrefaction as will enable us to show in a given case that the precise pattern and mode of putrefaction, down to the molecular details, could not have been other than it was. I do not say that the progress of science, or, indeed, our prescientific knowledge of natural regularities, carries no presumption of determinism. By a not unreasonable extrapolation from what we know, we can suppose that every detail of every event is determined to be just what it is by natural causes. But all our evidence is equally compatible with the view that causal determination is sometimes, or always, only approximate. The antecedent causal factors determine the gross outline of the result, but that only sets limits to the freedom or spontaneity of the agents' responses. The evidence we have, or any evidence we can foresee obtaining in the future, does not put us in a position to claim to know that determinism is true or to brand as irrational one who rejects it.[15]

At this point I would like to say something about the common view that a miracle (direct action of God in the world) would be a "violation of a law of nature". It is worth considering whether this is so, because it is often used against the believer in miracles. If the argument were explicitly set out, it would run something like this. "A law of nature tells us what *must* happen under certain circumstances. But in an alleged miracle what, according to the law, *must* happen does not. The man standing upright on the lake does not sink. But clearly what must happen must happen. Therefore. . . ."[16]

To be sure, even if a direct action of God would be a violation of a law of nature, I do not agree that this would render such actions impossible. The alleged impossibility of a freely falling body's reversing course and moving upward is, at most, an impossibility *within the natural order*, not an unqualified impossibility. The omnipotent author and sustainer of that order is not bound by it; he retains his freedom to act outside its constraints as well as within. But as I see it, we do not need to invoke this consideration, because there is no need to regard God's direct action on the world as a violation of a law of nature in the first place. Whether it is depends on the form that laws of nature take. We can envisage laws of which any direct action of God would be a violation. Such laws would specify unqualified sufficient conditions. Thus a law of hydrostatics might specify as a sufficient condition for a body sinking in still water (of sufficient depth) that the body be of a density greater than the water. If a man walks on still water, that would be a violation of *that* law. But, and this is the crucial point, we are never justified in accepting such laws. The most we are ever justified in accepting in the way of nomologically sufficient conditions is a law that specifies what will (must) ensue in the absence of any relevant factors other than those specified in the law. In other terms, the laws we have adequate reason to accept lay down sufficient conditions only within a "closed system", a system closed to any influences other than those specified in the law. We are confined to laws that carry riders like this simply because none of the laws we are capable of working with take account of all possible influences; even if a formulation took account of all influences with which we are acquainted, we cannot be assured that there are no hitherto unknown influences lurking on the horizon. A man standing upright on the surface of a lake will sink — unless he is being supported by a device dangling from a helicopter, or unless he is being drawn by a motor boat, or unless a sufficiently strong magnetic attraction is keeping him afloat, or. . . . When a galvanometer in working order is attached to an electrically charged body, the needle will move unless someone holds it still, or unless a strong gust of wind prevents the movement, or. . . . Since the laws we work with make (implicit or explicit) provision for interference by outside forces unanticipated by the law, it can hardly be claimed that the law will be violated if a divine outside force intervenes. No doubt that is not the sort of outside force scientists normally envisage, but that is neither here nor there. If we were to make the rider read "in the absence of outside forces of the sort we are prepared to recognize as such", our confidence in all our law formulations would be greatly weakened, for we have no significant basis for supposing that science has identified or can identify all the factors that can influence the outcomes it studies. Once we appreciate this point, we can see that "outside the ordinary course of nature" does not imply "a violation of a law of nature".

It will undoubtedly be replied that my argument depends on certain limitations of the present state of science, and when we develop a unified science, we will be in a position to exhaustively enumerate and interrelate all the factors that can influence a given sort of result. This will enable us to state unqualifiedly sufficient conditions, and the "in the absence of outside forces" rider can be omitted. Even now, though we are not in a position to *assert* laws of this form, we have good reason to suppose that there are such laws in force. My response would be to deny that we have sufficient reason to suppose that there are such laws. I recognize this to be an intelligible supposition, but we lack adequate reason to suppose it to be true. The course of science strongly suggests to me that nomological dependence is a "local" affair and it will be tight only to the extent that a system is closed to alien influences. I take the dream of a unified science in which all possible influences are systematically integrated to be just that, a dream.

4. Is Direct Divine Intervention Required?

There is much more to be said about the possibility of direct divine action on the world, but we must push on. Thus far I have been attacking the claim that direct divine action in the world is impossible and the claim that we can confidently rule out its actuality. But though I consider it a live possibility that God sometimes directly produces effects in the world, I am not at all inclined to restrict myself to this way of marking out those occurrences that are acts of God in some specially significant way. I also take it as a live possibility that God always acts through the natural order, and so I want to consider how to mark out the "special" acts of God on that assumption. There are several reasons for not restricting ourselves to the "direct intervention" account, even if we are not prepared to rule out its possibility.

First, even though divine intervention is possible, it is by no means clear that it ever does happen. I do not go along with Hume's argument in his famous essay on miracles that it is in principle impossible to be justified in believing that something has happened outside the usual course of nature, but I do recognize that we are rarely, if ever, in a position to justify conclusively such a claim. No matter how unusual or outlandish the occurrence, we cannot rule out the possibility that it was brought about by natural causes in a way that we do not currently understand. It is a truism that with respect to some occurrences attributed at one time to supernatural intervention we are, at a later time, in a position to give a scientific explanation, or at least to see the gross outlines of such an explanation. Mental illness and recovery therefrom is a signal case in point. We can be justified in dismissing the possibility of a naturalistic explanation only if we have (1) a complete description of the particular case and (2) a complete inventory of natural causes of that sort of occurrence. Armed with that, we might be able to show that there were no available natural causes that could have produced that result. But when are we in a position to do that? If we insist that what makes something a "special" act of God is that it is a direct act of God on the world, we cannot be assured that there are any "special" acts of God.

Second, not all the occurrences we feel inclined to treat as special acts of God even appear to be independent of natural causes. The contrary impression is fostered by preoccupation with the standard biblical "superspectacular" miracles: the parting of the waters of the Sea of Reeds, walking on water, changing water into wine, and so on. These do *appear* to stem from special divine intervention, whatever our final judgment. But other cases do not immediately strike us that way. Think of all the cases in which one takes oneself to have been guided or strengthened by God. When I take God to have guided me in making a decision, or to have enabled me to meet a crisis without collapsing, the phenomenology of the situation may present nothing outlandish. On the surface nothing untoward happens. In the guidance case I weigh the alternatives, think about them, pray about the problem, try to imagine alternative outcomes, and so on. In the strengthening case I simply meet the crisis, doing what seems called for at each point, perhaps frequently calling on God for help. Or consider a case in which I take God to have spoken to me. This *may* involve an apparent miracle—the clouds open and a booming voice seems to emerge from the empyrean vault. But more commonly we get something like the following: I ask God in prayer what I should concentrate on in my work, after which the thought forms in my mind that I should give priority to administration rather than scholarship, accompanied by a strong conviction that this is God's message for me. Again, on the surface nothing happens in a way that seems outside the order of natural causality. In all these cases we have events of quite ordinary sorts, occurring in contexts in which they frequently occur. Or again, consider events taken to be "providential", like the boy's emerging unhurt from the accident in which all others perished. This may be mildly unusual, but it is by no means unprecedented. It is easy to think of natural factors that would produce such a result—place and angle of impact, positioning of passengers, what each encounters in being propelled from his/her position. In all these cases one may believe that God is working outside the ordinary course of nature to strengthen one, to preserve the person from harm, or whatever, but one is not forced into this belief by an apparent absence of the right kind of natural causes. For all we can tell by an examination of the situation itself, these thoughts, capacities, or whatever were just as much produced by natural causes as other effects of those sorts.

Third, even where we believe that God is acting outside the natural order, that belief is by no means always crucial to our taking the occurrence to be an act of God in a specially significant way. Sometimes it *is* crucial. Here we must draw some distinctions within this vaguely demarcated class of "special" acts of God. The distinctions have to do with the special role or function we take the act in question to have, what sort of thing we take God to be up to in performing it, or, more generally, what we take to be so special about it. One historically important kind of specialness that does depend on divine intervention is the way in which an act of God is supposed to authenticate some person's claim to authority, to be delivering a divine message, or to be acting under divine instructions. Thus, according to Exodus 4, when God gave Moses his commission in the wilderness, he empowered Moses to validate his claims by performing certain miracles, for example, turning a staff into a snake and then back into a staff and turning water from the Nile into blood. God confirmed Elijah's claims to authority by sending fire from heaven to consume the offering made on Mt. Carmel. Jesus' status was confirmed, for many, by the wonders he performed. When this is taken to be the special significance of an act of God, it is essential that the act be thought of as direct. For the reasoning presumably runs like this. Moses did something that he could not do by his own natural powers; indeed, it was something that no creature could bring off by its natural powers. This could only happen if the creator and controller of the natural order set aside the usual rules in this particular instance and endowed Moses with special supernatural powers.[17] But he would not have done this had he not wished thereby to endorse Moses' claims. Therefore. . . .

If an occurrence is to elicit this reasoning, it must not only *be* outside the course of nature but must seem to be so. In fact, the latter is presumably sufficient in itself. If and only if the occurrence runs counter to what is generally believed to be the natural outcome of the antecedent situation will it be taken as an authentication of prophetic claims. Furthermore, it must be a publicly observed occurrence if it is to be effective. In this connection we should note that the effectiveness of this procedure depends on a certain cast of mind in the audience; in particular, it presupposes that the audience will be disposed to take direct divine intervention as the correct explanation of anything that strongly runs counter to what is confidently believed to be the course of nature. Hence it will fall flat with a contemporary scientistic audience that is predisposed to take such surprising occurrences as an indication that our scientific theories need to be revised. If *they* were to witness fire falling from heaven at Elijah's request on Mt. Carmel, their reaction would be, not "God has confirmed Elijah's authority", but rather "Back to the drawing board".

But by no means all occurrences that are regarded as acts of God in some specially significant way fall into these two groups. And many occurrences are taken to be special in a way that does not require the assumption of direct divine intervention. For one thing, there are God's "personal dealings" with creatures of which we spoke earlier—God's strengthening, guiding, enlightening, empowering, and speaking to the person. Again, there are all the cases that fall under the rubric of "providential care", personal and corporate. This includes, on the personal level, recovery from illness, survival of accidents, and the building of a career in ways not anticipated in advance. On the corporate level we have the rise and fall of nations, the preservation of a people from destruction, the growth of the Church and its guidance in making its basic decisions. In all these cases what is taken to be "specially significant" is the nature of the outcome, not merely as happening somehow or other but *as a carrying out of God's purposes.* We may believe in some or all such cases that God has brought about the outcome apart from natural causes, but that belief is not essential for our singling out these occurrences in the way we do. What we take to be special about them is simply that God has acted in such a way as to effect *this result*, that *this* is something that God *intended* to bring about. How God chose to do this is not the heart of the matter; it will be special in the relevant way whatever that choice. In these cases we are centrally interested in the character of the result whereas in the "authentication" cases the result could be, and often was, quite indifferent in itself, its significance residing in its being a sign of divine favor.

Many people think, and I myself at one time thought, that the belief that God enters into active interaction with his creatures, a belief crucial to the Judeo-Christian tradition, requires us to suppose that God directly intervenes in the world, acting outside the course of nature. But the considerations of this paper clearly indicate otherwise. Just by virtue of creating and sustaining the natural order God is in as active contact with his creatures as one could wish. Merely by the use of natural causes God carries out his purposes and intentions with respect to creatures, and this surely counts as genuine action toward them. If God speaks to me, or guides me, or enlightens me by the use of natural causes, he is as surely in active contact with me as if he had produced the relevant effects by a direct fiat. Indeed, as I suggested above, we do not even need the doctrine of continuous divine preservation in order to achieve that result; although if God is actively sustaining everything in being at every moment, this does, so to speak, give God's instrumental actions more immediacy. But even without that, God is still intentionally doing everything done by the natural order he creates. After all, when one human being directly interacts with another, by speaking to or embracing the other, the agent is making use of aspects of the natural order, exploiting physical and psychological regularities; we do not know how to do it otherwise. And surely this does not imply that we are not in active contact with each other in such transactions. However necessary direct intervention may be for the authentication of messengers, it is not required for genuine divine-human interaction.

5. Special Acts of God without Direct Intervention

Because of all these considerations I am motivated to find some other way to bring out what makes some acts of God "specially significant", some way that does not require us to view them as outside the course of nature. Before launching into this, let me underscore something that has been at least implicit in my discussion. I am very much opposed to trying to limit God either to working within the course of nature or to direct intervention. In my view both the traditional "supernaturalists" and the scientistic "revisionists" are wrong in seeking to restrict God to one *modus operandi*. I am not charging them with deliberately trying to dictate God's procedure. No doubt each side sees itself as delineating the only possible alternative. But as I have been arguing, both sides are wrong in denying the possibility of the other side's suggestion. Since I take it that in speaking to me God could be working either through the course of nature or outside it, I am content to leave it up to God which way he prefers. And I will not insist on determining which way he has chosen before listening to his word. End of sermon.

In seeking a way of construing events within the natural order as "special" acts of God I am entering onto well-trodden ground. The "revisionist" theologians who reject the view that God sometimes acts outside the natural order have been much concerned to explain why some naturally determined events, rather than others, are taken as "miracles", "acts of God", or "revelations of God". I find in their discussions two suggestions, one of which I shall reject as inadequate, but the other of which I find more promising.[18]

The most obvious suggestion to be found in the writings of, for example,

Paul Tillich and John Macquarrie on this subject is that what distinguishes the "special" acts of God is something about the way in which they are experienced and responded to. According to Tillich

> A genuine miracle is first of all an event which is astonishing, unusual, shaking, without contradicting the rational structure of reality. In the second place, it is an event which points to the mystery of being, expressing its relation to us in a definite way. In the third place, it is an occurrence which is received as a sign-event in an ecstatic experience.[19]

Here I want to concentrate on the third condition, that the occurrence is received "in an ecstatic experience". I am not sure exactly what Tillich means by this, but it is clear that in such an experience one has the sense of being "grasped" by something fundamental in reality and for human life. Tillich often speaks of being grasped by "the power of being", the "ground of being", the "mystery of being".[20] He calls on Rudolph Otto's analysis of numinous experience in terms of the *mysterium tremendum et fascinans* to flesh out his account.[21] Furthermore, the occurrence calls out, or tends to call out, what Tillich calls "ultimate concern", a reaction that involves such components as an absolute commitment, an absolute trust in a promise of salvation, and total devotion and worship.[22] In this experience it seems that the ultimate is present and manifesting itself to one. It is a searing and transforming experience that can reshape one's entire life, providing a focus and organization for one's existence.

Now I do not wish to deny that what are taken to be specially significant acts of God can be, and sometimes are, received and reacted to in this way. Nor do I wish to minimize the importance of such experiences for the individual and for the shaping of religious communities and religious traditions. However, an appeal to these experiences does not suffice to give a general account of what differentiates these "special" acts of God from other events, and this for two reasons. First, we do not always react in so extravagant a fashion to what we take to be a specially significant act of God. I would agree that if a person were completely indifferent and blase in the face of such an occurrence, that would be a good, and perhaps conclusive, reason for denying that he took it to be an act of God. But it seems clear that I *can* take God to have sustained me or guided me without being shaken to the roots of my being by the experience. Quite devout people see many or most occurrences as constituting God's dealings with us; yet many of them never have a Damascus-road experience. So we *can* take something as a "special" act of God without receiving it in the ecstatic fashion Tillich specifies. The second point is that when the ecstatic experience does occur, it can, and often does, *result* from our supposing the occurrences to be an act of God rather than *constituting* that supposition. When I become aware of the boy's "miraculous" survival of the accident, I take this to be a case of God's providential care, and this may then lead me to have the experience of being grasped by the "power of being", of being in the presence of God. Since in these cases my taking the occurrence as an act of God causes the experiential reaction, the former can hardly be constituted by it.

Note also that Tillich's account is restricted to events that are "astonishing" and "unusual". This leaves aside all the "ordinary, on the surface" occurrences we were discussing earlier as special acts of God.

But, as intimated above, the ecstatic experience is not Tillich's whole story. Even in the passage just quoted he also speaks of "an event which points to the mystery of being, expressing its relation to us in a definite way". Rather than take the time to unpack this rather cryptic formula, I shall turn to John Macquarrie, whose development of this line of thought is more lucid.

> What is distinctive about miracle is God's presence and self-manifestation in the event.[23]

In speaking of the crossing of the Sea of Reeds Macquarrie writes:

> . . . this significance is really God's grace and judgment.[24]

Again:

> The miracle focuses the presence and action that underlies the whole and makes sense of the whole.[25]

From this point I would like to take the ball and run with it myself. Since Tillich and Macquarrie think of God as Being-Itself in a way that seems to them to preclude thinking of God as literally an agent who carries out intentions and acts to achieve his purpose, they do not attempt to develop the concept of an act of God with which I am working. Nevertheless, the above quotations from Macquarrie suggest to me something that I can work out as follows. In taking my coming to a decision or my forming a certain thought as an act of God (of guidance or communication) I suppose this event to be a "self-manifestation" of God's purposes (or a fragment thereof). Even if I take everything that happens in the world as an act of God, still I specially regard these events as acts of God, not because they *are* acts of God in any stronger, different, or more basic sense than myriads of other happenings I just let float by, but because in these cases I have some idea as to what God is up to. I discern, or think I discern, a bit of the divine purpose. These events "focus" for me "the presence and action that underlies the whole and make sense of the whole". Why do I take only some of the ideas that float through my mind to be cases of God communicating with me, even though I regard all my nonvoluntary ideation as acts of God? Because in those special cases I have some idea as to what God is trying to accomplish: for example,

I take it that God is forming in my mind the idea of concentrating on administration, along with a strong sense of conviction, because that is what he wants me to do. Why do I regard the escape of the boy from the wreck as a special act of God? Because I think I can see why God saved the boy, but I do not think I can see why God arranged other details of the accident as he did. Even if everything that happens is carrying out the divine purpose, it is only seldom that we have, or think we have, some insight into what that is. It is these cases that we take, in a preeminent sense, to be acts of God. Thus when I speak of "special" acts of God, the specialness attaches to our talking rather than to the action itself. This may seem to lay us open to our own criticism of the first suggestion from Tillich as being too subjective. But the criticism of that suggestion was not that it made the discrimination rest on *some* reaction of the subject, but rather that it made the discrimination rest on experiential and emotional reactions of the subject. Our account is rather in terms of how the subject is thinking about the matter, what the subject believes about it.

Note too, in case this needs emphasizing, that it is only the demarcation of "special" acts of God that is made to rest on human reactions. Members of this class share with innumerable other happenings the objective feature of being acts of God, a feature that attaches to them however we think, feel, or experience.

But if we believe that all or most naturally determined events *are* acts of God, do we not think that we see what God's intention is for any such event, however insignificant and nonspecial it appears, namely, that this event occurs. If I believe that each movement of each leaf in the wind is done by God, do I not thereby also believe that each of those movements carried out God's intention that it occur? This must be admitted. How then can I maintain that it is only where I take something to be a "specially significant" act of God that I take myself to discern a bit of the divine purpose? I think the answer must be that in those special cases we think we discern a *bit more* of the divine purpose. We think that we see at least a little way into what God's purpose was *in* bringing off that event, for what further purpose that event occurred. This is clearly the case with respect to the "superspectacular" miracles, where those who regard them as acts of God see them as instrumental in the furtherance of national destiny, or the work of the Church, or the validation of prophets. Again, when we single out a pattern of events as an instance of providential care (e.g., the building of a career in science or the ministry in the face of hardship, failures, and obstacles), we think we see, to some extent, why God would be interested in doing that, how this furthers his purpose for mankind. Finally, the same point holds for God's "individual dealings with us". When I take a piece of ideation to be a message from God, I think I know, at least in part, what God meant to be communicating, and hence I think I know for what immediate purpose God brought it about that those ideas formed themselves in my mind at that time. Again, when I suppose God to have guided me in making a decision to go into teaching rather than the law, I believe that I have some inkling of the purpose for which God guided my deliberations in a certain way, namely, to lead me to make that decision and thereby to make such contributions as I can to my fellow human beings in that mode of activity.

I do not suppose that this is the whole story of what is involved in "special" acts of God. Indeed, I do not suppose that there is a sharp line between the special ones and the ones we acknowledge in a blanket fashion. If it is a matter of degree how special we take a certain act of God to be, our interest or involvement in the alleged divine purpose may well play a large role in determining the degree of "specialness" for us. And there may be other complexities as well. But I believe that the main lineaments of the situation are as I have depicted them.

6. Conclusion

Thus we can think of God's action in the world as pervasive, if not all-pervasive, whether or not anything ever happens outside the ordinary course of nature. And whether or not this is the case, we can understand why it is that we pick out some small subclass of happenings to be taken as divine action in a special way.[26]

NOTES

1. Paul Tillich, *Systematic Theology*, London: Nisbet, 1953, vol. 1, p. 274.
2. Ibid., p. 296.
3. Aquinas, *Summa Theologiae* (*ST*), Ia, Q. 103, art. 5. Aquinas, *Summa Contra Gentiles* (*SCG*), III, 64.
4. *ST*, Ia, Q. 103, art. 7. *SCG*, III, 72, 74.
5. *ST*, Ia, Q. 105, art. 4. *SCG*, III, 89, 90.
6. *ST*, Ia, Q. 105, art. 5. *SCG*, III, 67, 70.
7. I neglect the possibility that there should be foreseen but unintended consequences of divine action. I take it that it is results we are aiming at without also bringing about a host of results we are not aiming at. I assume that God can, and does, bring about just what he intends to bring about, no more and no less. (Remember that we are limiting ourselves here to states of affairs that are wholly within God's voluntary control. The possibility of states of affairs that are not will be discussed below.)

Peter van Inwagen has suggested to me that God might create a world without deciding all of its structure. For example, he might will that there be some number of atoms between 10^{43} and 10^{44} but leave it to chance just how many there will be.

A similar point can be made as to the exact form of natural laws. This suggestion poses a different sort of challenge to the thesis that everything naturally determined is intentionally brought about by God. Here the alternative is not that there are foreseen but unintended consequences of divine choices, but rather that certain features of the causal process were not chosen by God at all. If this is an intelligible supposition I do not know how to rule it out. But I am not convinced at this point that it makes sense to think of God's leaving certain details of the basic structure of the universe "to chance".

8. Cf. Aquinas, *SCG*, III, 69, 70.

9. This term was introduced by the sixteenth-century Jesuit theologian Louis de Molina. For a discussion of this type of knowledge, together with historical references, see R. M. Adams, "Middle Knowledge and the Problem of Evil", *American Philosophical Quarterly, 14*, April 1977, 109-117.

10. John Macquarrie, *Principles of Christian Theology*, 2nd edition, New York: Charles Scribner's Sons, 1977, p. 248.

11. Gordon Kaufman, "On the Meaning of 'Act of God' ", in *God the Problem*, Cambridge, MA: Harvard University Press, 1972, pp. 134-135.

12. Paul Tillich, *Systematic Theology*, p. 129. One cannot help noting that in this passage Tillich, to use his own terminology, seems to be absolutizing the natural order of causality and making an "idol" of it.

13. Macquarrie, *Principles of Christian Theology*, pp. 247-248.

14. Revisionist theologians also object on theological grounds to supposing that God sometimes directly intervenes in nature. They take such behavior to be "unworthy" of God, since it presupposes a lack of power or foresight, a defect of will or intellect. They assume that only if God were unable to set up the natural order in such a way as to achieve all his purposes by its normal working would he seek to carry out any intentions by direct intervention. But why should we assume that God would prefer to attain his goals only by working through the natural order if he could? What basis do we have for that assumption? Even if we can see why God should choose to work sometimes outside the natural order (and traditionally it has been thought that God would choose this route in order to authenticate his messengers), we certainly cannot see why he should choose to work exclusively through the natural order. It seems to be presumptuous for any human being to claim that degree of insight into the divine preference order.

15. For a more elaborate version of this line of thought see Peter van Inwagen, *An Essay on Free Will*, New York: Oxford University Press, 1983, pp. 198-201. The argument of this paragraph has been quite independent of considerations from quantum mechanics. If that were brought into the picture, the prospects for establishing determinism would be even dimmer.

16. It is worth noting that this argument can be mounted only on a fairly strong interpretation of natural laws, according to which they have modal force. Laws as mere records of observed regularities or mere extrapolations of observed regularities, or mere universally true conditionals, will not do the trick.

17. It does not matter whether we think of God as endowing Moses with supernatural powers or think of God as turning the staff into a serpent himself. In either case God has acted outside the natural order—either to bring about an event in the universe directly or to endow some creature with supernatural powers. In either case the direct action of God, in connection with the claims made by the human being, is taken to validate those claims. Some miracles are more naturally viewed in one of these ways, and some in the other. It is more natural to think of *Moses* as turning

the staff into a serpent (having been granted the special power to do so by God), whereas it is more natural to think of God sending down the fire on the sacrifice, after Elijah calls on him to do so.

18. These two suggestions are intimately blended in the writings of theologians such as those I will be citing, Paul Tillich and John Macquarrie. If I were trying to represent the views of these people, I would present the matter differently. My purpose here is to distinguish two ways in which one might try to answer our question and to evaluate each.

19. Tillich, *Systematic Theology*, p. 130.

20. See, e.g., ibid., pp. 24, 124, 126.

21. Ibid., pp. 239-240.

22. Paul Tillich, *Dynamics of Faith*, New York: Harper, 1957, chapter 1.

23. Macquarrie, *Principles of Christian Theology*, p. 250.

24. Ibid., p. 251.

25. Ibid., p. 253.

26. This paper has profited greatly from comments by Robert Audi, Richard Creel, Alfred Freddoso, James Keller, Alvin Plantinga, and Peter van Inwagen.

PART THREE

Evolution and Creation

CHRISTIANS GET THE BEST OF EVOLUTION

James F. Ross

1. Introduction

Could humans have evolved, yet be capable of life forever with God?[1] Evolutionary hypotheses invite us away from the baleful ambiguities of dualism, from talk of our bodies and souls as if they were two things, with the soul the true self, the body a disposable shell. They challenge us, suggesting ways as well, to reconceive our nature more coherently in view of our conjectured origins and our revealed destiny.[2] They are, as Teilhard de Chardin thought, a "light" to the theologian.[3]

1.1. A QUESTION OF HUMAN NATURE, NOT CAUSATION

The problem concerns the *nature* of man, particularly as understood by the Catholic Church and other important Christian churches: that humans are *by nature* both material beings, not ghosts in machines, and, though embodied, *apt* for unending life with God; that for any of this no change in *what* we are is required or is even possible. (I do not explore dualist readings of that conception in this essay.)

The problem is only *apparently* about how humans are produced originally, whether by evolution or direct creation; it is *substantively* about how to describe our nature consistently and intelligibly. I am looking for an account of human nature that literally fits the Christian conception I mentioned, as to the undeniable materiality, mortality, and unity of the person. Imagining evolution as systems of spread-out causation, where complexity builds rapidly by simple rules that "follow" an overall bias, say, natural selection, "frees the mind". It reminds one that an adequate account of human nature must place humans squarely at home in the physical universe, perhaps even among the objectives to which all nature is directed.

I have narrowed the issue a little, emphasizing that intelligent beings, and probably living beings in general, are not merely resultant but emergent from micromatter and have active powers not possessed by their microparts. These parts, in any mere aggregation or physicochemical interaction alone, are in-

223

capable of such active powers, but in "obediential" capacity (see I, 6 below) are a perfect medium for them. So most of this essay is about some conditions for emergent being, which could, of course, appear in nature by evolution.

"Scientific" materialists think humans are not suitable for eternal life. They think humans, like plants, are composed of structures that pass away with their realizations. Biblical fundamentalists think humans are not suitable for evolution from prehumans but are fit to be made only directly by God. Maybe, indeed, enspiriting *is* specially related to God (so I believe). Still, humans and all material living things belong to one natural system along with inanimate things. Humans are, nevertheless, *apt* for life with God.[4]

Evolution is a goal-directed *spread-out* way of coming to be from secondary causes. It is like a natural system of assembly lines and model-years, with an "inner" account of design changes (perhaps some version of "random variation", "adaptation", and "natural selection"). The processes might even, for all we know, be ordered to a cosmic outcome, as embryonic development is ordered to the mature organism.

Living things generally seem to belong to a "spread-out" system of design changes. In saying that, I make no attempt to deny that details of evolutionary theory, especially those relating microgenetic changes to gross organ changes, are sketchy and in some respects anomalous.[5] Still, it would be an unusual living organism that could *not* belong to *any* evolutionary system. That is because material living things replicate their designs (with variations) in their offspring, ensuring design preservation when generation is successful, along with inevitable design changes due to the functioning and malfunctioning of the reproduction process. So we look to the *nature* of humans. Are humans *apt* to have evolved from prehuman life forms? Is there something about humans that makes it *impossible* that they are the output of the causal systems characteristic of living things generally?[6]

1.2. A QUESTION OF UNITY IN BEING

If humans are fit to have evolved, the cosmic physics, the life system (Teilhard de Chardin's biosphere), and the psychic system (Teilhard's noosphere) have to allow for the unity of being of intelligent material things, like the unity in living things that differs from the mere aggregation, the connecting and compounding, of nonliving things. Living things are alive all over, with one life, not the way a steel beam is rigid all over by the bondings of each molecule to its neighbors, but more the way a computer is "on" by an "all-over" power. *How* are humans—who inhabit the material, the biotic, and the noetic realms—unities, integrated with the whole cosmos, yet irreducible to the matter that composes them?

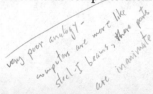

[handwritten note] very poor analogy — computers are more like steel I beams, they are inanimate.

Imagining a "spread-out" process by which quanta organize into light, then atoms, then alive and intelligent being, exposes the *scale* of what we need to do: to resolve a question about *what* humans really are by reexamining the whole cosmos.

1.3 EVOLUTION SUGGESTS EMERGENCE,
BUT EMERGENCE DOES NOT REQUIRE EVOLUTION

In fact, evolution is mostly resultant. The supposed evolution of life and intelligence suggests that there is emergence in nature (described below, I, 6), not just "resultance" (as when pine needles adapt to altitude), yet no evolutionary hypothesis is part of the emergence doctrine I explore. In fact, neither requires the other. Even if humans came directly from the hand of God, like tin soldiers from a toy moulder, humans are still emergent things, in the sense of "emergence" I explain below (I, 6). Nevertheless, the kind of thing humans *have* to be, in order to be at all, is a kind of thing *suitable* to appear in the cosmos by evolution, though it would appear that some "triggering" event is required (see section V below). That much philosophical analysis may be able to establish. Whether or not humans did so appear is a factual issue for both science and religion, one which is not settled by philosophy.

I am content for now with clarifying a bit what it is for human nature to be emergent, relative to micromatter, and how that is the basis for the active ability to live forever with God. This offers an alternative to dualist accounts of human nature and opens broad areas of metaphysics for a new look.

1.4. PROSPECTS FOR ANALOGY OF BEING: PSYCHIC VS. MATERIAL

Beyond the material I think there is another dimension of reality, psychic or spiritual, characterized by "psychic force", "psychic energy". Within this realm causation is displayed according to *meaning* and is, thus, perceptible to the understanding alone. Such causation is, in effect, agency that operates within perceived meaning, within displayed meaning (and feeling), with lawlike regularity and upon material things, like humans and objects. (This is not a new suggestion; many, like Jung and Teilhard de Chardin, have advanced it.)

That kind of causation configures—in terms of meaning, purpose, and value—events and things accessible to understanding alone. These configurations cannot fully be explained by any account of the micromatter because the laws of microstates cannot distinguish the meaningful from the nonsensical and the valuable from the empty.[7]

In the longer run we have to explain how humans are materially subsistent *psychic* beings and why there are no cases of materially subsistent *intelligent*, but nonpsychic, things, where the causation involved is merely the basic physical causation operative everywhere on matter. (That, obviously, is a falsifiable claim should someone succeed in making such a thing.) The main point to establish (but not in this essay) is that spirit, in which humans share, is a distinct way of being from matter and is required for intelligent life. That hypothesis too, if refined, will eventually be testable when human cognition, especially the unconscious and the will, is better understood. It could also be *refuted* should a genuinely cognitive computer be produced.

1.5. INITIAL APPROXIMATION

For the moment an approximate notion of intelligent being, as a kind of living being, will do. Emergence is to be understood in a way that does not require that any distinct "force" (energy or causation) beyond the universal physical forces be involved, and, in principle, it does not: that is, the emergence of life from matter may not require psychic being, even if the emergence of intelligent being does. Whether some unknown force, say, *élan vital*, is required for the emergence of life from micromatter, or whether it is the organization (the form) of micromatter into life systems that gives the appearance of some force or vitality, need not be considered here.

In the special case of beings that inhabit the realm that is God's, the spiritual realm, besides a formal cause that is emergent (e.g., organization-into-a-rose-bush, organization-into-a-human) intelligent being requires an *efficient* causation, both of beginning and continuing to be, which is (only) analogous to the causation of material beings.

1.6. HUMANS BOTH NATIVE AND EMERGENT

Humans are not some "imported alien entity" in the cosmos; they are natives of the material world. They are of nature and not a miracle. Humans will, if St. Thomas Aquinas (*De potentia dei* 5, 5-10) is right, and I think he is, dwell in the cosmos forever. How can something so different in its active abilities from its microcomponents belong to the *same* universe as they? How is human being "harmonized", unified, with the cosmos? It is unified by the fact that it is emergent being, being that "boils up" from micromatter into something *subsistent in* it.

Generally speaking, for humans to be emergent is for humans to subsist in micromatter by being *necessarily* composed of carbon-based molecules, constructed of *systems* of such molecules (groups of such molecules formed into subsystems), and yet for "being-a-human", as a structural organization of organic molecules, to be absolutely inaccessible from the micromatter. This inaccessibility is of three kinds: (a) mere obediential potency of the micro-matter; (b) analogy of being between macromatter and the subsistent thing; (c) formal inaccessibility of the emergent structure system from a true cosmic physics. I will discuss the first kind here, the second kind in section I, 7, and the third in section III.

Now, if we could inspect all "possible" states of micromatter, generated from arbitrary "entry" states by the laws of physics alone, no subpatterns of states could be identified as "being a human being". This is the first kind of inaccessibility.

Consider ink molecules and messages. Because the "possible" patterns of ink molecules include every inscribable message, all writable nonsense, and all arrays that neither are nor fail to be writings (e.g., blots, blob, and blurs), messages can subsist in ink marks as in a medium, but there is no way, even from the most comprehensive knowledge about ink, to construct from it either the syntax or the semantics of any system of messages. There is nothing about *ink* or the *states* of ink that provides more than the passive capacity ("obediential potency") for messages. Thus, something, whether a human or a message, is emergent with respect to a medium (or class of media) just in case it cannot *be* except in the medium, although its structure is inaccessible from the medium, which has only "obediential potency" for the structure.

Organic micromatter is the only medium possible for a human, whose flesh and bone of its essence (as far as we know, at least as to its beginning and development), whereas sound waves are an alternative medium for any inscribable message. A message does not have one kind of matter "of its essence".[8]

Humans exist materially, but not *in a subject*, the way an apple's shape exists *in* the apple and is *of* the apple. I am not a being in a material being or beings. *Subsistence is existence in a medium but not in a subject.* The materially subsistent thing does not *inhere* in its medium or its components; it does not "belong to" or "characterize" the medium, the material, or the component. Rather, the material thing — *in* the medium (say, micromatter), *of* the matter (say, carbon-based molecules), and *out of* the components (cells, organs, systems) — *is* absolutely. It *exists* and can endure a complete change of components at a great enough "remove" (e.g., a change of atoms, perhaps of cells, but probably not of organs). Relatively to micromatter a human is a subsistent thing. Absolutely, it is a really existing subject. Subsistence, which is existence in a medium, and out of stuff, but not in a subject, can come about either by resultance or by emergence. In the case of humans the ex-isting thing, subsistent materially, is emergent, not resultant.

Resultant things, as I said, can subsist materially, too. Simple aggregates and simple compounds do not result in a subsistent thing: a pile of sand is not a hill subsisting in the medium sand. But radios subsist materially because they are beyond the active abilities of their components both to begin to be and to organize in that way. They exist in a medium, are the *subject* both of prediction and inherence, and yet are not *in* a subject. The emergence-resultance distinction is a distinction among subsistent things, things that exist in a medium but are ultimate subjects in being. (Note that this use of 'subsist' is not congruent with important theological uses [e.g., about the Trinity] but is fashioned for this job.)

1.7. HUMAN BEING AND MATERIAL BEING ARE ANALOGOUS (ANALOGIA ENTIS)

Emergent being makes substantial being (in contrast to qualitative or quantitative being) analogical. By that I mean literally that the being of a stone is different from that of a plant, which is different from that of an animal, which is different from that of an intelligent thing.[9] That is the second kind of inaccessibility between micromatter and emergent being. Emergent beings are mutually inaccessible because global emergence (see section III) brings about real analogy of being among material subjects, *analogia entis* (say, among microparticles, plants, and people) and because such differences in being cannot be analyzed as respects (whether finite in number or not) in which the entities differ (in fact, analogical difference of being cannot be analyzed as a lattice of "*features*" in which entities agree and differ).[10]

To say something "emerges" in nature is to say, not by what *process* it appears, but rather that it subsists in material components, as does a radio, but, unlike a radio, "inaccessibly from them" (in the ways under discussion) and independently of them as individuals. Some evolution, like other production methods, is emergent; most is resultant. Most causation is neither evolutionary nor emergent. Thus, the three notions—*causation*, *evolution*, and *emergence*—are distinct, although the latter two involve the first, while neither the second nor the third involves the other. A brick is a resultant of its components, arranged, and so is a house; neither evolves. A plant, an animal, or a human is not a resultant; each is emergent, relative to micromatter, whether or not it evolved. Emergence may be either local or global. Human emergence is global (see section III, 3).

1.8. IS THIS NOVEL?

Perhaps aligning *emergence* so that humans are a natural but special case of emergent being (i.e., materially subsistent immortal beings[11]) is novel. Perhaps also novel is identifying global emergence by the possession of the three kinds of inaccessibility already mentioned: (a) mere obediential potentiality of the matter, (b) analogy of being, irreducible to a lattice of similarities, and (c) formal features of the universe that make certain "realms" of laws formally inaccessible from a true cosmic physics (see section III). Otherwise, the overall viewpoint is Aquinas', with some elements from Aristotle.[12] It is not new to say humans are unities in being, are material but able to live with God, and might have had prehuman ancestors. The surprise is how little we understand this, and how mighty a task it is to explain global emergence and then to *show* that humans are a case of it.

2. A Theological Reflection

Is there a conflict between evolutionary theory and the Christian faith? Not if humans *did*, in fact, evolve from prehumans. A true account of evolution (or of anything else) is compatible with what is divinely revealed. An approximate one may not be. Its rough edges may scrape the religious substance. Similarly, religious belief, unrefined by new reflection, may snag the fabric of science.

CONTEXT AFFECTS CONTENT

Revelation, formulated propositionally, varies semantic context with historical context.[13] For instance, that the truth of "the dead will be resurrected" requires that the resurrected be composed of the same flesh and bones they possessed at death or at some other time is unlikely given present scientific knowledge. In the Middle Ages it might have appeared to be part of what is meant.

"Theological" questions are typically phrased in "secular" terms: for example, is sin "estrangement from oneself"? Does one see God in the very flesh one dies in? Does transubstantiation alter molecules chemically? So theologians make secularly phrased answers, of which "humans might have evolved from prehumans" and "humans did not so evolve" are paradigm cases. These answers they build from Scripture and the history of the faith, as well as from what they understand of science.[17]

There is a two-way exchange between science and religion. The faith is formulated to resolve ambiguities revealed in "old" certainties by new contexts, as when Christians adopted elements of Platonic philosophy, following Augustine's "spoils of the Egyptians" doctrine (*De doctrina christiana*). They then had to answer, for instance, whether souls preexisted embodiment. The believing community rejects formulations not adequate to its religious understanding and allows others to become normative, and even to remain normative (because religiously serviceable) after their "secular base" (say Platonism or Aristotelianism as "science") deteriorates. The fundamentalists' denial that man evolved is a salient religious response (in secular terms) to

secular questions. It illustrates, too, how religious disagreements, even errors, arise in responding to secularly embedded religious questions.[15] Some
group of believers has to be wrong on the matter because some say humans
could not have evolved from prehumans and others say that humans could
so have evolved, compatibly with the Scripture. Unraveling religious faith
into secularly phrased assertions is theological; the *authorizing*, proclaiming,
of such responses is *religious* (as it occurs in acts of councils, conventions,
creeds, preaching, liturgy, ritual, and even in song).

Theologians, characteristically, use philosophical constructions. They have
to when addressing whether humans, destined as revealed, are fit to have
evolved. Their results will eventually come to the believing community for
incorporation or rejection, as I described.

This is not just *my* view, a tendentious description of part of theology and
of the development of doctrine. It has historical and theological respectability,
even authority. It is illustrated in the very process by which biblical literalists
reject human evolution on religious grounds. From a similarly respectable
Christian tradition I adopt an antidualist "Christian anthropology", along
with the respectable objective of providing for the "special creation" of
humans, which I explain here.[16]

3. Emergence and Inaccessibility

A thing is "emergent" in *contrast* to something, say, "resultant" or
something "original". It is emergent *relatively* too: for instance, human being is emergent relatively to physical being (being, all of whose aptitude is
in principle comprehended by physical laws, and all of whose successive states
are explicable by principles exhibited universally in nature).

Something can be *emergent locally*, say, in some subsystem, region, epoch,
or subdomain of the world: for instance, messages in ink marks, or *emergent
globally*, in the whole cosmos conceived in a certain way: for example, as
a system of quanta that models a certain formal system or systems.

A *thing* is emergent just in case its constitutive system (its organization-
into-something) is emergent. (In Scholastic terms, it is emergent just in case
its form is not a resultant of changes in "prior" things.) Thus, English sentences
are emergent in print marks on pages, just in case the system ~ English
sentence ~ is emergent relatively to the system(s) ~ physical marks on paper ~ .
(I use the symbol ~ ~ to mark names of systems.)

Clustered with the notion of "emergence" are ideas like *not reducible*,
not a logical consequence of, *not predictable from*, *superadded to*, and so
forth. Locke believed thought was superadded to the primary qualities at God's

will. He and others believed colors to be superadded to the primary qualities, and life to inanimate matter. Other connotations are undisturbed in my alignments. But superaddition in the sense of "origin by *fiat*" is excluded. *Emergence* is a contrary of *superaddition*, just as it is of *resultance* and also of *supervenience by increasing complexity*. Both the latter allow, in principle, for theoretical reduction. Superaddition blocks reduction by absence of *any* natural connection; emergence blocks reduction by the formal and epistemic inaccessibility of *existing* natural connections. Two kinds of inaccessibility have already been indicated. This is the third.

3.1. THE FORMALITY (THE FORMAL STRUCTURE) OF THE UNIVERSE[17]

Taken as a whole, the world is a model of some formal system(s). Every fact is a case of a structure within a consistent formal system;[18] every fact has logical form. That is a necessary condition for being at all. The world has to be a "model", an "interpretation", of some purely formal structure. (You might think that it may, in part, model one formal structure and, in remainder, disparate ones. I think I can show that to be inconsistent.[19]) Each formal structure has its own formal characteristics: for instance, the pure formality of the world is consistent; otherwise it could not have a real model. Just as we can ask about any formal system whether it is consistent, so we can ask whether it is set-theoretic, whether it is complete, and whether it has regions of "truths" that are inaccessible to one another in various ways.

The whole cosmos cannot model a *complete* formal system. For instance, the extension of space-time is a model for real number theory, as are many other physical relations. Every real number truth is "true of" space-time and has a "space-time" interpretation in every region of space-time. The facts of nature, including the physical properties of space-time, are a material interpretation, a model, of a Gödel-incomplete system. The designs of all the facts of the cosmos, taking "all" distributively, not collectively, are not derivable, by any consistent set of transformations, from anything less than all of them.

3.2. THE COSMOS IS GÖDEL-INCOMPLETE

Metonymically that is so, because any adequate system of which the cosmos is a model is Gödel-incomplete. Besides, in its overall particulars the universe cannot be a model of a system that is not Gödel-incomplete. That is because there are real paths in space where $C = 2\pi r$ where π is a real number.[20]

The world is an *interpretation* of a formal system F just in case every "design" in F is illustrated in the world. That is quite different from the sense in which the world is a *model* of system F. The world is a *model* of an *adequate* formal system just in case *every* truth about the world is an instance (formally) of some truth, some design, in F. Not every design in F needs an instance in the world, but no instance in the world can be of a design not in F. For example, simple quantificational logic is not an adequate formal system for the world because there are facts whose form, design, is not contained in quantified logic: for instance, causal conditionals and various kinds of necessities. Wittgenstein was, of course, right that no "scientific", "ideal" language (as such a language was imagined at the beginning of the century) *could* contain the statement of every truth. Without disagreeing, I repeat a corollary: every fact has logical form. The world is a model of one or more formal systems. If not a *single* system, then *any* single formal structure is incomplete for the world in the sense that there are facts whose form lies *outside* the expressive capacity of the formality. If the world *is* a model of one (or more) single formal systems, it (and each) must be Gödel-incomplete, even if no fact in the world lies outside the expressive capacity of some formality.

Thus, treat everything that is the case W (actually) as a design having form (along with content which we ignore for now, except to note that any difference of content requires another instance of some design having form). F is *adequate* to W just in case there is nothing in W whose design is not an instance of some form that is a truth of F. Because any adequate formal system for the world will have to contain real number theory, to provide the form for such general truths as "any circle has its circumference equal to pi times its diameter", any formal system will be incomplete; it will have a locus of truths not derivable, not provable, in the system. There is nothing surprising about this or new either, though it does suppose there are real features of physical things, space, and time that sufficiently ground number-theoretic statements about the world, so as to make such statements genuinely true-of and true-in the world.[21]

3.3 NOW WE ENTER THE REALM OF SUPPOSITION

Take the "region" of universal laws of physics and chemistry concerning, say, the cosmos regarded as quanta: there may be another "region", say, laws of intelligent being, that is not transformationally accessible from the first. The one kind of laws might be underivable, formally, from the other. In that case phenomena satisfying the one kind of laws would be absolutely emergent with respect to phenomena satisfying the other.[22] For my purpose, phenomena or systems are globally emergent just in case they are absolutely emergent with respect to all phenomena, or systems, comprehended by a true cosmic physics.

Now suppose there *are* globally emergent phenomena, that life and intelligence are globally emergent. Have such suppositions utility toward explaining the way psychic (spiritual) reality is subsistent in matter? I think so. So far I have no cogent argument that life and intelligent being *are* globally emergent. Reconsidering the questions about human nature may eventually disclose arguments.

My hypothesis is that there are "regions" of natural systems that are formally inaccessible from a true cosmic physics. It is not that such regions are logically independent of one another; they are not. It is not that the laws of physics might have been true when the laws for living (material) things or intelligent material begins might not have (whether or not there are things of both kinds). Now, suppose one region of laws cannot be true without the other, though one region, matter, can have instances without the other's doing so.[23] Still, one does not *imply* the other in the sense that there does not exist a formal system containing the one realm of law, in which the other is derivable by permitted transformations. The two regions (of laws) are not coderivable in any consistent formality. You might say that *living thing* implies *material thing* (and so for the relevant laws), but that is not so if immaterial life is possible. And to say the reverse, that matter implies immaterial being, is to use 'implies' in a sense different from the technical notion of "derivation by transformations permitted in a purely formal system".

This is stronger than nonreducibility, though that follows, too. It is logical dependence (of a certain kind of life on matter) without derivability (of the structure of that life from the structure of matter). Yet it is not even contemplated that we are dealing with mere superaddition by divine fiat. Instead, I am saying that if an intelligent material being cannot exist immaterially, though there can be immaterial intelligent beings, still the principles, the structures for intelligent material being, cannot be derived from the principles, the structures for material being, within any consistent formal system. This is the third kind of inaccessibility.

Humans, on such a view, are emergent beings, essentially embodied and enspirited, that cannot exist except subsistently in material systems of a certain complexity.[24] Humans, on this view, can exist forever in favorable material conditions that do not have to resemble the conditions of their emergence or origin except insofar as is absolutely necessary so as to sustain their characteristic activity.[25] Saying humans cannot exist emergently except in material systems does not require that humans evolve from prehumans, though perhaps other reasons require it.[26]

I need, now, for the sake of further specificity, to go beyond the initial requirement of global emergence: that the constitutive structure (laws) of the thing, say intelligence, be cosmically inaccessible (as defined) from the physics of the cosmos (that is, the cosmic physics).

4. Emergent Systems

(1) *Emergence* has to do with systems. Systems are realities with laws and logical relationships: for instance, systems "plug together" into larger systems. A computer is a system of component systems. So is DNA. Emergent systems have materially realized systems as modules, like words on paper or sounds. Some emergent systems, when realized materially, constitute emergent beings: for example, humans and dogs. Others constitute the biosphere, the system of living material things.

(2) *Things with components* can have *different components* (over time, not *instanter* or *ab initio*), and abstract particulars, not genuine individuals, can exist in different media (say, sound and writing as media for statements). That is true of resultants, like chairs and radios, as well as emergents, like animals and people. Active, internally controlled change of components is also necessary for emergent things, but not so for resultants. We can call that "contingency downward", to contrast with the next feature.

(3) Organization of components to "system entry level" *necessitates* the being of the thing (e.g., a cat). We can call that, in contrast to "contingency downward", "necessity upward". The right parts, put together "right", will give you a radio or whatever with physical necessity. That holds for both the emergent and the resultant, too. The relevant difference is that with a resultant there is something about the parts that determines "the right way" to put them together. With *emergent things the "right way" for the parts comes from the whole to be made and, typically, from an advanced developmental stage (maturity) of the whole to be "made"*.

(4) The nature of an emergent thing cannot be predicted except by analogy, by experience with analogous "styles" in nature: for example, understanding whale propulsion from the study of birds in flight. Knowing the properties of egg-tempera on hardboard would not allow one to envisage an unseen Wyeth painting, but knowing that, the subject, and some Wyeth oils, one might envisage it. Perhaps the way we envisage prehistoric creatures from fossils is from analogies to other things.

(5) The emergent thing (cat) *subsists* componentially and materially. It is what exists (a cat, a human, a bird). It is the subject of change and an agent (where appropriate). Once in being, it has to continue to be by exchanges of its conponents with its environment and, in extreme cases, by exchanges of the biotic and chemical *kinds* of components. Sometimes even the medium of being can be exchanged, for instance, a *composition* can be reduced from performance to score.[27]

(6) *Systems emergent*. A system is an active input-transformation-output structure, usually with many "entry" positions and many "exits", too. For instance, a digestive system can be entered by feeding, injection, and insertion of food. A broadcast system can be exited by receivers and interceptors;

a highway system by many terminals. Systems do not absolutely need "initial" or "start" positions or "out" or "stop" positions: for instance, a five-part canon can be entered anywhere if the *order* is right and be terminated at will. To get an emergent thing from components, we need emergent systems.

Active, energized systems that operate on an energy basis additionally to that of their components are, synchronically, logical structures (a flow chart of logical transformations) and, diachronically, processes. They contrast with passive systems. Distinguish a traffic system, which operates on the energy of the autos and stoplights, from a computer, whose main current powers all the component systems. A system with a main current is "live", "on", "on line", "up", in being as a unit. Thus, ~ English-sentence ~ can be potential (not passive) as a system of rules, or an *active system* as, for instance, energized as part of the process ~ Expressing oneself-in-English ~ when someone is in fact speaking or writing English. I am, here, interested only in active, energized systems—systems in process.

An emergent system cannot be "reduced" to its component systems for the various reasons I have mentioned. The most interesting, and purely speculative, though, is *cosmic* inaccessibility, which occurs because (a) the structure of the *emergent* thing is of a formality disparate from that of the microparts (the cosmos is not a model of a single formality) or (b) the structure of the emergent thing falls in a *region* of the formal system not transformationally accessible from the cosmic physics. The latter option is, I think, true. Besides, the energy of some active systems is different from physical energy. The energy that powers the lines and voices of the actors of a play and the hearts and hearing of the audience is physical (or, perhaps, vital); the energy for the process (the active system) of *understanding* is psychic, spiritual.

Consider a case of *local* emergence. Suppose a radio receiver is ultimately a resultant. Nothing about the system explains why it yields Poulenc's *Gloria* now and Shakespeare's *Hamlet* later. Nothing about the radio system explains the internal semantic structure of *Hamlet* linguistically or of Poulenc's *Gloria* harmonically and rhythmically. The entities, the play and the *Gloria realized* (brought into real being—*a sounding*) by successive states of the radio, are constituted as structures that cannot be explained, either as to their origin or as to conservation by the components and capacities of the radio system. The radio is simply *capable*, as a medium of production, for the sounding to be realized. *Relative* to the radio system the pieces heard are emergent. Nevertheless, each *sound* is *resultant* from the radio, beginning with its initial "recipient" state followed by a causal "entry" state (the radio signal for the first note or rest) and the succeeding entry states, with the whole system "on" with electrical energy.

Emergent systems have to be *realized* in a medium (say, mechanically, electrically, chemically, etc.) for their realizations to *be* anything (whether we are talking about statements, music, plays, philosophy, cognitive states, or cognizing beings). Yet, the "whole truth" about how one gets from entry states to output or exit states in such a system cannot be told decompositely as a story about the components because *reduction* is logically blocked on account of (a) merely obediential potency, (b) analogy of being, and (c) formal inaccessibility (see above).

(7) *Realizations happen necessarily.* When the "entry" conditions are satisfied, realization is necessary: among inscriptions, for example, an English sentence emerges *necessarily* once entry positions are filled. An array of components can sometimes realize more than one system, and thus double emergence is possible (an inscription that is both an English and an Italian sentence, or a palindrome).

(8) *Realizations need components.* Systems (for example, radio circuitry or a traffic system) need parts: for example, wires, roads, and such. Recursive, self-same, components are possible, but only in systems that come into being from the top down, not from the bottom up. Otherwise components have to belong eventually to different systems. Even with recursion (a sentence made with words made of words made of sentences of words, and such) the components, the system, and the emergent things (realizations) all have to be different.

(9) *Impossibility of prediction "upward".* In general one cannot predict the emergent, or even guess at it adequately, from the components and their laws (except by analogy to other systems).[28] Thus, you cannot predict ~ English grammar ~ from a list of English words or from the general laws of physics and the construction of typesetters. In fact, prediction "backward" has not been successful yet: we have not discovered from the output of English discourse either a satisfactory generative or transformational grammar. We have not "recovered" the system (structure) from its output.

There is no system (where the ultimate components are not recursions of the same system) which cannot be realized by components that are logically independent, and by different components at different times, and, in many cases, by components of logically independent types (for example, sounds and inscriptions).

(10) *Subsistent being in a material medium.* System realizations, even within the system ~ English sentence ~ , are *things*, typically, that really exist, like a sentence. A system realization that is nonrecursive requires a medium for being (say, "matter") and components (say, dots) but need not *itself* be a material being. Thus a statement, a thought, a conjecture, can really exist, expressed in sound or writing, and *not* be a material thing. That snaps the stranglehold of materialism on being. *We* have being materially but are not just material things.

Thus, *War and Peace* subsists in ink marks (and they, in turn, result from their component molecules). The semantic structure of the chapters cannot be analyzed into the physics and chemistry of the printing or of any other medium in which the novel is composed or preserved: for one thing, the same marks in the same order could have had a different meaning. *Emergent systems satisfy laws for their successive transformational states that their modules and ultimate components do not.* One reason for this is that the same states could have had other components.

The full physics, chemistry, sociology, and history of bats in a cave might explain the pattern of bat dung on a cave floor. Still, if from one hundred feet above the floor, in bright geologists' worklights, the pattern displays the complete first thirty-two Latin verses of the Gospel of St. John, *that* could not be explained by explaining the origin of each droplet's position. That could only explain how the pattern happens to have the "shape" it has. You cannot explain what is *there* without supposing *another* reality, that Gospel. Nothing about the history of droplets would explain that the pattern is Latin, grammatical, coherent, or that it *says* anything at all! Even if the bats' flight paths were constrained by passage ways that formed the letters, the message is emergent relative to bat dung.

(11) *Higher systems by nesting.* Systems nest in systems as components, as nodes for a "higher" system. A protein atom is a system; so too, a peptide; and so forth. Suitably arranged in a hospitable environment, they "realize" (by satisfying an "entry condition for") a DNA molecule that as a whole is an entry unit in a larger system of "genetic information transfer". As a node in the larger system, ~ genetic information transfer ~ , it uses the chemical-level properties to affect molecular actions that, within the conservation of energy principles, reproduce it and its information transfer activity.

Looked at from the point of view of individual molecules, nothing very dramatic happens when DNA replicates. There are minor chemical interactions. But macromolecularly the phenomena are startling (and took decades to discover and explain, even in part). At the chain level it is incredible, wondrous, astounding, and, as the persistence of cancer shows, not understood at the appropriate systems level yet.

Semantic laws require suitable units (say, words) that belongs to word-contrast systems and are formed from systems of sounds and marks. Satisfying the "entry" conditions to a "higher" system—whose laws operate only on systemized "chunks", on modules that are themselves systems, and whose laws are not contained by, or reducible to, those of the chunks—is the logical mechanism for emergence. Once the emergent systems are *meaning* systems, there is no limit to the abstractive complexity and power over the matter that can be achieved.

My speculation is this: more complex *cognitive* beings evolve neuron structures whose electrochemical states are the base nodes (modules) for representation of the being itself to itself as situated in its environment, and of its environment presented to it as represented-to-itself. These representations thus have an overlapping subjective *focus* (like overlapping spotlights) that begins to unify consciousness. These states are only *entry* nodes in still further systems, *meaning* systems, constituted and transformed by semantic and psychic laws.

To judge and feel become active capacities when enough complexity of focused cognitive representation occurs. Not simply enough physical capacity, but enough cognitive *activity*. Why? Because complex cognitive activity is the threshold for a *psychic energy* system—a differently energized thing.

Nothing, so far, differs from what might be a scientist's general view that selfhood arises from increased thought capacity; even when I say that when a certain level of thought capacity is actually reached, there is an internal organization of the whole cognitive being, even down to its living cells (with detectable molecular results), into a specific kind of thing having different life capabilities from very similar beings with more limited thought capacities (e.g., some higher apes). This is an analogue of Aristotle's principle that there is *one* life of a living being regardless of how many parts of it are alive: for a plant "to be" is "to live", for a rational being "to be" is "to be cognitively".

With action-thought capacity of a certain abstractive power *psychic being emerges*. That is where a scientist might demur, wanting evidence that the system is energized differently as well as organized emergently.

5. Physical Organization and Psychic Energy: Energy Manifested in Meaning

I speculate further that when a system of systems becomes complex enough, it is organized by a different energy that acts in parallel with the physical forces of the components, converting physical action and chemical events into parallel phenomena and vice versa, just as meaning can supervene (nonreductively) on the physics of printing, even account for patterns of *type* and be *affected* by properties of type (e.g., visual ambiguity makes meaning ambiguity sometimes).

Psychic energy makes meaning-to-us. It converts somatic relations into subjective meaning, and that into feeling (e.g., nausea). It is not merely chemical, electrical, or magnetic energy that polarizes the visual appreciation into revulsion when someone observes that the rolled chocolate cake one is enjoying looks like a dog turd. Psychic energy, manifested by and condensed into *meanings* (like capacitors or like some "chips"), is present in the physical energy system. Just think of a thought "complex" (say, your financial fears, beliefs, objectives, satisfactions, etc.) that processes, like a "money chip", daily events into your reactions and choices about purchases.

A cognitive being generates thoughts by meaning-relationships, most of which are not even accessible to the thinker. Thought ability and even its content are mainly unconscious, inaccessible to introspection and, often, even to inference about oneself. That is why we call that "realm" of cognition, feeling, understanding, "the unconscious". And most of the time we fail to take account of the fact that the unconscious, as *directive* (of external action), is *biased and goal-oriented* (in ways variously explained by diverse theories from Aristotle's conception of the happiness sought by the whole being, to Augustine's view of our seeking God, to Freud's repression theory, and to Jung's compensation theory). The *bias* of unconscious thought (toward overall well-being, I think) unifies the emergent being into a self. (Not a phenomenal subject of action, but a real agent.)

Psychic force is *still* natural force, but subsistent, among humans, in systems obeying physical laws in their entirety. Psychic force *manifests* itself in us in the enormous energy of meaning. Experience generates experiences, like revulsion, excitement, attraction, and love, that move us *bodily*. Bodily states and movements become for us psychic by acquiring meaning and generating feelings (like fear, shame, content, delight). Such meaning systems are *modules* (like the "form" of a chip) in a larger system that includes our overall thought, action, and automatic bodily functions and automated cognitive ones—an overall cognitive system that may be inconsistent in various ways and have incoherent response mechanisms when "first-level" inconsistencies "surface" in experience. Thus there is room for the psychotic, the neurotic, the irrational, and the wrong in our cognitive behavior.

The human, including its subthought and feeling systems, has its being from the energy that organizes it into what it is, energy that its states psychosomatically manifest. That energy, in turn, is from the being of God.[29]

A telephone argument subsists in the electrical energy of the telephone system but has its being from the expressed opinions and feelings of the parties, which might have been exchanged via radio or letter instead. *The energy system of subsistence need be, not the energy system of being*, but only of the matter or its medium (in this case the latter). Thus, with focused consciousness there emerges, in a psychic energy system, a psychic material being. I mean that humans are psychic beings "all over", not "in their minds". The mind is not "a place" or "in a place", nor is cognition "in one's head". The life energy, what makes us human beings, is actively *everywhere* in the body.[30] It is analogous to physical energy, just as human being is analogous to inorganic being.

That is the general outline of how a system of material beings (e.g., atoms) may in principle develop emergently into an entity that in its constitutive organization (in what formally determines *what* it is) is a psychic being (a human). The human *presents* (realizes, makes real) a distinct *dynamis*, force, *energia*, energy, and thus, is, as a whole, a distinct being that was essential for its coming to be. Yet the material realization is in principle separable from the material realization that is not necessary for the human continuing to be, provided only that a suitable "material base" be maintained.

One might dispute the need for a distinct organizing energy; however, if there is such an energy, it would explain what death is essentially. That energy seems to be what disappears when a living thing dies. It dies all over, just as it lives all over, and for it dying is ceasing to be, just as for it being is living. That has both religious and metaphysical import because distinguishing psychic energy from physical energy is a basis for saying man is enspirited over and beyond being an overall rational unity, without postulating any duality of *entities*. It is not an account of man by behavorial output, as distinctly intelligent (a classification of no great reliability), but an account of the energy of the material system by which the individual (the person) is made to be. Distinction of energy is distinction by origin, causation, and continuance of being.

Suppose one denies there is a distinct realm of psychic energy. One might still grant my other points about emergence, systems nesting, and the hypothesis that it is by the internesting of cognitive systems (not neural states, which are only the entry nodes for the cognitive systems) that an overall intelligent material being (the person) is emergent. Such an emergent being is *more* than a mental-state/material-state unity. It is, rather, a matter-energy composite, unified in being, subsistent in matter, and a person all-over, not just in some parts, some powers, or some states.

Many analytic steps are required to "fit" Christian anthropology and the prospects of evolutionary science. But a general outline is discernible and looks plausible: (1) We have, like Aquinas, spirit—the psychically energized system realized in matter, individuated and "identified" (as to which spirit it is) by the matter (cells and organs) animated. (Spirit is not a substance but a form.) (2) The person's beginning-to-be would be (as Aquinas also says) dependent on the suitable material organization of secondary matter, for example, on a certain brain complexity and even on cognitive experience in humans both specifically and individually. (3) The person's continuing being is accounted for by the reality it participates in: psychic energy, a manifestation of the being of God. (4) The person, an emergent reality, matter enspirited in a psychic system, is thus capable of existence resurrected (but, probably, not disembodied).

That humans are not capable of a disembodied existence accords with the view that matter (materialization) is essential to them but also demands the permanence of physical energy, raising a problem of physical eschatology. The cosmos must endure forever in some form.[31]

What might destroy this picture by its anomaly? Is it evolution or materialism? Is it "emergence" in general or some special problem when what emerges is a different being from its components? Surely not the latter. Cells are different beings from their components; so are chairs, and that is not even emergence. Statements are different beings from their sentential expressions, and that *is* emergence.

Nor is *evolution* the anomaly, as is so widely supposed. No special difficulty for a view of emergent spirit, and of an enspirited thing, dependent in being upon materialization, arises from evolution as a developmental hypothesis. Whether we are talking about emergent evolution (as I delineated it), or resultant evolution, or even instantaneous creation, and whether we take the "anthropic illusion" of crucial physical quantities in the cosmos seriously or completely ignore it, there is exactly the same difficulty: How can an actually immortal being be a material, corruptible thing and yet be, throughout, a single, substantial thing — not an accidental union of distinct kinds of substances (Plato or Descartes) or a spirit *generating* matter or appearances (idealism)? Whether man is created *tout court*, instantly and directly by God, or develops from "approximations" into emergent psychic being, does not affect that issue. How can an enspirited material being capable of life forever with God be a thing that is through and through *one* thing, corruptible and mortal, not some combination of distinct things, or in some part really real and another only apparent?

Whether bodily resurrection of some kind is needed (both logically and religiously) is the same for any view that holds that humans are inherently immortal and, despite material limitations, somehow survive of their own capacity one in being. (Many Christian groups have not resolved whether surviving death is a natural ability or a gift condition of man.) The special philosophical problem is to explain with suitably *articulated* steps what emergence is and how psychic (re)organization *constitutes* a different sort of being from the nearest prehumans. Evolutionary theories do not cause the problem, which is *there* regardless of how humans came into being. Rather, evolutionary theories contribute to the solution by making us look, through intermediate steps, for the *structures* by which a unitary being, as man is, would have to exist, whether or not evolved.

6. Special Creation?

Suppose there is no logical or physical impediment — perhaps, indeed, a natural necessity and inevitability, given our cosmic position — in the evolutionary emergence of humans, then what contact with God makes us in "his image and likeness"? It need not have been an event; it may be an analogy of nature, as Aquinas thought. But suppose an event was required besides.

Would a sudden, first, active awareness of God in a few beings (say two), otherwise "ready and able" for self-consciousness and autonomy, do for a "special creation of the soul"? I think so, especially if it consisted in a polarizing encounter that created an opposition of "I" and "you".

Why not suppose for "special creation" that prehuman cognitive development crossed the borderline to psychic being through the emergence of a rational unconscious? The thought-judgment-feeling-action-appraisal was unified by the bias of the rational appetite (the will), but "focused self-awareness", the basis of *agency* had not yet developed. "Crossing that barrier" to unified self-awareness is both a natural process looked at developmentally (though no one but God could have known "looking upward" from photons that the borderline was there) and yet is, from each human's point of view, its "special creation", its coming into being, its *inhabiting* the realm that is God's. The idea is that some prehumans were psychic beings (with unconscious rational being), but not persons, not humans, a kind of "missing link". Consciousness is needed for agency (*suppositum*).

The triggering experience by which unconscious rational cognition first organized into human selfhood was probably a *polarizing* encounter with God, by opposition to an external law-giving self, one that *focused* their consciousness into being "self-aware" and *acting*. It is this organization of *consciousness*, personhood, on the surface of the encompassing human unconscious, that is transmitted and enlarged socially in their human offspring.[32] Such a "triggering" experience makes the human condition calamitous, *ab initio*; it is the recognition of God as *opposed* self. The first *human* act, like the first Satanic act, was to reject the sovereignty of God's Will.[33] It was, in Newman's words, "aboriginal catastrophe". It is the condition of all mankind, a condition, as Augustine thought, that only God can correct.

I am not equating "psychic energizing of the cognitive system" with consciousness, but rather with the encompassing "unconscious" by which a cognitive being is a rational animal, but not a person. I am suggesting that being a rational animal, as whales and porpoises may be for all we know, is not enough for personhood (*suppositum*). It is the condition in which a being is ready and able but still needs to be "sparked" into selfhood by activity. Personhood, selfhood, is consequent on psychic being and results from an encounter with God, the beginning of history, allowing escape from a kind of autism. This encounter is analogous to the repeated encounters with the objective in each child's development with its parents, until in maturity it has to live (relatively) unbounded by its parents, as lawmaker to itself, while acknowledging objective moral law, of course. The human condition is thus transmitted along with selfhood by socialization, living in human history.

Every creature comes into being by divine power, so "special creation", no matter what it is, could be aptly described only in terms of "activity" implying a change of the basis of predication from the point of view of the creature alone and not involving a succession of acts in God. That being so, "special creation", if thought to be religiously indispensable in the Scripture story, can be accommodated by the conditions I mentioned and, no doubt, by other conditions quite different. I find the conditions hypothesized attractive because it feels "right" that the human condition should be "aboriginal" and should involve alienation from God, a situation that only God can put right. The historical process of righting the human condition, once enacted through revelation, is reenacted in each human life with grace.

7. Cosmic Comments

(a) Humans are material and immortal beings, not a mixture; (b) the whole human survives death and lives forever (at least all who are "saved"); (c) all humans are "specially created" in the image of God and (d) are yet essentially material. These fit what I have sketched. Still, what would things have to be like overall in nature for all this to be true, and is that compatible with the way they seem, religiously and scientifically? And how is conscious thought related to psychic being? These questions invite further speculation.

TO BE IS TO CONTINUE TO BE

When the chemical environment was "right" and the first "nodes" for satisfying the abstract formulae for material living things (being an "open system" with certain generative, reproductive, appetitive, and nutritive activities) were reached by the first molecules to do so, there must also have been enough ready material and environmental hospitality for the process to continue on its own. I mean, absent a comet's whipping in to pulverize the earth, the conditions to *start* life are "formally" (that is logically, according to the abstract laws of living systems) sufficient to sustain the process over cosmic epochs: they would (hypothetically) necessarily lead to its further development and, whenever emergence thresholds are reached, to emergent being.

Imagine "living material being" being defined functionally and abstractly as an entirely material organization that is actively an open energy system in a hospitable environment, with complete unit functions and species roles in a nested bioecology, and manifesting some or all of the following functions (or substitutes for them): growth, death, nutrition, and reproduction (both internal and as a whole). Various material formulae in carbon-based molecules (at least two million actual species, perhaps twenty times that, on earth alone) have actually satisfied that system design and are capable of DNA realizations. Infinitely many more may be possible. And as the notion of bioecology is made more abstract, entirely different constituent capacities might be substituted to the same effect: for example, "life stability" might be substituted for nutrition with regard to a silicon-based system that "lives" at 5 degrees above absolute zero.

A biosystem is by its formal structure a persisting *developing* system (in a suitable environment). *Evolution is a logical consequence of material life suitably situated.* Emergent evolution, as I delineate the idea, is a *contingent* though inevitable outcome given the right initial conditions, constants, quantities, and such. So, as a rule of thumb, to be is to continue to be, and, for a life system, to continue to be is to evolve. This is analogous to the way the structures that account for the synchronic difference of words in meaning also explain the diachronic development of meaning and of expressive capacity of natural languages.[34]

In the absence of interference, life develops. Without disabling interference, living things adapt, variegate, fit into all the available environmental niches, and differentiate into various living kinds. That provides units, each living or of life, capable of modular combinations into emergent things, provided there are structures (systems) with "entry positions" for such modules as they happen to be distributed in nature.

Man is not a cosmic accident or incident but the inevitable, emergent, though defeasible, consequence of the initial conditions (such as cosmic constants, the number of the initial particles, and such) and of various logical necessities both as to the properties of particles and the general principles they "instantiate", "model", or "provide an applied semantics for". (Death cannot just be a breakdown in a system, as in a radio; it is the disintegration of the *basis* for the system because components "act on their own".) I mean to suggest not that man is *the* object, but that he is *a* purpose, or goal, of the cosmos. (There is an "anthropic illusion" caused by the peculiar "fitness" of the cosmos for the appearance of humans that suggests that it exists for humans.) If there is such a goal, it may be far different, and far future. The process that produced one kind of psychic being subsistent in matter might (for all we know), in cosmic eons at high energy, cross the emergence borderline again and again. If it does *not*, that would need explaining. That is not to suggest that evolution of the whole life system and of the cognitive beings (noetic system) is not teleologically ordered, as is the development of each living thing. I think it quite likely that it is so ordered, but to an end we cannot yet conceive.

Rather, the inevitability (relatively to general cosmic contingencies) of development of life on earth, of differentiation of life-forms leading to human beings, and the fact that there is an orderly single system of interbalanced phases, epochs, of earthly life (whatever the explanatory mechanism) seem to be at the heart of the general evolutionary hypothesis and also of the "anthropic illusion": that the universe is "for" the emergence of man because nothing else can "explain" its general contingencies.

For now we need only be confident that the known facts and the best-established explanations do not preclude that cognitive beings, emergent psychic beings, developed inevitably (but defeasibly) from simple life-forms. And we must be particularly careful to distinguish the emergent psychic being — cognitive being with unconscious thought, organized so as to be ready and able for selfhood, that is, for self-conscious feeling and action — from the *further* organization of conscious life in psychic being. For that may progress both by evolution and by *grace* toward a unified consciousness that imitates Christ.

8. Conclusion

Being differentiates analogously by emergence. *To be* for a stone is different from *to be* for a plant (for which *to be* is *to live*), or an animal (for which to *be* is *to live sentiently*), or a human (for whom *to be* is *to rational-animalize*, as D. P. Henry phrased it).

Human evolution in the cosmos, which is either anthropically "illusory" or anthropically biased, is inevitable in the way that any outcome is hypothetically necessitated by the underlying principles and contingent initial conditions. But it is not logically necessary, even on the hypothesis that enough photons came into being. For, if evolution of the biosphere with humans is emergent from micromatter, nature might "expand" physically forever and never display an emergent phenomenon. And still it is a matter not of chance but of hypothetical necessity whether one of the emergent structures of nature is exemplified. That is why I remark that there is either an anthropic "illusion" of the cosmos or else an outright anthropic bias.

The view I develop, nonreductive evolutionary naturalism (as Ernan McMullin calls it), is only one alternative regarding the origin of man. But it is not a mere alternative, say to a dualism that maintains there is a plurality of substances, rational and material, in man (Descartes), or a plurality of substantial forms, rational and corporeal (Bonaventure), or a single spiritual substance accidentally united to matter (Plato), or a merely apparent matter (Neoplatonism), or a mind-dependent phenomenal body (Kant), or a mind-dependent sensible world (Berkeley). All those positions have been disavowed by the Christian religious tradition.

Each of these views is inconsistent with the explicit promise of bodily resurrection by Jesus and is internally inconsistent as well (a point I cannot expect to establish here). In fact, I turn the question around: Is there another view of human nature that accords as well or better with Christian teaching about life with God and the hypothesis that human life evolved on the earth?

One final point. As St. Thomas said in *De potentia dei*, the only cause of being is the power of God, and all natural causes act as instruments of that power: the higher cause is more immediate to the effect than the instrumental one. Thus God, the only cause of being, is more immediately the cause of the being of each human, whether evolved or not, than its own parents or its food or its environment. God is, then, as much the cause of each person's being as if he had breathed being into whole adult humans, like life into toy animals, one by one.

I do not naively suppose that if one spatiotemporally rearranges the right kinds of material particles long enough and carefully enough, one will get an immortal, enspirited material being. One would have to know how, as God does.

To get the best of evolution, Christians need to live forever with God. That is what is *promised* in Scripture, *advanced* by the emergence of human life in the biotic sytem and *achieved* by the cooperation of the Spirit over millennia: the Kingdom to come, a world without end.[35]

NOTES

1. If so, we are the first of evolution's "perfect products", intelligent material beings *able* to live forever with God. Because the latter information comes to us by revelation and is part of the "good news" for mankind, Christians get the best of evolution. That is true substantively in their ability to live forever, as well as dialectically in the sense that (contrary to nineteenth-century fears) evolutionary hypotheses invite and aid a deeper understanding of both man and nature and, consequently, of God and revelation. For more on this, see note 3. For more on fears about evolution see Roland M. Frye, "So-Called 'Creation Science' and Mainstream Christian Rejections", *Proceedings of the American Philosophical Society*, 127, 1983, 61-70.

For instance, Karl Rahner in *Theological Investigations* is explicit that Jesus, the Redeemer, "is a moment of the history of God's communication of himself to the world—in the sense that he is part of the history of the cosmos itself. He must not be merely God acting in the world but must be part of the cosmos itself in its very climax. This is the fact stated in Christian dogma: Jesus is true man; he is truly part of the earth, *truly a moment in the biological evolution of this world*, a moment of human natural history." (See Gerald A. McCool, editor, *A Rahner Reader*, New York: The Seabury Press, 1975, pp. 166-172. Italics added.) Note that Rahner says that it is a Catholic dogma that Jesus is a moment in biological evolution. He even repeats the claim a few lines later: "All this is Catholic Dogma." I mention this in light of my comments about theology in section II, below, and to make clear that my general position is theologically respectable and, in fact, as both Rahner and

Teilhard de Chardin saw (note 3, below), human life and the being of Jesus ought not be explained as the intervention of the miraculous and alien into the cosmos; it is the hypostatic union that is supernatural. As Rahner says, "It must also be underlined in this connection that the statement of God's *Incarnation*—of his becoming *material*—is the most basic statement of Christology" (McCool, *A Rahner Reader*, p. 169, italics in original). I admit I do not like the semantic form of "God's becoming material", but the general idea is exactly what I am developing: that humans are *by nature* material (and so is Jesus) but able (in sense one, see note 4) to live forever with God, yet wholly integrated into nature, thus, truly perfect products of biological evolution. Christians get the best of evolution because, with nature perfected with grace, they gain life forever with God.

2. We cannot exclude, at the outset, that humans may coexist with an "offspring" species that may evolve from them, perhaps by their own intelligent manipulation of the evolutionary process in nature. Such hypotheses invite us to predict from our scientifically illumined religious vantage that humans will occupy the cosmos forever, along with whatever forms of life develop. In a word, successor speciation from humans will not replace the humans who have existed and will exist resurrected forever. And if that speciation is a retrenchment, a devolution, perhaps due to human genetic malfeasance, they, too, will probably nevertheless be psychic beings capable of life with God. Will they require redemption, being of a different nature, as it were? This is an example where evolutionary hypotheses enlarge our imagining, offering a broader perspective on the faith, generating from secular contexts questions requiring religious answers secularly phrased. (See section 2.)

3. See Ernan McMullin, "Teilhard as a Philosopher", *Chicago Theological Seminary Register 60*, 1964, 15-28, and his remarks, p. 50, in "How Should Cosmology Relate to Theology?" in A. R. Peacocke, editor, *The Sciences and Theology in the Twentieth Century*, Notre Dame, IN: University of Notre Dame Press, 1981, pp. 17-57.

4. By "apt" here I mean "have the active ability for". There are two relevant senses of "active ability": to-be-able to play Chopin, to-be-able-and-*disposed* to play Chopin. The second ability for life with God depends on grace where the intentional object, "life with God", is understood as a transparent (thought of) intentional object of one's disposition. There is a dispute as to whether we should regard men's opaque seeking after God, Augustine's "*cor inquietum dum requiescat in te*", as the *telos* of human nature, as man's (opaque) objective by nature or by gift. I think life with God is man's *telos*, as an opaque intentional object of human nature, like what one reaches for when falling in a strange dark place. It is surely thought in the Catholic tradition that humans are by nature indestructible and "for" the knowledge and love of God. Thus, they are, in the first sense, able to live with God forever.

I know there is another hypothesis, that humans are capable naturally of life with God by acting rightly (for which grace is required, in fact) but are also "capable" of spiritual destruction, so that death is the cessation of being for them. That, as far as I know, is not "good doctrine". But such a view, too, has interesting and enlightening aspects within the evolutionary perspective.

5. See D. S. Bendall, editor, *Evolution from Molecules to Men*, New York: Cambridge University Press, 1983.

6. I say nothing here about the origin of life from inanimate matter, except to conjecture that even if it is by evolution, it is probably emergent. It is not relevant here whether life originated on earth and evolved here or arrived extraterrestially, as F. Hoyle speculates. Nor do I address the equally interesting issue of whether humans are exempted from differentiation with *successor* species and exempted from having

branching species. Evolutionary eschatology is as little advanced as physical eschatology. See Freeman J. Dyson, "Time without End: Physics and Biology in an Open Universe", *Reviews of Modern Physics*, *51*, 1979, 447-60.

7. Displayed meaning is contrasted with "contained", "transmitted" meaning, like the telegraph signal in wires that is distinct from the message carried. Jerry Fodor has pointed out that explanations of information-transfer will not amount to explanations of cognition, which involves response to and creation of displayed meaning.

8. That is not to say that *no* meaning or expression has one kind or even one piece of matter "of its essence". Take, for example, autographic art; see Nelson Goodman, *Languages of Art*, Indianapolis: Bobbs-Merrill, 1968.

9. Roughly, for a stone, to be is "to materialize stonily" (to act like the sort of matter that it is); for a plant, to be is to live (to vegetate); for an animal, to be is to animalize (to act as an animal); and for a human, to be is to rational-animalize. There is no such thing as "mere" existence, "just being actual", as naive modal actualists suppose, in the face of the obvious fact, throughout the history of philosophy, that metaphysical systems that countenance both being and change, have to have two kinds of causation and at least two modes of being (consider Plato, Aristotle, Kant, Berkeley, Leibniz, and Aquinas). (On the notion of two kinds of causation see J. F. Ross, "Creation II", in A. J. Freddoso, editor, *The Existence and Nature of God*, Notre Dame, IN: University of Notre Dame Press, 1983, pp. 115-141, and J. F. Ross, *Philosophical Theology*, Indianapolis: Hackett, 1981, pp. 35-85 and 222-278.) Though I cannot go into refinements here, I remark that if there really is emergence as I describe it, then there is an adequate ground in nature (before we even begin to discuss the analogy between creatures and God) for real analogy of being (*analogia entis*) within the category of substance. (For brevity I use Aristotle's categories: they are, of course, only rough.)

10. See J. F. Ross, *Portraying Analogy*, New York: Cambridge University Press, 1981. See the analogous argument as to why analogy of meaning cannot be analyzed as a lattice of semantic features, though it can be modeled as contrasting displays of meaning-relevant, coapplicable, distinct words.

11. This is not a comprehensive analysis of emergence. Emergence of a thing requires a background system that is Gödel-incomplete, where the emergent portion is within the underivable realm, while the medium and component portions belong to the derivable realms. Emergence is *not* defined in terms of unpredictability (see P. Henle, "The Status of Emergence", *Journal of Philosophy*, 39, 1942, 486-493; A. Pap, "The Concept of Absolute Emergence", *British Journal of the Philosophy of Science*, 2, 1952, 302-311); or as effect that exceeds its cause (see A. O. Lovejoy, "The Meaning of 'Emergence' and Its Modes", in E. S. Brightman, editor, *Proceedings of the 6th International Congress of Philosophy*, 1926, New York: Longmans, Green & Co., 1927, pp. 20-33; and C. R. Morris, "The Notion of Emergence", *Proceedings of the Aristotelian Society, Suppl. Vol. 6*, 1926, 49-55); or as a gap by which the laws of the emergent system *cannot consistently* belong to the same "axiom system" as those of the components (or media); or as some kind of arbitrary superaddition of properties by divine fiat (Locke).

I do not, at this point, say anything about whether the secondary sense qualities are emergent relative to the neural medium of brain states but speculate only that living things and human beings are emergent relative to their micromatter, whereas molecular being is resultant and not emergent relative to atomic being. Further, I do not yet commit as to whether atomic being is resultant or emergent relative to quarks, hadrons, leptons, and similar constituents.

12. I do not pretend to show that disembodied existence is *impossible* for humans. That is another matter. I treat it as neither a necessary nor a natural state. For instance, the first experience after death for an individual may be as resurrected.

The philosophical underpinning for my view has not been augmented much since the Middle Ages, except by Teilhard de Chardin, even though it seems the only way to integrate the revealed destiny of mankind with the lawlike unity of all of nature. Furthermore, I do not endorse what A. Peacocke diagnoses as panpsychism in Teilhard's theories. (See A. Peacocke, *Creation and the World of Science*, Oxford: Clarendon Press, 1979, p. 159.) Panpsychism just avoids the analogy of substantial being in the opposite direction from monistic materialism. It is a position, despite Leibniz's efforts, without a future.

Karl Rahner, *Theological Investigations*, seems quite close to views I develop, including the analogy of being, in holding that humans are both material and enspirited, that the general biotic system is evolutionary and, yet, that history is goal-directed toward the Kingdom of God, and that the cosmic system is emergent in key respects. I have not, however, found a worked-out analysis of emergence or of spirit-matter unity to attribute to him yet. So these reflections are more schematic than demonstrative, to be reinforced in my book *Creation* and in other papers. For the present, let me just say that what is much more important to the notion of emergence, which earlier literature, cited above, shows is not adequately defined by unpredictability and irreducibility, is the real *analogy of being* that everyone but Rahner seems to miss.

I agree also with Peacocke that biological scientists are right to reject "vitalism", "the view that some entities or forces other than physical chemical ones are present and operate in biological organisms and constitute their distinctness", because it is empirically "a dead end". I, too, talk in terms of nonreducible systems that "internest" into higher structures. But I do not, as metaphysician, rule out vitalism and psychism as hylomorphic real structures in things. I certainly think there is a psychic, spiritual, realm of being inhabited by God, which is only analogous to material being.

13. If Christians did not know that the very same being could be composed of different cells at different times, they might explain bodily resurrection (of which they are assured in Scripture) as reassembly of the same cells as were put into the graves. Eventually a general resurrection would require more atoms than ever existed. Would a situation where not everyone could be reassembled out of preexisting parts turn resurrection, at least for some, into reincarnation? I think not. But one might have thought so without such facts to consider.

14. See J. F. Ross, "On the Nature of Philosophical Theology", *Union Seminary Quarterly Review*, 26, 1970, 3-17. See also "Verification or Certification? The Place of the Community in Theology", *Soundings*, 53, 1970, 208-214.

15. I am, of course, distinguishing theologians' activities from the response of the believing community.

16. I do repudiate, but not with any reasoning offered here, the argument that the persistently dualist imagery of Scripture is any indication of how to explain human being, beyond excluding reductive materialism. Nevertheless, I do not try to show that dualist accounts of human nature are incompatible with Scripture or even with evolutionary theory but instead try to sketch a nondualist, nonreductive, emergent-evolutionary account that fits the prospects of science and the revealed destiny of man. Its origins are in medieval hylomorphism.

17. See "Mathematics, Philosophy of" by Charles Parsons in Paul Edwards, editor, *Encyclopedia of Philosophy*, New York: Collier, 1967. See also the articles on "Logic", "Set Theory", "Gödel", and "Formal Systems" in the same work.

18. That seems to be necessitated because no fact is without logical relationships, such as incompatibility with other states of affairs.

19. See "Mask of God", my third O'Hara lecture, University of Notre Dame, 1982, to be incorporated, in substance, into my forthcoming book *Creation*.

20. I recognize that this argument rests upon our taking "true of w" to obtain, even if real number theory is "true of w" *only* by abstraction, and even if there cannot be infinitesimal intervals that can be "occupied" for infinitesimal times.

21. There is a problem, which I bypass for now, about what is the truth-making relation. It has to be dealt with elsewhere.

22. It is important to remember that emergence is not satisfactorily defined in terms of unpredictability "upward" and nonreducibility "downward," as A. Peacocke, *Creation and the World of Science*, still treats it. (See again the papers cited in note 11, above.) Rather, a triple inaccessibility, that includes unpredictability and irreducibility, but requires analogy of being and formal inaccessibility, is needed.

23. I speak here without adjusting for the more general context provided by Duns Scotus' doctrine of the disjunctive transcendentals, in which it is not possible that a material thing exist unless a living, thinking, immaterial thing exists.

24. I do not rule out a miraculous preservation of a human, disembodied; but such a state is not naturally possible, nor is it the state in which humans, resurrected, are to live with God. Furthermore, reembodiment may not require material of the same biotic kind as beginning to be does.

25. So, one molecule, complex enough, might do.

26. Scotus' and Ockham's view that God can do anything that he does via *secondary* causes, without such causes, can only be true to the extent that the "secondary cause" is not *logically* involved in the effect, for example, as a human parent is in a particular child. See Aquinas, *De potentia dei*, V, 5, 1 (also III,2). In fact, it may turn out that prehuman ancestors are similarly involved in the identity not only of humans but of the species. In that case, the very same humans who evolved *could not* have been created directly without ancestors.

27. Just how independent an emergent thing can be from its components and its medium depends on whether it is an individual whose matter is essential to it and, in the case of humans, of-its-essence. See Aquinas, *On Being and Essence*. An abstract particular, like a statement, can have many media. A "form", according to Aquinas and Aristotle, could be "received in many kinds of matter".

28. Arthur Peacocke holds very similar views: for instance, that humans are emergent, irreducible to their microstructure, and unpredictable from it. See Peacocke *Creation and the World of Science*, pp. 119, 167; see also K. Denberg, *An Inventive Universe*, London: Hutchinson, 1972, pp. 153, 156. But notice, emergence is not explained in these works beyond such notions as inventive, unpredictable, and irreducible. That is not enough.

29. See J. F. Ross, "Creation", *Journal of Philosophy*, 77, 1980, 614-630, and "Creation II", including the reviews of the latter by D. Burrell, *International Journal of Philosophy of Religion*, and W. Mann, *Religious Studies*, forthcoming.

30. Both Descartes and Aquinas, with quite different conceptions of the soul, held that the soul is *everywhere* in the body.

31. I used to think that this objection was practically insuperable until I read Freeman Dyson's speculations, so much like the thought of Aquinas in spirit (*De potentia dei*, 5), and realized that physical eschatology, as science, is yet an infant. See Dyson, "Time without End".

"Looking at the past history of life, we see that it takes about 10^6 years to evolve a new species, 10^7 years to evolve a genus, 10^8 years to evolve a class, 10^9 years to evolve a phylum, and less than 10^{10} to evolve all the way from the primaeval slime to Homo Sapiens. If life continues in this fashion in the future, it is impossible to set any limit to the variety of physical forms life may assume" (p. 453). Dyson then considers quite explicit, and apparently physically possible conditions, under which life could continue forever.

32. Arthur Peacocke says "the sense of self, of being a person, arises only in so far as we interact and communicate with *other* persons. Our selfhood seems only to be constituted if we are in personal contact with others" (Peacocke, *Creation and the World of Science*, p . 144). That is a widespread opinion, with which I concur. It is what suggests the idea of a "sparking", an "antiautistic" encounter of un-self-conscious rational being with God, by which the first human persons (self-aware, originators of actions subject to moral appraisal) appear.

33. See St. Anselm, *De casu diaboli*.

34. See James F. Ross, *Portraying Analogy*, New York: Cambridge University Press, 1982.

35. See Dyson, "Time without End".

EVOLUTIONARY EXPLANATIONS OF
RELIGION AND MORALITY:
EXPLAINING RELIGION AWAY?

William H. Austin*

Though the self-styled "scientific creationists" reject most elements of the contemporary scientific consensus in cosmology and geology as well as evolutionary biology, it seems most unlikely that the movement would exist if it were not for Darwinism. On the whole, historically, religious thinkers of all degrees of sophistication have found it easier to make their peace (once a clear scientific consensus emerged) with cosmologists' and geologists' findings than with those of Darwinian and neo-Darwinian biologists. There are no doubt several reasons for this, but the main reason, briefly stated, seems to be that Darwinian theory has been suspected of having unacceptable *moral* implications. Among Protestant theologians of moderately to very conservative persuasion the main factor determining their attitude toward Darwinism has been whether they thought its scientific content could or could not be successfully separated from its moral-and-metaphysical penumbra.[1] For their part biologists (with some notable exceptions such as Julian Huxley, Jacques Monod, and C. H. Waddington) have typically held that the separation can and should be made, thus helping to maintain what John Habgood has called "the uneasy truce between science and theology".[2]

Recently, however, Edward O. Wilson, an eminent zoologist and one of the principal founding fathers of the nascent discipline of sociobiology, has violated this truce in a striking way. Furious controversy has attended the sociobiological program of extending neo-Darwinian theory to explain the behavior and institutions of wasps, antelopes, people, and other social animals. No one minds much about the wasps and antelopes; it is the programmatic application of sociobiological principles to the explanation of human beings and their cultures that has drawn the fire.

Reading about the controversy, one could get the impression that Wilson is the only sociobiologist, or the only important one, or at least the only important one who theorizes about human beings. He is not. In some ways the best source on human sociobiology is Richard Alexander's *Darwinism and*

Human Affairs, which is less rhetorical in style than Wilson's *On Human Nature* and less brash (with more empirical backing) than Richard Dawkins' *The Selfish Gene*.[3] Wilson is, however, the only one I know of who gives more than passing attention to matters of religion, and for that reason I will focus on his work and some of the many large issues it raises.

In *On Human Nature* Wilson strongly advocates scientific materialism (a.k.a. scientific naturalism or scientific humanism) as an alternative to religious worldviews, superior both as an interpretation of the world and as a source of moral guidance. This is a familiar enough stance so far, but Wilson differs from most scientific humanists in holding that people cannot do without myths. We are genetically programmed to be myth-makers and myth-followers; we need a mythology ("defined in the noble sense", p. 201/208)[4] to engage our loyalties and direct our energies. Wilson does not define these terms, but it appears that by a "mythology in the noble sense" he means a credible worldview, incorporating our scientific knowledge and expressed in a literary way that makes it capable of firing people's imaginations and enthusiasms.

Among available (or potentially available) mythologies the chief candidates, according to Wilson, are scientific materialism, Marxism, and "traditional religion" (a category within which he unfortunately makes no discriminations). Marxism he dismisses as a fatally flawed version of scientific materialism, which by ignoring biology has saddled itself with a hopelessly inaccurate and inadequate theory of human nature. (In other contexts, and from another point of view, he treats Marxism as simply a variant form of religion. Either way we need not give it independent attention, on Wilson's view.)

Traditional religion, Wilson recognizes, cannot be dealt with so summarily. Though it has lost its credibility for many, there are still many for whom it retains much of its old power. Its strength is that it has something that scientific materialism presently lacks: a literature (in the literary, not the scholarly, sense) capable of engaging people's loyalties. The weakness of scientific materialism is that the evolutionary epic is yet to be written. When we have it, it will include a tale of cosmic history and above all the saga of the triumphant march of human knowledge, as well as the history of life forms. These are its materials, but plagued as we are by the two-cultures split, they have not yet found their poets. (It may be that one purpose of his book is to do something about this. He seems to be trying hard there to capture the interest of potential poets among his readers. This may account for the somewhat strange rhetorical style of the book: he is trying to be both scientific and eloquent, and the resultant product is often obscure, confusing, and resistant of philosophical analysis.)

While we await the appearance of the evolutionary epic, what advantages does scientific materialism have in the conflict with traditional religion? Wilson mentions, but does not dwell upon, the repeated defeats theologians suffered in their conflicts with science before the truce. He stresses much more strongly the claim that scientific materialism will triumph because sociobiology will soon be able to explain, in purely materialistic terms, the sources of religious belief and practice. Already, he thinks, "traditional religious beliefs have been eroded, not so much by humiliating disproofs of their mythologies as by the growing awareness that beliefs are really enabling mechanisms for survival" (p.3). Hitherto this "awareness" has not been securely grounded in any well-established scientific theory. But now

> As I have tried to show, sociobiology can account for the very origin of mythology by the principle of natural selection active on the genetically evolving material structure of the human brain.
> If this interpretation is correct, the final decisive edge enjoyed by scientific naturalism will come from its capacity to explain tradition religion, its chief competitor, as a wholly material phenomenon. (p. 192/201)

A little later, summarizing his arguments for the superiority of "the scientific ethos", he repeats the claim with a new twist or two:

> the possibility of explaining traditional religion by the mechanistic models of evolutionary biology . . . will be crucial. If religion, including the dogmatic secular ideologies, can be . . . explained as a product of the brain's evolution, its power as an external source of morality will be gone forever. . . . (p. 201/208)

In short, Wilson is claiming that by explaining religion sociobiologists can discredit it. Obviously, many things about this claim call for clarification. "Explaining religion" is quite a global notion; just what aspects of religious belief and practice are to be explained? And in what sense of 'explain'? Decades of philosophic analysis have revealed how subtle and multiform the notion of explanation is, and "how deep into the traditional problembody . . . of philosophy . . . questions of explanation cut".[5] I will not elaborate on these questions here; it seems the better strategy is to go ahead with an examination of Wilson's claim, introducing distinctions as they become necessary.

We do need to distinguish at the outset among senses in which religious belief might be "discredited". In the most obvious sense to discredit a belief is to show that it is false, or at least that its degree of rational credibility is lower than had been thought. But there is also a psychological sense, in which a belief is discredited to the extent that people find it less persuasive and find themselves less likely to hold it, regardless of whether the change in belief is rationally justified. It seems quite possible that Wilsonian (or Freudian) explanations of religious beliefs might be more efficacious in discrediting them in this psychological sense than in the logical/evidential sense. Further, a belief or system of beliefs might be discredited as a source of practical (including moral) guidance. Here again the previous distinction is germane. One might show that a belief, even if true, does not have the practical consequences it was thought to have; or, on the other hand, an explanation of a belief might have the psychological effect of rendering it *de facto* less likely that people will act upon it.

It is not entirely clear which among these senses of 'discredit' Wilson has in mind. I will assume for the sake of discussion that he is not proposing that religious belief is to be discredited only in the psychological sense. And, as the above quotations suggest, I will assume that he is claiming *both* that explaining religious beliefs will show them false (or at least lower their degree of rational credibility) *and* that, whatever their status as theoretical propositions, traditional religion will be shown to be a poor source of moral guidance (or at least not as good a source as scientific humanism).

My discussion of Wilson's project will come in four stages. Many people would say that his program is hopelessly misguided from the start, either because explanations of beliefs cannot discredit them or because phenomena of human culture (such as religion) are not susceptible of biological explanation. I will argue that the arguments for these claims are inconclusive and thus that Wilson's program needs to be considered on its merits. Then I will examine Wilson's attempted explanation of religion and argue that it is at best a rather weak form of explanation, unlikely to discredit anything very strongly. Even if Wilson's explanations can be made strong, they will proceed in large part by showing how religion has been adaptive, which may seem to be a strange way of discrediting it; I next examine this suggestion. Finally, I will consider the prospects of scientific materialism as an alternative source of moral guidance and strength.

1. Summary Judgment Denied

Consider first the claim that an explanation of why someone holds a belief would show it false or reduce its degree of rational credibility. Obviously not simply any kind of explanation would do the job. If I explain why someone holds a belief by pointing to all the excellent arguments he or she has mustered in support of it, I hardly discredit the belief. We are concerned with the kind of explanation that offers what Alston has called "reason-irrelevant" causal conditions for religious belief, that is, "conditions which do not include acquiring, considering, or possessing good reasons for the belief".[6] Wilson means to offer this kind of explanation, of course.

But an obvious objection comes immediately to mind. Surely, one would think, the extent to which it is rational to hold a belief depends solely on the logical relation between the belief and the available evidence. How could a *causal* explanation of the belief's being held have any bearing on the matter?

The principle that the rational credibility of a proposition is a function of its relation to the relevant evidence is hard to dispute, and I do not propose to dispute it. But I do not think it follows that a causal explanation of someone's believing a proposition would be altogether irrelevant. For the rationality of believing a proposition is not purely a function of its relation to the evidence in hand. Sometimes the evidence in hand is not *enough*; sometimes what rationality requires is that we seek out more evidence before actually assessing the hypothesis in question. In principle it is almost always an open question, or rather at least an open-able one, whether more evidence should be sought.

Are there cases in which causal explanations of beliefs would provide reasons for reopening the question of their credibility and seeking further evidence? One such case would seem to arise when someone has (in large part, at least) accepted a proposition on the authority of an expert. Presumably he or she has done so on the assumption that the *expert's* belief stems from rational assessment of evidence. A causal explanation of why the expert holds the belief could cast doubt on that assumption and suggest that it is time to look into the matter oneself or (if that is not feasible) to find another expert.

Similarly, when one has been relying not on an external authority but on one's own intuitions or hunches, one's confidence in them might well be reduced if a causal explanation were forthcoming. A special case here is provided by a person's "basic beliefs" — those that are held, not on the basis of evidence, but rather because they seem of themselves so solid, luminously certain, inescapable, or the like. These are the ultimate evidence statements, against which nonbasic candidates for belief are assessed. Now if someone offers a causal explanation for my holding some belief that I have taken as basic, the issue of the potential relevance of the explanation is not preempted by the "relation to evidence" criterion, since by definition the belief is not held on the basis of evidence. What then? If someone could show me that a basic belief of mine was implanted by hypnotic suggestion or was caused by a neurosurgeon tinkering with the circuitry in my brain during an operation, I would remove it from my roster of basic beliefs. I suspect that the "luminous certainty" would evaporate in such an event, but even if it remained, I would no longer trust it. The proposition in question, no longer basic, would become a candidate for assessment on the basis of evidence.

I have not argued that causal explanations of beliefs provide evidence against them, only that they are relevant to the process of rational belief assessment in the sense that they can provide reasons to take a harder look at the evidence, and demand more and better evidence, than one might otherwise have thought necessary. This modest point is obviously not enough to sustain the claim that explaining a belief could discredit it, but it does block the argument that it would be pointless in principle to examine Wilson's explanations.

A second line of argument, much used against sociobiology in general, seeks to establish that the phenomena of human mental and cultural life are in principle not susceptible of explanation by means of the principles of evolutionary biology or any other natural science. (So Wilson cannot discredit religion by explaining it, since he cannot explain it.) The key idea here is that human behavior and culture cannot even be appropriately described, let alone explained, without the use of irreducibly intentionalistic terms like 'purpose', 'meaning', 'significance', 'rationality' — terms outside the vocabulary, corresponding to realities beyond the reach, of the natural sciences.

From a slightly different angle the point can be put as follows. When we set about explaining things, we have two quite distinct explanatory patterns to work with: in one mode we explain things by appeal to natural laws and efficient causes; in the other we appeal to purposes, intentions, and the like. Von Wright has termed these the "causal" and the "teleological" patterns, respectively.[7] The claim then is that the causal pattern is the appropriate one for the natural sciences and the teleologial pattern is the appropriate one for the human sciences: no marriage between them (much less an incorporation of one into the other) is possible. The arguments for this claim are many, diverse, and not infrequently obscure. This is not the place to try to sort out the many subtle issues that are involved.[8] For our purposes it is enough to note that a standard line of counterargument exists and has not yet been shown nonviable. The gist of it is that there is another pattern of explanation, in which purposive-seeming behavior is shown as the outcome of more or less complex feedback mechanisms. Such explanatory mechanisms, which seem clearly to belong in essence to the causal family, open up the possibility of replacing teleological explanations with "quasi-teleological" ones, as von Wright calls them. ("Pseudoteleological" might be better, but for convenience I will follow von Wright's terminology.) Whether higher-order human intentional behavior — as opposed to the sort of animal behavior that we feel tempted to describe as purposive, while wondering if this is only a metaphor — can really be explained in this way remains to be seen. But the matter is under vigorous debate, and as long as the question remains open, it would be premature to rule out Wilson's project as impossible in principle.

The quasi-teleology line is a natural one for an evolutionary theorist to take: natural selection is itself a feedback process, and many of its neurophysiological products are uncontroversially explained as cybernetic mechanisms. Wilson occasionally makes explicit use of the terminology of cybernetics, and it appears more frequently (encased in a formidable mathematical apparatus) in a more recent book he wrote jointly with Charles

Lumsden, a physicist: *Genes, Mind, and Culture*.[9] In that book they develop a theory of "gene-culture coevolution", by means of which they try (among other things) to answer a simple argument that *seems* to tell forcefully against the thesis that genes are substantial determinants of human culture: culture changes quite rapidly, and natural selection on genes is a slow process. The nub of their reply is that how fast natural selection works depends on how fast the relevant environment changes, and human culture changes the relevant environment rather quickly (being, after all, itself an important *part* of the relevant environment). The authors develop mathematical models according to which gene-culture coevolution could bring about substantial changes in gene frequencies in a relatively short time — a thousand years, say. If this works, it raises a problem that Wilson seems not to have noticed: How to account for the persistence of maladaptive, genetically based cultural traits? As we shall see, an important step in Wilson's argument is that the ease with which human beings are indoctrinated into dogmatic religious or quasi-religious ingroups (illustrated by our many contemporaries who, having rejected traditional religion, eagerly embrace some cult or other) can be understood as the genetic relic of our hunter-gatherer ancestors' adaptation to an environment of warring tribes, a relic that survives to plague us now. But why does it survive if gene-culture coevolution can work so fast?

   High-road intentionalists are unlikely to be swayed by *Genes, Mind, and Culture:* its models are too hypothetical, and it deals explicitly only with rather rudimentary mental and cultural phenomena. It seems more immediately addressed to those social scientists, such as behaviorists or the anthropologist Marvin Harris,[10] with his intriguing research strategy of "cultural materialism", who agree that natural-science methods should be applied in the study of human behavior but deny any substantial role to genetics. The argument between Wilson and such people, interesting as it is, is something of a side issue for our purpose. A cultural-materialist explanation of religious belief would seem to have just as much (or as little) tendency to discredit such belief as would a sociobiological one.

2. Wilson's Account of Religion

   Let us turn now to Wilson's account of religion. He recognizes that the explanation will not be easy to produce. Religion constitutes "the greatest challenge" for human sociobiology, for two reasons (pp. 175f./183). First, it is a uniquely human phenomenon, so sociobiologists cannot get much help from their knowledge of other social animals. Second, its effectiveness depends on its true function and workings being well disguised, since "religion is above all the process by which individuals are persuaded to subordinate their immediate self-interest to the interest of the group". ('Brought' would be a better word than 'persuaded', since Wilson's point is that the effectiveness of the process depends on the individual's not being aware of what is going on.)

Some background: For a long time a major problem in evolutionary theory was to account for "altruistic" behavior on the part of animals—behavior in which an individual sacrificed or risked its life or its reproductive potential to the benefit of others. (Note that 'altruism' is defined purely in terms of results, not intentions.) A commonly cited example is the bird that gives a warning call when it sees a hawk, at the risk of calling the hawk's attention to itself.

People who hoped to fashion an "evolutionary ethic" welcomed such cases as showing that nature is not so red in tooth and claw after all. But they posed a theoretical problem. Granted, a group whose members act "altruistically" toward others will do well in competition with groups whose members do not. But *within* the group the "selfish" individual is likely to have more descendants than its "altruistic" competitors. Most theorists were convinced that, in all but rare and extraordinary circumstances, natural selection at the individual level would override group selection. Genes that disposed their bearers toward 'altruistic" behavior would be strongly selected against, and the behavior should be expected to disappear. The breakthrough that sociobiologists see as having made their discipline possible was the observation that what counts, from a natural-selection perspective, is not the number of descendants one has, but the number of replicas of one's genes that appear in subsequent generations, whether in one's own descendants or in those of relatives. Since in sexually reproducing organisms an individual shares at least half its genes with siblings, an individual's "inclusive fitness" would be better served if it sacrificed its life to save three brothers than if it saved itself at their expense.

This "kin-selection" hypothesis accounted nicely for the long-standing puzzle of the sterile castes in social insects (Wilson's original specialty). How could a gene that caused females to be sterile (except in the special environment provided the queen) possibly be maintained in a population? By a quirk in the reproductive mechanisms of the species involved, females actually share a greater proportion of genes with their sisters than with their parents or potential offspring. Thus a system could evolve in which the inclusive fitness of a worker was maximized by her devoting her energies to taking good care of her mass-productive sister, the queen.

But not all animal "altruism" is directed to close relatives. To explain things like the mutual grooming of unrelated monkeys, sociobiologists have postulated "reciprocal altruism": it is worth my while to devote some energy to grooming you if you will do the same for me. Obvious problems arise, suggested by one of Dawkins' memorable chapter titles: "you scratch my back, I'll ride on yours". Considerable ingenuity has gone into their solution, but we cannot pursue the topic further here.[11]

Since explanations of animal "altruism" have been among the foundational achievements of animal sociobiology, it is understandable that Wilson looks to human altruism as a promising candidate for evolutionary explanation. But here a familiar complaint seems especially apposite: sociobiologists take intentionality-laden terms like 'altruism' (and 'slavery' and 'rape'), apply them metaphorically in describing nonintentional animal behavior, explain the behavior, and then try to apply the same explanatory mechanisms to the intentionalistic human behavior. Wilson does not address this issue in his chapter on altruism. As a result, his discussion sheds more light (a fair amount) on the ways in which our altruistic inclinations can become entangled with disguised self-interest than it does on altruism itself.

Wilson's explanation of the origins of religion might be described as "Durkheim geneticized". In the long prehistory of mankind, when the greater part of the species' genetic capital was fixed, and learning rules were encoded in some of the more primitive parts of the brain, people lived in hunter-gatherer bands of close relatives, struggling with a hazardous environment (other bands being among the hazards). In those circumstances groups whose members were programmed to feel a fierce emotional loyalty to the group, and to respond swiftly and unhesitatingly to the symbols of the group's identity and its leader's authority, were more likely to survive and leave descendants with similar programming. The institutions of religion were the most effective instrument.

Note that this account depends on some assumptions, not implausible but not solidly established either, (1) that our ancestors lived in bands of close relatives (necessary if kin selection is to be decisive) and (2) that their social institutions resembled those of Durkheim's aborigines or other contemporary survivals of the stone age.

He gets onto shakier ground when he discusses historical religions. Here he admits that the particular forms institutions and beliefs take are very much subject to the vagaries of cultural evolution, but he insists (on largely a priori grounds) that they will evolve in ways that enhance the "Darwinian fitness" of their practitioners. He stresses the frequency with which religion is the instrument of the economic, military, or political subjugation of one group by another. But it is not at all clear that the subjugators typically have more children. On the contrary, it might seem they are more likely to limit their families and enjoy the good life.

In any event, religion is not *always* a means of subjugation. Challenged to account for Mother Teresa, Wilson points out that "she is secure in the . . . knowledge of her church's immortality" (p. 165/173). He cites Jesus' saying that those who believe will be saved and those who do not will be condemned, as he had earlier cited Tertullian's dictum "the blood of martyrs is the seed of the church" as evidence that the purpose of religious altruism is "to raise one group over another" (p. 149/155). Well, in a sense; but we are now a long way indeed from *productive* advantage.

There are several practices, common in historical religions, that do not seem to enhance the reproductive fitness of their practioners. Altruism like Mother Teresa's is one. Another is *proselytization* of nonkin, which may strengthen the group to which the proselytizers belong but also dilutes the advantage of belonging to a strong group by bringing in unrelated competitors. Kin selection will no longer work when proselytization of (or altruism toward) nonrelatives is the phenomenon to be explained. Whether reciprocal altruism or group selection can be successfully substituted remains to be seen. At any rate, explaining the transitions from the institutions of tribal religions, founded on kin selection, to those of proselytizing religions, maintained in some other way, is a major challenge for Wilson. Another challenge is posed by hermit saints and cloistered contemplatives, whose ascetic world-renunciation would seem to enhance neither their own reproductive fitness nor anyone else's. To be sure, these patterns of religious life have not been prominent in all religious traditions, but the problem for a theorist of Wilson's persuasion is to explain why the ideal of ascetic world-renunciation should (or even how it could) arise and persist as frequently as it has.

In short, though Wilson has provided moderately plausible explanations of the origin of religion and the continuing phenomenon of ready indoctrinability, there are significant features of historical religions that seem hard to explain in his terms. But his is a first attempt; perhaps others (or Wilson himself if he returns to the subject) will be able to meet the challenges? Here I want to argue that in the present and foreseeable state of evolutionary theory the explanations a sociobiologist will be able to provide are likely to be relatively weak explanations, and thus to have relatively little capacity to undermine the practices and beliefs they explain.

To make good this claim, I need to indicate what I mean by the strength or weakness of an explanation, show why a weak explanation is a weak discrediter, and show why sociobiological explanations of religious phenomena are likely to be weak. Of necessity the discussion will be too brief and crude to do justice to the complex issues involved. Only a rough suggestion of the necessary argument can be given.

What I call the strength of an explanation is a function of four factors. (One crudity is that I shall be speaking as if there were a one-dimensional measure of the strength of an argument, which seems most unlikely. How many dimensions there actually are in "strength space" I cannot say.) For simplicity of exposition I will suppose — what many would dispute — that a theoretical explanation can be regarded as an argument, with a statement describing the phenomenon to be explained as its conclusion, and with premises that include principles of the theory in question as well as statements describing relevant actual or hypothetical factual circumstances. One factor in the overall strength of an explanation will be the tightness of the logical relation between its premises and its conclusion, ranging from entailment on down through various grades of what is most often called inductive strength.

Another determinant, or dimension, of the strength of an explanatory argument is the precision and specificity with which its conclusion describes the phenomenon to be explained. For instance, if what we want to explain is that 73 percent of the members of a given population are female, an explanatory argument whose conclusion is merely that there should be more females than males will be weaker than one whose conclusion is that three-fourths of the members will be female.

The probabilities of the premises of the argument provide a third factor. The more confident we can be that the circumstances described in the extratheoretical premises actually hold (or held), the stronger the argument. Similarly, if the theoretical principles used in the explanation are relatively well-established, with an extensive record of prior explanatory success, the explanation will be stronger than if they are relatively untried theoretical conjectures. In relation to the theoretical apparatus a fourth factor is also relevant to the strength of an explanation. If a body of theory includes several alternative explanatory mechanisms or models, then an explanation that invokes one of them and gives good reasons to suppose the others not to be involved will be stronger than one that leaves alternative explanatory possibilities in the field. Thus if we explain some phenomenon as a result of kin selection and can show that in the circumstances reciprocal altruism and group selection could not have been involved, then our explanation is stronger than it would have been if we had had to allow that with different assumptions about the circumstances (less plausible, perhaps, but not excluded) a reciprocal-altruism explanation could be forthcoming.

What makes all these factors relevant to the strength of a causal explanation is that they all bear on the degree of confidence we can have that the explanation has really specified the cause, and the whole cause (which may of course be a combination of causal elements), of the phenomenon in question. We are supposing, for the sake of argument, that a causal explanation of a belief can discredit it. But surely its capacity to do so depends on how complete it is and on how well-grounded it is. A somewhat plausible account of what *might* have caused a belief will do little to undermine it.

We can expect sociobiological explanations of religion to be rather weak, for the same sorts of reasons that only weak explanations are available for many phenomena we would like to have explained (the demise of the dinosaurs, the large brains and scant hair of human beings, the fact that so many organisms reproduce sexually when they could pass on *all* their genes to the next generation by asexual reproduction). One source of weakness is that for so many of the most interesting phenomena the explanation involves reference to properties of bygone populations and environments, about which we are not in a position to establish high probabilities for our statements. Another difficulty, noted by many authors, is that evolutionary theorists have available to them a variety of explanatory mechanisms but very often lack the necessary information to determine which is (or are) operative in a given case. Maynard Smith has stated the problem concisely:

> We have three mechanisms [mutation, selection, and migration] which we believe to determine the course of evolution, and we have a mathematical theory which tells us that these processes can produce their effects at levels we cannot usually hope to measure directly. . . . The measurement difficulty is serious. It means that we can think up a number of possible evolutionary mechanisms, but find it difficult to decide on the relative importance of the mechanisms we have conceived.[12]

The severity of the difficulties is heightened when phenomena of human culture are the objects of explanation. One can reject the argument that culture is in principle inaccessible to natural-scientific explanation and still recognize that our available theoretical apparatus and stock of relevant factual information are less adequate for the explanation of cultural phenomena than for those of anatomy and physiology. Further, as Wilson himself pointed out, religion presents special difficulties in addition to those pertaining to other aspects of culture.

So, for the foreseeable future we can expect sociobiological explanations of religion to be rather weak at best. That does not mean that they would be without intellectual value; sometimes a weak explanation is as much as we can reasonably expect. It does mean, I have argued, that they would be of little force to discredit religious belief.

How might Wilson reply? He might say simply that I am being too pessimistic about the prospects of evolutionary theory: that while sociobiologists do not have strong explanations for religious phenomena now, they will be able to provide such explanations sooner than I think. One could discuss this reply at length, but the most reasonable terminus of discussion would be that we shall have to wait and see. Another line Wilson might take, of greater theoretical interest, is to claim that I have erred in focusing on the strength of sociobiological explanations in some absolute sense of "strength" — or, rather, on their strength as compared with that of the explanations we sometimes achieve in more tractable domains. What matters, he might say, is whether they are stronger than relevant competing explanations. The competitor he himself would probably cite is the explanation that people have their religious beliefs because God implanted the beliefs in them. A philosophical defender of Wilson might, instead, consider the relevant alternative explanation to be that people hold the beliefs because the evidence favors them. Wilson or his defender could then argue that even if the sociobiological explanations are weak, they are stronger than the relevant alternative. To assess that argument is beyond the scope of this paper. I also cannot deal here with the issue whether explanations must be strong if they are to discredit what they explain, or only stronger than certain competitors. But the issue is clearly an important one and needs attention.

3. Religion as Adaptive

Suppose that strong evolutionary explanations of religious belief were forthcoming. They would still have a special feature that might seem to render them ill-suited to the role of underminer. After all, an evolutionary explanation of x proceeds in large part by showing how x is or has been adaptive (or else by showing that it is a consequence of y, which is or has been adaptive).[13] To say that religious beliefs are adaptive sounds like, if anything, a reason to accept them, not reject them.

Consider, for instance, how Marvin Harris explains two items of belief that seem bizarre and irrational to most persons outside the religious traditions in which they appear—the sacred cow of India and the Jewish and Islamic ban on pork.[14] As to the cow, Harris argues that cattle have been, and still are so absolutely vital to the economy of village India that the cattle population must be maintained at all costs. Now in ordinary times it would do no very great harm to kill and eat a few marginal or superannuated cows. But in time of famine the starving farmers will be subject to a desperately strong temptation to eat their cattle, even though that would destroy the basis of their future livelihood. An absolute ban on cattle-killing is therefore needed, and (Harris suggests) nothing less forceful than a sacred taboo will suffice to sustain the ban in times of terrible hunger. The taboo protects people from the temptation, quite possibly irresistible without it, to sacrifice their future survival to relieve their present distress—though of course in the most extreme situations it may require them to sacrifice their lives so that their community may survive.

Similarly, Harris offers an economic rationale for the Jewish and Muslim ban on pork: pigs are forest creatures, and it is uneconomic to try to raise them in the hot, arid lands whence came the Torah and the Koran.

These accounts are rather plausible and show how a functional explanation can make sense of seemingly irrational practices and beliefs.

Does that mean that the explanations vindicate the beliefs? Here we need to distinguish between the belief that a practice is good to follow and the belief that it was enjoined by a deity. If the beliefs in question are that a deity or deities laid down the prohibitions on eating pork and killing cattle, respectively, then the explanations seem to enhance their credibility by removing an obvious objection: Why would a wise and benevolent deity issue such arbitrary and capricious injunctions? On the other hand, the explanations are also compatible with, and in similar fashion enhance the credibility of, the priestcraft theory of the origins of religious beliefs and practices. (Clever priests did cost-benefit analyses, concluded that slaughtering cattle and raising pigs were highly uneconomic propositions in the environments in question, and devised formidable sanctions against these undesirable activities.) Further, explanations like Harris' fit fairly readily into a Darwinian framework: somehow the idea arises that pigs are unclean animals in a more than physical sense,[15] and a society that embraces this idea is more likely to survive in an arid environment than one that does not.

There is another important point. Showing how religious taboos are adaptive in the various environments in which they originate counts against the hypothesis that there is one and only one god, unless we suppose that this god calls himself or herself by different names and gives widely varying accounts of his or her nature to different peoples at different times and places. This suggestion, while welcome in some quarters, has seldom been acceptable to adherents of monotheistic, proselytizing religions that claim universal authority. If that is the kind of religious tradition we are considering, and if we want to give the same kind of explanation for each of these religious prohibitions (as opposed to saying that Yahweh forbade pork, and the Indian ban on killing cattle came about in some quite different way), then the priestcraft explanation or the natural-selection explanation (or some combination of them) appears to have an important advantage. So these explanations of religious beliefs as adaptive may have a sting in their tails after all. They are particularly damaging in the context of the general problem of conflicting religious traditions, sharpened by a nontheological account of how the conflicting traditions arose.

Thus, on balance, an explanation of a practice as adaptive would seem to count against the claim that it was divinely enjoined. But it might still seem to count in favor of the claim that the practice is good to follow. Not only specific injunctions like those we have been considering but also more general systems of religious belief offer guidance for conduct in a variety of ways. To the extent that they are explained as adaptive, they might seem to be vindicated as guides to conduct, whatever we might think of them as systems of theoretical propositions.

Let us return to Wilson and ask how he would respond to the latter suggestion. I think there would be two main points in his reply. One is that whatever traditional religion can do for us, the new mythology of scientific materialism, richly and vividly expressed in the evolutionary epic, will be able to do at least as well. I will return to this point in the next section.

Wilson's other point would be that while some features of religious belief are still adaptive, others — including the most crucial ones — are adaptations to a long-bygone environment and thus dysfunctional in the world we now live in. These crucial features, common to traditional religion and to the dogmatic secular ideologies that have replaced it in some quarters, are *dogma* and *ingroup exclusivism*. That is, Wilson thinks it is characteristic of traditional religions and surrogates such as Marxism (1) to seize upon ideas and elevate them to the status of sacred, unquestionable dogmas and (2) to divide the world harshly into Us and Them, and preach and practice a fierce loyalty to Us and a ruthless hostility to Them. Such tendencies were adaptive for hunter-gatherer bands, but highly hazardous for us, who must live together in complex interconnected cultures.

It is worth mentioning, in response, that the mere fact that an organic or behavioral feature of an organism was originally an adaptation to a bygone environment does not in itself show that the feature is now maladaptive. The currency among evolutionary theorists of expressions like 'preadaptation' and 'the opportunism of evolution' reflects the fact that features originally selected as adaptive in one environment may also be, with more or less modification, adaptive in a new environment. So the claim that a feature adapted to a past environment is now dysfunctional must be established by an independent argument.

However, where dogma (as Wilson understands it)[16] and ingroup exclusiveness are concerned, the argument is not far to seek. The interesting question is whether they really are necessary features of "traditional religion". Wilson is pessimistic about the prospects of liberal religion. A survey of which religious groups are prospering today, and which are not, suggests it is at least possible he is right. So let us consider, if only briefly, his arguments for scientific naturalism as an alternative source of moral guidance and strength.

4. The Alternative of Scientific Naturalism

There is a striking asymmetry in Wilson's treatments of ethics and of religion. From the beginning it has been part of his program to provide biological explanations of the sources of ethical beliefs as well as religious ones. One famous passage may be recalled: "What . . . made the hypothalamus and the limbic system? They evolved by natural selection. That simple biological statement must be pursued to explain ethics and ethical philosophers, if not epistemology and epistemologists, at all depths".[17] Equally notorious is the suggestion that "scientists and humanists should consider together the possibility that the time has come for ethics to be removed temporarily from the hands of philosophers and biologicized".[18]

We should not, in our shock, overlook the key word 'temporarily' in that last quotation. The idea appears to be that ethics is to be returned to the philosophical moralists once they have absorbed the relevant biological information and learned to give it due weight. There is no comparable suggestion that religion should be returned to the hands of the theologians in due course. Theology is to be discredited by evolutionary explanations; ethics is not. Why the difference?

It may be that Wilson is involved here in a deep and serious inconsistency. Suspicion grows when we read in *On Human Nature* that an understanding of the "raw biological causation" of belief in universal human rights "will be more compelling in the end than any rationalization contrived by culture to reinforce and euphemize it" (p. 199/206f.). So biological explanation of a belief can actually strengthen it!

There seem, actually, to be two distinct inconsistencies here. The inconsistency involved in Wilson's differential treatment of ethics and religion can be mitigated, if not eliminated. He would say that particular moral principles, for instance Kant's, can be discredited by biological explanation; but the enterprise of moral philosophy (in contrast to that of traditional theology) would not be discredited, since moral philosophers are not shackled by dogma. The second inconsistency, that biological explanations are sometimes supposed to undermine beliefs and sometimes to strengthen them, remains. To resolve it Wilson would need to revise his argument by specifying further conditions which must be met if an explanation is to discredit (or to strengthen) a belief.

In any case, what Wilson *cares most about* is that "traditional religion" should be discredited "as an external source of morality". By "an external source of morality" I think he means a source from which moral norms could be derived quite independently of any consideration of our biological needs, norms further which would be capable of overriding any that are based on such consideration. His argument is that if religious belief and practice can be shown to have a biological origin, they will have lost their claim to derive from a transcendent source that would justify overriding biological imperatives.

As an example of the kind of norm theologians have been capable of coming up with, ponder John Henry Newman's declaration that it would be

better for sun and moon to drop from heaven, for the earth to fail, and for all the many millions who are upon it to die of starvation in extremest agony . . . than that one soul . . . should commit one single venial sin, should tell one wilful untruth, though it harmed no one, or steal one poor farthing without excuse.[19]

It is that sort of thing, I suggest, that Wilson wants above all to block. For Wilson, as for Hume before him, the ultimately most important objective is that religious doctrines should never be taken as sources of moral guidance that would diverge from the guidance we can get from consideration of human nature, naturalistically understood.[20]

This brings us back to the question Just what sort of guidance *will* knowledge of our evolutionary history provide us? It is important to recognize that Wilson is *not* suggesting, in the manner of Julian Huxley, that we can discern in the evolutionary process a pattern on which we can model our behavior or a direction to be followed. In *that* sense he could agree with Richard Alexander's forthright answer to the question "What does evolution have to say about normative ethics, or defining what people *ought* to be do-ing?" — "Nothing whatsoever".[21]

For Wilson evolutionary knowledge is relevant in a quite different way. His thesis is that people make their moral decisions and judgments (and ethicists construct their systems) on the basis of their moral intuitions, their deep emotional likings and aversions. As long as we do not understand the sources of these feelings, we are swept along helplessly by them. But in fact they are governed by elements in the limbic system, which have an evolu-tionary history. When we have deciphered that history we can "shift from automatic control based on our biological properties to precise steering based on biological knowledge" (p.6/7).

One is tempted to respond that knowledge of how the ship and its in-struments are constructed does nothing to tell us in what direction we want to steer. This rejoinder is not completely fair (playing with people's metaphors often is not), but it does raise a problem that Wilson does not solve. He sees the problem: "we are forced to choose among the elements of human nature by reference to value systems which these same elements created in an evolu-tionary age now long vanished" (p. 196/203). That is, when we understand the sources of our deep intuitions and emotional reactions, they will lose their status as oracles (another favorite metaphor), and we will be free to choose which ones to follow, which ones to resist, and which ones to give more weight than others. But the problem remains: we have no basis for making these choices other than guidelines drawn from those same intuitions. Wilson goes on to assert that "this circularity of the human predicament is not so tight that it cannot be broken through an exercise of will", but he still does not address the problem of criteria of choice. Reading between the lines, one senses that he stands in the long line of thinkers who have believed that once the obstacles and false guides they have variously identified are cleared away, reasonable people will be able to agree on central moral questions.

Wilson undoubtedly both underestimates the extent to which we are able even now to make intelligent choices among our inherited emotional guides and exaggerates the extent to which knowledge of their biological sources will help us do so. Moral philosophers have been at this enterprise for some time now. Wilson's underestimate of what they have accomplished probably stems from his failure to distinguish between two quite different ways in which philosophers have appealed to moral intuitions. One way (the one he has in mind) is to appeal to intuition as sanctioning sweeping moral principles (justice is fairness, do unto others. . . , maximize liberty) and draw out their consequences. The other approach is to take as starting points people's intuitive reactions to specific situations or types of situation, in particular those concerning which people's intuitions agree, and then look for moral principles that will give the greatest possible coherence to the greatest number of them. The principles can then be applied to give guidance in situations where our intuitions fail us or clash. On this approach, moral principles are justified in a way roughly analogous to the way scientific hypotheses are justified by their success in making sense of empirical data.[22]

The mode of moral theorizing I have just so crudely sketched can be and has been pursued without reference to evolutionary biology, but the latter can potentially make a modest contribution to it. If the way people respond to a particular type of situation can be shown to be the result of adaptation to an environment unlike ours, that could provide a reason to set it aside when we are looking for principles to make systematic sense of our intuitions — to treat it as a piece of bad data, so to speak. As we saw earlier, showing that something is an adaptation to a past environment does not automatically discredit it. But if the intuition in question were already a difficult case, hard to reconcile with others, explanation of it as adaptive to a past environment would give reason to quit trying to fit it in. On the other hand, if an intuition were shown to be presently adaptive (in the biological sense), that would be a reason to give weight to it.

While Wilson expects the biological-knowledge component of scientific naturalism to provide ethical *guidance*,[23] he does not see it as a source of emotional *strength*. Unlike most "evolutionary ethicists", he is convinced that people do have deep needs that traditional religion can satisfy—needs for security, for a sense of meaning and mission, for a feeling of personal and group identity, and the like. Scientific materialism as we now know it cannot meet these needs. But, Wilson believes, scientific materialism enriched by the evolutionary epic will be able to. On the face of it this seems dubious. One can see how the evolutionary epic might be stirring and inspiring, might provide a sense of meaning, of being part of a great enterprise. (Remember that the tale of the growth of human knowledge is to be integral to it.) But it is hard to see how it could provide the serene security, the firm sense of personal and group identity, that traditional religions have (often) provided their followers. Can we have *these* things without dogma and ingroup exclusiveness? That is the painful question.

Wilson has a remarkable answer. The gist of it is that satisfactions for our basic emotional needs are rather freely substitutable, one for another.

> A kind of principle of the conservation of energy operates among them, such that the emphasis of any one over others still retains the potential summed power of all. . . . Although the means to measure these energies are lacking, I suspect psychologists would agree that they can be rechanneled substantially without losing strength, that the mind fights to retain a certain level of order and emotional reward. (pp. 199f./207)

The suggestion seems to be that we can rather easily do without security and ingroup identity if we have a stirring vision and the exaltation of discovery. I wonder about that.

Wilson stakes a lot on the principle of substitutability of emotional satisfactions. He also relies crucially on the appearance of the evolutionary epic, which is hardly a sure thing. It seems fitting, therefore, that he titles his last chapter "Hope" and concludes it by invoking the mythic hero Prometheus. He quotes a passage wherein Aeschylus has Prometheus say, "I caused mortals to cease foreseeing doom". The Chorus asks, "What cure did you provide them with against that sickness?" Prometheus replies, "I placed in them blind hopes".

To say that Wilson's hopes are "blind" would be an exaggeration (even if it is his own exaggeration). But it is no exaggeration to say that one would like to see a more solid basis for them.

NOTES

* I am indebted to the editor of this volume, Ernan McMullin, for helpful comments and suggestions.

1. I have drastically simplified the picture, of course. For an extended treatment see James R. Moore, *The Post-Darwinian Controversies*, Cambridge: Cambridge University Press, 1979.

2. John S. Habgood, "The Uneasy Truce between Science and Theology", in A. R. Vidler, editor, *Soundings*, Cambridge: Cambridge University Press, 1962, pp. 21-41.

3. Richard D. Alexander, *Darwinism and Human Affairs*, Seattle: University of Washington Press, 1979. Richard Dawkins, *The Selfish Gene,* New York: Oxford University Press, paperback, 1978 (first published 1976). Edward O. Wilson, *On Human Nature*, Cambridge, MA: Harvard University Press, 1978, and New York: Bantam Books, 1979.

4. Page references to *On Human Nature* are given in the text. The numbers before and after the slash refer to the Harvard and Bantam editions respectively.

5. Georg Henrik von Wright, *Explanation and Understanding*, Ithaca, N.Y.: Cornell University Press, 1971, p. vii.

6. William P. Alston, "Psychoanalytic Theory and Theistic Belief", in John Hick, editor, *Faith and the Philosophers*, New York: St. Martin's Press, 1964, pp. 63-102; see p. 82.

7. See the book cited in note 5. It might be better to speak not of two patterns but of two clusters of patterns, and to dub them something like the "causal/mechanistic" and "teleological/intentionalistic" clusters. The terminology is uncouth but perhaps tolerable in the decent obscurity of a footnote. 'Causal' by itself can be misleading, since some authors treat motives as causes. 'Mechanistic' by itself can suggest two narrow a conception. 'Teleological' does not cover the kind of case in which we explain someone's belief by pointing to her or his good arguments. Wesley Salmon's 'statistical relevance' model would join Hempel's models in the "causal/ mechanistic" cluster.

8. For a good brief presentation of the intentionality argument in relation to sociobiology, see John R. Searle, "Sociobiology and the Explanation of Behavior", in Michael S. Gregory, Anita Silvers, and Diane Sutch, editors, *Sociobiology and Human Nature*, San Francisco: Jossey-Bass Publishers, 1978, pp. 164-182.

9. Charles J. Lumsden and Edward O. Wilson, *Genes, Mind, and Culture*, Cambridge, MA: Harvard University Press, 1981. For a precis, with commentary by a wide range of scientists and philosophers, see *The Behavioral and Brain Sciences*, 5, 1982, 1-37. For a popular presentation see Lumsden and Wilson, *Promethean Fire*, Cambridge, MA: Harvard University Press, 1983. This book gives (pp. 189-192) an annotated bibliography of the sociobiology literature.

10. Marvin Harris, *Cultural Materialism: The Struggle for a Science of Culture*, New York: Random House, 1979.

11. See the books cited in note 3 and, of course, Edward O. Wilson, *Sociobiology*, Cambridge, MA: Harvard University Press, 1975.

12. John Maynard Smith, "The Limitations of Evolutionary Theory", in Ronald Duncan and Miranda Weston-Smith, editors, *The Encyclopedia of Ignorance*, Oxford: Pergamon Press, 1977, pp. 235-242; see p. 236.

13. Evolutionary theorists differ as to the relative importance they attach to natural selection and adaptation, as opposed to genetic drift and other alternative mechanisms of evolutionary change. No one would deny that adaptation is a factor, but some think that many particular features are better explained as by-products or, in cases where alternatives differ little in adaptive value, as results of genetic drift. For a lucid and vigorous, if one-sided, critique of overreliance on selectionist explanations see S. J. Gould and R. C. Lewontin, "The Spandrels of San Marco and the Panglossian Paradigm: A Critique of the Adaptationist Programme", *Proceedings of the Royal Society of London*, B 205, 1979, 581-598. The point about multiple hypothetical explanations is also treated in this paper.

14. Marvin Harris, *Cows, Pigs, Wars, and Witches*, New York: Vintage Books, 1978 (first published 1974), pp. 6-38.

15. Harris points out that pigs have inefficient cooling systems, so in a hot climate (though not in their natural habitat) they wallow in their excrement in a desperate attempt to cool themselves. Among people who already have a concept of uncleanness in a religious sense the idea that a physically unclean animal is also religiously unclean is likely to occur to someone.

16. Obviously, a crucial question is whether dogma, and the concomitant notion of religious commitment, has to be understood in Wilson's way. I have explored elsewhere some ways in which liberal theologians might interpret dogma and commitment: William H. Austin, *The Relevance of Natural Science to Theology*, London: Macmillan and New York: Barnes & Noble, 1976, pp. 108-113.

17. Wilson, *Sociobiology*, p. 3.

18. Ibid., p. 562.

19. John Henry Newman, *Certain Difficulties Felt by Anglicans in Catholic Teachings Considered*, Westminster, Maryland: Christian Classics, 1969, vol. 1, p. 240.

20. I have argued the point with respect to Hume's *Dialogues* in "Philos's Reversal", forthcoming in *Philosophical Topics*.

21. Alexander, *Darwinism and Human Affairs*, p. 276.

22. For detailed discussion see Norman Daniels, "Wide Reflective Equilibrium and Theory Acceptance in Ethics", *Journal of Philosophy* 76, 1979, 256-282.

23. For reasons of space I have concentrated on the theoretical issue and not undertaken to discuss Wilson's few suggestions (brief, vague, and/or not strikingly novel) as to lessons moralists might learn from biology. For a good treatment of the whole subject see Peter Singer, *The Expanding Circle: Ethics and Sociobiology*, New York: Meridian, 1981. There are also several good articles in Gunther S. Stent, editor, *Morality as a Biological Phenomenon*, Berkeley: University of California Press, 1980.

PRODUCTION AND PROSPECT:
REFLECTIONS ON CHRISTIAN HOPE
AND ORIGINAL SIN

Nicholas Lash

1. An "Aboriginal Calamity"

Darwin's *Origin of Species* interested Newman but did not greatly disturb him. "I do not fear the theory", he wrote in 1868, "I do not see that the *accidental* evolution of organic beings is inconsistent with divine design—It is accidental to *us*, not to *God*".[1] The implied restriction on our ability to comprehend the "pattern" or "meaning" of things reminds us of his enduring debt to Joseph Butler.[2] For Newman the "followability"[3] of the world is always bounded by nescience.

This comes across strikingly in a powerful statement of the doctrine of original sin in the *Apologia*, which can serve as text or backdrop for the remarks that I wish to make in this essay concerning the relationships between evolutionary views of human origins and Christian doctrines of redemption:

> To consider the world in its length and breadth, its various history, the many races of man, their starts, their fortunes, their mutual alienation, their conflicts; and then their ways, habits, governments, forms of worship; their enterprises, their aimless courses, their random achievements and acquirements, the impotent conclusion of long-standing facts, the tokens so faint and broken of a superintending design, the blind evolution of what turn out to be great powers or truths, the progress of things, as if from unreasoning elements, not towards final causes, the greatness and littleness of man, his far-reaching aims, his short duration, the curtain hung over his futurity, the disappointments of life, the defeat of good, the success of evil, physical pain, mental anguish, the prevalence and intensity of sin, the pervading idolatries, the corruption, the dreary hopeless irreligion, that condition of the whole race, so fearfully yet exactly described in the Apostle's words, "having no hope and without God in the world"—all this is a vision to dizzy and appall, and inflicts upon the mind the sense of a profound mystery, which is absolutely beyond human solution.[4]

And what, Newman asks,

273

shall be said to this heart piercing, reason-bewildering fact? I can only answer, that either there is no Creator, or this living society of men is in a true sense discarded from His presence. . . . *if* there be a God, *since* there is a God, the human race is implicated in some terrible aboriginal calamity. It is out of joint with the purpose of its Creator.[5]

Notice four things about that passage. In the first place, it is anthropocentric, not in the sense of supposing that "man is all that matters", but only in the sense that it focuses its description of darkness on the predicament of *human beings* as products of, agents in, and interpreters of the process of the world.

In the second place, far from appealing to the Scriptures to correct or contradict the stories told by scientists, Newman's references to "blind evolution" and to "the progress of things, as if from unreasoning elements, not towards final causes" represent an attempt to weave the scientific narratives into a larger description of our darkness.

In the third place, the doctrine of "original sin", as evoked by Newman, does not "solve" the problem, "explain" the mystery, illuminate the darkness. It asserts that how things are and are perceived to be is no transient circumstance, no temporary reversal in some otherwise "optimistic" narrative of natural and human progress. How things are is how they have ever been, right from the beginning: the "calamity" in which we are "implicated" is "aboriginal".

In the fourth place, the way things are and have ever been is said to stand in contradiction to God's creative purpose. But what place is there, in Newman's dark vision, for a characterization of the world as God's "good" creation? The question is unanswerable if, under the influence of certain strands in eighteenth-century natural theology, we suppose that belief in the goodness of creation is arrived at by "reading off" the more attractive or intelligible features of the furniture of the world and then fitting the "darker" patches into this bright picture.[6]

The classical Christian doctrine of creation neither rests upon nor presupposes any necessity of appeal to some form of what Kant called the "physico-theological argument".[7] It does not, as it were, express a balance struck in favor of theism by a disinterested spectator of the order (and disorder) of nature. The classical doctrine is derived from the practical recognition of the absolute dependence of us, and of all things, on that unfathomable and adorable mystery which in the Christian tradition we call "God".

The confession of God as Creator is, in a phrase of Langdon Gilkey, "the epitome of religious speech".[8] And to confess the *goodness* of God's creation is to acknowledge the absolute dependence (of us and of all things) to be creative, constitutive, life-giving, salvific. In other words, within the Christian as within the Jewish tradition the structure of discovery is from the experience of God as redeemer to the confession of God as Creator, not the other way round.

As "the epitome of religious speech", the affirmation of divine creation is appropriately located in the first book of the Jewish and Christian Scriptures and the first article of the Christian creed. But we need to bear in mind why it is that the doctrine of creation was elaborated at a relatively *late* stage in the history of the Jewish people's experience of God as the power that sets his people free.

With these remarks I am in danger of overstepping the boundaries of what was intended merely as a preliminary sketch of the doctrine of original sin. I shall therefore move on and risk some brief comments on the general background to our discussion in debates concerning the ways in which scientific and theological descriptions may be correlated. Having done so, I shall take up again each of the four topics that I have just indicated.

2. The Quest for Coherence

The Christian, according to Ernan McMullin, "has to aim at some sort of coherence of world-view, a coherence to which science and theology, and indeed many other sorts of human construction like history, politics and literature, must contribute".[9] What kind of coherence could this be, and how might it find expression?

As a first step, consider the case of the person who conducts his business, from Monday to Friday, on the assumption that economic affairs are regulated by immutable "iron laws" of economic necessity and who nonetheless devotes some part of each Sunday to praying for the relief of poverty. Is there not, here, some incoherence or inconsistency of "worldview"? Perhaps not, but how is the issue to be decided?

According to Arthur Peacocke human beings "will not be satisfied with a perspective of the world which indefinitely fragments their experience".[10] But the fragmentation, to be painful, must be *felt*. And many Christians (and others) do seem to "get by" surprisingly well in spite of the apparent contradictions that persist between, for example, their scientific and religious (or political and religious) convictions, attitudes, expectations, and policies.

Moreover, even if we do attempt to bring to unified expression (and hence to unified speech) the complexity and variety of our experience, there are devices at hand for rendering contradiction tolerable by giving it the appearance of rationality. For example, apparent contradictions or inconsistencies between religious and scientific truth-claims can be dealt with (even today) by embracing the kind of positivism according to which only the physical sciences (and disciplines which conform to what are—questionably—taken to be their procedures) can furnish us with "objective knowledge" and by then celebrating the consequent surrender of all cognitive claims on behalf of theology as evidence of the "maturity" of a faith liberated from infantile theological "realisms".[11]

A more widespread strategy for neutralizing apparent contradiction is that which appeals to, or presupposes, a dualistic account of the relationships between soul and body, mind and matter, spirit and flesh, history and nature. It is worth remarking that an account of the relationsips between science and theology which rests upon the metaphysical assumption that the items which constitute the furniture of the world can be exhaustively distributed between two classes of entities, facts, events, or objects (classes which we might label "mental" and "material") usually comes up with a doctrine of God as "Supermind". But such a doctrine, *thus derived*, is unstable. The consistent metaphysical dualist who seeks positive, "categorial" descriptions or models of the mystery of God is obliged to choose, in the last resort, between a God conceived as immensely impressive mental event (and yet even the greatest "idea" in the world remains an idea—in the world) or a God conceived as the most powerful of "the things that go bump in the night": the paradigm of the paranormal. And before neither of these idols of our imagination is is seemly to bow down in worship. We made them; they did not make the world.

There is a third direction in which coherence may be sought at too high a price: namely, by seeking to conflate the languages of science and religion into the grammar of a single discourse. Such attempts usually seek to "fit" religious symbols into a pattern constituted by scientific imagination. The result (I shall suggest later in this essay) has usually been to understate the tragic.

So far all I have done is to indicate my belief that we are ill-advised, as Christians, to seek for coherence of worldview either by denying the cognitive character of theological discourse, or by (implicit or explicit) recourse to metaphysical dualism, or by collapsing the languages of science and religion into a single pattern of description.

It is, undoubtedly, incumbent upon us to seek to unify—in action, imagination, and understanding—our fragmented experience. But is "coherence of worldview" an entirely appropriate description of our goal?

Consider, first, the notion of "worldview". I find it dangerously "spectatorial". It is, undoubtedly, incumbent upon Christians to attempt some formulation of their hope, some unified account of where they take themselves, and all people, and all the world, to be in relation to the mystery of God. Insofar as those things of which they seek to speak consist of "processes", of states of affairs with a "whence" and a "whither", and of some discerned *directionality* between beginnings and endings, the formulation of Christian hope will exhibit a *narrative* character: it will tell a story. But the story it tells is of states of affairs (and their prospects) of which we are not only products, participants, and interpreters but also, in some measure, responsible agents, organizers, and executants. There is, therefore, a self-involving, or *autobiographical*, element in the narratives of Christian hope.[12] It is this feature of religious and theological language which is insufficiently brought out, it seems to me, by the concept of "worldview".

Second, what of "coherence"? I have already suggested some of the ways in which coherence may be sought at too high a price. Our capacity for the energetic construction of illusions seems almost limitless. We always want to see further than we can; to make more sense than we can of the complex, conflictual variety of our experience; to transmute the obscurity of hope into the clarity of possessed explanation. And it seems as if the "larger" the story that we seek to tell, the greater the temptation to attribute a higher degree of "followability" to the process than experience warrants. All our projects and constructions—physical, social, and linguistic—are bounded by constraints. Beyond "coherence" our quest is, or should be, for something more like "adequacy" or even "truth". Coherence may be a necessary condition, but it is not a sufficient condition, of the truth of the stories in which we articulate our hope and symbolically unify our fragmented experience.

Finally, a word about conflict. It is still widely believed that the relationships between science and theology, and especially between the biological sciences and theology, in modern times have been usually conflictual, and theology ever the loser.[13] "Every schoolboy knows" that T. H. Huxley had the better of his confrontation with Samuel Wilberforce in Oxford in 1860.

It would, however, seem more accurate to say that *genuine* conflicts or disagreements between science and theology (and why should we rule out the possibility that such conflicts or disagreements can, indeed, occur?[14]) are exceedingly difficult to detect and accurately to specify because the "large-scale" confrontations that take place can usually be seen, with hindsight, to have been clashes not between "science" and "religion" (or "theology") but between incompatible, and perhaps incommensurable, "worldviews", "philosophies", or "religions" and their respective conceptions of what would count as good or successful science.[15]

3. Anthropocentrism

In light of those disgracefully brief remarks about the larger issues in the background of our discussion, we now turn to the first of the four topics that I placed on the agenda: namely, the problem of "anthropocentrism".

Let me tentatively propose the thesis that there is an *asymmetry of in-*

terest differentiating scientific from theological inquiry such that it is improper for the former and proper for the latter to be, shall we say, "anthropically focused". To say that "anthropic focusing" is scientifically improper is just another way of saying that any attempt to present such trends as may be discernible in cosmic or biological evolution as "all . . . pointing to man" is, in a phrase of Peacocke's, "understandable but unscientific".[16] Such attempts are understandable: it would not be surprising, it would not even necessarily be reprehensible, if I found my history, or that of my family, or class, or nation, or species, or planet, or galaxy, more absorbingly interesting than any other. But, however intelligible or even (in certain respects) justifiable such concentration of interest might be, all attempts to weave the evidence (cosmological or biological) into a single narrative, a story whose "plot" and purpose is the production of the human, are mythological in character and cannot constitute scientific explanations.[17] From a scientific point of view the human is neither the "center" of the cosmos nor the "crown" of evolution for the simple reason that, scientifically speaking, the cosmos has no center, and biological evolution no single central line or crowning achievement.

We talk less readily (or, at least, less innocently) than our forebears about "primitive" peoples and "master" races. We have learned to be wary of ethnocentricity. But it seems to have required the development of potentially destructive nuclear technology and the mounting evidence of our profligacy in the consumption and devastation of natural resources to bring home to us that anthropocentrism—in the sense of the assumption that the human race is the center of a world which exists simply to further human needs and ambitions—is, we might say, only a special case of the arrogance of ethnocentricity. The pride which puts us at the "center" of a world conceived as our private property contributes more powerfully than the destructive forces of "nature" to the dislocation and disruption of the process of things.

The scientist, then, in pursuit of "objectivity" seeks to avoid "anthropically focusing" his account of evolution. But original sin, our primal destructive egocentricity, learns to wear the mask of disinterestedness. Consider the ways in which the negative aspects, the "costs" of evolution, are stated and calculated. Scientists, anxious to avoid inappropriate anthropomorphism, sometimes present failure, and suffering, as "structural necessities"[18] for the survival of existing forms of life and for the production and vitality of new biological "wealth". Is such description quite as "neutral" as it seems?

"Darwinism", it has been suggested, "was an extension of *laissez-faire* economic theory from social science to biology".[19] And when Peacocke, following G. G. Simpson, says that the nineteenth-century "picture . . . of the biological world as 'struggle for existence' has given way to a more precise view of the process of survival . . . as an advantage in differential reproduction",[20] one cannot help wondering whether it is simply coincidence that the shift from talk of "struggle" to talk of "advantages in differential reproduction" and of "more efficient utilization of resources" neatly corresponds to the shift from the rhetoric of nineteenth-century capitalism to the more sanitized language of modern bureaucratic management. The anthropocentrism that we throw out of the front door, in the name of scientific disinterestedness, may creep in at the back. Ideology is infinitely ingenious.

Let me now turn to the other side of the picture: to the suggestion that the "anthropic focus" is appropriate for theological inquiry at least in the sense that such inquiry legitimately focusses on the predicament of *human beings* as products of, agents in, and interpreters of the process of the world. Whether or not it speaks of anything else, the Christian Gospel certainly speaks of human beings, their origin and destiny, "*principium*" and "*finis*". The doctrine of creation speaks of our "whence" and the doctrine of redemption of our "whither". These are but two aspects of a *single* statement, to the effect that we are not simply created, "absolutely" produced beyond all structures of causality, but created by a love that is unswervingly stronger than our weakness, destructiveness, and mortality. Effective transformative cherishing is, we might say, God's mode of production.

We shall return to this. For the moment I want to insist that acknowledging theological interest to be legitimately *focused* on the human predicament in no way licenses the *confining* of that interest to the human. Such disastrous restriction of interest is fostered by those dualisms of mind and matter, history and nature, spirit and flesh, to which I have already referred. Under their influence the "natural", "material" world is relegated to the status of the stage or floorboards on which is played out the "drama" of man's redemption, a drama of which an increasingly interiorized and privatized account is given.

If such dualisms are resisted, if theologians learn to welcome the insistence that human history is but an aspect of "natural history", that human beings are simply one kind (however distinctive and interesting) of organized matter, then the question arises as to whether redemption, the healing of the human, is intelligible except as an aspect of the healing of the *one* world of nature.

To put it another way. If the doctrine of creation speaks of *our* "whence", it does not do so exclusively. It speaks, by implication (as the gradual development of Jewish and Christian doctrines of creation indicates), of the whence of all things in heaven and on earth and under the earth. And if the doctrine of redemption is but the other element of a *single* theological story, then in speaking of *our* "whither" it speaks, by implication, of the "whither" of all things. In order to make sense of this we need (among other things) to recover important differentiations in the notion of "sin" as "distance" from God's presence and purposes. We always tend prematurely to moralize the mystery of the negative, but "sin" is an ontological, before it is an ethical, category. Perhaps we could say that the unique contribution of human beings to the "sin" of the world consists in the fact that we are the point at which darkness and destructiveness, in becoming self-aware, become not simply "distance" from God but acknowledgement of responsibility for the "resistance" which is the ethical (human) form of such distantiation. We are the guilty conscience of the world. It is from the tree of the "knowledge" of good and evil that we eat.[21]

It is often said that only with the emergence of human self-consciousness did it become "possible for actions and events to occur in the universe contrary to God's creative purposes".[22] I do not see how we could know this. We only discern God's *purposes* in glimpsing his *promise* and the manner of its fulfillment. If effective cherishing, God's mode of production, undergoes (as we learn from Gethsemane and Calvary that it does) suffering and death in order thereby to "overcome" them, then it seems that *all* suffering and death require such conquest and, in requiring it, are shown to be in some sense "contrary" to God's creative purpose. The mystery of evil is *far darker* than appears in our moralizing self-dramatization. Perhaps the important thing is never to suppose that we know very much about the purposes of God.

Theological reflection, as consideration of the being and action of the mystery of God, legitimately focuses on the human predicament because it is *here*, above all, that all our "solutions" and "explanations" are circumscribed, silenced, set within a larger nescience.

It is, said Polanyi, "the height of intellectual perversity to renounce, in the name of scientific objectivity, our position as the highest form of life on earth, and our own advent by a process of evolution as the most important problem of evolution".[23] The important word there is "problem". For all our complexity and excellence, beauty, power, and ingenuity, it seems as though, if we are the "center" of anything, we are the center of "sin", of the self-assertive disruption and unraveling of the process of things, at least on our small planet. We have found out a great deal about the processes of the world's production. But what are we to say, with assurance and without illusion, about its prospects? What *kind* of a question is this, and how might it be appropriately formulated? It is time to turn to our second topic: that of the relationship between scientific and theological narratives, and the possibility of telling a *single* true story whose subject matter would be (to paraphrase Aquinas' definition of the subject matter of theology) *all* things in relation to God their origin and end.[24]

4. Theology and the "Constituted Sciences"

According to Durkheim, as the division of labor increases, as "collective existence" becomes increasingly "organic", the social role of religion diminishes.

In particular, with the development of scientific knowledge religion surrenders its *cognitive* function to the "constituted sciences". "The true function of religion", he said, endorsing what he took to be the characteristic standpoint of the religious believer, "is not to make us think, to enrich our own knowledge . . . but to urge us to action, to help us to live".[25] He thus expected religious "cult" — as the public, symbolic expression of commitment to a way of life — to survive the supplantation of religion's cognitive function by scientific modes of knowledge.

However, because forms of worship reflect the *actual* circumstances of social existence — distorted, conflictual, "anomic" — they must also express a "project", a hope for and practical commitment to a redeemed or healed world. Religion, as the articulation of hope, therefore retains for Durkheim a conceptual element in moral or practical discourse: "there has to be a theory about" that faith which is commitment to a way of life. "Such a theory is without doubt bound to depend on the different sciences, as soon as they come into existence". But although such theory depends upon the constituted sciences, it goes beyond them. "Science is fragmentary, incomplete. . . . Life cannot wait. Theories which are aimed at helping people live and act are by that very reason compelled to be ahead of science and to force it to a premature conclusion."[26]

Durkheim's rationalistic positivism — which led him systematically to reduce the dimensions of the human quest for freedom and truth to *two*: "action" and "scientific" theory — inhibited him from sufficiently considering the possibility that there are modes of *cognition* that are not reducible to theoretic, "scientific" knowledge. As a result, he could give no satisfactory account of the "theories which are aimed at helping people live" (even the use of the *term* 'theory' here is anomalous and, on his own showing, misleading).

Suppose we acknowledge, with Durkheim, that the practical discourse of hope necessarily "depends on" the constituted sciences, just as both, in turn, depend on the whole range of everyday experience and commonsense discourse. Suppose, further, that — eschewing Durkheim's positivism — we allow the possibility that the discourse of hope expresses *cognitive* claims concerning how things "ultimately" are and may be made to be. Suppose, thirdly, that Christian theological forms of the discourse of hope express the conviction (in the face of all temptation to foreclose the future by unwarranted prediction, totalitarian control, or the despairing acceptance of present bondage as irredeemable) that *all* we "know" concerning our ultimate future, concerning the "whither" of us and of all things, is that the world *has* a future — a fulfillment, a freedom, a healing — in God. Suppose, in other words, that Christian hope paradoxically "enriches our knowledge" by protecting our nescience from illusion: that it functions, in Karl Rahner's formula, as "the guardian of the *docta ignorantia futurae* for the history of mankind in general".[27]

If we put these suppositions together, something like the following account of the relationship between science and theology would emerge. In the first place, the "larger narrative" of Christian theology, concerning the "whence" and "whither" of things, would depend upon, be disciplined and informed by, our common human experience and the constituted sciences — whose "fragmentary" conclusions it would seek to incorporate. In the second place, this "larger narrative" is, or purports to be, cognitive in character in answering (or, at least, clarifying[28]) a twofold question which the scientist, *qua* scientist, cannot ask.

"Why is there anything at all?" may not be a proper or intelligible question. If it is not, and can be shown not to be, then that would be the end of the matter. On the other hand, if it is a proper or intelligible question, it is, nevertheless, not a "scientific" question (and hence has no "scientific" answer) because it is not a question concerning this or that particular feature (however pervasive or fundamental) of the world. If it is a proper question, it is not a question for the specialist: it is a question which anyone can ask. In the Christian tradition "God" is the answer to this question, an answer which we did not provide and which we do not understand.[29] Insofar as it is a question about the dependence, or "production" of all things, the answer is a confession of faith in God as Creator. Insofar as it is a question about the prospects for or purpose of all things, the answer is a confession of hope in God the redeemer, who has "made us for himself".

However, even if God is the answer to the twofold question which contingent reality poses by its very existence, a question the asking of which is constitutive of specifically human existence, he is *not* the answer to any particular, "categorial" question or the fulfillment of any particular circumscribed hope. To suppose otherwise, to make God the answer to some particular question, to fit him into some broader explanatory schema, is idolatry. It is always idolatrous to attribute divinity to some particular feature of any "world" of which *we* seek obstinately to remain the defining center.

Because we do not understand the answer to the question what are we, confession of faith in the mystery of God protects our ignorance, disciplines our tendency to suppose that we know more than we do. As the guardian of *docta ignorantia*, Christian theology, which depends for its formation and formulation on the constituted sciences, disciplines their pretension to "expand" from "fragmentary" achievement into exhaustive explanations of the world.

Thus, for example, it has often been supposed that conflicts between theology and evolutionary theory arise from their offering irreconcilable accounts of the "production" of human existence in space and time. But theology (if it knows its job) does not offer an alternative account of man's production; it depends upon the constituted sciences. The real conflicts, I suggest, have to do with "prospects" rather than with "production". They arise when evolutionary science, having forgotten its "fragmentary" character, expands into a comprehensive explanatory system, "evolutionary epic", or utopian mythology[30] which purports to "know the answer": to lift what Newman called "the curtain hung over [our] futurity".

It is not surprising that in the nineteenth century, parascientific evolutionary myths of human "progress" should often have received from theology, not the critical questioning and demythologizing they required, but endorsement, because there is an undying conflict, *within* Christian theology, between attempts to turn trust into satisfactory explanation and those forms of Christian hope which acknowledge that it is only in darkness that we apprehend the love which moves the sun and the other stars.

But is this darkness not perhaps temporary? Might not further investigation, or social improvement, diminish or abolish it? We are brought back to our third topic: the "fall" of man, the "aboriginal calamity" in which we are all "implicated".

5. *"In the Beginning"*

The first thing that needs to be said under this heading is that there is, or at first sight appears to be, a *prima facie* conflict between evolutionary accounts of human origins and doctrines of "special creation": doctrines of (for example) the "infusion" into organic matter, by direct divine intervention, of "spiritual" capacities or an immortal "soul". This problem need not detain us, however, because doctrines of "special creation", which I take to be affirmations of the uniqueness before God of the human species, only conflict with evolutionary theory in the measure that they presuppose those metaphysical dualisms of "matter" and "mind", "flesh" and "spirit", which we have already discounted. The difference between human beings and other animals is evident, striking, and of inestimable significance. But in order to account for that difference, no *dualistic* doctrine of special creation is called for. Quite the contrary: such forms of the doctrine can only serve illusorily to isolate human history from other aspects of that natural history of which it indubitably forms a part.

(Christian fundamentalists, a category which includes a distressingly large number of sophisticated philosophers of religion, sometimes suppose that the dualisms which I am contesting have biblical warrant. It requires, however, only the most elementary familiarity with the language and thought-forms of both Old and New Testaments to appreciate that the biblical distinctions in which such warrants are discerned are—to put the matter as simply as possible—distinctions drawn between mortality and vitality, not between classes of entity. The Scriptures were not written by Descartes, or even by the disciples of Plato.)

The story in the second and third chapters of Genesis does not contrast the way things are with the way they once were. It contrasts the way they are and have ever been with how they should, in principle, be. Whereas the creation account in chapter one lyrically depicts the "familiar world which we know from our experience" and declares *this* world to be God's "good" creation, chapter two, "describes everything precisely as it is *not* in our experience".[31] And the story in chapter three tells us that we bear responsibility for the fact that things are not as they should, in principle, be.

"Paradise" is "God's own personal garden",[32] where we are not. It is not the occasionally flowering wilderness that we inhabit. There never was a time of "primal innocence". But if the author of Genesis, for whom — according to the conventions of his culture — what is true "in principle" is true "*in principio*", had denied that there was once such a time, *he* would have been denying that God's creative purpose, God's intention to have *us* inhabit *his* garden, is more fundamental and more effective than human pride and folly.

How might we, as modern Christians, express what the author of Genesis expressed in the language of "beginnings"? Perhaps by declaring — in the Easter faith that reads Jesus' journey through the darkness of death as a journey, not into chaos, but into the light of God's presence — that being God's garden is the *destiny* of the world. Our declaration of trust in God's creative goodness is a confession of hope, not in future "innocence" (what could this possibly mean?), but in present and future healing and homecoming.

In what might such healing and homecoming consist? Positively, we do not know. Negatively, we know that it does *not* consist in escaping from our finitude, for it is precisely the attempt to do *this* which constitutes that contradiction or negation of createdness which we call "sin". The flight from reality, the refusal to be humble before the facts, the refusal to work with the materials at our disposal, the attempt to do violence to the patterns and limits of the created order — whether by reactionary projects of "restoring" an imaginary past, or by totalitarian projects of utopian construction, or by despair's embrace of annihilation: *this* is "the ultimate (and original) sin".[33] The boundaries of the perceptibly possible may continually shift, but it is with the possible that we must work. And we do so in the conviction that, in ways which we cannot depict before their outcome, "all shall be well and all manner of thing shall be well".[34]

It is only in hope that the world of our experience can be discerned to be God's good creation, and it is only in the redemptive transformation of that world that it can be made to be what it "in principle" is: God's own personal garden in which we were made to dwell, but from which we continually sustain our banishment by refusing — through dominative ambition, oppression, despair, fantasy, or ecological rape—to work with the patterns and within the limits of its design.

The paradigmatic limit is that of mortality, and it is in the rejection or acceptance of mortality that the power of "original sin" and of its creative transformation by God's healing grace is above all displayed. For the Christian this means focusing one's consideration of the matter on the manner of Christ's dying.

The second Adam, like the first, is a gardener (this, at least, is what Mary Magdalen took him to be, on Easter morning). But his crowning achievement consists in that which in the garden he undergoes—as a matter not of resignation but of the execution of his Father's will.

If this is true, not only of Jesus but of "everyman", what does it say about the "prospects" or outcome of human history? At least it seems clear that whatever it says is subversive of all *hubris* and all strategies of domination. And yet if what this Adam thus achieves is, even *thus*, achieved, then the story of creation (a narrative which we cannot, except in the darkness of hope, *complete* in advance of its outcome) may yet be hoped to be the story of a garden grown and worked in toil, yet in whose last making "there shall be an end to death, and to mourning and crying and pain"[35] and "no more night".[36] (The story ends where it began: in God's own garden.)

There is a footnote that needs to be added concerning the concept of *common human nature*, or, if you like, concerning the function of the myth of "monogenism". A theological anthropology, or doctrine of the human, will "depend upon" the constituted sciences of biology and genetics. But genetic fraternity is not enough, because we are curious animals that do not only breed and feed but also speak and make plans. For us to share a common *human* nature, we should have to share a common hope and common language. There is, in other words, an ethical or political as well as a biological component to the concept of human nature. But there is also, on a Christian account of these matters, an eschatological component inasmuch as human beings are declared to have not only a common origin but also a common destiny: a common "whither" as well as a common "whence". The redemption of the human race would be the imperishable constitution or creation of that common humanity which, in so many ways, we manifestly lack.

6. Darkness and Hope

I would have preferred the argument of this paper to have been more straightforward, to have fulfilled less tortuously my brief to describe the relationships between evolutionary views of human origins and Christian doctrines of sin and redemption. Quite apart from the limitations of my competence, however, there were several factors which militated against such simplicity.

In the first place, scientific and theological discourse have drifted so far apart that they seem, by now, almost to operate with different "grammars", different "criteria of meaning, truth and value".[37] In the second place, theological discourse has itself become so irreducibly pluralist as to make it exceedingly difficult to know, on any particular issue, whether one is dealing with genuine disagreement or with mutual incomprehension. This is not necessarily bad news, nor does it necessarily threaten the unity or consistency of the faith which theology reflects, but scientists misunderstand the character of theological enquiry if they *expect* it to issue in a discourse as unified as their own.

I have emphasized, more than once, the *unity* of the doctrines of creation and redemption, a unity to which the creeds give summary, symbolic expression, but which has (since the seventeenth century) again and again been neglected or implicitly denied. I have suggested, first, that the structure of discovery is from the experience of God as redeemer to the confession of God as Creator; second, that the Christian doctrine of God is an acknowledgement and celebration of the *principium* and *finis* of the world, of the "whence" and "whither" of us and of all things. To emphasize unity, however, is not to deny distinction: the distinction between creation and redemption, "whence" and "whither", production and prospect, is irreducible. Perhaps we can say that the doctrine of redemption, the declaration of our hope, provides specifically Christian content to the Christian doctrine of divine creation. That is why I said that the declaration of the *goodness* of God's creation is a statement not merely of memory, let alone of "observation", but of hope.

I have also suggested that a similar interweaving of memory and hope, of descriptions of production and expressions of prospect, is detectable in the public uses to which scientific narratives of cosmological and biological evolution are put.

The increasing recognition, in both theology and the philosophy of science, of the indispensability of the narrative mode suggests one important direction in which collaborative exploration might proceed. I do not believe that either scientists or theologians *only* "tell stories",[38] but stories they do both undoubtedly tell.

Stories have plots; they impute "followability" to their subject matter. We do not like the dark, and in our fear of darkness, we are always tempted to attribute to the world and its processes a greater degree of "followability" than facts and experience warrant. One of the contributions of Christian theology, I have suggested, consists in the simultaneous assertion both that the world *is* "followable", that—by God's grace—it has plot, point, and purpose,[39] and that such "followability" as we discern is, in the circumstances of our darkness, always bounded by a larger nescience.

If our circumstances and prospects are as dark as Newman's sketch of original sin suggests — and, in spite of Mozart and Chartres, the delicate diversity disclosed to the microscope, and the wonder of an unforced smile, I believe them to be so — then this is, or should be, no surprise. The context of the confession of God's good creation, the context of our celebration of God's good garden, remains (for the Christian) the garden of Gethsemane and the hill of Golgotha on which the tree of life was planted.

NOTES

1. John Henry Newman, *The Letters and Diaries of John Henry Newman*, XXXIV, Oxford: The Clarendon Press, 1973, p. 77. Newman was commenting on [R. M. Beverley], *The Darwinian Theory of the Transmutation of Species Examined by a Graduate of the University of Cambridge*, London: James Nisbet and Co., 1868.

2. One remembers that, opposite the title page of *The Origin of Species*, Darwin set not only quotations from Whewell and Bacon but also a passage from Butler's *Analogy*.

3. Cf. W. B. Gallie, *Philosophy and the Historical Understanding*, London: Chatto and Windus, 1964, p. 45. "Every successful work of history . . . must be followable, as a unity, in the way that a story is" (ibid., p. 68).

4. John Henry Newman, *Apologia Pro Vita Sua*, edited by Martin J. Svaglic, Oxford: The Clarendon Press, 1967, p. 217.

5. Ibid., pp. 217-218.

6. Cf. Karl Barth's devastating and witty critique, in *Church Dogmatics*, III/1, Edinburgh: T. and T. Clark, 1958, pp. 388-414, of the degeneration of Leibnizian 'optimism' culminating in Abraham Kyburtz's *Theologia Naturalis et Experimentalis* of 1753, the whole of which "can be sung to the tune of 'Now thank we all our God' " (p. 402).

7. Whereas it can be argued that what Kant himself called the 'cosmological argument' is not a form of "argument from design" at all but stands, philosophically, closer (for example) to Aquinas' version of what I have called the classical Christian doctrine: cf. Brian Davies, "The Intelligible Universe", *New Blackfriars, 63*, 1982, 381-389. Davies follows Antony Flew in deploring the extraordinary confusion that surrounds uses of the expression 'cosmological argument'.

8. Langdon Gilkey, "The Creationist Issue: A Theologian's View", in David Tracy and Nicholas Lash, editors *Cosmology and Theology*, Concilium, 166, New York: The Seabury Press, 1983, p. 61.

9. Ernan McMullin, "How Should Cosmology Relate to Theology?" in A. R. Peacocke, editor, *The Sciences and Theology in the Twentieth Century*, Notre Dame, IN: University of Notre Dame Press, 1981, p. 52.

10. A. R. Peacocke, *Science and the Christian Experiment*, London: Oxford University Press, 1971, p. 8.

11. Cf. Don Cupitt, *Taking Leave of God*, London: SCM Press, 1980.

12. Cf. Nicholas Lash, "Ideology, Metaphor and Analogy", in Brian Hebblethwaite and Stewart Sutherland, editors, *The Philosophical Frontiers of Christian Theology*, Cambridge: Cambridge University Press, 1982, pp. 68-94.

13. For a sketch of late nineteenth-century rearguard actions cf. John Kent, *From Darwin to Blatchford. The Role of Darwinism in Christian Apologetic 1875-1910*, London: Dr. Williams's Trust, 1966.

14. There are, of course, methodological devices for *stipulating* that conflict cannot occur, but their existence hardly decides the matter.

15. As random illustrations, cf. Gilkey, "The Creationist Issue"; my review in *The British Journal for the History of Science, 14*, 1981, 202-204, of Harry W. Paul, *The Edge of Contingency: French Catholic Reaction to Scientific Change from Darwin to Duhem*, Gainesville: University Presses of Florida, 1979; James R. Moore's fascinating review-article, in *The British Journal for the History of Science, 14*, 1981, 189-200, of N. C. Gillespie, *Charles Darwin and the Problem of Creation*, Chicago: Chicago University Press, 1979; M. J. S. Rudwick, " Senses of the Natural World and Senses of God: Another Look at the Historical Relation of Science and Religion", in *The Sciences and Theology in the Twentieth Century*, pp. 241-261; Robert M. Young, "The Impact of Darwin on Conventional Thought", in Anthony Symondson, editor, *The Victorian Crisis of Faith*, London: SPCK, 1970, pp. 13-35.

16. Cf. Peacocke, *Science and the Christian Experiment*, p. 91.

17. See Ernan McMullin's illuminating discussion of appeals to the "anthropic principle" in "How Should Cosmology Relate to Theology?" pp. 40-47.

18. Cf. Peacocke, *Science and the Christian Experiment*, pp. 135-139.

19. Young, "The Impact of Darwin," p. 15.

20. Peacocke, *Science and the Christian Experiment*, p. 137, following G. G. Simpson, *The Meaning of Evolution*, New Haven: Yale University Press, 1950, p. 222. The same passage from Simpson (in a different edition) is appealed to in Peacocke's more recent work, *Creation and the World of Science*, Oxford: Clarendon Press, 1979, pp. 164-165. Here, the stoicism of Peacocke's position is even more apparent. All the emphasis is placed on the "need to learn how to *bear* suffering" (p. 182, my stress; cf. p. 246). But *who may say such things?* The wretched of the earth, or those who speak from the strongholds of social power?

21. If we assume, as I would wish to do, that "sin" and "freedom" are antithetically related: that "freedom" is fundamentally a matter of "proximity" to God and conformity to his purposes; then it follows that "freedom," like "sin," is an ontological category: that "self-possession" is a more fundamental matter than available *choice*.

22. Peacocke, *Creation and the World of Science*, p. 193.

23. Michael Polanyi, *The Tacit Dimension*, London: Routledge and Kegan Paul, 1967, p. 47, cited with approval by Peacocke, *Creation and the World of Science*, p. 72.

24. "Omnia autem tractantur in sacra doctrina sub ratione Dei, vel quia ipse Deus vel quia habent ordinem ad Deum ut ad principium et finem", *Summa Theologiae*, Ia, q. 1, art. 7.

25. Emile Durkheim, *The Elementary Forms of the Religious Life*, London: George Allen and Unwin, 1915, p. 416. I have preferred the translation offered by W. S. F. Pickering, editor, *Durkheim on Religion*, London: Routledge and Kegan Paul, 1975, p. 145.

26. Durkheim, *The Elementary Forms of the Religious Life*, pp. 430-431; translation from Pickering, *Durkheim on Religion*, p. 160.

27. Karl Rahner, "Possible Courses for the Theology of the Future", *Theological Investigations*, XIII, London: Darton, Longman and Todd, 1975, p. 33.

28. I have in mind Rahner's admirably cautious formula that "the answer given in revelation clarifies the question a man asks" ("The Foundation of Belief Today", *Theological Investigations*, XVI, London: Darton, Longman and Todd, 1979, p. 9).

29. "Belief in the creator God cannot be an explanation" because "God's act of creation is unconditional and absolutely free", Edward Schillebeeckx, *Interim Report on the Books 'Jesus' and 'Christ'*, London: SCM Press, 1980, p. 113.

30. To claim that such mythological "expansion" of scientific theory is unwarranted is not to imply that scientific theory can avoid, in practice, exercizing some socially symbolic or "mythic" function: cf. Mary Hesse, "Cosmology as Myth", in Tracy and Lash, *Cosmology and Theology*, pp. 49-54.

31. Henricus Renckens, *Israel's Concept of the Beginning*, New York: Herder and Herder, 1964, p. 157.

32. Ibid., p. 200.

33. The Bishop of Salisbury (John Austin Baker) and Others, *The Church and the Bomb*, London: Hodder and Stoughton, 1982, p. 108. Cf. Schillebeeckx, *Interim Report*, pp. 116-117.

34. Cf. Nicholas Lash, "All Shall Be Well: Christian and Marxist Hope", *New Blackfriars*, 63, 1982, 404-415.

35. Revelation 21:4.

36. Revelation 22:5.

37. Cf. Hesse, "Cosmology as Myth", p. 54.

38. Where the relationships between narrative and other forms of theological discourse are concerned, see Lash, "Ideology, Metaphor and Analogy".

39. For a lucid expression of the alternative judgement cf. Frank Kermode, "The Unfollowable World", *The Genesis of Secrecy*, Cambridge, MA: Harvard University Press, 1979, pp. 125-145.

TEILHARD: EVOLUTION AND CREATION

Christopher F. Mooney, S. J.

Pierre Teilhard de Chardin is surely one of the most fascinating people in the intellectual history of the twentieth century. Unknown before his death in 1955 at the age of 74, he immediately gained a notoriety and a renown which would have altogether amazed him during his life. He succeeded in disturbing scientists as well as philosophers and theologians, and finds today both strong support and violent opposition among Christian and non-Christian alike. He has been called a genius, a harbinger of a new and strong Christianity, and also a dangerous innovator, saved from ecclesiastical condemnation by his good faith alone. For some he is a daring thinker of great depth and originality, for others simply a scientist who has wandered from his exacting professional disciplines of geology and paleontology to speak in the poetic language of a personal religious experience.

All of these paradoxical reactions to the thought of Pierre Teilhard de Chardin are in some measure justified. They spring from the paradox in the man himself. Teilhard was a Jesuit and a priest, a scientist, a philosopher, a theologian, a spiritual prophet, and a seer. He was a man of enormous personal charm. He suffered deeply during his life, and yet that life was one of high adventure. His scientific writings fill ten large volumes. His anthropological, philosophical, theological, and spiritual writings fill another thirteen volumes. Then there are volumes of letters and spiritual journals. In the last twenty-five years he has had three biographers and has been the subject of thousands of critical articles and over a hundred books.

I would like to ask and answer two general questions in these pages. First, what did Teilhard want to do as a thinker, and why? Second, how did he carry out his intellectual enterprise on the various levels of his thought? The answers to these two questions will illumine the central theme in all his work.

1. A Guarantee for the Future

First, then, what did he want to do as a thinker, and why? Without fear of contradiction, I think we can say that Teilhard de Chardin was primarily a visionary, a seer. He once wrote, "Nothing is profane to those who know how to see".[1] Teilhard *saw* something and wanted to show others what he saw. He wanted to be a guide for others, and yet he suffered deeply for wanting to be a guide. He was severely disciplined by the Vatican authorities of his time; he spent most of his life in exile from his native Paris; and he was forbidden to publish anything of a philosophical, theological, or spiritual nature. Why, then, did he want to be a guide? Because, as Donald Gray has well noted, Teilhard saw with crystal clarity the disjointedness of two creation stories, two explanations for the world in which we live. There was first the sacred creation story of the Bible, the Genesis story, the prelude to redemptive history in Christ, the sphere of the sacred, to which Teilhard was totally committed. Then there was the creation story that began in the nineteenth century, the product of modern science, a story whose most recent and popular narrator has been the scientist and television personality Carl Sagan. In contrast to the sacred creation story of the Bible, the scientific creation story said that creation was a very long process, an evolution, that creation was not yet finished. This second story was not at all interested in talk about God or Christ, since it took place in the sphere of the secular, a sphere to which Teilhard, as a scientist, was also totally committed. Teilhard saw that those who told the first story left out everything that appeared in the second story and were largely unconcerned with the phenomenon of change in human life. On the other hand, he knew that the second story was valid, because as a geologist and a paleontologist he had come to understand evolution from the inside. But this second story left out a whole history of inwardness; it left out the study of what was most peculiar to the human species, namely, thought, spirit, growth in personal interrelatedness. Teilhard's overall project, therefore, was to unite these two stories, the redemptive story or process, and the cosmic story or process, and to expand the second story so that science would deal with the phenomenon of thought and reflection. For his experience as a Christian convinced him that God was responsible for both these processes, and he wanted others to see what he saw. Let me quote for you some passages from his writings between 1917 and 1940 to illustrate the intensity of his desire to make people see.

> There are in reality two types of minds and two only, those who never get past the perception of multiplicity nor feel any need to do so, and those for whom the same perception of multiplicity must necessarily resolve itself into some unity. The pluralists and the monists, those who do not see and those who do. . . . I know it looks ridiculous and vain to play the part of being misunderstood. And yet, I honestly believe that I see something and I wish that something to be seen. . . . I want to teach people how to see God everywhere, to see Him in all that is most hidden, most solid and most ultimate in the world. These pages put forward no more than a practical attitude, or, more exactly, perhaps, a way of teaching how to see. . . . Seeing. We might say the whole of life lies in that verb.

That is why the history of the living world can be summarized as the elaboration of ever more perfect eyes within a cosmos in which there is always something more to be seen. . . . To try to see more and better is not a matter of whim or curiosity or self indulgence. To see or to perish is the very condition laid upon everything that makes up the universe by reason of the mysterious gift of existence. I repeat that my only aim in these pages, my whole driving power, is to try to see.[2]

Why did this disjointedness in two sets of data, this apparent disunity between these two stories of creation, the religious and the secular, bother Teilhard so much? And why was he so intent that his readers see the unity which he saw? The reason is that his whole life experience, and therefore his whole system of thought, was a response to what he felt to be the most pressing need of humanity today, namely the assurance of some successful outcome for the human enterprise, some hope for the future. He said many decades ago that the focus of all human anxiety and fear today is the future, the sense of being responsible for the future and for human life on our planet. Long before it was fashionable, Teilhard proclaimed that the whole of modern culture was oriented toward the future. What reasons are there for us to hope in the future? What guarantees are there that we have a future? Teilhard believed that there were enough people focusing upon reasons for despair in the human future; he wanted to focus unilaterally upon reasons for hope. Some lines from 1940 and 1954 give us a sense of this concern of his for our contemporary fear of the future.

The whole psychology of modern disquiet is linked with the sudden confrontation of space-time. . . . Conscious or not, suppressed anguish, a fundamental anguish of being, despite our smiles, strikes in the depths of our hearts and is the undertone of all our conversations. . . . In the first and most wide-spread degree, the 'malady of space-time' manifests itself as a rule by a feeling of futility, of being crushed by the enormities of the cosmos. . . . Sickness of the dead end — the anguish of feeling shut in . . . Fear of being lost in a world so vast that man seems to have lost all significance. Fear of being reduced to immobility. Fear of being unable to find a way out. . . . In the great game being played, we are the players as well as being the cards and the stakes. Nothing can go on if we leave the table. Neither can any power force us to remain. Is the game worth the candle, or are we simply its dupes? We will never take a step in a direction which we know to be blocked. There lies precisely the ill that causes our disquiet.[3]

Let us imagine, Teilhard wrote toward the end of his life, that a group of miners are trapped through an accident deep down in the earth. For these miners to summon up the courage needed for the difficult struggle to climb back up the shaft, they have to presuppose two things: some opening exists at the other end, and that when that opening is reached, there will be air to breathe again and light to see. Now this is the case with our own generation. They are confronted with the realization that it is they themselves who

are responsible for the march of humankind, an enterprise of staggering proportions, demanding long and painful labor, the end of which seems infinitely
far away. It is useless to urge modern men and women to throw their energy
behind such an effort if there is the least possible suspicion either that the
world is hermetically closed or that the opening at the other end leads to
what is inhuman or subhuman. A death which is total, into which our whole
earthly achievement disappears forever; or, what comes to the same thing,
a survival which is humanly deformed and on a level lower than the noblest
aspirations of humanity: either one of these dismal prospects would be enough
of itself to inject into the marrow of human action the incurable poison of
weariness, discouragement, and fear. The taste for life would be stifled, and
the magnificent *élan* of humanity would eventually come to an end.

2. Science, Philosophy, Religion

Teilhard's overall project, then, is to elaborate a guarantee for the human
future that would bring the two creation stories together. This guarantee is
in reality three guarantees, elaborated on three different levels of his thought,
the scientific, the philosophical, and the religious. Once he has these guarantees, he draws from them some very important consequences for human living,
and especially for Christian spirituality. So let us see now how he elaborates
these guarantees and draws these consequences.

On each level of his thought Teilhard asks a question regarding human
life and then provides a master idea that is the key to answering that question. The question on the first level of his thought, the scientific level, is
this: What has been happening over the centuries to the phenomenon of
life? For this biological phenomenon seems to be the antithesis to the physical
phenomenon of entropy: while entropy is a disintegration of energy in the
universe, life seems to represent energy on the increase. Teilhard's answer
to his question about the phenomenon of life focuses upon the pattern of
the past which has been uncovered by modern science, and his master idea
is what he calls the law of complexity-consciousness. He starts with a fact:
in all known life the more developed consciousness will always correspond
experimentally with the more complex organic structure. This is seen most
clearly, of course, in the human person, where the most complex organic structure, the human brain, corresponds with the most sophisticated consciousness
which we know, namely, the capacity for reflection. For Teilhard this scientific fact shows not simply that there has been change over millions of years
but that there has been what he calls "genesis", from the French word *genèse*,
which means change in successive stages, change which is oriented toward

[handwritten marginal note: no, capacity for reasoning: a chimp can reflect, but it cannot reason!]

[handwritten margin note at top: wrong — not degree of consciousness, but rather unique capacities amongst organic beings, to reason.]

some goal, or more simply, directional change. This scientific fact also accounts for his coining the term "cosmogenesis", namely, directional change in the universe. More importantly, however, he believed that this scientific fact showed that the goal of the evolutionary process is the human species, which at the present time has both the highest organic complexity and the highest degree of consciousness. This human consciousness, this power of reflection, is for Teilhard the key to the evolutionary process. In a world where change is directional, where it is a genesis, it is clear that the movement of evolution has been in the direction of the human person, and therefore in the direction of human consciousness, in the direction of spirit, mind, thought, and love.

Teilhard now moves to a second level, and the question on this level is, not what has been happening to the phenomenon of life, but what is happening to the phenomenon of *human* life. Having pointed to the pattern of the past revealed by the law of complexity-consciousness, Teilhard now asks where this pattern is leading, where is the evolutionary process going, and what does it all mean? The master idea on this second level is Teilhard's analysis for the role of love-energy in human development. For there is no reason at all to suppose, says Teilhard, that evolutionary development, by which growth in complexity brings growth in consciousness, should cease with the arrival of the human person. For this arrival of human beings in the cosmos is only the crossing of the first threshold of reflection. Whatever significant human change there is must now take place on the other side of this threshold, not in the biosphere, but in that sphere which corresponds to the sphere of human mind and human thought, a sphere which Teilhard calls the "noosphere". Evolution today, on the other side of this first threshold of reflection, should be called, not "cosmogenesis", but "noogenesis", to indicate that what is going on in the human realm is a development of consciousness and interiority.

But what kind of development? Where is this development going? We see here the importance of Teilhard's master idea on this second level, namely, the role of "love energy". This is the energy which unifies, the same energy *[handwritten margin note: wrong]* which unifies molecules, but which on the human level operates in the realm of interpersonal consciousness. Teilhard uses the phenomenon of electromagnetic waves to illustrate how his master idea on the first level, the law of complexity-consciousness, operates also on the second level and meshes with his new master idea of unifying love energy. Through technology humans have made an enormously complex use of electromagnetic waves to enable them to share thoughts over vast distances. Someone with an idea in the remote mountains of Tibet can communicate that idea immediately to anyone *[handwritten margin note: rather mediated]* in this country provided there is the requisite technological complexity in the use of electromagnetic waves. Another image used by Teilhard to illustrate the operation of this unifying human energy is the image of the coil. Evolution, he says, is a coiling: the movement is not in a direct line but in the form of a coil. Unifying energy pushes up the coil by tightening it, thereby moving humanity closer and closer together around the surface of the earth. What is humanity moving toward? To understand Teilhard's answer, we have to think on the scale on which he thought, a scale of millions of years. What he envisioned at the end of the coiling process was a point, which he called Point Omega, which represented for him an experience of community for the human species which we can at present only dimly perceive, a kind of common sharing of consciousness, what he calls an experience of "more being". Human progress for Teilhard is thus synonymous with growth in consciousness for the human species, that is to say, growth in the capacity for union, or *wrong.* in the capacity for love. This growth in the capacity for union and love began when the first threshold of reflection was crossed with the coming of thought, and continues now and will continue in the future, again over a period of millions of years, up to the second threshold of reflection, which is the Omega Point.

Teilhard was very conscious, of course, that many objections can be made to this vision of the human species moving toward greater and greater unity. The most telling objection is obviously our experience of disunity. All around us we see disruptions, revolutions, transitions of all types. We also have experienced in this century manifestations of unity which have been radically disruptive, that of totalitarianism in all its forms, unities which have been bad for humanity. Finally, we have the existence of evil in the world, the presence of hatred, the very antithesis of love. Teilhard was very sensitive to these types of objection and elaborated three answers. First, we cannot deny that there has been a steady growth in the unity of consciousness of the species. All we have to do is to contrast how humans related to each other a thousand years ago, or five hundred years, or even a hundred years ago, to see how differently we now relate to each other on a global scale. Tensions and turmoil continue in the political order today precisely because of this growing sense of interdependence of everyone upon everyone, as well as upon the growing sense of the dignity of all human beings. We are a very different ?? species today from the times when humans allowed other humans to be enslaved. Secondly, the totalitarianisms which have pressured the species in so many ways in the twentieth century are examples of good energy gone awry. For these totalitarianisms have used force to unify peoples, and not love and freedom. Third, Teilhard admits that his understanding of progress as growth in consciousness has engendered a serious misunderstanding. For him growth in consciousness means growth in the *capacity* for love and union among humans, not growth in love itself. Insofar as human progress means the growth in our *capacity* for love, it also means that we are growing in our capacity to refuse love.

? Is Adam, then, substantial, by nature, inferior to us?

[handwritten margin note: not greater power, but greater — i.e. wider, opportunities!]

Thus, in spite of his strong emphasis upon the movement toward higher consciousness, Teilhard admits to a profound ambiguity in all human progress. Greater power to love seems to mean greater temptation to refuse love. But again, human progress for Teilhard takes place, not in a straight line, but rather in a coiling movement. The same cycle is repeated, and each time there is a little advance. Each new crisis is the product and the result of a previous achievement. Each new advance thus increases the temptation to stop or to regress. The future success of evolution in Teilhard's analysis thus appears to be jeopardized from the inside by the frailty of human love. This is why he was searching for some guarantee that humanity would ultimately use its freedom well, by finally choosing to love rather than to hate, to unite rather than to disperse. Within evolution, however, he could find no such ultimate guarantee. Hence at the end of this second level of his thought he begins his search for some guarantee outside the evolutionary process. He finds it by postulating, not proving, the existence of an Omega which is, not a Point at the end of the process, but rather a personal and divine source of love. This postulate is something like Pascal's wager. The last part of Teilhard's great work, *The Phenomenon of Man*, develops this idea of a divine personal Omega. Only such a transcendent absolute, he argues, "loving and lovable at this very moment," can activate the love energy of the world and bring the evolutionary process to a successful completion.

Many have pointed out that what Teilhard is really trying to do, in postulating a divine personal Omega who alone can activate the love energy of the world, is to develop a proof for the existence of God, an ultimate pledge of hope for the species. But in truth, all that Teilhard has come up with at the end of *The Phenomenon of Man* is a conjecture, a philosophical hypothesis, a necessary assumption, perhaps, but not a proof. He himself is the first to acknowledge this. This is why Teilhard, the scientist, was forced to move to a third level of his thought, the level of Christian theology, in order to find some ultimate source of hope for the human species. He had to appeal to Christian revelation to move from the level of a philosophical hypothesis to the level of an historical fact. At the very end of *The Phenomenon of Man* Teilhard has an epilogue entitled "The Christian Phenomenon." Here he identifies the Christ of revelation with the Omega of evolution and by so doing gives to evolution not some vague termination but the well defined reality of the historical Jesus. It is the historical Jesus who is the ultimate guarantee that the human species will survive. For Christianity tells us that there is a very precise goal for this creation which God has brought into existence. This goal is the second coming of Jesus, the Parousia. Christianity also tells us that, in the person of Jesus, God has actually entered into the evolutionary process. The second coming at the end of time has been preceded by the first coming at the time of the Incarnation, which Teilhard calls a prodigious biological operation. Since we know from Christian faith that Jesus has entered into the biological process, as this has been discovered by science, and that he will bring this process to a successful completion at the end of time, Teilhard is able to speak of the process, on this third level of his thought, no longer as a biogenesis or as a noogenesis, but as a Christogenesis. This third level also has its own master idea: Christ as the physical center for the evolutionary process and the source of love energy in that process.

We should note that Teilhard's Christology is very different from traditional Christology. Unlike theologians before his time, Teilhard began to use two sources of knowledge, corresponding to the sources of the two creation stories. The first was the data of Christian revelation, especially the cosmic texts of St. Paul in the eighth chapter of Romans, the first chapter of Colossians and the first chapter of Ephesians. All these texts are concerned with the lordship of Christ over the whole of creation, spiritual as well as the material. It is clear also in St. Paul that there is a strong physical relationship between Chirst and the cosmos. This physical relationship, of course, is emphasized by St. Paul's theological reflection upon the mysteries of the Incarnation and the Holy Eucharist. It is not surprising that Teilhard focuses his theological attention not only upon the Parousia, and the Incarnation, but also on the Eucharist, as the symbol of physical and organic unity between Christ and the cosmos, and also on the phenomenon of the Church, looked upon as the microcosm of the unity of the whole human species. These data of Christian revelation are then compared, on this third level of Teilhard's thought, with a second source of knowledge, the data which science has discovered about the evolutionary process, data which give an inductive vision of the world and human beings. Teilhard is trying, not to cast these two sources of knowledge, these two sets of data, into a single mold, but rather to confront them with each other and to compare them. He is always convinced, however, that a pole of truth exists and that these two sources of knowledge somehow meet in common vision in the future, since God is the source of both sets of data.

We said at the start that Teilhard was trying to unite the Christian creation story and the human creation story. But when he does bring them close together on this third level of his thought, what he sees is not just intellectual coherence but also some extraordinary consequences for human living, and especially for Christian living. There are therefore some very distinctive Teilhardian emphases in Christian spirituality. On this level of Christian faith he wants to be a guide to survival in the area of knowledge, yes, but he also wants to be a guide to action.

3. *Christian Spirituality*

Teilhard's spirituality may be described as a spirituality of creation and creativity. Teilhard summons us, as do the prophets and the seers, to a human task. Why? Because he sees the human task as a collaboration with God's creative action, which in and through the historical evolutionary process builds up the Body of Christ. You can see, of course, that on this level of spirituality the master idea of "Christ as a physical center" is another way of speaking of the more traditional doctrine of the divine omnipresence. Teilhard's great work of spirituality is *The Divine Milieu*, completed in 1927. Unlike the English word 'milieu', the French word '*milieu*' means both center and environment, and so you can see why Teilhard uses the phrase 'Divine Milieu' as a name for the person of Jesus. Jesus is the divine atmosphere, the divine omnipresence ceaselessly at work in creation. In another essay Teilhard speaks of the world as a crystal lamp, illumined from within by the light of Christ. Hence Teilhard's call to the Christian is to collaborate with God as he is experienced in the secular world. The effort of the Christian must be not so much to *bring* God to the secular world but to *find* God there. This, of course, is a very different emphasis from the one we have been used to in Christian writings. This collaboration is terribly important to Teilhard's spirituality, because in his system of thought the end of the evolutionary process will not come until certain necessary preliminary stages are accomplished in and through this collaboration between God and human beings. The final building up of the body of Christ, in preparation for the second coming at the Parousia, is in fact conditioned among free human beings. This collaboration, Teilhard says, is a necessary, though obviously insufficient condition for the coming of the Parousia.

Teilhard uses a vivid image to illustrate this human collaboration with the creative action of God leading to the Parousia, that of the master artist and the apprentice. In the shop of the master artist the apprentice does all the preliminary work. In the case of a painting, it is the apprentice who sketches the outlines of all figures in the painting, who chooses perspectives as well as colors, and who begins to sketch in the details of the painting. As time proceeds the master artist inspects the painting, makes adjustments and suggestions, as well as highlighting the consequences of emphasizing one or other detail in the painting. Finally, the apprentice can get no further with this preliminary sketch and must call in the master artist to complete it. The work of the apprentice is thus the necessary condition for the completion of the painting, since it is his preliminary sketch and his ideas which constitute the contours and the content of the painting. But his work is also insufficient, since only the master artist has the requisite skill and knowledge to bring the painting to its successful conclusion.

This creative spirituality of Teilhard, this collaborative effort between the
human and the divine, can be a very costly form of Christian discipleship.
In *The Phenomenon of Man*, Teilhard notes that "the human epic represents
nothing so much as a way of the cross."[4] In *The Divine Milieu* Teilhard develops his great theme of the passivities of life, those of growth and those
of diminishment; those events in our lives over which we have no control
and which inevitably bring with them fear, anxiety, and pain. The ultimate
passivity, of course, is death. And this phenomenon of death has an enormous importance in Teilhard's spirituality. Death is not a friend, but it is
not an enemy either. The reason is that death is central to the whole creative
process, and not just a single part of the redemptive process. Here again,
there is that characteristic change of emphasis: death can be lifegiving, whether
it is one of our intermediate deaths or our final death, and detachment is
essential to creative growth.

> The great victory of the Creator and Redeemer in the Christian vision, is to
> have transformed what is itself a universal power of diminishment and extinction
> into an essentially lifegiving factor. God must in some way or other make room
> for himself, hollowing us out and emptying us, if he is finally to penetrate into
> us. And in order to assimilate us into him, he must break the molecules of our
> being so as to recast and remodel us. The function of death is to bring about this
> opening up of our innermost selves which God desires. It will force us to undergo
> the disunion he is waiting for. It will put us into the state organically needed if
> the divine fire is to descend upon us. And in that way its fatal power to decom-
> pose and dissolve will be harnessed to the most sublime operations of life . . . Jesus
> on the cross is both symbol and reality of the immense labor of the centuries, which
> little by little raises up created spirit to restore it to the depths of The Divine Milieu.
> He represents, and in a true sense he is, creation as it reascends the slopes of being,
> supported by the hand of God, sometimes clinging to things for support, sometimes
> tearing itself from them in order to transcend them, and always compensating by
> physical suffering for setbacks caused by its moral failures . . . The Cross is not
> something inhuman but superhuman. It has been placed on the crest of the road
> that leads to the highest peaks of creation. The Christian's task is not to swoon
> in its shadow but to climb in its light.[5]

This emphasis in Teilhard's spirituality upon creation and creativity has
been responsible for what is perhaps the most serious objection to his Christian writings, namely, that he has a sense neither of sin nor of the mystery
of evil. In *The Divine Milieu*, for example, there is no development of any
purgative way. Teilhard deliberately avoids talking of sin and the reformation of one's life. Why? Well, as we noted already, he was concerned in his
total system of thought with generating optimism and hope. His experience,
although probably not ours to the same extent, was of a theological tradition
which drew very pessimistic conclusions from the human experience of sin,

especially original sin. In one of his theological essays Teilhard says that this theological tradition "cuts the wings of our hope for humanity."[6] He blamed an overemphasis on sin for the unconcern on the part of many Christians to build the earth and to contribute to the human enterprise. Teilhard would not deny, of course, that there is risk in choosing optimism regarding life rather than pessimism. But he would say that there is just as much risk in choosing pessimism. A good example of such pessimism is *The Imitation of Christ*, a classic of Christian spirituality, but one which is very negative, emphasizing mistrust of the world, separation as much as possible from its activities, and offering no invitation at all to life and creativity. But just because Teilhard does not talk about sin explicitly, this does not mean that it is not there, but just that it is not emphasized. We already noted his emphasis upon the frailty of human love, the refusal of community with others and with Omega, the failure of the whole evolutionary process. This can only be attributed to a failure of love or the presence of sin. Also we must remember, Teilhard's emphasis on human progress was an emphasis upon growth in the capacity to love. Human progress is therefore not the same as moral progress. Human progress in the Teilhardian sense necessarily involves the possibility of moral regress in individual lives. Indeed, no more terrifying pages on hell have ever been written by any master of the spiritual life than those to be found in *The Divine Milieu*.

I have tried to focus upon Teilhard de Chardin's passionate desire to find unity and coherence between the two creation stories, the one based on faith in the divine, the other upon faith in the human. If he could make others see what he saw, Teilhard felt, then he could assuage modern anxiety by offering us hope for the final success of human evolution, for the ultimate survival of all that the earth has developed in complexity and consciousness, all that is *best* in the world. This hope he rooted in the person of Jesus in whom the love of God Omega is revealed. Only what God has done in Christ can bring assurance that human creativity is indeed a participation in divine creativity, and that the outcome of the whole enterprise will therefore be on the side of life and not on the side of death.

4. Conclusion

We conclude by asking one final question: Can Teilhard's thought be true? We are all aware of the criticism that his writings are onesided and unbalanced, that he seems to have left out or deemphasized whatever does not fit into an optimistic outlook on world developments, on human history, on theology, on spirituality. How then can such thought be true? The most obvious answer to this objection is that visionaries are not "balanced" people. They are people with a message. Being "balanced" is an extremely difficult thing for any visionary intent upon delivering a message. What kind of truth does Teilhard's evolutionary system have, then? Biological truth? Philosophical truth? Theological truth? Is Teilhard's message therefore false because it is unbalanced? What are his criteria for truth? He himself tells us that he has two criteria for truth. The first is coherence. Does his message make sense out of the world around us? Does it unify the experiences we have in life? "If a system of thoughts", says Teilhard "enables us to grasp a little more of the world and helps us to harmonize its elements, we can be sure we are closer to the truth. Truth is nothing but the total coherence of the universe in regard to each of its elements".[7] Teilhard's second criterion for truth is fruitfulness, personal, social and cultural. Does his message lead to a creative human life? Teilhard would say that we must first do what he suggests that we do, and then we shall find out whether what he says is true.

As a final judgment, then, on the evolutionary system of Pierre Teilhard de Chardin, I think we can say that whether one is favorable or hostile to his efforts to elaborate a guarantee for success of the evolutionary process will depend in large measure upon one's theological, spiritual and intellectual temperament. Such temperament will determine whether one can resonate with the style of Christian living which Teilhard urges upon us, with the fundamental harmony of the universe which he tries to transcribe for us. He once wrote to a close friend that people made a big mistake in comparing his writings to those of Darwin. What they should do, he said, is to compare his writings with the music of Richard Wagner. Teilhard wanted to be not only the apologist for hope and survival, but their musician as well. Like any great musician Teilhard wanted to create a mood and an attitude toward life which would unify all things secular and sacred in a single movement toward the future. Let us end with his own words.

> All over the earth at this moment, at the heart of the new spiritual atmosphere created by the appearance of the idea of evolution, there flow the currents of love of God and faith in the world, the one current highly sensitive to the other. In me, by pure chance, the ratio of each has been favorable and their fusion has taken place spontaneously, too weak yet to be propagated with explosive force, but still sufficient to make it clear that fusion itself is possible and that some day or other the chain reaction will come.[8]

NOTES

1. Pierre Teilhard de Chardin, *The Divine Milieu*, New York: Harper & Row, 1960, p. 38.
2. *Christology and Evolution*, New York: Harcourt Brace Jovanovich, 1971, p. 101; *The Making of a Mind*, New York: Harper & Row, 1965, p. 269; *The Divine*

302   Christopher F. Mooney

Milieu, p. 15; *The Phenomenon of Man*, New York: Harper & Row, 1959, pp. 31, 35.
3. *The Phenomenon of Man*, pp. 227, 229; *The Appearance of Man*, New York:
Harper & Row, 1965, pp. 208-209; *The Phenomenon of Man*, pp. 230-231.
4. *The Phenomenon of Man*, p. 313.
5. *The Divine Milieu*, pp. 68-69, 87-88.
6. *Christianity and Evolution*, p. 79.
7. *Human Energy*, New York: Harcourt Brace Jovanovich, 1962, pp. 54-55.
8. *The Heart of Matter*, New York: Harcourt Brace Jovanovich, p. 102.

INDEX OF NAMES